D1037374

# Lifespan Development

Second Edition

by

**Sharleen L. Kato, EdD**
Family and Consumer Sciences Department Director
Seattle, Washington

Publisher
**Goodheart-Willcox Company, Inc.**
Tinley Park, Illinois
www.g-w.com

Copyright © 2018
by
**The Goodheart-Willcox Company, Inc.**

All rights reserved. No part of this work may be reproduced, stored, or transmitted in any form or by any electronic or mechanical means, including information storage and retrieval systems, without the prior written permission of The Goodheart-Willcox Company, Inc.

Manufactured in the United States of America.

ISBN 978-1-63126-540-2

2 3 4 5 6 7 8 9 10 — 18 — 21 20 19 18 17

**The Goodheart-Willcox Company, Inc. Brand Disclaimer:** Brand names, company names, and illustrations for products and services included in this text are provided for educational purposes only and do not represent or imply endorsement or recommendation by the author or the publisher.

**The Goodheart-Willcox Company, Inc. Safety Notice:** The reader is expressly advised to carefully read, understand, and apply all safety precautions and warnings described in this book or that might also be indicated in undertaking the activities and exercises described herein to minimize risk of personal injury or injury to others. Common sense and good judgment should also be exercised and applied to help avoid all potential hazards. The reader should always refer to the appropriate manufacturer's technical information, directions, and recommendations; then proceed with care to follow specific equipment operating instructions. The reader should understand these notices and cautions are not exhaustive.

The publisher makes no warranty or representation whatsoever, either expressed or implied, including but not limited to equipment, procedures, and applications described or referred to herein, their quality, performance, merchantability, or fitness for a particular purpose. The publisher assumes no responsibility for any changes, errors, or omissions in this book. The publisher specifically disclaims any liability whatsoever, including any direct, indirect, incidental, consequential, special, or exemplary damages resulting, in whole or in part, from the reader's use or reliance upon the information, instructions, procedures, warnings, cautions, applications, or other matter contained in this book. The publisher assumes no responsibility for the activities of the reader.

**The Goodheart-Willcox Company, Inc. Internet Disclaimer:** The Internet listings provided in this text link to additional resource information. Every attempt has been made to ensure these sites offer accurate, informative, safe, and appropriate information. However, Goodheart-Willcox Publisher has no control over these websites. The publisher makes no representation whatsoever, either expressed or implied, regarding the content of these websites. Because many websites contain links to other sites (some of which may be inappropriate), the publisher urges teachers to review all websites before students use them. Note that Internet sites may be temporarily or permanently inaccessible by the time readers attempt to use them.

*Cover image: Samuel Borges Photography, India Picture, Dragon Images, Monkey Business Images, Ruslan Guzov / Shutterstock.com*

# Introduction

*Lifespan Development* is a book about people—how people grow, change, and mature throughout the life stages from birth to old age. Young children learn to walk, talk, spell, jump, and tell jokes. Teens learn to become more independent. Adults take on more responsibilities for themselves and others. In this book, you will learn about the things that people have in common in their physical growth, cognitive or intellectual development, and in their social and emotional maturation. You will also learn how people differ individually, due to a combination of genetic heredity and personal experiences and environment.

Families often go through similar developmental stages. In the family life cycle, couples get married and have children. They care for, nurture, and discipline their children to help them become responsible members of society. Families exist in an ever-changing environment. Coping with divorce, remarriage, job stress, and special needs such as physical disabilities, learning disorders, and socio-emotional disorders are the daily realities of many families. In this book, you will learn strategies that provide for individual and family needs and promote lifetime human development.

As the stages of human growth and development are explored, you will learn about the developmental theories of Erikson, Piaget, Vygotsky, and Kohlberg. These theories will help you understand how and why people develop and learn throughout each stage of the lifespan. Because careers in education and training and human services often require more extensive knowledge of lifespan development, this book also provides an overview of these career areas.

The more you understand lifespan development, the better you will understand the capabilities, motivations, and expectations of those around you. This includes your family members, fellow students, coworkers, and those you care for or work with in professional settings. Even better, it will give you a better understanding for your own life's journey.

# About the Author

Sharleen L. Kato, EdD, loves teaching as well as learning. She is a Professor at Seattle Pacific University where she encourages students to become creative and successful by understanding and caring for the people in their lives. She believes that understanding lifespan development is the first step to appreciating the differences and similarities between individuals, and this in turn leads to stronger work teams, families, and communities. Dr. Kato has taught undergraduate students for over 25 years. She currently serves as the Family and Consumer Sciences Department Director. Dr. Kato holds a Doctorate in Education, a Master's in Human Ecology, and an undergraduate degree in Home Economics. She travels extensively spending at least two weeks each year serving in an orphanage, teen home, and prenatal clinic in the Philippines.

# Reviewers

The author and publisher are grateful to the following reviewers who provided valuable input to this edition.

**Samantha M. Abel**
Family and Consumer Sciences Teacher
Shawnee Mission East High School
Prairie Village, Kansas

**Jennifer D. Adams**
Family and Consumer Sciences
  Education Specialist
FCCLA State Advisor
Alabama Department of Education
Montgomery, Alabama

**Rose Benzenhafer**
Family and Consumer Sciences Teacher
Sunbright High School
Sunbright, Tennessee

**Shaunda Brittain**
Family and Consumer Sciences Teacher
FCCLA Advisor
Lexington High School
Lexington, Tennessee

**Deborah Fanning**
Family and Consumer Sciences
  Department
Child Services Coordinator
FCCLA Co-Sponsor/FTA Sponsor
Scottsboro High School
Scottsboro, Alabama

**Megan Johnson-Burns**
Family and Consumer Sciences Teacher
Skyline High School
Dallas, Texas

**Carol Lafferty**
Family and Consumer Sciences Teacher
Blue Valley North High School
Overland Park, Kansas

**Marcia H. LaLonde**
Family and Consumer Sciences Teacher
Ballard High School
Seattle, Washington

**Sharon Mang**
CTE Department Chair
Greensburg Community High School
Greensburg, Indiana

**Karen Testi Palmer**
Family and Consumer Sciences Teacher
Sammamish High School
Bellevue, Washington

**Ann Pogue**
Family and Consumer Sciences Teacher
Education and Training Internships
  Teacher/Coordinator
South Grand Prairie High School
Grand Prairie, Texas

**Susan Sain**
Family and Consumer Sciences Teacher
Marion County Schools
Jasper, Tennessee

**Jolene Schlemmer**
Family and Consumer Sciences Teacher
Lincoln Southwest High School
Lincoln, Nebraska

**Mollie Wassner**
Family and Consumer Sciences Teacher
Washington High School
South Bend, Indiana

**Whitney Weaver**
Family and Consumer Sciences Teacher
Deer Park High School South
Deer Park, Texas

# Contents in Brief

# Contents

# Part 2
# Stages of Human Growth and Development

# Chapter 8
# Middle Childhood: Ages 6 through 10 . . . . . . 170

# Chapter 9
# Adolescence: Ages 11 through 19 . . . . . . 204

## Chapter 12
## Older Adulthood: Age 66 Plus . . . . . . 288

## Part 3
## Strategies Promoting Lifetime Human Development
### Chapter 13
### Child and Adult Care Resources for Families . . . . . . 318

## Chapter 14
## Providing for Individual and Family Needs . . . . . . 342

# Part 4
# Career Preparation and Opportunities
## Chapter 15
## Preparing for Careers . . . . . . 374

# Chapter 16
# Career Paths in Education and Training . . . . . . 402

# Chapter 17
# Career Paths in Human Services . . . . . . 424

# Features

## Case Study ???

## Cultural Connections

## Health Connections

# *Safety* Connections

# Promotes Successful Learning

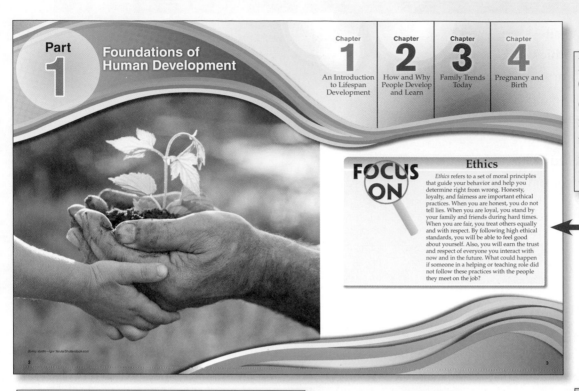

## Part 1 — Foundations of Human Development

| Chapter 1 | Chapter 2 | Chapter 3 | Chapter 4 |
|---|---|---|---|
| An Introduction to Lifespan Development | How and Why People Develop and Learn | Family Trends Today | Pregnancy and Birth |

### FOCUS ON — Ethics

*Ethics* refers to a set of moral principles that guide your behavior and help you determine right from wrong. Honesty, loyalty, and fairness are important ethical practices. When you are honest, you do not tell lies. When you are loyal, you stand by your family and friends during hard times. When you are fair, you treat others equally and with respect. By following high ethical standards, you will be able to feel good about yourself. Also, you will earn the trust and respect of everyone you interact with now and in the future. What could happen if someone in a helping or teaching role did not follow these practices with the people they meet on the job?

**Focus On** Offers insight on ethical issues you will encounter throughout the lifespan.

**Objectives** Objectives summarize the learning goals for each chapter.

---

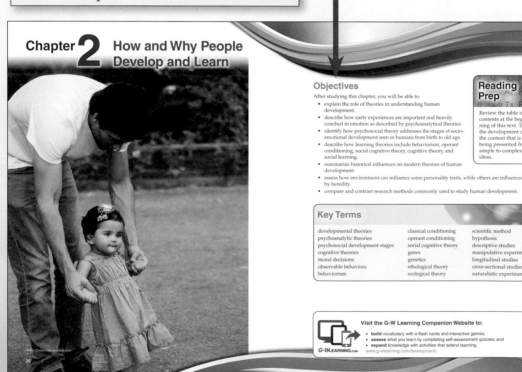

## Chapter 2 — How and Why People Develop and Learn

### Objectives

After studying this chapter, you will be able to

- explain the role of theories in understanding human development.
- describe how early experiences are important and heavily couched in emotion as described by psychoanalytical theories.
- identify how psychosocial theory addresses the stages of socio-emotional development seen in humans from birth to old age.
- describe how learning theories include behaviorism, operant conditioning, social cognitive theory, cognitive theory, and social learning.
- summarize historical influences on modern theories of human development.
- assess how environment can influence some personality traits, while others are influenced by heredity.
- compare and contrast research methods commonly used to study human development.

### Reading Prep

Review the table of contents at the beginning of this text. Trace the development of the content that is being presented from simple to complex ideas.

### Key Terms

| | | |
|---|---|---|
| developmental theories | classical conditioning | scientific method |
| psychoanalytic theories | operant conditioning | hypothesis |
| psychosocial development stages | social cognitive theory | descriptive studies |
| cognitive theories | genes | manipulative experiments |
| moral decisions | genetics | longitudinal studies |
| observable behaviors | ethological theory | cross-sectional studies |
| behaviorism | ecological theory | naturalistic experiments |

**Visit the G-W Learning Companion Website to:**

- **build** vocabulary with e-flash cards and interactive games;
- **assess** what you learn by completing self-assessment quizzes; and
- **expand** knowledge with activities that extend learning.

G-WLEARNING.com   www.g-wlearning.com/development/

**Reading Prep** Activities address literacy skills for college and career readiness.

**Key Terms** Presents the new terms you will learn in the chapter to expand your vocabulary.

# Enhances and Extends Learning

## Core Skills

For college and career readiness, these activities link chapter content to various academic areas such as writing, reading, speaking, listening, and math.

## Critical Thinking

Questions challenge you to use higher-level critical thinking skills when reviewing chapter concepts.

## Research

Apply various research methods to explore chapter topics and complete activities.

---

### Summary

The study of human development encompasses all the aspects of human growth from birth through old age. These include the progressive changes seen in physical growth, intellectual or cognitive abilities, and socio-emotional development.

Development occurs in an orderly and gradual manner. Every person's rate and timing of development is unique. No two people develop exactly the same, although similarities can be seen throughout stages of life.

A lot is known about human development, but there is still much more to learn. Today, debates continue about several prominent issues. How much of development can be attributed to genetics? How much can be attributed to environment? This is the nature versus nurture debate. Whether development occurs slowly over the lifespan or is a result of abrupt changes is also debated. Lastly, whether development is directed by the person or a caregiver continues to be pondered. In all three of these issues, the answer is *both*. What is not yet answered is *how much*?

### Vocabulary Activity

Write each of the terms on a separate sheet of paper. For each term, quickly write a word you think relates to the term. In small groups, exchange papers. Have each person in the group explain a term on the list. Take turns until all terms have been explained.

### Critical Thinking

1. **Determine.** At which age are you at your prime in life? Why?
2. **Analyze.** Do reality television shows harm participants?
3. **Predict.** How do you predict that you will grow and change between now and when you are age 30?
4. **Identify.** If you could choose any age to be today, what age would you choose? Why?
5. **Draw conclusions.** Observe a teacher who uses the andragogy teaching method. Why do you think this method was chosen?
6. **Evaluate.** Do you think that people of different ages can be close friends? If not, why not?
7. **Assess.** Which aspect of development is most important to overall growth and development?
8. **Compare and contrast.** Choose one year from your life as a child and another from your teen years. How are you the same? How are you different?
9. **Make inferences.** Make a photo picture collage of a celebrity or someone you know from infancy to present age. What factors may have affected the visible growth and development changes? What invisible changes do you assume?
10. **Cause and effect.** How might eating the same unhealthy meal for lunch and dinner for the next five years affect your development?

### Core Skills

11. **Writing.** Write a two-page paper about how you have grown and changed physically, intellectually, emotionally, and socially since your first day of high school.
12. **Speaking.** Practice and give a one minute speech on why studying human development is important.
13. **Listening.** Ask a parent or another adult how they have changed since graduating from high school.
14. **Reading.** Read a biography about someone's life. How has that person grown and changed over his or her lifetime?
15. **Math.** Find the birth length of yourself or someone else your age. Compare your birth length to your current height. What is your percentage growth?
16. **CTE Career Readiness Practice.** Presume you are the human resources director of a small business. Recent research shows that employees who have good eating habits and total wellness have a positive impact on productivity. You are forming a workplace *Wellness Council*. Get together with your council members (two or more classmates) and brainstorm a list of several possible ideas for encouraging healthful eating and wellness among employees. Then narrow the list to the three best options. How would you implement one of these options? How would you get employees involved? What criteria will you use to determine how well employees are meeting healthful living goals?

### Research

17. Search for an electronic news article about aging or a medical breakthrough on extending the lifespan. Is the article from a scientific, medical, or well-known educational institution? Avoid articles that lack objectivity.
18. Choose a decade from the past century. Research the social, political, economic, and historic events of that decade. How might these events have affected someone who was a teen during this decade? Create an electronic presentation of your findings to share with the class.

### Event Prep

19. Arrange to interview an older adult about how both heredity and environment influenced his or her development through the lifespan. What traits did he or she inherit? What events had a great influence on development? Prepare a list of questions you would like to ask prior to the interview. After the interview, create a scrapbook to record the interview questions and responses. You may wish to expand your project by developing an FCCLA *Power of One* project for *Family Ties*. Use the FCCLA *Planning Process* to guide your project planning. See your FCCLA adviser for further information.

---

## Vocabulary Activities

Activities that review and reinforce chapter vocabulary terms and their definitions.

## Event Prep

Individual and team activities suggest ways to expand projects for competitive events.

## Checkpoint

Questions that appear throughout the chapter test your reading comprehension.

### Checkpoint

1. What is a neonate?
2. Describe a neonate's physical characteristics.
3. How is the health and wellness of a newborn determined?
4. Describe newborns' reflexes and their abilities to hear, feel, touch, see, and taste.
5. What are some of the family adjustments that occur when a newborn comes home?

# Encourages Exploration of Chapter Topics

## Cultural Connections
Learn about other countries and cultures as related to the text material. Activities reinforce learning.

often sag. Muscle loss also affects range of motion, and movements become slower. Physical activities such as strengthening exercises can slow this process, improving both physical appearance and abilities.

Other signs of aging cannot be seen externally. Internal body organs age and lose some efficiency of their function. The brain shrinks and pulls away from the skull. Blood flow to the brain decreases. As the heart's capacity decreases and blood vessels harden, the heart might have to pump harder to get blood to other organs. Lungs have a lower air capacity. The digestive system slows, often resulting in constipation. Incontinence, which is involuntary urination or defecation, may occur as health problems increase. Although these changes are normal, some happen faster for those who live sedentary lifestyles.

### Changes in Sensory Skills

Sensory changes from middle adulthood continue throughout older adulthood, 12-1. *Presbyopia*, a slow decrease in the ability to focus on nearby objects, progressively worsens. The ability to adjust from light to darkness, from low glare to high glare, and to see objects in the side view becomes more challenging. Other vision conditions often develop. Eye doctors recommend scheduling visits at least every 1–2 years, but sooner if changes in visual acuity are noted. Doctors recommend having hearing tested annually to help detect changes in hearing.

### Vision Conditions

The most common vision conditions in older adulthood are cataracts, glaucoma, macular degeneration, and diabetic retinopathy. As people age, the lens of the eye thickens causing cloudy or distorted vision. This condition is known as cataracts. Colors are not as bright, and details become blurry. For a while, eyeglasses can help clarify vision. As the disease progresses, however, surgery is necessary. A simple laser surgical procedure can restore the lens to clearer vision.

#### Health Connections — Biological Theories on Aging

In addition to biological changes that adults experience as they age, such as physical decline, there are also theories on aging. These theories offer explanations as to why the body deteriorates or functions differently from younger adulthood. Following are three of the most common biological theories on aging:

- **Cellular clock theory**—Cells need to divide to rejuvenate and to perform effectively in body functions. Cells can only divide about 75–80 times throughout life. When cells have trouble dividing, the body cannot perform optimally. Leonard Hayflick theorized that since cells have a time limit in dividing, the maximum age of life expectancy is between 120–125 years.
- **Free-radical theory**—Cells metabolize and produce byproducts, or free radicals.

*Free radicals* are unstable oxygen particles that damage other cells and interfere with regular body functions. Free radicals damage DNA, which can lead to many diseases and disorders.

- **Hormonal stress theory**—The body's reaction to stress changes as the body ages. Instead of reacting quickly to stress, the body remains in a state of stress longer than in previous stages of the life cycle. As a result, the body's immune system weakens, which leads to higher risks for illnesses and diseases.

**Speaking Activity**

With a partner, discuss the three biological theories on aging. Of the three, does one sound more likely than another? Do you have another theory for why aging occurs?

## Health Connections
Examine health issues related to lifespan development.

## Safety Connections
Provides tips about how to prevent accidents and promote safety throughout all stages of the lifespan.

#### Cultural Connections — Promoting Cultural Diversity

Cultural background influences the family unit, especially children within the unit. *Culture* includes holidays, food customs, religions, and traditions. A country's holidays can include all of these aspects and convey a value to children and the rest of society. For example, Thanksgiving in the United States is a family holiday where members share a meal, family time, and mention for what they are grateful. Other countries have holidays unique to their culture, which also communicate values. In Israel, students do not attend classes for Rosh Hashanah to celebrate the New Year. In Uruguay, Constitution Day is a national holiday celebrating the first constitution, which influences the government and people.

**Research Activity**

Select three other countries and research one holiday from each country. Is there a U.S. holiday similar to this holiday? Which values are represented by each holiday?

Children can often be exposed to negative images and messages. Without more sophisticated problem-solving skills, children are vulnerable. Parents and caregivers should talk to children about the dangers and limit media exposure based on their personal values and standards. Parents may also preview movies, shows, or websites before their children watch or visit them to determine if the content is appropriate. Caregivers may also choose to watch shows with children or to monitor computer time. If any questionable topics come up or if children have questions, parents are there for a teachable moment.

 **Checkpoint**

1. According to Erikson, w...
   childhood need to solve...
2. Describe relationships...
3. Describe relationships...
4. What is bullying? Give...
5. List three ways children...

### Special Needs

Children between the a...
cognitive, and socio-emotio...
special needs become more...

Many screenings are av...
ing tests are usually admini...
problems that may have de...
reading tests are other com...

Vision problems that oft...
include hyperopia and myop...
that results in difficulty seein...
condition that results in diffi...
may have a vision problem i...
ing, showing light sensitivity...

During the toddler years, more teeth develop. By the time toddlers reach their second birthday, most have all of their primary teeth with the exception of their second molars. This changes the look of their smile and facial features.

### Motor Skills

During the toddler years, children learn many new gross- and fine-motor skills. At the beginning of the toddler years, toddlers are often just learning how to take a few hesitant steps without support. Throughout the toddler years, they learn to walk quickly, 6-2. Toddlers also learn to pull a toy on a string, run for short distances, kick, throw, walk backward, and climb stairs more easily. As toddlers explore their world, they move constantly. They fall and get back up many times an hour. Caregivers should provide a safe environment, but encourage this active exploration as much as possible.

*Monkey Business Images/Shutterstock.com*

6-2 The term *toddler* refers to the way children "toddle" as they walk during this stage.

#### Safety Connections — Childproofing

Childproofing, or the process of ensuring a home is safe for children, is especially important for toddlers. During the toddler stage, toddlers are walking and exploring their world. They may grab on to furniture or loose items to help them balance. They are also curious and have enough fine- and gross-motor skills to open cabinets and get into bottles or liquids that may be harmful to the skin or even poisonous. Monitoring the movement of toddlers is always important and necessary. The following guidelines can help you childproof a home and make watching toddlers somewhat less stressful.

- Place sharp objects out of reach.
- Keep windows closed or open windows slightly and lock in place.
- Ensure medicine, kitchen, and other cabinets have childproof locks.
- Use outlet and power strip covers.
- Install child protection gates at tops and bottoms of staircases.
- Keep up-to-date on new safety regulations and product recalls for items such as cribs or certified child safety seats.

**Writing Activity**

What other precautions could you take to ensure the safety of a toddler? Expand these guidelines by adding five more childproofing tips. Then inspect your home for child safety and write an action plan to address any safety concerns you noticed during your inspection.

# G-W Integrated Learning Solution

**The G-W Integrated Learning Solution** offers easy-to-use resources for both students and instructors. Digital and blended (print + digital) teaching and learning content can be accessed through any Internet-enabled device such as a computer, smartphone, or tablet. From the following options, choose the ones that work best for you and your students.

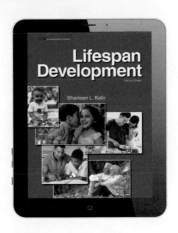

The easy-to-navigate **G-W Learning Companion Website** for *Lifespan Development* offers students multiple opportunities to increase comprehension of key concepts and reinforce learning. The website complements chapters of the text and is available to students at no charge. www.g-wlearning.com/development/

The **Online Learning Suite** for *Lifespan Development* is available as a classroom subscription. It combines the digital student text and workbook in digital format.

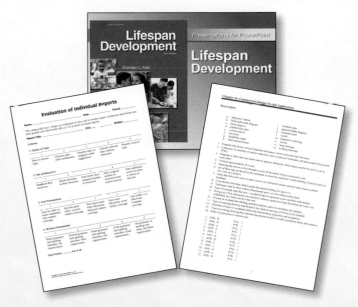

The Online Instructor Resources provide extensive support to instructors. Available in one accessible location, support materials include Instructor's Presentations for PowerPoint®, ExamView® Assessment Suite, lesson plans, answer keys, and more! The Online Instructor Resources are available as a subscription and can be accessed at school or at home. These resources are also available on CDs.

Are you looking for a **Blended Solution**? G-W offers the Online Learning Suite bundled with the printed textbook in one easy-to-access package for school districts and instructors seeking a combination of print and digital tools. With this option, individual students and instructors have the flexibility of using solely print, solely digital, or a combination of print and digital versions of *Lifespan Development* educational materials to best meet their particular learning/teaching styles.

# Part 1

# Foundations of Human Development

Sunny studio—Igor Yaruta/Shutterstock.com

## FOCUS ON

# Ethics

*Ethics* refers to a set of moral principles that guide your behavior and help you determine right from wrong. Honesty, loyalty, and fairness are important ethical practices. When you are honest, you do not tell lies. When you are loyal, you stand by your family and friends during hard times. When you are fair, you treat others equally and with respect. By following high ethical standards, you will be able to feel good about yourself. Also, you will earn the trust and respect of everyone you interact with now and in the future. What could happen if someone in a helping or teaching role did not follow these practices with the people they meet on the job?

# Chapter **1** An Introduction to Lifespan Development

Blend Images/Shutterstock.com

4

# Objectives

After studying this chapter, you will be able to

- discuss how human development involves physical, intellectual, and socio-emotional development.
- identify how development occurs in an orderly and gradual manner.
- describe how every person's rate and timing of development is unique.
- explain how physical, intellectual, and socio-emotional development are interrelated.
- summarize the current issue of nature versus nurture in human development.
- compare and contrast pedagogy and andragogy.

## Reading Prep

Before reading this chapter, review the introductory material preceding Chapter 1. Textbooks generally provide a preview of the book and how the material is presented. Did this material help you understand how to use this book?

## Key Terms

human development

physical development

gross-motor skills

fine-motor skills

cognition

cognitive development

socio-emotional development

heredity

environment

nature versus nurture debate

continuity

discontinuity

pedagogy

andragogy

## Visit the G-W Learning Companion Website to:

- **build** vocabulary with e-flash cards and interactive games;
- **assess** what you learn by completing self-assessment quizzes; and
- **expand** knowledge with activities that extend learning.

G-WLEARNING.com   www.g-wlearning.com/development/

Look around you. Your friends, your family, the bus driver, the barista at the coffee shop, your teacher, the child you babysit—all are unique. They are different ages, come from diverse backgrounds, and possess unique natural abilities, experiences, talents, skills, and interests. Their resources vary greatly including income, education, and family support. Yet there are similarities, especially with those in the same age group. In other words, people are similar to one another in some ways and different from one another in other ways, **1-1**.

## What Is Human Development?

Of course, not all people are exactly alike, but people do go through similar stages of development. A 6-year-old is very different from a 13-year-old. Both are different from an infant, a 20-year-old, or an elderly person. Why? Throughout peoples' lives, they grow and change. This process is called **human development**. Human development is an amazing, gradual process in which people change from birth through adulthood.

Development occurs throughout the lifespan as people grow and learn. In the first five years of life alone, babies learn to roll, crawl, stand, walk, run, hop, and skip. They learn to laugh, talk, joke, and sing. They learn to feed themselves. They learn to trust and to interact with others through words and gestures. Children learn to count, spell, and write. They learn to build friendships and care for others. They become industrious and learn self-control. They learn to organize their activities. Later as teens, they learn independence. Their minds process more complex ideas. As teens transition to adulthood, they take on more and more responsibility for themselves and others. Throughout adulthood, people continue to develop and change from young adulthood all the way through old age.

*Andresr/Shutterstock.com*

**1-1**  Although these young people are in the same age group, they differ in physical traits, personality, and style.

## Checkpoint

1. What is human development?
2. List six skills children often learn during the first five years of life.
3. When do people often learn independence and begin to process more complex ideas?

# Types of Development

The average lifespan in the 21st Century is 78 years. That is almost 30 years longer than the life expectancy in the previous century. Nutrition, medicine, better sanitization, and lifestyles have all contributed to this increased lifespan. People change and develop over their lifespan in several major ways. They change physically, cognitively, socially, and emotionally (hereafter referred to as socio-emotional development).

In each stage of life, people can be described by their physical, cognitive, and socio-emotional differences. In later chapters, you will learn about typical physical, cognitive, and socio-emotional development from birth through old age. Here are a few highlights.

## Physical Development

Throughout life, people change in size and height. People often judge children's ages by the way their bodies look in height and overall proportion of parts. This is called **physical development**— the changes in size, body composition, chemical make-up, and height that occur as humans develop from birth to adulthood. Although all people grow and change physically at different rates, scientists and researchers agree on general guidelines or expectations of which changes are common in each stage of development.

Babies gain weight and grow in length rapidly. Their teeth become visible as they break through the gums, **1-2**. These first baby teeth fall out and new ones replace them. Their hair thickens and becomes more plentiful. In younger children, the head is proportionally larger in relation to the body than in older children.

In the teen years, growth in both height and weight continue. Bodies change in ways beyond height and size, however. As a teen enters puberty, his or her body begins to change in preparation for possible parenthood. Muscle and fat tissue begin to redistribute and accumulate. Chemical changes also occur within the body.

qingqing/Shutterstock.com

**1-2**  This baby is beginning to grow his first teeth, which is a physical sign of development.

During adulthood, muscle and fat tissue continue to redistribute. The body begins aging rather than regenerating or growing. Arteries harden and eyesight changes. Hair and skin change. Sleep patterns change. As a person reaches older adulthood, the physical body slows both in function and activity level.

With these changes in height, body size, and chemical change also come differences in physical abilities. Individually, people differ in balance, strength, coordination, and energy levels to perform both gross- and fine-motor skills. **Gross-motor skills** involve large muscle movements such as crawling, walking, and jumping. **Fine-motor skills** involve small muscle movements such as cutting with scissors, typing on a keyboard, and writing with a pen or pencil. You will learn about both gross- and fine-motor skills throughout the life stages as you study human development.

## Cognitive Development

As humans, you think. You perceive, sense, organize, memorize, recall, reason, problem solve, and imagine. All of these actions or processes involving thinking and knowing are called **cognition**. The way people change and grow in how they think over the stages of life is called **cognitive development**. In each stage of life, mental abilities change. These changes are due to both social interaction and brain development.

Think about when you were in kindergarten. As a 5-year-old, you approached a problem differently from the way you do today. Your ways of learning changed significantly, and as a result, teachers present information in a much different manner. Their expectations of your involvement in learning change, too, **1-3**.

Part of cognitive development is the advance and expansion of the use of language. Babies progress from babbling and cooing to speaking words and sentences. Throughout childhood, children learn new words daily. By the teen years, they can articulate complex thoughts as language progresses throughout the stages of life.

*YanLev/Shutterstock.com*

**1-3**  Your ability to learn new subjects has significantly changed since childhood.

As people develop, moral issues become more prevalent. Moral issues deal with what a person judges to be right or wrong. Moral decision making is included under the category of cognitive development. This is because moral decision making involves problem solving and reasoning.

In moral development, people are able to understand and approach problems differently based on their life stage. For example, a 3-year-old may struggle with the concept of sharing toys. A teen may struggle with the decision to participate in illegal behavior. An adult may face challenges with decisions regarding relationships with coworkers or family members.

## Socio-emotional Development

The ways in which you feel about yourself and interact with people change throughout your life. **Socio-emotional development** refers to changes in the way a person's social relationships, feelings, social skills, self-esteem, gender identity, and ways of coping with situations change over time.

Babies learn to trust and depend on their caregivers. Young children learn about themselves and become aware of others. Learning to control emotions is an important part of this stage. Students learn to wait their turn, form a line, raise their hand, and listen as their parent or teacher is giving instructions.

Children learn to make friendships with their peers. They form a concept of themselves. They begin to appreciate that people can act one way, but feel differently on the inside. Children learn to care about others. They also learn how to cope with stress. They begin to see differences in others' abilities and talents.

Teens learn to identify themselves in different roles. They make decisions and choices that affect their adult life. They learn to take responsibility for themselves, care for others, and form intimate relationships with others, **1-4**.

Adults learn to form relationships with others, too. These relationships often result in choosing to parent children. In many capacities, adults become caregivers. They are employees and employers. They are responsible for their own health and well-being and many times that of others. Their moral decisions can carry significant consequences.

*Monkey Business Images/Shutterstock.com*

**1-4**   Forming close relationships is a part of development.

## Checkpoint

1. List the three major ways in which people develop over time.
2. Define *gross-motor skills* and *fine-motor skills*. Give an example of each.
3. What is cognition?
4. Define socio-emotional development.

# Principles of Human Development

There is a lot known about the way humans grow and change over time. At the same time, there is a lot that is unknown. Over the years, what people know continues to change. For example, the way society views children changes throughout generations. In earlier times, people often believed children were blank slates ready to be formed by their parents' intentions. Today, people believe that children learn through experiences, but have inborn tendencies and abilities, **1-5**.

People also view teens differently today than in previous decades. In the past, people considered teens to be young adults. There was no transition period between childhood and adulthood (as people now believe and term *adolescence*). Adult responsibilities, including marriage and childbirth, were often hoisted on young teens.

In the past, people even viewed adulthood differently. People commonly believed that upon reaching adulthood, no further development occurs. Today, tremendous physical, cognitive, and socioemotional changes occur throughout adulthood. These changes are not just seen as aging, but a refining in many abilities.

Although the details of what people know about human development will continue to increase, four basic guidelines can be established. That is, these are ideas believed to be true about how people develop. Human development is relatively orderly and takes place gradually. The ways in which people develop are interrelated, and among individuals, development varies.

Juriah Mosin/Shutterstock.com

**1-5** Reading is a taught skill, but this child's curiosity and tendency toward learning is innate.

## Human Development Is Relatively Orderly

Development occurs in an orderly manner. For example, children learn their alphabet before they can read. They learn to walk before they run. They learn to ride a bike before driving a car. Although not everyone proceeds in exactly the same manner, as people develop, their abilities build on each other in an orderly way.

By understanding how people develop, you can make relatively accurate and useful predictions. Understanding the orderly stages of development helps you deal with people in a manner that is appropriate to their abilities and understanding. You can forecast and make reasonable predictions about people based on their present and future stages in life.

## Human Development Takes Place Gradually

While some changes occur within minutes, most changes take weeks, months, or years to complete. Consider height as an example. The physical changes that occur from birth through adolescence are enormous. A growth spurt might occur over a few months or a year, but for the most part, these changes are gradual. You may not notice growth from month to month unless someone tells you. Perhaps you experienced a growth spurt in late childhood or early adolescence, **1-6**. You probably did not feel yourself growing, but shortening pants legs and remarks of others are simple reminders.

Likewise, your brain development and cognitive changes are astounding. These changes also occur over time. Perhaps you did not notice your changing reading abilities until the books seemed simplistic and immature. Over time, you can see how friendships change, too.

## Human Development Is Interrelated

As children learn to walk, they also learn to say a few words. At the same time, fine-motor skills develop and they begin to feed themselves. Children explore their world with a curious mind. They remain tied to their caregivers, sensing anxiety when the caregiver is out of sight.

*Yuri Arcurs/Shutterstock.com*

**1-6** Most people experience growth spurts during adolescence.

### Cultural Connections — Universal Development

Although social norms, holidays, and languages vary among cultures, the physical, cognitive, and socio-emotional development of the people within each culture is fundamentally universal. For example, the official language of Jordan is Arabic and the official language of Brazil is Portuguese. Even though the languages in each country are different, the cognitive development of people in Jordan is not drastically different from people in Brazil. In both countries, children still learn their native languages in similar ways, are able to pronounce their first words at about the same time, and learn to speak in the same age group. Similar to the cognitive development of children, the physical and socio-emotional development of Jordanian and Brazilian children are not country-specific. Children will physically progress in about the same way and similarly experience social situations. Although cultural customs differ from one country to another, the types of human development are transnational.

#### Writing Activity

Rent two short foreign films from the library featuring young children or teens. While watching each film, notice how the characters are similar to the characters in the other film. In what ways do they differ? Write a journal entry comparing your life experiences with the characters from the films.

Physical, cognitive, and socio-emotional development occur together. They are interdependent of one another. In other words, they are mutually dependent and supporting. Development in one area coincides with development in another area. For example, a young child who is behind in physical coordination is often behind in cognitive and socio-emotional development. If the same child is helped with physical coordination, cognitive and socio-emotional development are often enhanced.

One theorist who recognizes interrelated physical, cognitive, and socio-emotional development is Abraham Maslow. Maslow's *Theory of Human Needs* arranges the types of needs in five levels, **1-7**. The base level includes physical needs to survive such as air, water, food, clothing, and shelter. The second through fourth levels include psychological needs such as security, love and acceptance, and esteem. The final level, self-actualization, is to fully realize one's own potential. This is a lifelong process. According to Maslow, a person cannot meet these higher-level needs until first meeting the basic needs.

## Human Development Varies Among Individuals

Although development is orderly and predictable, the outcomes and rate of development vary by individual. Many different factors cause these differences. First, genetics and **heredity** (traits people are born with) are different for everyone. Next, a person's experiences and **environment** (all of a person's surroundings and the people in them) are not exactly the same. This is true even for brothers and sisters raised together. Because both heredity and environments influence development and no one is exactly alike, you can expect individual variations in developmental characteristics. There are differences in the ages when people experience events that will influence their development. The bottom line is that everyone grows and changes at a different rate and on a different time schedule.

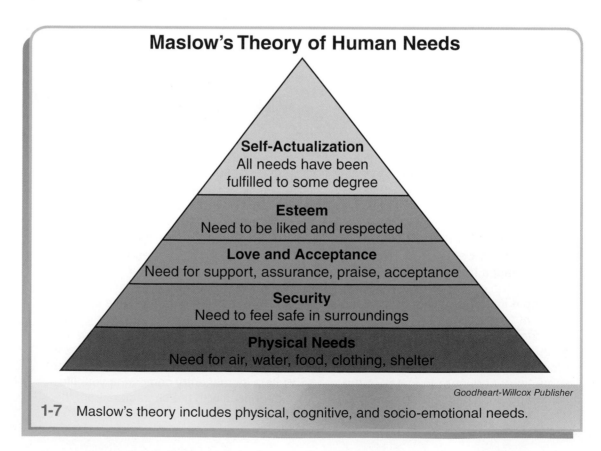

**Maslow's Theory of Human Needs**

**Self-Actualization**
All needs have been fulfilled to some degree

**Esteem**
Need to be liked and respected

**Love and Acceptance**
Need for support, assurance, praise, acceptance

**Security**
Need to feel safe in surroundings

**Physical Needs**
Need for air, water, food, clothing, shelter

*Goodheart-Willcox Publisher*

**1-7**  Maslow's theory includes physical, cognitive, and socio-emotional needs.

## Checkpoint

1. Name the four basic guidelines about how people develop. Give an example of each.
2. How can understanding the orderly stages of development help you deal with people in a manner that is appropriate to their abilities and understanding?
3. According to Maslow, what are the five levels of human needs?
4. List two factors that cause human development to vary among individuals.

## Key Issues in Development

Human development takes a lifetime. Many milestones along the way mark the journey from newborn to old age, **1-8**. A fascination with how people grow and change over time is evident in people's interest in those around them, especially celebrities or newsmakers. Movie stars and other news generators are all sources of interest and speculation. How does a child dreamer actually become a professional baseball player, a gifted teacher, or a brain surgeon? How does a young child develop into a criminal? People want to know.

People are fascinated and curious with newsmakers. As a person becomes famous, people have questions. What are this person's likes and dislikes? Where does the person live? Is the person married? Does the person have children? How articulate is this person? Curiosity often does not stop there, however.

*Thomas M. Perkins/Shutterstock.com*

**1-8** From grandchild to grandparent, many changes take place along the way.

As a person's fame rises, the questions often increase. How did this person become who he or she is today? What was the person like as a child? Who are the person's parents? Where did the person grow up? Which schools did the person attend? Who were the major influences in his or her life? How will the rise to fame impact this person?

This example highlights three important issues in human development. First, is the *nature versus nurture debate*. How much of who people are relates to genetics and how much relates to environment? Are there some traits that are genetic and others that are created by environment?

Second, and very much related, is the issue of *continuity versus discontinuity*. Do changes in development occur because of the slow progression of change or do they occur as a result of something abruptly changing?

Lastly, and again related, is the issue of motivation. Who directs people's growth and development? Do people direct themselves through exploration and interactions? Do others, such as parents, teachers, and friends, direct growth and development? These three issues continue to be the subject of debate and controversy.

## Nature Versus Nurture

How do you describe yourself to others? Are you outgoing? Are you shy? Do you have brown hair and eyes? How might you describe your body type? Are you thin or are you heavy? You have many traits, abilities, and tendencies. Some of these you may attribute to genetics. Others you assign to your environment.

*Junial Enterprises/Shutterstock.com*

**1-9**  This teen has similar physical features as her father.

If you have brown eyes, you may credit this to your father. You are likely correct since eye color is an inherited trait, **1-9**. If you are thin, you may credit this to your mother. Could your weight, however, have more to do with your eating habits than heredity? Perhaps you eat healthful foods such as fruits and vegetables and avoid junk foods high in sugar and fat. You are also physically active every day. If you were not carefully monitoring your weight, would you still be thin? Body dimensions and traits may be easier to trace to genetic or environmental influences, but for many traits, identifying the source can be difficult.

The debate between genetic versus environmental influences on development is often called the **nature versus nurture debate**. This is the choice between heredity as a source of your development and the environment. Tremendous progress in the last two decades has helped identify traits more influenced by heredity and those influenced more by environment. For most traits, other than physical characteristics such as eye and hair color, both genetics and environment play a part. The next chapter will cover the issue of nature versus nurture in more depth.

## Case Study ???

### Nature Versus Nurture

Imagine Cara, a shy and reserved girl, sitting in class nervously waiting for her turn to read aloud. Next to her sits her classmate Kenny, who is bursting with energy and can hardly wait for his turn to read. When Kenny's turn comes, he speaks loudly and confidently, even when he stumbles over words.
- Were Cara and Kenny born that way?
- Was Cara taught to be shy by her shy parents? Is shyness a natural part of who she is?
- If Kenny were born with a tendency to be shy, would he have been as outgoing if raised in Cara's family rather than his own?

## Continuity Versus Discontinuity

Have you heard stories about yourself from when you were a young child? Do you remember kindergarten? What were some of your experiences and feelings in elementary school? How are you similar to the person you were as a seventh grader? Some who study human development believe that people are essentially the same from birth to death. Personalities remain intact. People who are quick to explore the world around them remain so. Those who are hesitant around new people and experiences stay that way. Although people grow and change, they essentially stay the same. Developmental changes are relatively slow, but steady. This process of development is called **continuity** for its stable nature.

Perhaps development is not continuous and slow. Possibly, development happens instead as the result of sudden changes that occur throughout the lifespan. A child enters preschool. At this abrupt change in his or her daily routine, the child reacts and makes strides toward becoming more independent. Perhaps other changes such as a parental divorce, the death of a sibling, or a move to another city further promote the child's independence, **1-10**. This process of development, spurred by abrupt changes, is called **discontinuity**.

Both continuities and discontinuities are likely to affect a person's development throughout the lifespan. You may be born with certain tendencies, but as each of you experiences different life events, you change and adapt as necessary. A person's hesitancy toward new experiences may change as he or she encounters new experiences that are not chosen. Anger problems may become continuous as a person faces new experiences that trigger similar emotional responses. Perhaps these same anger responses may be thwarted when a negative consequence, such as losing a friendship, occurs as a result of an emotional response.

## Pedagogy Versus Andragogy

Babies develop into children. Children grow and mature into teens. Teens become adults. Who directs this development? Does development occur naturally? Do others such as parents or caregivers lead development? Some people believe that human growth and development relies heavily on another person guiding or mentoring learning. This teacher- or parent-directed method of learning is often referred to as **pedagogy**.

*StockLite/Shutterstock.com*

**1-10** Moving away from your school and friends can be an abrupt change in life.

## Health Connections    Teaching Styles

One teaching style that utilizes the theory of andragogy is the Montessori method of teaching. This teaching style encourages children to direct themselves in learning and play activities instead of the teacher leading them through activities. Children can explore their own interests through the five senses and can learn to guide themselves at their own pace. This andragogy style of teaching differs from the pedagogy style of teaching because the Montessori teacher is less direct in instruction.

Montessori teachers prepare the environment around the children and supply activities that are both self-directing and self-correcting. Children are placed in classrooms by three-year age groups. These classrooms foster social interaction, in which the older students can help explain what they have learned to younger students. This also reinforces the older children's learnings. From exposure to watching older students, the younger students can direct their own activities to test, recreate, and gain experiences.

### Speaking Activity

Compare the pedagogy teaching style to the andragogy teaching style. With a partner, debate the pros and cons of each teaching style.

Cheryl Savan/Shutterstock.com

**1-11**  Independent learning can mean reading about developments in your area of interest.

Some people believe that development is self-directed from the earliest stages of infancy. This is termed **andragogy**. Proponents of andragogy believe that a child interacts with his or her environment very early in life, directing learning as growth and change occurs.

Which is correct? Probably a combination of both pedagogy and andragogy is an accurate assessment. Young babies and children direct much of their learning as they explore their world. Parents and caregivers provide stimulating experiences that promote learning. As people mature, they become more independent and self-motivated, **1-11**. Learning environments appropriately change from teacher-directed instruction of pedagogy to self-directed instruction. Andragogy utilizes experiences and maturing social roles of the learner. Guidance and mentoring can be used. For example, as a teen takes on more responsibility by babysitting children, the teen learns what works and does not work in keeping the children safe and entertained. The children's parents may leave instructions, but the teen learns the responsibilities of the job through self-directed learning.

## Checkpoint

1. Make a list of some of your own personal characteristics and describe whether the traits are a result of nature or nurture.
2. Define the terms *continuity* and *discontinuity*.
3. Compare and contrast pedagogy and andragogy.
4. What are you learning through pedagogy? What are you learning through andragogy?

## Why Study Human Development?

There are many reasons to study human development. You interact with people daily in your family, school, job, and recreation. Studying human development gives insight into what to expect of the people in your life based on their stage of development. This understanding may enhance relationships as you work with children, other teens, and adults at different stages of life. You will be better able to appreciate and relate to people at different stages of development, **1-12**. You will have more insight into your own life both now and in the future. Knowing more about your own stage of life may motivate you to consider choices you make that will affect your life.

*Lisa F. Young/Shutterstock.com*

**1-12** Understanding different stages in lifespan development can help you connect with other people.

## Checkpoint

1. How will studying human development help you as you interact with people daily?
2. How will studying human development enhance your relationships with others?
3. How can studying human development affect your life?

## Summary

The study of human development encompasses all the aspects of human growth from birth through old age. These include the progressive changes seen in physical growth, intellectual or cognitive abilities, and socio-emotional development.

Development occurs in an orderly and gradual manner. Every person's rate and timing of development is unique. No two people develop exactly the same, although similarities can be seen throughout stages of life.

A lot is known about human development, but there is still much more to learn. Today, debates continue about several prominent issues. How much of development can be attributed to genetics? How much can be attributed to environment? This is the nature versus nurture debate. Whether development occurs slowly over the lifespan or is a result of abrupt changes is also debated. Lastly, whether development is directed by the person or a caregiver continues to be pondered. In all three of these issues, the answer is *both*. What is not yet answered is *how much*?

## Vocabulary Activity

Write each of the terms on a separate sheet of paper. For each term, quickly write a word you think relates to the term. In small groups, exchange papers. Have each person in the group explain a term on the list. Take turns until all terms have been explained.

## Critical Thinking

1. **Determine.** At which age are you at your prime in life? Why?
2. **Analyze.** Do reality television shows harm participants?
3. **Predict.** How do you predict that you will grow and change between now and when you are age 30?
4. **Identify.** If you could choose any age to be today, what age would you choose? Why?
5. **Draw conclusions.** Observe a teacher who uses the andragogy teaching method. Why do you think this method was chosen?
6. **Evaluate.** Do you think that people of different ages can be close friends? If not, why not?
7. **Assess.** Which aspect of development is most important to overall growth and development?
8. **Compare and contrast.** Choose one year from your life as a child and another from your teen years. How are you the same? How are you different?
9. **Make inferences.** Make a photo picture collage of a celebrity or someone you know from infancy to present age. What factors may have affected the visible growth and development changes? What invisible changes do you assume?
10. **Cause and effect.** How might eating the same unhealthy meal for lunch and dinner for the next five years affect your development?

## Core Skills

11. **Writing.** Write a two-page paper about how you have grown and changed physically, intellectually, emotionally, and socially since your first day of high school.

12. **Speaking.** Practice and give a one minute speech on why studying human development is important.

13. **Listening.** Ask a parent or another adult how they have changed since graduating from high school.

14. **Reading.** Read a biography about someone's life. How has that person grown and changed over his or her lifetime?

15. **Math.** Find the birth length of yourself or someone else your age. Compare your birth length to your current height. What is your percentage growth?

16. **CTE Career Readiness Practice.** Presume you are the human resources director of a small business. Recent research shows that employees who have good eating habits and total wellness have a positive impact on productivity. You are forming a workplace *Wellness Council*. Get together with your council members (two or more classmates) and brainstorm a list of several possible ideas for encouraging healthful eating and wellness among employees. Then narrow the list to the three best options. How would you implement one of these options? How would you get employees involved? What criteria will you use to determine how well employees are meeting healthful living goals?

## Research

17. Search for an electronic news article about aging or a medical breakthrough on extending the lifespan. Is the article from a scientific, medical, or well-known educational institution? Avoid articles that lack objectivity.

18. Choose a decade from the past century. Research the social, political, economic, and historic events of that decade. How might these events have affected someone who was a teen during this decade? Create an electronic presentation of your findings to share with the class.

## Event Prep

19. Arrange to interview an older adult about how both heredity and environment influenced his or her development through the lifespan. What traits did he or she inherit? What events had a great influence on development? Prepare a list of questions you would like to ask prior to the interview. After the interview, create a scrapbook to record the interview questions and responses. You may wish to expand your project by developing an FCCLA *Power of One* project for *Family Ties*. Use the FCCLA *Planning Process* to guide your project planning. See your FCCLA adviser for further information.

# Chapter 2

# How and Why People Develop and Learn

Rehan Qureshi/Shutterstock.com

# Objectives

After studying this chapter, you will be able to

- explain the role of theories in understanding human development.
- describe how early experiences are important and heavily couched in emotion as described by psychoanalytical theories.
- identify how psychosocial theory addresses the stages of socio-emotional development seen in humans from birth to old age.
- describe how learning theories include behaviorism, operant conditioning, social cognitive theory, cognitive theory, and social learning.
- summarize historical influences on modern theories of human development.
- assess how environment can influence some personality traits, while others are influenced by heredity.
- compare and contrast research methods commonly used to study human development.

## Reading Prep

Review the table of contents at the beginning of this text. Trace the development of the content that is being presented from simple to complex ideas.

## Key Terms

| | | |
|---|---|---|
| developmental theories | classical conditioning | scientific method |
| psychoanalytic theories | operant conditioning | hypothesis |
| psychosocial development stages | social cognitive theory | descriptive studies |
| cognitive theories | genes | manipulative experiments |
| moral decisions | genetics | longitudinal studies |
| observable behaviors | ethological theory | cross-sectional studies |
| behaviorism | ecological theory | naturalistic experiments |

## Visit the G-W Learning Companion Website to:

- **build** vocabulary with e-flash cards and interactive games;
- **assess** what you learn by completing self-assessment quizzes; and
- **expand** knowledge with activities that extend learning.

G-WLEARNING.com    www.g-wlearning.com/development/

Imagine yourself standing in the checkout line at a grocery store. The line is slow moving and as you wait your turn, you have a hard time ignoring a nearby young child who is throwing a temper tantrum. The child kicks, screams, and lies on the floor and cries. Why? Did the child's mother say *no* to a request for a toy? Maybe the reason is much more complex. You think about why this behavior is occurring and what motivates the child's actions. Your opinion is based on past experiences and knowledge. Your opinion may be different depending on whether you know the young child, or if the child is a stranger to you. Is the child tired, hungry, or too young to understand? Does the child not get enough attention? Is this a behavior that is usually rewarded?

## The Role of Developmental Theories

People have opinions about why others act the way they do. Researchers and scientists explore the many ways in which humans grow and develop. They are motivated by the intrigue of understanding how humans develop. They observe people, perform experiments, and draw conclusions based on their studies and earlier studies that others have done. As a result of observation and experimentation, scientists and researchers formulate developmental theories. **Developmental theories** are comprehensive explanations about why people act and behave the way they do and how they change over time.

Why should you learn about developmental theories? In doing so, you will better understand the capabilities, motivations, and expectations of those around you, **2-1**. This includes family members, fellow students, coworkers, and those you care for or work with in professional settings. Understanding developmental theories will give you a broader picture of how people develop and change over time. You will not have to rely only on your own limited personal experiences

*Diego Cervo/Shutterstock.com*

**2-1** By learning about development theories, you will better understand what others are capable of doing and why.

and observations. Most importantly, understanding developmental theories can make you a more empathetic person. *Empathetic* means to be understanding or sensitive to the feelings, thoughts, and experiences of others.

## Checkpoint

1. How do researchers and scientists explore the ways in which humans grow and develop?
2. What are developmental theories?
3. Why should you learn about developmental theories?
4. What does empathetic mean?

# How Early Life Experiences Affect People Over Time

Many theorists have held different ideas about how and why humans develop and change the way they do. Some theorists believe that much development happens at an unconscious level and is buried in emotions. These ideas are called **psychoanalytic theories**. Psychoanalytic theorists analyze the symbolic meaning behind behaviors. They often believe that early life experiences are important in development.

## Freud's Theory

Sigmund Freud was a pioneer in applying psychoanalytic theory. With the goal of restoring psychological health, he helped his patients talk through their issues. As he talked with more and more patients, he began to create a developmental theory that focused on early life experiences. He believed that what happens early in life affects a person for years to come. Although his theory is not considered scientifically sound today, he opened the door to a new way of understanding development.

## Cultural Connections   Shoulders of Giants

Changing historical views of health combined with recent developments in health and psychology influence modern theories on human development. As more information becomes available and understood, scientists and researchers are able to expand on preexisting information and develop new research and theories. Each theorist partially relies on information available during the time, including society views and norms, psychological studies, and knowledge from the medical field. Thus, historical information can influence modern theories. For example, Erik Erikson's psychosocial theory developed at a specific era in history. Erikson, a student of Freud, studied the principles of Freud's psychoanalytic development. Erikson was determined to branch from Freud's school of thought and incorporate his own ideas. Through additional observation and research conducted in various countries, Erikson developed and expanded his own theory.

### Speaking Activity

Isaac Newton once wrote to a colleague, "If I have seen a little further, it is by standing on the shoulders of giants." What did Newton intend when he wrote this phrase? Working with a partner, discuss your thoughts.

# Erikson's Psychosocial Theory

Erik Erikson appreciated Freud's work, but believed that both early and later life experiences affect development. He felt that development is a social process and people are motivated by their desire to connect with other people. Erikson believed that all humans develop in eight stages, **2-2**.

| Erikson's Psychosocial Developmental Stages | | |
|---|---|---|
| **Stage** | **Age** | **Description** |
| **Trust versus mistrust** | Infancy (birth to 1 year) | Babies learn about trust from their caregivers who meet their needs including food, attention, physical contact, interaction, and safety. When needs are not met, babies do not learn to trust others and the world is perceived as unpredictable. |
| **Autonomy versus shame and doubt** | Toddler (1 to 3 years) | Toddlers learn how to control their physical bodies by feeding, toileting, dressing and undressing, and making strides in physical development. As toddlers learn new skills, they become self-confident. A lack of control or independence can make them feel like failures and cause shame and doubt. Often, this is caused by caregivers punishing them for not doing things right. |
| **Initiative versus guilt** | Early childhood (3 through 5 years) | Through discovery and exploration, young children learn about the world and their place in it. They learn what is real and what is imaginary. They learn to take initiative for their place in the world. Criticism and punishment can result in guilt for their own actions. |
| **Industry versus inferiority** | Middle childhood (6 through 12 years) | Children develop competencies both at school and at home. They develop a sense of self and confidence by becoming competent in the outside world. If children are compared negatively to others, feelings of inferiority can surface. |
| **Identity versus identity confusion** | Adolescence (13 through 18 years or older) | Preteens and teens begin to understand and experiment with a number of different roles. A task during this stage is to integrate multiple roles such as sister, daughter, student, athlete, friend, and employee into one consistent role. If a central or core identity is not established, role confusion exists. |
| **Intimacy versus isolation** | Early adulthood (19 through 39 years) | During later adolescence and early adulthood, intimate relationships form. These relationships should involve sharing one's self emotionally. Success in this stage is based on success in earlier stages. Failure to establish intimacy results in emotional or psychological isolation. |
| **Generativity versus stagnation** | Middle adulthood (40 through 65 years) | Adults in midlife begin to place emphasis on assisting others through sharing culture with the next generation. This can be done in many ways including rearing children, teaching others in the workplace or community, or passing on cultural values. A lack of generativity leads to stagnation. |
| **Integrity versus despair** | Older adulthood (66 years and older) | In the last stage of life, adults review their life and reflect on its meaning. If people are satisfied with the meaning of their life and involvement, there is a sense of integrity. Without it, despair emerges at the end of their life. |

*Goodheart-Willcox Publisher*

**2-2**  According to Erikson, personality can develop in ways that are healthy or unhealthy.

According to Erikson's **psychosocial development stages**, people must successfully resolve a psychological and/or social conflict before moving to the next stage. If they do not, their unsuccessful resolution will affect their future stages of development. For example, in the first stage, babies must resolve the conflict of trusting or not trusting others, especially those who care for them. Babies must learn to trust that they will be fed when they cry and comforted when they need comforting. If babies do not have their needs met, they will not easily trust others throughout life. If babies' needs are met, they will become trusting people capable of having trusting relationships. Erikson was careful to point out, however, that there must be a healthy balance for optimal development. If needs are always met to an extreme, a baby may become overly trusting.

What about the other stages? According to Erikson, the stages continue to work similarly throughout life. In early childhood, preschoolers face the conflict of learning to develop initiative by carrying out plans versus taking advantage of others. For example, a preschooler may come up with a plan to "play school." She wants to be the pretend teacher. She also wants her younger sister and neighbor to play as her students. They go along with her plan, but as she becomes bossy, they lose interest. The preschooler needs to take the initiative to carry out her plan to play school. At the same time, she has to learn to make the game enjoyable for others. Resolving initiative versus guilt issues are important during this stage of life and will have lifelong results.

During the elementary school years, children must master important social and academic skills, **2-3**. Erikson calls this conflict *industry versus inferiority*. By not keeping up with their peers, children will feel inferior or less important. Again, Erikson was careful to point out that there must be a healthy balance for optimal development.

*iofoto/Shutterstock.com*

**2-3**  Making friends, learning to read, and learning how to add and subtract are just a few of the important social and academic skills children must learn during middle childhood.

During the teen years, individuals must resolve the conflict of *identity versus identity confusion*. Questions such as the following all become important: Who am I? How am I different from others? How do others see me? What are my interests? What will I do with my life?

Erikson did not stop with adolescence. He believed that development occurs throughout a person's life. People are always changing and developing. Even people in older adulthood must face psychosocial conflicts that will help them eventually face death.

## Checkpoint

1. What do psychoanalytic theorists analyze? What do they often believe?
2. Which theorist was a pioneer in applying psychoanalytic theory?
3. According to Erikson, which conflict must individuals resolve during the elementary school years?
4. According to Erikson, which conflict must individuals resolve during the teen years?

# How People Process Information and Learn

Ideas about how people process information, think, and learn are called **cognitive theories**. Cognitive researchers seek to explain the differences in how people think throughout the stages of life. They look for explanations of how cognition changes throughout the lifespan. The most well-known researcher was Jean Piaget. Many cognitive theorists have followed Piaget's work, including the researcher Lev Vygotsky.

## Piaget's Cognitive Theory

Piaget recognized that children do not think like adults. He also realized that babies are alike in how they think. Children are alike in how they think. Teens are alike in how they think. Lastly, adults are alike in how they think. Piaget described the stages of cognitive development in four stages, **2-4**.

So why do young children think differently from teens? Piaget believed young children base their thinking on what they know. When children think the moon is following them or that babies are delivered at the front door, their beliefs make sense to them based on their limited experiences. As they gain more experience, their way of thinking will change and adapt.

Although many researchers have added to people's understanding of how thinking occurs, Piaget's four stages of cognitive development remain important. His theory helps people understand how children are active in their own development and learning. They need a lot of exposure to experimentation, discovery, and firsthand experiences.

## Vygotsky's Sociocultural Theory

Numerous researchers and scientists have challenged Piaget's theory. Many have challenged his view that all humans develop through experimentation with

## Piaget's Stages of Cognitive Development

| Stage | Age | Description |
|---|---|---|
| **Sensorimotor** | **Birth to 2 years** | Babies begin to learn about the world through exploring with their mouths, grasping objects, and using other senses. Learning relies on reflexes, but moves to more sophisticated behaviors. |
| **Preoperational** | **2 to 7 years** | Toddlers and young children begin to learn to communicate through language or other symbols. They do not make broad generalizations about things they learn, but learn specific knowledge. As they progress through this stage, they begin to understand concepts such as reversibility and consequences. |
| **Concrete operational** | **7 to 11 years** | Children in this stage can make generalizations and understand reversibility and consequences. They understand that an action or behavior can cause a chain of events resulting in a different result. They can group, subgroup, and make classification hierarchies. They become more logical during this stage. |
| **Formal operational** | **11 years and older** | Individuals become more logical, concrete, and can process abstract thoughts during this stage. They can make predictions about cause and effect, use analogies and metaphors, and entertain "what if" questions. Objects do not need to be seen to be considered. |

*Goodheart-Willcox Publisher*

**2-4**   Piaget viewed intelligence as a process that helps people adapt to their environment.

objects. Instead, others believe that the social and cultural environment shapes human cognitive development. Cognitive development does not just happen, but occurs because humans interact with other people, not just objects. They learn language. They learn how to use tools such as pencils, computers, art media, and other tools that aid communication. Generation after generation, older people pass this knowledge to younger people.

Vygotsky was one well-known researcher who believed that children are social beings and develop their minds through interactions with parents, teachers, and other knowledgeable people, **2-5**. For example, when Mackenzie's teacher shows her how to fold and cut a paper heart, she may later repeat her teacher's instructions to herself. Through this and many other interactions, she will learn to be a skilled problem solver. This internalization of problem solving will continue throughout life as Mackenzie interacts with mentors.

*Monkey Business Images/Shutterstock.com*

**2-5**   Vygotsky believed that social interaction is critical to cognitive development.

### Kohlberg's Theory of Moral Development

Imagine that you really need a medication, but do not have enough money to pay the pharmacy. Would you steal the medicine from the pharmacy? What if having the medicine is a matter of life and death? Lawrence Kohlberg asked a similar question to children, teens, and adults. How do people decide what is right and what is wrong? In doing his research, Kohlberg identified three different levels of thinking that people go through in making **moral decisions** (personal decisions that evaluate what is right and what is wrong).

In the first level, people make decisions based on whether or not they will be punished or rewarded. All children are in this level. In the second level, people's moral decisions are motivated by laws and how they might be perceived. Some older children and many youth are in this level. In the third level, some teens and many adults make moral decisions based on principles such as justice.

Because Kohlberg observed men and boys to develop his theory, some researchers believed that his findings did not include the way women and girls make decisions. Carol Gilligan was one of these researchers. She believed that the idea of justice was typical of males, but less typical of females. She believed that many women used the idea of care for others as a motivating factor in making moral decisions.

## Checkpoint

1. Which theorist described the stages of cognitive development in four stages? What are these stages?
2. According to cognitive theory, why do young children think differently from teens?
3. Describe Vygotsky's sociocultural theory.
4. What are moral decisions?
5. Describe Kohlberg's three levels of thinking that people go through in making moral decisions.

## How Experiences Cause People to Behave in Certain Ways

Researchers and scientists have long been interested in how people think and learn. Early researchers and scientists believed that people were essentially blank screens. Just like a computer, people are products of data entered. When data is entered, an outcome will result. When talking about people, these results are called **observable behaviors** (the things people do and say or the way they act).

Why does 8-year-old Tyler hit others on the playground? Does this behavior occur because he was modeled aggressive behavior at home? Did an older brother or sister hit him? **Behaviorism** is the belief that people's behavior is determined by forces in the environment that are beyond their control, **2-6**. In what is often described as the *nature* (what you were born with) versus *nurture* (what you have been taught) debate, behaviorists believe that nurture wins.

*Rob Marmion/Shutterstock.com*

**2-6**  According to behaviorists, how people behave depends solely on what they are taught, not what they are born with.

## Pavlov's Classical Conditioning

Ivan Pavlov demonstrated the idea of behaviorism through his infamous experiment with a dog. The dog, which had a natural innate tendency to salivate when in the sight of food learned to salivate at the sound of a bell. This happened after a training period when a bell would ring each time the dog was to be served food. After awhile, food was no longer needed for the dog to salivate—only the sound of the bell. Since that time, this has been termed **classical conditioning** (behaviors that are associated with emotional responses).

Does conditioning have to be that direct? Can conditioning happen without a trainer? Behaviorists answer *yes*. A parent may be unaware that he or she is teaching a child to be afraid of something, such as swimming or dogs. Perhaps the parent takes a loud deep breath and tenses his or her muscles or voice—all signs of fear. Repeating those reactions may result in a child having the same fears. Likewise, hearing a favorite song can bring positive thoughts based on an emotional experience you associate with the song. You may remember a certain moment, friend, food, or joke. Hearing the song makes you feel good. Positive, negative, or neutral experiences affect people and a range of emotional associations, attitudes, and behaviors result.

## Skinner's Operant Conditioning

B.F. Skinner was well-known for identifying the basic principle of operant conditioning. **Operant conditioning** is the repetition of behaviors when reinforced. People tend to repeat behaviors that have a positive effect. If you receive a good grade on a project, you may use a similar strategy on a future project, **2-7**. Repeated high grades on tests and projects may result in you believing that you are good in math.

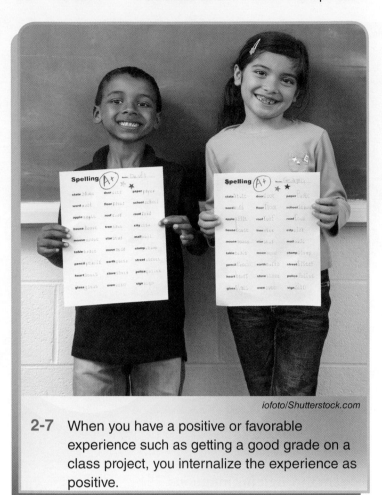

iofoto/Shutterstock.com

**2-7** When you have a positive or favorable experience such as getting a good grade on a class project, you internalize the experience as positive.

Skinner saw that to make the behavior stick, the reinforcement must be gradually removed in an unpredictable pattern. Sometimes you are reinforced, whereas other times you are not. He believed that these stages were crucial to learning. As a result, you still believe that you are good in math and try harder each time you complete a project or take an exam. Your behavior has changed. Behaviorists call this learning.

Behaviorism in the form of operant conditioning became quite popular in American education. Providing continuous positive reinforcement when a new skill or behavior is learned, followed by gradual removal of the reinforcement, is believed to result in a permanent behavioral change. Negative reinforcement, or punishment, is also believed to be very important.

You have probably observed the effects of behaviorism when working with children. Encouraging children for their efforts, modeling positive behaviors, and maintaining a positive attitude can have a significant effect on their behavior by making interactions pleasant and fun.

## Social Cognitive Theory: Taking Behaviorism One More Step

Is behaviorism really that simple? Imagine that you are babysitting several active young children. They are arguing over toys, whining and complaining, and physically hurting one another. Despite all your encouragement, modeling of appropriate behavior, and a positive attitude, you are having difficulty getting the children under your care to behave appropriately. If simple positive reinforcement and punishment is all that is necessary, why do children not learn and behave the way people want them to? Also, if behaviorism really works, why can people not use behaviorism to control behaviors in adults?

Albert Bandura argued that people are very different from Pavlov's dog. They are much more complex. He argued that people, whether children or adults, watch and imitate other people's behaviors, despite whether or not there are rewards and punishments involved, **2-8**. People are affected by rewards and punishments, but their reaction to rewards and punishments are filtered by their own perceptions, thoughts, and motivations. He called this **social cognitive theory**.

Social cognitive theorists believe that a child who observes a kind act may later imitate the same act toward a classmate. Another learns how to swear or eat healthy by imitating other people's actions. The same experiences, however, will not have the same result on every person. How a person responds is based on personal reaction and how he or she processes the information. A child who observes aggressive behavior may become aggressive or a person who avoids conflict. The result all depends on how the person processes the information and his or her cognitive abilities.

Lisa F. Young/Shutterstock.com

**2-8**   A teen may tackle a tough math problem by imitating a teacher.

## Checkpoint

1. What is behaviorism?
2. Who demonstrated the idea of behaviorism through his infamous experiment with a dog? What has this been termed?
3. What is operant conditioning? Who was well-known for identifying this principle?
4. What is social cognitive theory?

## Which Theory Is Correct?

There are hundreds of theories about the ways humans develop. This textbook covers just a few. Which theory is the most correct? No one theory should be regarded as the absolute truth. Humans are much too complex to describe using simplistic theory.

Although there are many different and sometimes conflicting ways to explain human development, most are valid to some extent. Some theories may fit better than others. Sometimes theories may conflict. The conflict between two theories, however, often leads to more valid insights. You can benefit from understanding several approaches to development and applying them to people of all ages with whom you interact.

Throughout your life there will always be more theories that emerge as knowledge about human development grows. This makes studying lifespan development exciting. For example, in recent years scientists have been debating the origin of specific characteristics or traits of people, such as mathematical problem-solving abilities. Is this an inborn trait or a learned trait? Theories about the development of specific traits are discussed in the next section.

## Checkpoint

1. Which theory is the most correct?
2. What can often develop from the conflict between two theories?
3. Give an example of a debate that has been occurring among scientists in recent years.

# What Causes People to Develop Specific Traits?

This question has been asked repeatedly. Is it nature or nurture? Are a person's personality traits, abilities, skills, and tastes a result of *heredity* or a result of *environment*? Most researchers today will answer *both*. The question is not a matter of "which," but "how much?" How much does heredity affect people's traits? How much does their environment or home life affect them? The challenge for researchers to answer the question of "how much?" is that heredity and the environment interact in complex ways.

## How Does Biology Influence Development?

Do you have blue eyes, freckles, brown hair, the ability to sing, or athleticism? Certain traits such as these are passed to you from your parents through a complex process at the time of conception, **2-9**. At that moment, specific instructions about you including hair and eye color, among thousands of other traits, are in your genes. **Genes** are the part of your DNA (deoxyribonucleic acid) molecule and are found in every one of your body cells.

Monkey Business Images/Shutterstock.com

**2-9**  There are certain traits you have in common with family members related to you biologically.

The instructions found in your DNA do not change over your lifetime. These instructions, which make you who you are, remain constant. Your DNA does not change. If your DNA carries the instructions for brown eyes, this eye color will remain the same throughout your life. Genes control many things about you including your physical traits, brain development, and your personality and temperament.

No single gene determines a particular behavior as human behavior is extremely complex. In recent years, however, **genetics** (the study of genes) have started to show patterns about how just one gene can be associated with different inherited disorders. The most common example given is how an extra chromosome 21 is responsible for Down syndrome. *Down syndrome* is a disorder that causes a delay in physical, intellectual, and language development. Genetic research will likely uncover more and more associations between traits and groupings of multiple genes.

When considering factors that influence human development, genes are just a part of the story. There are many genetic and environmental factors that are connected to the development of any trait. There is still much that is unknown, however, about the specific combinations of genetic and environmental factors that determine traits. Just because a person has the genetic makeup to have a trait, does not mean that the trait will develop. Assigning traits and behaviors based on biology is called **ethological theory**.

## How Does Environment Influence Development?

Even though genes determine your individual traits, the environment can manipulate some traits. Scientists and researchers are finding many ways in which the environment affects growth and development. Social and emotional traits are affected by the environment, but physical traits are, too. For example, the human brain continues to grow and develop long after birth. When children are exposed to stimulating and interactive environments, their brains physically respond differently from the brains of children who have not had the exposure. The brain development of critical pathways needed for strong connections affects children's cognitive skills. Assigning traits and behaviors based on environment is called **ecological theory**.

### Family

Families affect human development in profound ways. They offer the most immediate setting for human development. Children have their most frequent interactions with family or caregivers in the home, daycare, or school.

Many research studies suggest that the quality of the home environment is especially important to children's development and that these influences are very complex, **2-10**. Good parenting and a stimulating home environment are consistently associated with better outcomes for children. For example, family interactions and activities that stimulate language and cognitive development also promote social development. At all ages, family members teach children how to trade or share toys, resolve conflicts, recognize and express emotions in acceptable ways, and interact with others in socially appropriate ways.

*Iakov Filimonov/Shutterstock.com*

**2-10** Stress in the home has an effect on the health of teens and adults.

Families matter. Researchers and scientists agree on this. Families, however, differ greatly in terms of their basic parental abilities and skills, their financial resources, sibling relationships and birth order, extended family involvement, and values. The same parents can have a different effect on different children within the same family. How and why families matter are much more complicated questions that have yet to be completely answered.

## Peers

Although families have the greatest social influence on a child's early development, peers have a greater impact during later childhood and adolescence. Friendships or the lack of friendships, social power and status, and acceptance and belonging all affect social and emotional development. Peers offer equal status, a relationship that does not exist in child-adult relationships. Friendships change as children grow and develop. Relationships between boys and girls change, too. Peer relationships also help children and teens interpret their own culture through unique language, fads, music, and fashion. For adults, peers form the basis of social networks that lead to social and emotional health and development.

## Community

Research has often focused on the impact family and peers have on development. Newer studies also examine the role community plays. The community offers a physical environment in which to live and grow. A person's community is the neighborhood, town, or city in which he or she lives, **2-11**. School is also part of a person's community. The community factors that affect development are endless.

Some researchers see a relationship between people's self-worth and the way they view their environment. People of all ages may derive their self-concept according to how others view their neighborhood. For example, children living in poverty may see themselves differently from their more affluent classmates. In the community in which they live, they may interpret this to mean that they are not as valuable as wealthier classmates. Although this situation does not always result in lower self-esteem, this result is possible.

Factors such as diversity and the average income and education of residents may impact the outcomes of children as behaviors are modeled. Affluent families may have more relationships outside the community that provide both positive and negative social models than families with a lower income. Other factors such as the number of single parents and of children per adult resident might affect children raised in the neighborhood.

*forestpath/Shutterstock.com*

**2-11** Communities can have a profound effect on a person's development.

Negative social environments may deprive children of positive social models and expose them to antisocial behavior. Violence is a concern in American society. The effects of family and community are often blamed for the increase in violence. One boy may learn that aggression and violent behavior is prohibited in school and the potential for being punished may deter him. Another boy may be encouraged to exhibit aggressive behavior as his parents and community encourage a "boys will be boys" attitude.

In addition, communities collectively share values. Resources such as libraries, swimming pools, music venues, youth day camps, and scouting programs provide enriching experiences that enhance social and cognitive development, **2-12**. The availability of resources does not guarantee their use, however.

## Economic Resources

Do parents of different socioeconomic conditions raise their children in different ways? The answer is most likely yes. Do these translate into a better family environment that promotes optimal development for those with more resources? The answer to this question depends more on the quality of parent-child interactions than on economic status.

Families that are economically advantaged may be better able to provide housing in areas that offer more support services. Parents may have higher self-esteem, which in turn directly affects their child's self-esteem. They may be able to provide stimulating resources such as books, travel, and other educational experiences.

Families with fewer economic resources may still efficiently use them in child-rearing processes that promote optimal development. Less economically advantaged parents may spend more quality time playing and talking with their children. Most researchers today agree that family interaction is vitally important in optimal development of youth.

## Media

Teachers often hear students mimicking television characters, reciting movie trailers, or singing advertisement jingles. Students are surrounded by media. Television, movies, videos, podcasts, video games, music, and the Internet bombard people both inside and outside the home. Media has a lot to offer people including consumer news, current events, entertainment, sports, education, and popular culture. Easy accessibility makes media influence even more prevalent.

*Jaimie Duplass/Shutterstock.com*

**2-12**   If youth are valued in a community, greater resources for children and teens are often provided.

## *Safety* Connections                  *Evaluating Websites*

While conducting independent online research, you will be presented with several sources of information. How can you decipher which websites are valid and which are unreliable sources of information? When evaluating websites, look for these indicators in the web address to make sure you are looking at a safe, reliable Internet source.

- *.gov.* These websites are a government resource containing accurate national and international information.
- *.edu.* These websites are for particular schools and universities. Information is educational and reliable.
- *.org.* Information from these websites comes from a recognized nonprofit organization and is safe.
- *.com.* This is the most common website. Information may not always be reliable. Check information against other reference materials for validation.

### Research Activity

The next time you are conducting online research, identify the source of information by determining the type of website. Then, read about the organization, government department, university, or other source of information to further assist you in determining the validity of information.

The media is often blamed for many negative social trends in American society including aggressiveness and violence, early sexual experimentation, and interest in harmful substances such as alcohol and cigarettes. Some teen girls' preoccupation with body image is often blamed on enhanced celebrity body images seen in the media. Do media really have such a negative effect on development in youth?

Here is what researchers know. Media affects everyone differently. Your age, experiences, values, and your media literacy all affect how you interpret a message. Because no two people are alike in all areas, how media affects development will also vary. Media messages can be helpful or harmful to children and teens. Their effect may not be immediately apparent. When a child watches a superhero fight, he or she may mimic the actions immediately while playing. Long-term effects of viewing violence in media may occur over time, however, as certain messages are frequently repeated. Less is known about long-term effects, both positive and negative, on the development of youth.

## Case Study ???

### Social Media Interactions

You have befriended a young girl named Anna. You babysat her when she was younger and have remained her older friend and mentor. Anna is 10 years old, quite shy, and a bit socially awkward. Most of her friends use social media to keep in touch with one another. Anna is begging her parents for their permission to let her sign up for a social media profile. Her parents are hesitant as they worry about the inappropriate advertising and potentially dangerous interactions with adults. They would rather not see another reason for Anna to sit in solitude, even if that includes interacting online with her peers. They want her to be a physically active "normal" child like they once were. Anna's parents asked for your opinion.

- What are the dangers present for children who spend time using social media?
- How might using social media help Anna to develop her interpersonal skills? How might it hinder her social development?
- Is there an appropriate minimum age for using social media? If so, what is that age?
- Are your ideas based on a personal theory or are they based on something else?

## Health Care

Imagine researchers find a genetic predisposition for various disorders such as health-related or learning issues. The next logical step is to look for ways in which the environment can be manipulated to lessen or eliminate the issue. Medical treatments including medications and procedures can often lessen a genetic characteristic. Some genetic medical conditions can be lessened with medication and therapy combined. The availability of health care, proper nutrition, and physical activity are the most obvious ways to manipulate the environment.

## Nutrition

Children and teens need nutritious foods to physically grow and function. Adults need nutritious foods to maintain health. The nutritional needs of children and teens are constantly changing as they go through tremendous bodily changes in their move toward adulthood. A lack of proper nutrition can also affect cognitive development. For example, inadequate nutritional intake can result in loss of knowledge, brainpower, and productivity. The ability to learn in school diminishes (shorter attention spans and memory) when there is a lack of nutrition.

Good nutrition and an active lifestyle are thought to improve health and performance in school and at work, but they also affect social and emotional development. Self-esteem may also be affected. For example, more adolescents become overweight due to poor nutrition and lack of activity. Media and peer pressure demand that females look thinner and males get bulkier. These societal pressures lead many children, teens, and adults to engage in less healthful eating behaviors.

## Physical Activity

How does physical activity affect development? Childhood and adolescence are vital times for promoting the development of motor skills such as hopping, jumping, skipping, shooting a basketball, learning a dance move, or kicking a soccer ball, **2-13**. Most children are naturally active, but may not have the opportunity to play and explore because of space or safety concerns. Because their parents or caregivers do not encourage them to be physically active, they may lead more sedentary (non-active) lives. Sedentary lifestyles can lead to poor health at any life stage.

Obviously, fresh air and activity are good for physical development. Physical activity can also increase blood supply to the brain by causing new *capillaries* (blood vessels) to grow, which produces cognitive benefits. Of course, physical activity alone does not cause increased cognitive abilities. When combined with other enriching experiences, physical activity may have a positive impact on thinking and learning.

Monkey Business Images/Shutterstock.com

**2-13** Childhood and adolescence are important stages for promoting physical active behaviors that can last a lifetime.

## Checkpoint

1. What is ethological theory?
2. What is ecological theory?
3. How can a person's heredity influence some personality traits?
4. How can a person's environment influence some personality traits?

# Research Perspectives and Methods

Researchers use the scientific method to seek answers to questions about human development. The **scientific method** starts by asking questions about observed behaviors. Through these observations, a **hypothesis**, or possible answer, is formulated. A hypothesis is similar to a prediction about something that can be tested. Usually this is done by collecting data, or information, **2-14**. For example, surveys may be collected or observations made. The hypothesis can then be rejected or supported. If the hypothesis appears to be supported, then the researcher forms a theory about the cause or relationship between the observed behaviors. The theory is then tested again and again using different situations and people.

There are many ways to collect data to test a hypothesis. One way is to collect descriptive data. **Descriptive studies** use information that describe people and situations such as their age, attitudes, or behaviors. You then simply count the different responses. For example, how many 11-year-olds versus how many 18-year-olds think they should be getting allowance from their parents? How many teen males were texting while involved in a car accident?

| Common Research Gathering Methods | | | |
|---|---|---|---|
| **Method** | **Description** | **Advantages** | **Disadvantages** |
| Case study | A case study outlines one particular person or situation and evaluates the response within the scenario. These situations can usually not be repeated in another situation. | • Specialized situations can provide specialized information that may otherwise be unavailable. | • Case studies are usually atypical and not reflective of a common situation. Researchers must be careful when generalizing conclusions. |
| Interview | The researcher has a prepared set of questions to ask the subject and engages in direct communication. | • Information gathered is directly from the subject.<br>• Emotional and physical responses can also be observed. | • Questions can be intentionally or unintentionally biased.<br>• Subjects may respond to the interviewer with "the right answer," or what they suspect the interviewer may want to hear.<br>• Subjects may not be comfortable discussing topics with the interviewer. |

*Goodheart-Willcox Publisher*

**2-14**  When studying people as the subject matter in research, these research methods are frequently used.

(Continued on next page)

| Common Research Gathering Methods | | | |
|---|---|---|---|
| Method | Description | Advantages | Disadvantages |
| **Observation** <br> Laboratory setting | Subjects are brought into a laboratory to be observed in behavioral or physical responses. | • The observation room is controlled. <br> • External factors are removed from the setting. | • The setting is unnatural to the subject, which may influence responses. <br> • The subject is usually aware that he or she is being monitored, which may influence responses. |
| Natural setting | Naturalistic observation (used in field experiments) uses a setting that is natural and normal to the subject to observe responses. | • The subject may be more comfortable in a usual setting than in a lab setting. <br> • Subjects may not realize they are under observation, which may create a more genuine response. | • The observer has less control over the environment and therefore less control over external factors that may influence responses. <br> • The subject may still be aware of the researcher's presence, which may influence responses. |
| **Standardized test** | Tests are created to measure response for multiple people. | • Procedure for testing is orderly. <br> • Allows comparison to hundreds of other people. <br> • Scoring is procedural and less likely to be biased. | • Some people are not good test takers, which may not accurately reflect their performance. <br> • Environment may influence test performance. |
| **Survey** | The researcher prepares a list of questions to give to multiple people. | • Responses can be anonymous. <br> • The researcher is removed from the line of direct communication, allowing participants to feel at ease in responses. <br> • Can be used to discover a variety of information; surveys are easily customizable. | • Survey questions can be intentionally or unintentionally biased. <br> • Subjects may respond in a way they feel is "the right answer" to the survey question or fear consequences. <br> • Surveys may not ask all pertinent questions, which can lead to skewed information in data results. |

*Goodheart-Willcox Publisher*

**2-14** (Continued.)

Some data is collected by keeping all the variables that affect behavior the same except for one. These are called **manipulative experiments**. For example, when asking a group of teens whether or not they should receive an allowance from their parents, the group could first be divided into two groups. One group would hold part-time jobs, the other would not. By manipulating this one variable, the outcome could change. Then again, the manipulated variable (having a job) may have no impact on the teens' opinion.

Sometimes researchers want to know whether or not data changes over time. In **longitudinal studies**, the same individuals are observed over a period of time. Liam may be asked his opinion on allowance as a teen, and then again as an adult. By following the same individual over time, the researcher can begin to understand variables that cause change.

Researchers are creative in using the scientific method. Sometimes they compare groups of various ages at the same time (**cross-sectional studies**). Sometimes groups are only observed and observations are recorded (**naturalistic experiments**).

## Ethical Research

Although creativity is important, researchers must follow ethical standards. This means they must ensure the people being observed are safe and not harmed, either during the experiment or afterward, **2-15**. Information gathered must be kept confidential. The research must be considered moral. Those observed must give their permission. Studies involving children must be extra diligent in making sure they follow ethical standards. Researchers must obtain permission from the child's parents or guardians, and cause no harm. The scientific method demands truthfulness and diligence in seeking to further people's understanding.

*Alexander Raths/Shutterstock.com*

**2-15**  This researcher is explaining the safety involved in her research, which is an important part of following ethical standards.

## *Safety* Connections          *Research and Ethics*

Ethics is integral when conducting research experiments. When research involves people as the study, the rights of experiment participants are relevant and necessary. Universities, hospitals, and research laboratories often have ethics committees to evaluate the legitimacy of proposed experiments. Ethics committees review the overall purpose of the experiment and means of gathering information to determine if research is ready to be properly and ethically conducted. Below are criteria that ethics committees check for during investigation as well as rights of the research participants.

- Participants must be informed of the purpose of the experiment and *consent*, or agree, to participate in the study. They must also be informed of their right to exit the research participation at any point during the experiment.

- If information about the experiment is withheld to prevent influence to the participant's responses, the researcher must inform the participant, or *debrief* the participant of the entirety of the experiment upon experiment conclusion.
- The researcher must protect the physical and mental well-being of the participants. This includes appropriate behavior from the researcher.
- Information about participants must remain confidential and anonymous, unless agreed upon otherwise.

### Research Activity

Find a research experiment of your choice from another period of time. Using the above criteria, determine whether the experiment was ethical or unethical. How did you come to your conclusion?

## Checkpoint

1. What is the scientific method?
2. Which data collection method uses information that describes people and situations?
3. Describe how data is collected for manipulative experiments.
4. What is the difference between longitudinal studies and cross-sectional studies?
5. List four ethical standards researchers must follow.

## Summary

In trying to understand the precise nature of human development, researchers and scientists conduct numerous observations, experiments, and studies. They form theories from their work. Theories provide an explanation for observations made over time and both explain and predict behavior.

Psychosocial theory, advocated by Erikson, addresses the stages of social and emotional development in humans from birth to old age. Learning theories include behaviorism, operant conditioning, social cognitive theory, cognitive theory, and social learning. All of these theories are valuable in the field of human growth and development. No one theory, however, should be regarded as the absolute truth.

What makes humans develop specific traits? Researchers and scientists continue to explore the impact of heredity and environment on development. This includes the effects of family, peers, community, economic resources, media, and health issues such as nutrition and physical activity.

Researchers use a variety of ways to observe and understand behaviors using the scientific method. Hypotheses are tested and theories formulated. Conducting ethical research is of utmost importance. Through careful and diligent analysis, understanding of human development increases.

## Vocabulary Activity

Remind students that many words can be divided into parts. Those that can be divided into two or more parts have a core word, or *root* and an *affix*—something that is attached to the word. There are two types of affixes attached to root words: *prefixes* are added before the root word and *suffixes* are added after the root word. Tell students that knowing how to analyze words can help them figure out the meanings of those they do not know. Have students review the terms list and identify words that have roots and affixes.

## Critical Thinking

1. **Analyze.** Quietly observe your classmates. Why do you think they behave the way they do? With a partner, discuss your findings.

2. **Identify.** Observe children at play. Give an example of social learning theory in action.

3. **Assess.** Can you change someone's impatient behavior by always giving the same kind response? If so, could this cause lasting change?

4. **Determine.** Which family member are you most like? Is this due more to heredity, environment, or your social interactions with that person?

5. **Predict.** If a child has a parent who is very outgoing and one who is quiet and reserved, how might this impact their child? Would gender make a difference? Would it matter who spent the most time with the child?

6. **Draw conclusions.** Think about your emotional and social interactions with family and friends. What factors (such as sleep, stress, excitement, nutrition) have affected your interactions with others today?

7. **Evaluate.** If given a choice, would you choose to be extremely intelligent or extremely beautiful or handsome? Why?

8. **Compare and contrast.** Create a table comparing and contrasting the research methods commonly used to study human development.

9. **Make inferences.** Choose two well-known celebrities from the past. If these two individuals had a child, what characteristics of each might you predict?

10. **Cause and effect.** Choose a news story about a person such as someone who robbed a store or someone who built a new neighborhood playground. What do you think influenced this person to commit this act?

## Core Skills

11. **Draw conclusions.** What is the role of theories in understanding human development?

12. **Writing.** Using Erikson's theory, write a two-page paper reflecting on and giving examples of your psychosocial development.

13. **Speaking.** Demonstrate how classical conditioning can be used to change behavior.

14. **Listening.** Interview a young child and ask about the events of his or her day. How does the report relate to Piaget's theory?

15. **Reading.** Read a book that includes a relationship between at least two siblings. Describe how these fictional characters are alike and how they are different.

16. **Math.** Interview your family members and friends. Ask them about the origin of their most dominant physical and personality traits. Keep a tally of whether they most often refer to a biological or environmental origin. Tally the results. Which origin was cited the most? How often was the origin the same for both traits?

17. **CTE Career Readiness Practice.** Every action has a reaction, whether immediately seen or not. There are positive and negative consequences for different action and inaction. Make a list of five things you have done for which there were either positive or negative consequences. Put a plus sign (+) beside the positive outcomes and a minus (−) sign beside the negative outcomes. What could you do differently to change each outcome?

## Research

18. Conduct an Internet search to learn more about the difference between scientific observations, experiments, and longitudinal studies. How do scientists use these ways of studying humans to form theories and explain and predict human development? Share your findings with the class.

19. Find an online video that effectively demonstrates one of the theories described in this chapter. Share your video with the class and identify the reasons you chose this video.

20. Conduct further research on the theorists discussed in this chapter and their theories of human development. What historical influences most impacted their work?

## Event Prep

21. As a class, brainstorm a list of ethical education-related dilemmas. Working in small groups, choose one of the dilemmas on the list, debate the topic, and solve the dilemma. Create a five-minute video presentation outlining the group's view on the dilemma. You may wish to expand your project by participating in an Educators Rising *Ethical Dilemma Competition*. See your adviser for further information.

# Chapter 3 Family Trends Today

ClickPop/Shutterstock.com

# Objectives

After studying this chapter, you will be able to

- define *family* and describe how families play a part in society.
- identify the common family types currently found in the United States.
- summarize the family life cycle.
- assess unique challenges that culturally or ethnically diverse families may face.
- outline some of the challenges facing families today.
- determine how the economic environment affects families.
- recognize various special needs and disabilities that challenge children and their families.

## Reading Prep

In preparation for reading this chapter, read a newspaper, a magazine, or an online article on family trends today. As you read, keep in mind the author's main points and conclusions.

# Key Terms

family
family life cycle
empty nest
ethnic or cultural diversity
multiculturalism
ethnicity
stereotypes
prejudice
social system
natural environment
human constructed environment

human behavioral environment
child custody
joint custody
child support
maternity leave
paternity leave
Family and Medical Leave Act (FMLA)
recession mode
recovery mode
expansion mode

standard of living
special needs
disability
Individuals with Disabilities Education Act (IDEA)
Individualized Education Plan (IEP)
inclusion
specific learning disability (SLD)
giftedness
pullout programs

## Visit the G-W Learning Companion Website to:

- **build** vocabulary with e-flash cards and interactive games;
- **assess** what you learn by completing self-assessment quizzes; and
- **expand** knowledge with activities that extend learning.

www.g-wlearning.com/development/

"All happy families resemble one another, but each unhappy family is unhappy in its own way." When do you think this was written? Ten years ago? Last year? Surprisingly, Russian novelist Leo Tolstoy (1828–1910) wrote this over 130 years ago as the opening words to his novel *Anna Karenina*. Concern about dysfunctional and unhappy families is not a new topic. The concern for family stability spans the centuries.

Next time you are with a group of friends, try this experiment. Ask each of your friends to define the term *family*. People are all familiar with the concept of family. Most people have extensive personal experience with families. Coming up with one simple, all-inclusive definition, however, still proves to be difficult.

## What Is a Family?

According to the U.S. Census Bureau, the traditional definition of **family** means two or more people living in the same household who are related by blood (birth), marriage, or adoption. In broader definitions, *family* might be defined as a group of people related by marriage. Family could also be a group of people who share common ancestors. A very close-knit group of unrelated people might even be viewed as a family. Sometimes, teachers and coaches talk about a class of students or a sports team being a family.

Today, strikingly diverse possibilities make the traditional family just one family form. These differing forms inspire emotional debates over whether shared genes, a shared household, or other shared resources including emotional support define a family. The debates raise new questions for people to consider.

- Must families be based on marriage?
- Must everyone claim one primary family?
- Can a person be a part of multiple and equally important families?
- Must emotional and social support be present to constitute a family?

### Cultural Connections    Families in the Media

Families have always come in diverse forms, reflecting the many changes in the larger culture. The social environment, including films and television, affect the way people think about and view families.

Sometimes the media exaggerates family interactions for comedic or dramatic effect. Scripted shows may emphasize a particular event or setting, which may or may not accurately reflect the majority of home settings. Other times, producers will create reality television shows that feature families in unusual living situations. These families may be atypical, but they demonstrate a type of unique family diversity.

Many television shows and films portray a two-parent household. Sometimes, the film or television series has a clean, happy ending. This vision may contrast with actual family trends. Statistics reveal that some married couples stay happily together, but many marriages end through divorce.

#### Listening Activity

How has the media portrayal of a family differed over time? View one film or one episode of a television series from 60 years ago, one from 30 years ago, and a current film or television show. What differences and similarities do you notice in each of the family settings?

Such questions result in debates about family values at both the personal and the political level. Many people have strong feelings about their own family and families in general. Quite often their responses are emotional since families can be a source of great joy as well as pain and frustration. The full range of family experiences—some positive, some negative—help formulate opinions of "what a family ought to be." What is a family? If families are so common in society, why do people have such difficulty agreeing on a definition?

## Types of Families

Families form in a number of ways. Many people choose to marry while others choose to remain single. Children may be a part of the family unit through biology or adoption. Couples, through choice or infertility, may remain childless. Children may be born to a single woman. Single fathers may parent children. Different family types often form as society changes. Following are common family types currently found in the United States:

- A *nuclear family* consists of a husband and wife and their biological children. Parents of a nuclear family often share the responsibilities of raising their children, completing household chores, and supporting the family financially.

- A *single-parent family* includes a father or mother and his or her children, **3-1**. Single parents often face many challenges. All of the family's adult roles fall on the single parent. The single parent may hold all or most of the financial responsibility for raising the child. Relationships with parents, siblings, and friends can provide great sources of support, however.

- An *extended family* includes several generations living under one roof. For example, an extended family might include parents and their children, grandparents, aunts, uncles, or cousins. Family members must deal with more people living in the home. There are also more people to help handle the responsibilities and duties of raising children and caring for the home.

- A *stepfamily* forms when a single parent gets married. At times, *blended* is used to describe this family, but some believe this term is too simple. Afterall, two different family structures combine to form the new family unit, creating new role expectations to resolve. This is especially true when both parents have children from other marriages who will be living with them. Merging families requires many adjustments for everyone. Children may be resistant to stepparents entering their lives. Discipline from a stepparent may not be well received. Time, communication, and patience are required for effective family functioning.

*Andresr/Shutterstock.com*

**3-1**  A single parent may be separated, divorced, widowed, or never married.

## Case Study

### International Adoption Regulations

Kerissa and Nick, happily married for two years, had the opportunity to travel abroad. They cared for and worked with children in a village school who, for various reasons, are orphans. None had any extended family members to care for them. During their stay, Kerissa and Nick formed a special relationship with a young boy named Chris John. Their hearts broke as they said their goodbyes, knowing that nutritious food would be scarce. "If only we could take him home with us" Nick lamented. They vowed to each other that they would find a way to reunite with Chris John, hopefully through adoption. They knew that they were strong, stable candidates even though the adoption process might prove rigorous. They were surprised to find out that although they could go through the application process to adopt a child, the international adoption laws of that country would not let them choose a particular child. Instead, a child would be chosen for them based on preset parameters.

*   Do the international laws described above seem unreasonable to you?
*   Why might the international adoption laws described above be or not be in the best interest of the child? Why might they be or not be in the best interest of the adoptive parent?

---

*   An *adoptive family* forms when a married couple or a single person is legally granted permission by a state court to raise another person's child. The adopted child then becomes a permanent part of the family. There are many reasons people choose to adopt a child. Perhaps they cannot have children of their own. They may want to add to their current family. Helping a child in need of a home may also be a reason to adopt.

*   A *foster family* forms when an adult provides a temporary home for a child who is unable to live with his or her biological parents because proper care is not provided. Caseworkers place children in foster homes until they can find a permanent home for the children. Sometimes, children can return to their original home if the parents can prove they are able to provide necessary care. In many states, foster care stops when children are 18 years of age.

*   A *childless family* exists when a married couple does not have children. Some couples may be unable to have children of their own and do not wish to adopt. Other couples may not want to have children. They might prefer to aid other family members or focus on their careers.

## The Family Life Cycle

The term *lifespan* may seem like a synonym for *life cycle*, but the two words have different meanings. *Lifespan* refers to the duration of life for a living organism. *Life cycle* refers to the developmental stages within the lifespan. The **family life cycle** consists of six basic stages that many families go through as a normal part of life, **3-2.**

The *beginning stage* is the first stage of the family life cycle. During this stage, a couple forms a bond and commits to a lasting relationship. They marry and establish a home. The couple adjusts to life together and decides when, or if, they want to have children. Couples who choose to never have children remain in the beginning stage until they reach the mid-years stage.

# The Family Life Cycle

## The Beginning Stage

A couple marries and starts to build their lives together. This stage lasts until the couple has a child.

*Tyler Olson/Shutterstock.com*

## The Launching Stage

The couple's children leave home to live on their own. This stage ends when the last child moves out of the family home.

*Gina Smith/Shutterstock.com*

## The Childbearing Stage

The couple has their first child. This stage ends when the couple has their last child.

*Creativa/Shutterstock.com*

## The Mid-years Stage

The couple often faces an empty nest and may redefine their priorities. This stage lasts until retirement.

*Monkey Business Images/Shutterstock.com*

## The Parenting Stage

The couple raises their children through the school-age and teen years. This stage continues until children begin to leave home.

*Golden Pixels LLC/Shutterstock.com*

## The Aging Stage

The couple retires and focuses on their interests. This stage lasts through the eventual death of one and then the other spouse.

*Halina Yakushevich/Shutterstock.com*

**3-2**  Some families may skip or even repeat stages of the family life cycle.

When a couple decides to have their first child, they enter the *childbearing stage* of the family life cycle. During this stage, the couple assumes the roles of parents and accepts many new responsibilities. Having a child is costly and expenses increase significantly. Extra demands of time and energy are placed on the couple as they care for the child. A couple often has less freedom to do as many activities outside the home as they did when in the beginning stage. The childbearing stage of the family life cycle continues until the couple decides to not have any more children.

A family enters the *parenting stage* of the family life cycle when the first child starts school. Oftentimes, the childbearing and parenting stages of the family life cycle overlap for couples who have several children. Navigating the school system and balancing work and family issues are often more difficult during the parenting stage. School activities can cause the family's schedule to change. Parents face particular challenges as children enter the teen years and often seek more independence and less parental control.

The *launching stage* of the family life cycle occurs when the first child leaves home. Children may go to college or find a job and move into their own place. Some may get married and start their own families. As children leave home, schedule demands may lessen, and parents often have more free time.

The next stage of the family life cycle is the *mid-years stage*. During this stage, many couples often face an **empty nest** when the last child leaves home. Couples may feel a void in their lives when the home is empty and they are no longer focusing their resources on rearing their children. Couples may redefine their priorities. They may develop new interests as they learn to accept the empty nest. As their grown children become parents, the couple welcomes grandchildren into the family. The couple also starts to focus on retirement.

The *aging stage* is the final stage of the family life cycle. This stage lasts from retirement through the eventual death of one and then the other spouse. During this stage, couples may experience the birth of grandchildren or great-grandchildren. They may travel or visit with family. Couples may develop new hobbies. As a parent's health declines, grown children may need to provide additional care and assistance. When a spouse dies, the remaining spouse may need help coping with the loss.

The family life cycle may seem familiar, but is not the reality for everyone. As society changes, the function of the family also changes. Some people choose to remain single and live alone. Others become single parents. Couples break up. Divorces and remarriages occur. New families are formed. Grown children may leave home only to return later to live with their parents, perhaps bringing their children with them. At times, parents may accept the responsibility of raising their grandchildren. Other events can also cause the family to make many more adjustments. Family members can help one another face challenges by communicating openly and showing support for one another.

## Family Diversity

In the United States, people of different backgrounds, languages, races, ethnicities, religions, and socioeconomic classes live in one society. This is called **ethnic or cultural diversity**.

## Cultural Connections    Variations in the Family Life Cycle

Although the family life cycle traditionally occurs in six stages, these stages are not the pattern every family experiences. Stages in the family life cycle can overlap, not happen at all, or be revisited. For example, some couples choose to have a child at a younger age. By the time this child is in high school, the couple may decide to have more children. By the time the oldest child leaves the household, the couple will be in the launching stage with the oldest child and the parenting stage with the younger children. If the couple continues to have more children, they will also be in the childbearing stage.

Sometimes stages can happen out of order with intervening stages skipped. For example, statistics reveal an increase in households where children are raised by their grandparents. In these cases, the grandparents are in the parenting and aging stages. They have already experienced the launching and mid-year stages, but are revisiting the parenting stage to raise the grandchildren.

Another example is when a couple enters the parenting stage with their own children, but live with their parents. This living situation creates a three-generational household. The caretaking responsibilities fall to the second generation, or the *sandwich generation*. The sandwich generation provides for their own child or children, simultaneously taking care of their own parents.

### Writing Activity

Evaluate your own family life cycle. Which stages of the family life cycle apply to your parents and grandparents? Do you plan to experience all six of the family life cycle stages in order? Write a journal entry reflecting on your current and future family experiences and plans.

---

In earlier decades, minority families worked to fit in and become part of the majority culture. They learned the language, customs, and beliefs followed by the majority. Some people described this acceptance of the majority culture as a *melting pot*, assuming that different cultures and ethnicities were becoming more like one. A closer look at minority groups revealed that family customs and traditions were still being practiced while families also embraced the majority culture. A more appropriate description of the country's population today is *multicultural*. **Multiculturalism** is based on the idea that cultural identities should not be ignored, but instead should be maintained and valued.

Multiculturalism addresses differences in race, ethnicity, religious beliefs, life experiences, values, and socioeconomic status. **Ethnicity** is a person's identity with a particular racial, national, or cultural group and support of that group's customs, beliefs, and language. All these factors are part of *demographics*, or statistical qualities of the population.

Diverse families sometimes face unique challenges. Cultural **stereotypes** (preconceived generalizations) and **prejudice** (negative bias) can be difficult to overcome. Families play a critical role in socializing family members to accept, respect, and celebrate diversity in cultures.

### English Language Learners

Students who enter school in the United States with limited English skills are called *English language learners (ELLs)*. These students often have difficulty communicating, learning, and succeeding in school. Their parents and older siblings often have very limited English skills and may not speak the English language in the home. Sometimes no one at home can help them with homework because of the language barrier. Special instruction can help these students learn the English language and gain the necessary skills to succeed.

## Cultural Connections    Avoiding Stereotypes and Prejudices

Each family has challenges and operates differently. Although the types of families may be recognizable and classifiable, the family lifestyle cannot be easily determined. Attempting to discern family lifestyles according to the type of family may lead to stereotypes and prejudices. Stereotypes occur when a person is classified or judged according to one trait, such as gender, culture, or ethnicity. Stereotypes group people together and ignore individualism. Prejudices are similar and occur when judgments are passed on a person without getting to know the individual. Stereotypes and prejudices often form based on lack of information. The best way to break

a prejudice or stereotype is by becoming informed. Learning about other cultures and customs broadens personal knowledge and allows a connection to form with other people. Whether stereotypes or prejudices come from within the home or from outside the home, engaging in open communication can help break communication barriers.

### Research Activity

Research family customs in a culture unfamiliar to you. Identify the culture's common family type, roles, and other activities. Create an electronic presentation of your findings.

Children learn language very quickly. Many times, children and teens teach their parents and other family members the English language. Many immigrant families place a high value on educational success. High standards and expectations may accompany these values.

In addition to language instruction, students whose primary language is not English sometimes need more social and emotional support. Adapting to a new culture and language can be difficult. When students learn to accept, celebrate, and expect diversity, they will be better prepared to participate as adults in a multicultural society. Families can support both the celebration and acceptance of diversity.

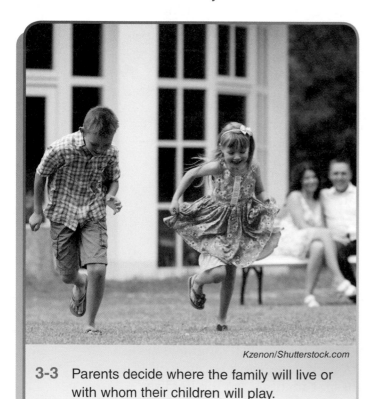

Kzenon/Shutterstock.com

**3-3**  Parents decide where the family will live or with whom their children will play.

## The Family as a Social Unit

Families come in various forms, reflecting the changes in the world around them. Whatever is happening socially, economically, and politically produces the cultural values and norms in which families exist. In other words, families exist within a social system. A **social system** refers to the organization of individuals into groups based on characteristic patterned relationships.

The family is a social system because its members group together to meet each other's needs and the needs of society. For example, families play a primary role in identity development of individual members. Families choose with whom to interact by establishing boundaries. Parents decide what are the acceptable rules and boundaries for family members, especially when children are young, **3-3**. These boundaries are constantly changing as the tasks of the family unit change.

Some boundaries are self-selected, whereas other boundaries may be imposed by laws, circumstances, or culture. For example, a family with school-age children interacts with the school system once a child enters school. Educating children is a requirement in the United States. A parent has the choice, however, to use the public school system, private schools, home schooling, or online schools.

## Changing Environmental Factors

A family's **natural environment** includes all living and nonliving things on Earth not influenced by people. For example, animals and plants are a part of the natural environment. The natural environment also includes genetic makeup of the individual family members as well as air, energy, water, land, and sources of energy and food. For example, imagine a genetic disorder passed from one generation to the next. The disorder may have great implications on the health and quality of life for family members.

People's interactions with the natural environment can cause changes that might affect the health and well-being of family members. For example, pollution can negatively affect air quality, making the air unclean and unhealthy. Air pollution can cause family members to develop respiratory conditions such as asthma.

The **human constructed environment** includes products produced for consumers to use. Fast foods, electronics, appliances, cars, and homes are just a few examples of the endless products made for consumers. This environment has a great impact on the family unit. For example, when cell phones were introduced, they changed the ways in which family members communicated with one another.

The **human behavioral environment** includes all the societal systems that regulate behavior and relationships between people. The judicial, educational, economic, religious, and political systems all play a part. Within these systems are laws, rules, and policies that regulate human behavior. City, county, state, and federal laws are all part of this environment as are school rules and employee rules and expectations.

## Health Connections — Air Pollution

The environmental condition of the region where you live is one factor in your natural environment that can affect your health and development. For example, if you live in an area with high amounts of air pollution, you may choose not to be outside as much as you might if you lived in a region with cleaner air.

Air pollution is caused by high amounts of such chemicals as carbon monoxide, sulfur oxide, nitrogen oxide, and lead in the atmosphere. Children, older adults, and people with respiratory conditions, such as asthma, are the most vulnerable to the effects of poor air quality. Short-term effects of poor air quality include irritation to the respiratory system, which can restrict the ease of breathing and increase the chances of developing a cough. Long-term effects include permanent lung damage, which reduces the ease of your body to fight against lung diseases.

To caution the public of current air quality, many weather reports include an *Air Quality Index (AQI) Rate*. This system ranges from 0 to 500. The higher the AQI rate, the greater the health concern is in your area.

### Speaking Activity

Working with a partner, discuss the following question: How would your lifestyle change if the air quality rate in your region was considered to be a constant health threat?

## Checkpoint

1. In your own words, define the term *family*. Compare and contrast your definition of family to the definition in this text.
2. List seven common family types currently found in the United States.
3. Describe the six stages of the family life cycle.
4. Define multiculturalism.
5. Why is the family called a *social system*?

# Concerns of Families

Families exist in an ever-changing environment. Dual-career families, separation, divorce, remarriage, and stepparenting—these are the daily realities of many families. Oftentimes, there are not enough hours in a day to take care of the responsibilities. Despite time-saving technologies such as prepackaged goods, home shopping, and labor-saving home appliances, families still feel their personal time is diminishing. In the past and in the present, many families have limited options. Part-time work may not be an option if a full-time salary is needed. Child care may cost more than salaries earned. Government assistance may not be available for older adults or children. The following describes some of the challenges facing families today.

## Divorce

Many marriage relationships in the U.S. falter or fail. Sometimes this happens early in a marriage. Sometimes it happens many years into the marriage, especially when children enter the picture or later when they leave home. Why do marriages fail? People report many reasons including loss of interest, feelings, or a missing sense of commitment. Conflicts and misunderstandings occur. Break-ups, separation, and divorce can feel tragic to those involved, especially children of the divorcing couples, **3-4**.

Divorce can have significant financial impact, especially for women. When children are involved, the impact can be lifelong. Often, the division of financial assets can be difficult. Child custody and support can be a source of heated disagreement.

*Gladskikh Tatiana/Shutterstock.com*

**3-4** When a marriage is failing, emotions run high and feelings of abandonment and rejection are common.

**Child custody** determines who has the legal responsibility for the child. In some cases, parents will seek joint custody. **Joint custody** is a legal agreement in which both parents provide care and make decisions for the child. **Child support** is also a legally binding agreement about financial responsibilities. Usually, lawyers are involved and legally binding court decisions are made concerning both child custody and support.

All family members are affected by the impact of divorce. Emotional challenges including loneliness, depression, and anxiety are common. Family members often need additional support from people close to them during this time. Support groups and counseling services can also help family members cope with their feelings in acceptable ways.

## Remarriage and Stepparenting

Many divorced adults choose to remarry quickly after their divorce. A new marriage and family life can be a source of significant stress for all family members. If children are involved, new relationships must be established between stepparents and stepchildren. Children also maintain a relationship with the other parent. If both parents remarry, children must learn to adjust to two sets of parents. This also means they have four sets of grandparents, as well as siblings and stepbrothers or stepsisters.

Family members may also have to accept more responsibilities. Children may feel anger or resentment toward their parent or the new stepparent. They may think they are being treated unfairly. Stepparents may struggle with disciplining stepchildren. Families may struggle financially as living expenses increase with more people living under one roof. Families can cope with these many changes by working together, maintaining a positive attitude, and keeping the lines of communication open.

## Workplace Issues

Work provides many things for families, the first of which is financial income and stability, **3-5**. Through paid work, families financially support their needs and desires. Although financial motivation is primary, there are many other benefits to paid work. Work provides social interaction and a way to utilize individual talents, skills, and abilities for a specific vocation.

Status is associated with different types of work, such as office work or manual labor. Families often identify themselves by the type of work parents do, where they live, and where their children go to school. Higher pay allows for spending on wants, not just needs. At the same time, people identify others and make assumptions about their personal characteristics based on stereotypes about their line of work. These assumptions can be both positive and negative, and are not always accurate.

*Diego Cervo/Shutterstock.com*

**3-5** Full-time work consumes many hours of a person's life.

Alexander Raths/Shutterstock.com

**3-6** Layoffs, firing, or company downsizing are experiences families face.

Sometimes jobs are lost involuntarily, **3-6**. The loss of a job, especially the main income for the family, can cause tremendous stress on all family members. Work contributes to the family's financial health, as well as their sense of identity. Preparing for a job market and the subsequent job search can be challenging. This is especially true if the person has not recently conducted a job search, or if the search lasts for an extended time. Many adults report that looking for a job can affect a person's self-esteem or self-worth. In a tough job market, unemployment not only affects financial stability, but a person's sense of place in the community. Work, whether paid or not, gives a sense of purpose and is important to adult development.

Sometimes job changes require relocation. Some families, such as military families, accept moving from one location to another as a part of life. Others who move less often find relocation to be extremely stressful as they must leave their friends, family, school, and community.

Entering a new community takes time and effort, as does finding a place to call home. Making new friends, starting new schools, and locating community resources take time and energy. Starting a new job can be a challenging transition as life revolves around meeting deadlines, dealing with new coworkers, and balancing home and family demands. This transition time is full of ups and downs for many families.

### Balancing Work and Family

A mother's job requires a business trip on the same day that her daughter's soccer team has a play-off game. A father's fishing trip, which was planned and paid for a year ago, is scheduled the same week. The young son chips a tooth and must undergo emergency dental work. A friend's mother dies and she needs emotional support. Work-life balance involves finding the right balance amid the many demands involving

- family and friends
- careers
- organizations and causes you choose to serve
- activities that promote physical, intellectual, and socio-emotional growth

## Health Connections — Strategies for Balancing Family and Work Life

At times, family and work life will conflict and overlap. Finding a solution may not always be easy, but is possible with planning and strategizing. The following are tips that may ease or prevent work-family conflicts.

- **Plan and schedule ahead.** Plan ahead to give others an opportunity to adjust to and work with your plans. Schedule activities in advance to avoid having conflicting plans.
- **Communicate.** Communicate your plans with family members and coworkers to keep them informed and to prevent last-minute changes to the family routine or workweek.
- **Show support.** Demonstrate support for other family members by sharing responsibilities to help manage family life. Show emotional support with a caring, positive attitude.
- **Prioritize.** Think about all the tasks that you need to do in a day and decide which are most important.
- **Enjoy quality time together.** Schedule quality time for the family to spend together. This may include vacations, meals, outings, or activities within the home. These bonding moments provide nurturing, memorable, lifelong effects.

### Writing Activity

Write a journal entry about a time when work interfered with another aspect of your life. How did you handle the situation? What could you do to manage the situation differently?

---

Families are often concerned about more than just finding balance. They also want to make a difference in the lives, organizations, and community to which they contribute. Work-life balance is a major cause of stress among families.

Many family and career transitions are made in early adulthood when the real challenges are in balancing competing demands. Traditionally, women transition in and out of the workforce more frequently than men in early adulthood due to parenting responsibilities.

Because many women bear children, maternity leaves are common. **Maternity leave** is paid or unpaid time off from work to care for a new child, **3-7**. Companies may also grant paternity leave to employees. **Paternity leave** is paid or unpaid time off from work that fathers may take after the birth or adoption of a child. In the U.S., the **Family and Medical Leave Act (FMLA)** allows full-time employed individuals to take job-protected leave without pay for the family transitions that involve close family members such as spouses, children, and parents. Even so, work and family issues require thought, planning, and flexibility.

*Zdorov Kirill Vladimirovich/Shutterstock.com*

**3-7** Six weeks time off is often the minimum companies offer for maternity leave.

## Job Stress

Work often takes more hours of an adult's day than any other activity including sleep. Work can affect family life in positive ways and can be a source of identity, financial security, socialization, and fulfillment. Work can also be a cause of frustration and stress. At times, this stress affects family relationships in a negative way. Feelings of frustration and disharmony at work can carry into family relationships in the form of impatience, short temper, anxiety, or worry. Young adults, especially those with young children, tend to be more easily dissatisfied with pay and working conditions than middle-aged or older adults. Middle-aged adults tend to carry more workplace responsibility.

# The Impact of the Economy on Families

Children and teens do not need wealth to become happy, productive adults. Even so, people today live in a money-driven economy. Children and teens, as members of families and communities, are not immune to the economic swings that affect people's well-being.

As the economy improves or falters, personal spending, unemployment rates, and prices of *consumer goods* (products and services people buy) rise and fall. New home sales fluctuate and the cost to rent an apartment or home changes, too. Corporations, schools, and the government respond by hiring or laying-off employees. In good times, more people are hired. Wages increase when the economy is good. When the economy changes slowly, families can adjust and plan. When changes occur quickly, they are often more difficult to alter and manage. These economic changes generally fall into three descriptions: recession, recovery, and expansion.

When the economy is in a **recession mode**, there is a slowing and decline in the economy. Unemployment goes up as do requests for government assistance such as unemployment pay and food vouchers. More families access food banks and subsidized school nutrition programs. Even if families do not need outside assistance, they tend to spend less on extras such as eating out, buying clothing, going to the movies, and vacations. Families tend to carefully monitor their spending and savings.

When the economy is in a **recovery mode**, things again start to look hopeful. Spending on consumer goods increases. Consumers purchase more clothes because they like them rather than just replacing damaged or outgrown items. They may purchase food items that appeal to individual family member's tastes rather than focusing on the basics. Families may spend more on entertainment. Families still tend to be more conservative in their spending and focus more on their savings, however.

When the economy is in an **expansion mode**, unemployment rates are usually lower and most people who seek employment can find jobs. There is a feeling of prosperity. People are more willing to spend on consumer goods, especially luxury items. Families may pay to see a movie in the theater rather than renting one to watch at home. Simply, financial resources give families choices they would otherwise not have, **3-8**.

Ways in which the economy influences the family are complex. Some families do not have the choice to spend or save more, even when the economy is in an expansion mode. They may be struggling financially due to limited income, responsibilities to extended family members, or other personal issues. Likewise, some families at the upper end of the economic scale may hardly feel the effects of a changing economy.

*Phil Date/Shutterstock.com*

**3-8** Families may travel more when the economy is in an expansion mode.

A family's **standard of living** is a measure of the wealth, comforts, and material goods available to them. Most families have a standard of living they aspire to meet. This could be the same as their current level of living. Many families, however, aspire to a higher standard of living. That is, they want to be able to buy better quality items, have a higher status in the community, buy a bigger house, or purchase more consumer goods. If this standard is out of reach, stress, frustration, and unhappiness can result. The ways people react to their level of living impacts the family environment.

## Children and Families with Special Needs

Children have a broad range of abilities and special needs, **3-9**. **Special needs** include physical disabilities, cognitive disabilities, emotional and behavioral problems, and learning disorders. They also include speech, vision, and hearing disorders. Special needs can be minimal or severe. The *Americans with Disabilities Act* defines a **disability** as a cognitive or physical impairment that impedes or limits common activities.

*Vitalinka/Shutterstock.com*

**3-9** Many children with special needs often follow the same pattern of development as other children.

Children with special needs often require extra help that is different from what is necessary for most other children. These needs may be temporary or lifelong. They may be the result of an accident, or they are present at birth and will be an issue throughout the child's lifetime. Taking care of a child with special needs can be extremely costly due to extra medical treatments, assistive devices, or special therapies. Families must often make many adjustments to help children with special needs achieve their full potential. Community resources, such as medical specialists, schools, or support groups, can provide help. Community resources to support all members of the family are critical.

When accommodations are made for children with special needs, they can partake in many of the normal activities of their peers. They can spend time playing and enjoying themselves. Although challenged, many families report positive outcomes from integrating special needs into their family life. Becoming more empathetic toward others, including older adults, and communicating more clearly with family members are often mentioned.

Disabilities and disorders come in many forms. The following sections will present a brief overview of physical disabilities, learning disorders, and social-emotional disorders.

## Physical Disabilities

Physical disabilities may involve mobility such as walking or standing. They may also involve the senses such as seeing or hearing. An altered or missing body part, such as an injured or irregularly developed arm, may present challenges. When accommodations are made for physical disabilities, children can partake in many of the normal activities of their peers.

Assistive devices, medical treatments, or surgeries may improve some physical disabilities. For example, a child who has difficulty seeing may need eyeglasses to enhance sight. A teen who loses a leg in an accident may receive a prosthetic limb and again learn to walk. Children with *cerebral palsy*, a disorder that affects gross-motor skills and muscles, may gain mobility through intense physical therapy or by using assistive devices or a wheelchair, **3-10**. Treatment depends on the severity and progression of the disability and availability of resources.

*Jaren Jai Wicklund/Shutterstock.com*

**3-10** Assistive devices, such as a wheelchair, can help a child with cerebral palsy be more independent.

## Learning Disorders

People vary cognitively, or in the ways in which they learn and process information. Some students learn quickly and easily. Other students struggle with traditional classroom instruction. Perhaps you always do well on projects, but score low on standardized tests. Some people excel at fixing objects and doing activities with their hands.

Learning disorders usually involve reading and writing and are often not detected until a child enters school during middle childhood. They may be detected earlier if a young child demonstrates difficulty in listening, learning to write letters or draw shapes, or counting. Educational therapists can help children with learning disorders.

## Social-Emotional Disorders

Social and emotional problems are often seen in behavioral issues that set children apart from their peers. These differences in temperament are more than just being shy or easily excitable. Social and emotional disorders often keep children from normal activities and hamper relationships. They can also affect a child's learning.

Social or emotional issues are hard to categorize or diagnose. Young children often have minor emotional or behavioral challenges. They have tantrums. They are learning new tasks and pushing the limits to become more independent. They may bite or hit a playmate. Sometimes these emotional challenges become severe and aggressive. Therapy may help children find ways to deal with their emotions and help parents gain appropriate skills to work with their children.

## Individuals with Disabilities Education Act (IDEA)

The **Individuals with Disabilities Education Act (IDEA)** is a federal law that governs how states provide early intervention, special education, and other services to children with disabilities. Part of the IDEA requires that public schools create an **Individualized Education Plan (IEP)** for each eligible student, **3-11**. An IEP includes specific educational goals to best meet the student's needs. An IEP also includes a placement agreement. The most common placement is **inclusion**, which means students with special educational needs spend all or most of their time in a general education classroom setting.

To develop an IEP, input from the parent or guardian is essential in understanding the child's special needs. Other members of the IEP development team often include

- at least one general education teacher
- a special needs teacher
- a school guidance counselor
- a psychologist
- a school administrator

Students who are eligible for an IEP must be determined to have a specific learning disability. A **specific learning disability (SLD)** includes disorders involving basic psychological processes that impair using or understanding language. These include the ability to listen, speak, read, write, spell, or calculate. SLDs do not include learning problems that come from vision or hearing impairment, motor disabilities, cognitive disabilities, emotional illness, economical, or cultural disadvantages.

*Ramona Helm/Shutterstock.com*

**3-11**  IDEA addresses eligible children's special educational needs from birth to age 21.

### Giftedness

Some children are described as *gifted*. **Giftedness** or exceptionality in learning is detected early. A child who is gifted might be particularly verbal with an advanced vocabulary. Maybe the child shows ability to reason or understand concepts at a young age, **3-12**. The child might read earlier than other children and remain at an advanced reading level.

Children who are gifted are usually ahead of their peers in one or more areas of intelligence. Gifted children usually excel in one or two areas, not necessarily in all areas. A child who is advanced in reading may struggle with peer relationships. Teachers should offer flexibility and allow all students opportunities for advanced learning.

wavebreakmedia/Shutterstock.com

**3-12** There are many signs of giftedness in children.

Intellectual giftedness can also be viewed as a special need as it often requires additional family support and resources. Sometimes conflict between siblings arises. Siblings may be treated differently, attend different schools, or be compared with each other. Meeting the needs of a gifted child can challenge both parents and children alike.

Should gifted children be separated from the regular class and placed in a classroom of gifted children? Many experts agree that this is a viable way to provide an enriching environment for gifted students. Some schools are set up just to serve gifted students. These schools can be expensive to run and exclusive. Because of this, many schools provide **pullout programs**, which allow children to leave the regular classroom for certain periods of the day or week. They offer flexibility as pullout programs allow students opportunities for advanced learning in a particular subject area along with social opportunities with peers.

## Health Connections   Signs of Giftedness

The ability to read at 2 years of age is a clear sign of giftedness, but signs of talent in children may not always be as obvious. Children who are gifted may also display subtle signs of their talent or mental capacity, including areas beyond the classroom. Following are some possible signs of giftedness in children:

- interests frequently change because the child has a strong desire to learn
- possesses an excellent memory and may recall details others have forgotten
- asks many questions that reflect critical thinking and expects detailed answers
- has a longer attention span and displays intense focus on a task
- quickly understands new activities or tasks with minimal instruction
- displays independent thought
- enjoys spending time alone to process thoughts
- has highly developed emotions and is extra sensitive

Environmental factors will influence the child's abilities. If the skill is not encouraged and allowed to flourish, the talent may become hindered for lack of opportunity to express and perform the skill set. Caregivers and teachers need to continue to encourage the child's talent to reach optimum development.

### Writing Activity

How might a parent or teacher encourage gifted children to further develop their skill set? Select three of the bulleted items and create a plan for encouraging child giftedness. You may consult reliable online or print sources.

## Checkpoint

1. How do divorce, remarriage, and stepparenting affect families?
2. Give an example of a workplace issue and describe how it can affect a family.
3. Beyond money to spend, how does a changing economy impact children and their families?
4. How does the *Americans with Disabilities Act* define a disability?
5. What is included in an IEP? Who helps develop an IEP?
6. What are pullout programs?

## Summary

The traditional definition of *family* means two or more people living in the same household who are related by blood (birth), marriage, or adoption. Today, strikingly diverse possibilities make the traditional family just one family form.

Different family types often form as society changes. Common family types include the nuclear family, single-parent family, extended family, stepfamily, adoptive family, foster family, and childless family.

The family life cycle consists of six basic stages that include the beginning stage, childbearing stage, parenting stage, launching stage, mid-years stage, and aging stage. The family life cycle is not the reality for everyone. As society changes, the function of the family also changes.

Divorce, remarriage, and stepparenting, and their subsequent challenges are realities of many families today. Workplace issues such as balancing work and family have an impact on family wellness. As the economy fluctuates, families feel the impact.

Some families are enhanced and challenged by meeting the special needs of family members. Special needs include physical disabilities, cognitive disabilities, emotional and behavioral problems, and learning disorders. Likewise, giftedness can present its own set of challenges.

## Vocabulary Activity

Work with a partner to write the definitions of the key terms based on your current understanding before reading the chapter. Then pair up with another pair to discuss your definitions and any discrepancies. Finally, discuss the definitions with the class and ask your instructor for necessary correction or clarification.

## Critical Thinking

1. **Compare and contrast.** Write your own working definition of the family. How does your definition differ from the definition given in this chapter?
2. **Predict.** How do changing demographics and diversity affect the health, welfare, and well-being of children? of adolescents?
3. **Draw conclusions.** How are families depicted in television and film today? Which fictional television family do you see as most true to life?
4. **Predict.** How might families look in 10 years and in 25 years? What changes may occur? How will families remain the same?
5. **Identify.** Choose a fictional single-parenting relationship depicted by television or movie characters. What are some of the advantages and disadvantages of this relationship?
6. **Analyze.** Think about several families you know. Which stages of the family life cycle have these families experienced? Were any of the stages skipped? Were any stages revisited?
7. **Make inferences.** What can members of stepfamilies do to improve their relationships with one another? What sort of resources might be available to help new stepfamilies adjust?
8. **Cause and effect.** How might society be different if parents had the financial choice and ability to stay home with their children for the first year of life?
9. **Determine.** If possible, should one parent stay home with their young children? Why or why not?
10. **Assess.** Do you think the U.S. lags behind other industrialized countries in regard to family-friendly policies such as parental leave for child care?

11. **Evaluate.** How might you be a resource to a family who has a child with special needs? What resources or talents do you have that could benefit both the parent and child?

## Core Skills

12. **Listening.** Ask each of your friends to define the term family. How are their definitions similar? How are they different?

13. **Writing.** Write a one-page paper answering the following questions: Must everyone claim one primary family or can a person be a part of multiple and equally important families?

14. **Speaking.** Make a list of the rules or expectations that are part of your family experiences. Working in small groups, discuss how these expectations formed boundaries for you.

15. **Math.** Choose a consumer good you would like to buy. Compare the cost of the good at three different stores or websites. Be sure to consider size, weight, or amount of the good, as well as any applicable shipping or handling fees. Which place offers the best price?

16. **Reading.** Read a book about a family going through a divorce. How are the family members affected by the impact of the divorce?

17. **CTE Career Readiness Practice.** You may have been taught to treat others how *you* would like to be treated. This is often referred to as *the golden rule*. Productively working with others who have a background different from yours may require that you learn to treat others as *they* wish to be treated. Conduct research on the Internet about cultural differences related to personal space, time, gestures or body language, and relationships toward authority figures. Create a T-chart that shows the difference and ways you would adapt your interactions to account for that difference.

## Research

18. Search for articles online about a person with a physical disability. How has medical science such as nutrition, medicine, or medical treatment helped him or her to live a better quality of life? Share your articles with the class.

19. Choose a family concern described in this chapter. Do a search for books that are available that might give more insight for families facing this challenge. Create a list of your findings to share with the class.

## Event Prep

20. Use the FCCLA *Planning Process* to create a project to help families work together to strengthen the family bond. Project topics may include understanding and celebrating diversity, strengthening relationships, nurturing children, managing multiple responsibilities, or overcoming obstacles. You may wish to expand your project by developing an FCCLA *Families First* project. See your FCCLA adviser for further information.

# Chapter 4 Pregnancy and Birth

Otna Ydur/Shutterstock.com

# Objectives

After studying this chapter, you will be able to

- analyze how good health before pregnancy can impact the health of the future developing baby.
- analyze how care during pregnancy including good nutrition, medical care, and a healthy lifestyle can lead to more positive outcomes for the mother and developing baby.
- describe how various prenatal complications including genetic disorders, the mother's age, health status, and environmental factors including drugs can affect the developing baby.
- describe the three stages of pregnancy and the developmental milestones that occur in each stage.
- identify and describe the three stages of childbirth.
- discuss how preterm labor, induced labor, breech presentation, oxygen deprivation, and the Rh factor can complicate childbirth.

## Reading Prep

Before reading this chapter, preview the illustrations. As you read, cite specific textual evidence to support the information in the illustrations.

## Key Terms

obstetricians
certified nurse-midwives
low birthweight
stillbirth
gestational diabetes
caesarean section
sexually transmitted infections (STIs)
bacterial STIs
viral STIs
HIV

AIDS
fetal alcohol syndrome (FAS)
sudden infant death syndrome (SIDS)
germinal period
zygote
blastocyst
embryonic period
embryo
fetal period

fetus
Braxton-Hicks contractions
natural childbirth
Lamaze method
doula
episiotomy
very low birthweight
induced labor
breech birth
oxygen deprivation
Rh factor

## Visit the G-W Learning Companion Website to:

- **build** vocabulary with e-flash cards and interactive games;
- **assess** what you learn by completing self-assessment quizzes; and
- **expand** knowledge with activities that extend learning.

**G-WLEARNING.com** www.g-wlearning.com/development/

This story of human development begins even before a baby is conceived, long before developing in the womb. In this chapter, care before and during pregnancy, challenges during pregnancy, and the stages of prenatal development will be discussed. Birth, the baby's grand entrance into the world, will be described. Issues after birth will also be discussed as this first important life stage is explored. Although you may often think that development begins at birth, you will learn that the information presented in this chapter covers the foundation of human development.

## Care Before Pregnancy Occurs

Care *before* pregnancy? Absolutely! Health and lifestyle behaviors can play a large part in both becoming pregnant and the success of a pregnancy. Most importantly, these factors can play a large part in the health of a baby. They may even have lifetime effects on both the mother and child.

An important first consideration for a woman who is planning to become pregnant or suspects that she is pregnant is to find good medical care. If possible, a thorough checkup before becoming pregnant is important to make sure the mother is healthy. Genetic testing (for possible risks of birth defects) can be done at this time. Any known health problems should be observed and managed, including family health issues or infections. When a woman suspects she is pregnant, she should confirm the pregnancy with a doctor and begin early medical care.

Eating a well-balanced diet of healthful foods is important during every stage of life, **4-1**. A woman's well-balanced diet, healthy body weight, and physical fitness before pregnancy can provide the right setting for optimal development of a baby. Before pregnancy, taking extra *folic acid* (a type of vitamin) is recommended. Folic acid promotes healthy brain and spinal cord development, some of the earliest organ developments during pregnancy.

Women should avoid alcohol consumption, drugs (including over-the-counter and prescription drugs), and smoking during pregnancy. Even secondhand smoke should be avoided. All of these can cause great harm to the developing baby. Chemical exposure can have negative lasting effects. Avoiding these things prior to pregnancy can have a positive impact on the future pregnancy as well. Pregnancies are most successful when women begin at a healthy body weight, are active, and have social and emotional support from family members and friends. When pregnancy does occur, a woman is ready to devote her cognitive, physical, social, and emotional resources toward supporting her developing baby.

*Bogdan Wankowicz/Shutterstock.com*

**4-1**   Fresh fruits and vegetables are a rich source of vitamins and minerals.

### Checkpoint

1. Why is good health care important prior to pregnancy?
2. What is the benefit of taking extra folic acid before pregnancy?
3. List three things women should avoid prior to and during pregnancy.

## Care During Pregnancy

Prenatal care is essential to give the best possible outcome for both the mother and baby. Good medical care, nutrition, and health practices are all important for optimal results. The healthier the mother is, the more positive the outcome of the pregnancy will be for her and her baby.

### Medical Care

An early task for a pregnant woman is to find good health care. There are many options. The most common is being under the care of a medical doctor. **Obstetricians** are doctors who specialize in pregnancy and childbirth. Women may choose to use their family doctor who provides general care. They may also choose **certified nurse-midwives**, or nurses who specialize in pregnancy and birth. Any of these medical professionals can provide good care for healthy women. If a woman is at risk from complications, she may need to see a doctor who specializes in the condition.

During the first medical exam, usually at around the eighth week of pregnancy, expectant mothers are screened for potential health problems. An expected due date is calculated based on the last menstrual period. A full physical exam is done and blood and urine samples are taken.

---

## *Safety* Connections     *Medical Checkups*

Regular medical care is vital in monitoring the health of women prior to and during pregnancy. The health status of the mother directly impacts the growth and development of the baby. During pregnancy, a woman attends regular checkups to ensure her pregnancy is progressing in a safe and healthy manner. The frequency of medical checkups increases throughout the pregnancy.

A checkup is scheduled once a month for weeks 4 through 28, twice a month from weeks 28 through 36, and once a week from week 36 until birth. At checkups, both the health of the mother and baby are monitored. At the first examination during pregnancy, the physician will speak with the mother to understand her lifestyle, family history, and father's family history. The physician will also conduct tests for potential health threats to the baby and determine a due date for the baby. In sequential medical visits, the physician will check blood pressure, heart rate, and weight of the mother. The physician may also conduct prenatal testing to screen for genetic-related diseases, potential birth defects, or threatening conditions to the mother. Maintaining scheduled medical visits is a critical part of pregnancy.

### Career Activity

What education and training is needed to become an obstetrician? Research the education requirements, job responsibilities, and salary of an obstetrician. Does this career interest you? Why or why not?

After the first visit, health care exams are usually scheduled every month until the last few months when visits are increased to every two weeks. During the last month, weekly visits are the norm. During these visits, weight is taken, blood pressure measured, and measurements are taken to determine the size of the developing baby.

## Nutrition

Even before a mother suspects pregnancy, she should eat in a healthy manner. Grains, plenty of fruits and vegetables, protein from meats, beans, or eggs, and dairy products are all important. During pregnancy, each meal becomes a meal for mother and baby. Because so much growth and development is occurring for the baby, good nutrition is vital.

To meet nutritional needs, women often need to eat an additional 300 calories daily beginning in the fourth month. Women who are at a healthy weight before pregnancy should gain between 25 and 35 pounds while pregnant, **4-2**. Women who are overweight or underweight before pregnancy may be advised differently.

Pregnant women should strive to eat healthful foods. Even so, most doctors recommend additional vitamin and mineral supplements. *Prenatal vitamins*, made just for pregnancy, contain extra folic acid, calcium, and iron. The additional supplements have several benefits. Folic acid helps reduce brain and spinal cord birth defects. *Calcium* helps build strong bones and teeth. *Iron* helps to reduce the chance of babies being born at a low birthweight. Babies are considered **low birthweight** when they weigh less than 5.8 pounds.

Some foods should be avoided during pregnancy. These include some fish and shellfish that contain high levels of mercury. Undercooked meats, poultry (such as chicken), and eggs should be avoided. Milk products that are unpasteurized, such as cheese, should also not be eaten. All of these foods can cause food-related illnesses that may affect the developing baby.

| Weight Gained During Pregnancy | |
| --- | --- |
| **Portion of Added Weight** | **Weight Gain in Pounds*** |
| **Baby** | 7–8 |
| **Uterus** | 2 |
| **Placenta** | 1.5 |
| **Amniotic fluid** | 2 |
| **Increased maternal blood volume** | 3–4 |
| **Increased maternal breast mass** | 2 |
| **Increased maternal stored fat and other nutrients** | 6–8 |
| **Increased maternal fluid retention** | 4 |
| **Total weight gain** | 25–35 |

*Numbers vary for women who are underweight or overweight at the start of pregnancy and for women pregnant with multiples. Consult a doctor for a specialized weight gain plan.

*Goodheart-Willcox Publisher*

**4-2**  During pregnancy, doctors carefully monitor women's weight gain to ensure optimal health of both the mother and the developing baby.

## Health Connections    Dietary Guidelines for Americans

The U.S. Department of Agriculture has created the *Dietary Guidelines for Americans*, a customized booklet of recommendations specific to American eating habits. These guidelines outline foods and nutrients that are lacking or consumed in excess in the American diet and offers recommendations for how to increase or reduce certain foods. According to the *Guidelines*, women prior to and during pregnancy typically lack iron, folate, and seafood in their diets. All three items are crucial to the development of the fetus and are also beneficial to the health of the mother. The *Dietary Guidelines for Americans* recommends the following advice for women prior to and during pregnancy:

### Folate
- *Prior to pregnancy:* Consume 400 micrograms per week.
- *During pregnancy:* Consume 600 micrograms per week.

### Iron
- *Prior to pregnancy:* Consume more foods with *heme iron*, a form of iron that is more easily absorbed by the body.
- *During pregnancy:* To help meet iron needs, an iron supplement may be recommended by a physician.

### Seafood
- *Prior to pregnancy:* Increase to about 8 ounces per week.
- *During pregnancy:* Consume 8–12 ounces of seafood per week, excluding swordfish, shark, king mackerel, and albacore tuna (no more than 6 ounces), which are high in mercury.

### Research Activity
Research food sources of folate and iron. How can folate, iron, and seafood be incorporated into the diet? Does your nutritional advice differ for women prior to pregnancy and during pregnancy?

## Lifestyle

A healthy lifestyle is vital to both mother and developing baby. A major factor in health and wellness during pregnancy is the impact of stress. Stress can have negative effects in all stages of life, which may include emotional and physical disorders. During pregnancy, stress has been associated with early births and low birthweights for newborns. How can stress be reduced during this time?

One of the best ways to reduce stress during pregnancy is for the mother to be surrounded with a support group. Friends, medical professionals, and family can all help to relieve stress by providing social and emotional support. Having an employer who is willing to accommodate any necessary job changes is important, too. For families in financial need, some government assistance programs, such as WIC (Supplemental Nutrition Program for Women, Infant, and Children) can offer support. WIC offers nutritional foods, classes, and health screenings. Finally, getting physical activity, both aerobic and stretching exercises, can aid in wellness, **4-3**. Together, these factors can reduce the chance of problems during pregnancy.

*hartphotography/Shutterstock.com*

**4-3**  Pregnant women who are not normally physically active should consult their doctor before starting a physical activity program.

## Checkpoint

1. Describe what happens during the first medical exam of pregnancy.
2. After the first medical exam of pregnancy, how often are exams usually scheduled?
3. What is unique about prenatal vitamins? Why are they important?
4. List four foods that should be avoided during pregnancy.
5. How can stress be reduced during pregnancy?

# Problems in Prenatal Development

Women have been giving birth since the beginning of time and in the vast majority of cases, pregnancy and birth goes well. Even so, some women have a greater chance of experiencing problems during pregnancy. Complications can make the pregnancy difficult and may affect the health of the mother. Often, these problems can have an effect on the developing baby. These problems range from family genetic disorders to environmental concerns such as drug use or radiation exposure.

## Genetic Disorders

Some problems associated with pregnancy are *genetic* (passed down through family genes). Prenatal testing can determine the possibility of some genetic disorders before pregnancy occurs, **4-4**. Others can be tested for during pregnancy, and some of these disorders can be treated. Other genetic disorders cannot be treated prior to birth.

## Case Study

### Genetic Screening and "Designer Babies"

Casey and Jared are planning to have another baby. They already have a 2-year-old son, Micah, who was born with a congenital kidney disorder. Micah has undergone numerous surgeries since birth, including a kidney transplant. He is doing well now, but still requires a significant amount of medical care. Due to financial reasons, Casey and Jared only plan to have two children. They would both love to have a healthy daughter. They would like to have a red-haired, brown-eyed girl who is smart, athletic, and tall. All of these traits are in their family. If Casey and Jared could, they would arrange for their future daughter to have all of these family traits.

- Should people be able to create a perfect baby? Why or why not?
- Should there be limitations to genetic screening? If so, what should these limitations be?
- If people are allowed to create a designer baby, what regulations would be needed to avoid creating a completely changed society with generally "perfect people"? Is there a danger in people all becoming alike?
- Since there is a clear correlation between certain diseases and their link to sex chromosomes, do you think genetic engineering to control diseases is a good idea? What are some alternative methods other than genetic engineering to help prevent sex-linked diseases?

## Genetic Disorders

| Name | Description | Effects | Treatment |
|------|-------------|---------|-----------|
| **Cystic fibrosis** | Caused by two faulty genes that interfere with the respiratory, digestive, and reproductive systems. The body cannot easily process mucus, which creates blockage within the body. | Digestive, reproductive, and respiratory issues. Effects range from mild to severe. | No cure exists, but treatments are available and vary depending on symptoms. Treatments may include medications, exercise, and dietary supplements. |
| **Down syndrome** | Caused by an extra chromosome. | Severe cognitive disability and delayed language development. Effects are not uniform. | Possible surgery, education specialists, and specialized learning programs. |
| **Fragile X syndrome** | Caused by a faulty gene. The X chromosome is unstable (fragile) and usually breaks. | Effects range from short attention span to a learning disability to severe cognitive disability. | Treatments vary, but may include specialized education and therapy. |
| **Huntington's disease** | Caused by an abnormal gene that provides instructions for producing a protein called *huntingtin*, which is suspected to play an important role in nerve cells in the brain. | Loss of some physical control, memory, and ability to rationalize. Often leads to depression and death from complications. | There is no cure, but medication is available to treat symptoms. Physical activity is also recommended. |
| **Phenylketonuria (PKU)** | Caused by two mutated genes that prevent the body from processing phenylalanine, an amino acid. | If undetected, can cause permanent internal damage and cognitive disability. | When detected early, a modified diet can prevent physical and cognitive damage. |
| **Sickle-cell anemia** | Caused by a recessive gene that alters the shape of the red blood cell. Affected cells are bowed instead of circular and do not properly carry oxygen throughout the body. | Effects range from no effect unless in high altitude areas to chronic illness to early death. | Blood transfusions, penicillin, and proper medication. |
| **Spina bifida** | Caused by incomplete development and formation of the spine. | Partial to complete paralysis, fluid buildup in the skull. | Corrective surgery, physical therapy, and a modified diet. |
| **Tay-Sachs disease** | Caused by a recessive gene. The body is unable to break down certain types of fats, which build up in the system and can block neural transmissions. | Cognitive and physical deterioration that usually leads to early death. | No cure exists, but a modified diet and medication can ease symptoms. |

*Goodheart-Willcox Publisher*

**4-4** Genetic disorders vary in effects and treatment.

Genetic disorders fall into several categories. The first are disorders associated with faulty genes or chromosomes. These are inherited or passed down from mother to baby. Sickle-cell anemia and cystic fibrosis are examples of inherited diseases.

Sometimes genetic disorders are caused by absent, damaged, or extra chromosomes. A genetic disorder caused by a chromosomal defect is Down syndrome. The risk of having a baby born with Down syndrome increases with the mother's age.

Many genetic disorders can be treated before or after birth. Heart or kidney problems may be detected prior to birth. Treatment can then be implemented immediately following birth or sometimes even before birth. When a mother's family history of preterm labor or **stillbirth** (delivery of a deceased baby) are known, special medical care during pregnancy may reduce the chances of occurrence.

## Mother's Age

A mother's age during pregnancy can impact the most important outcome of the pregnancy, the health of the developing baby. Age can also affect the mother's pregnancy experience and the mother's own health. Age at both ends of the spectrum, young mothers and older mothers, can complicate pregnancies and births.

### Teen Mothers

Teen pregnancy has consequences on both the mother and baby. Teen mothers are more likely to develop high blood pressure than older mothers. They are more likely to experience preterm labor and delivery resulting in low birthweight babies. Low birthweight babies face their own challenges including developmental delays that can last for many years. If the teen mother consumes alcohol or uses drugs, the impact is great during the early weeks of development when the brain and spinal cord are developing.

If the teen mother is just past puberty, her body is still in a growing stage. Her brain is still undergoing tremendous growth and change. When a teen mother is supporting the growth and development of a baby, fewer nutrients are available for her own growth and development. Many teen mothers do not receive early prenatal care, which can impact the health of both mother and baby.

Another concern for teen mothers is finding adequate emotional and social support. Having a baby in the teen years increases the likelihood of the mother and child being socially and economically disadvantaged throughout their lives. Stress often increases, especially if social support systems are not in place. For this reason, many high schools offer alternative school programs that allow teens to finish their schooling while learning parenting and life skills.

### Older Mothers

Many women choose to become pregnant after turning age 35. Most have healthy babies. The odds of having a healthy baby decrease, however, when compared to younger mothers. Conception often takes longer and the risk of having multiple babies (twins, triplets) is increased.

Older pregnant women are more likely to give birth to babies with birth defects and abnormalities. There are two main reasons. One is exposure to environmental toxins over her longer life. Two is the age of the fertilized egg.

## Cultural Connections    Teen Parenting

Becoming pregnant during the teen years has consequences on both the mother and child. The physical, emotional, and financial costs of raising and supporting a baby are extremely high. Babies have many physical needs, such as diapers, food, clothing, cribs, car seats, strollers, blankets, child care, and toys. These physical needs are costly.

Babies also need constant care and attention, both physically and emotionally. Babies need to be fed, clothed, cleaned, and changed. They need to know that when they cry, they will receive comfort. Babies need to feel safe and secure. Meeting a baby's needs can be emotionally and physically taxing on any parents, but especially on teens who are still growing and maturing themselves.

Teen parents must often put their own needs aside to first provide for and attend to the baby, which often leaves teen parents fatigued. With the new responsibilities of parenting, having a child during the teen years can prevent high school graduation and interfere with plans for higher education. If the mother has multiples or a baby with special needs, additional resources and support are necessary to provide proper care and optimal development for the baby or babies.

### Financial Activity

Estimate the financial cost for raising a baby in the first year by conducting an Internet search. How would becoming a parent impact a teen's life?

---

Over a lifetime, people are exposed to more and more environmental toxins. Secondhand smoke, cleaning chemicals, food pollutants, and medications are just some of the pollutants that can affect a developing baby.

Women begin their monthly menstrual cycle as older girls or young teens. They can continue this cycle at least 40 years, but all of their eggs exist from the start. By the time an older mother conceives, the older egg may be susceptible to genetic chromosomal abnormalities. This can result in birth defects such as Down syndrome. Because of these risks, prenatal testing is often done to prepare the mother and medical team in providing proper care for the baby.

When a mother is older, the pregnancy can be harder on her as well. **Gestational diabetes**, a type of diabetes that occurs only during pregnancy, is more common. Older mothers are at a higher risk for *miscarriage*, the early loss of a pregnancy. They are also more likely to have problems with labor and deliver their babies via **caesarean section** (surgical removal of the baby) than through normal vaginal delivery.

## Illness and Poor Health

A mother's health has implications for the developing baby. When a woman is ill or in poor health, her body may struggle to support both the health of the mother and that of the developing baby. Infections and viruses can have an impact depending on when they occur during development. For example, contracting rubella (German measles) during the first three months of pregnancy can cause infant blindness. A mother can pass some sexually transmitted infections to the baby during birth.

### Sexually Transmitted Infections

**Sexually transmitted infections (STIs)** are infectious illnesses that are spread primarily through sexual contact. STIs are also known as *sexually transmitted diseases (STDs)*. Some common sexually transmitted infections include genital herpes, gonorrhea, syphilis, chlamydia, and HIV.

STIs are often categorized as bacterial and viral infections, **4-5. Bacterial STIs** are caused by bacteria and can be cured with antibiotics if detected and treated early. Unfortunately some, such as chlamydia, often go undetected leading to *pelvic inflammatory disease (PID)*, which can cause infertility in women. Others, such as gonorrhea, have become more resistant to antibiotic treatments. Syphilis can lead to serious mental disorders and death. Although syphilis is more controlled than previously, outbreaks still occur.

**Viral STIs** are caused by viruses and cannot be cured. They cannot be treated with antibiotics. Some treatments can alleviate symptoms, but because there is no cure, the symptoms return. Genital herpes, genital warts, and human papillomavirus (HPV) are common viral STIs. *Human papillomavirus (HPV)* is prevalent in young adulthood and has been linked to cervical cancer. For this reason, many young females are given the HPV vaccination.

The **HIV** or human immunodeficiency virus causes the disease **AIDS** (acquired immune deficiency syndrome). HIV is spread through bodily fluids. Blood transferred during an infusion, shared needles, and unprotected sex are all possible sources of exchange. Once a person has HIV, the virus attacks the body's immune system. AIDS develops when the person's immune system is no longer able to fight illness.

All STIs can cause serious health problems. A mother could be infected and not realize she has an STI because she does not show any outward signs of infection. This can have dire affects on developing babies. An STI can enter a mother's bloodstream and reach the unborn baby.

Likewise, mothers with HIV/AIDS are more likely to infect their babies if proper medical care is not used. The virus has the most impact on the unborn baby during the first three months of development. After birth, babies are more likely to be sick from infections. Facial abnormalities are common in babies infected with HIV/AIDS.

## Environmental Factors

Some pregnancy problems and birth defects are the result of the unborn baby being exposed to harmful substances, **4-6.** These include such things as chemicals, illness and infections, and medications. Alcohol, drugs, and cigarettes also create an adverse environment for both mother and baby. Knowing exactly which agents in the environment are causing the problems can be difficult. A combination of several agents could be the problem. The level and length of exposure can also make a difference. Pregnant women should check with their health provider on what items to avoid.

| Sexually Transmitted Infections | | | | |
|---|---|---|---|---|
| **Name** | **Description** | **Symptoms** | **Health Risks to Fetus and Newborn** | **Treatment** |
| **Bacterial** | | | | |
| **Chlamydia** | Caused by the bacteria, *Chlamydia trachomatis*; is transmittable through any type of sexual activity | • No noticeable symptoms<br>• Vaginal or penal discharge<br>• Painful urination<br>• Fever<br>• If left untreated, may damage reproductive organs and cause sterility | • Can be passed to baby during delivery<br>• Eye infection during birth<br>• Pneumonia | Prescribed antibiotics |
| **Gonorrhea** | Caused by the bacteria, *Neisseria gonorrhoeae*; is transmittable through any type of sexual activity | • No noticeable symptoms<br>• Vaginal or penal discharge<br>• Painful and/or frequent urination<br>• Fever<br>• Abdominal pain<br>• If left untreated, may damage reproductive organs and cause sterility | • Can be passed to baby during delivery<br>• Blindness<br>• Blood infection | Prescribed antibiotics |
| **PID** | A severe infection caused by bacteria that moves into female reproductive organs (Chlamydia and gonorrhea can lead to PID) | • No noticeable symptoms<br>• Discharge<br>• Abdominal pain<br>• Fever<br>• Painful urination<br>• If left untreated, may cause sterility | • Eye infection<br>• Blindness | Prescribed antibiotics; in severe cases, surgery may be necessary |
| **Syphilis** | Caused by the bacteria, *Treponema pallidum* | • No noticeable symptoms<br>Early Stage<br>• Small, painless sore on affected area<br>Later Stages<br>• Body rash<br>• Fever<br>• Hair and weight loss<br>• Headache<br>• Sore muscles<br>• If left untreated, may cause permanent internal damage and death | • Can be transmitted to the fetus<br>• Stillborn birth<br>• Delays in development<br>• Postpartum death | Penicillin injection or prescribed antibiotics |

*Goodheart-Willcox Publisher*

**4-5** STIs can affect the fetus or newborn in cases of pregnancy.

(Continued on next page)

| Sexually Transmitted Infections | | | | |
|---|---|---|---|---|
| **Name** | **Description** | **Symptoms** | **Health Risks to Fetus and Newborn** | **Treatment** |
| Viral | | | | |
| **AIDS/HIV** | Virus that destroys white blood cells and interferes with the body's ability to fight illnesses and diseases (HIV can lead to AIDS) | Early Stage<br>• Fever<br>• Fatigue<br>• Sore or swollen muscles<br>Later Stages<br>• Weight loss<br>• Body sores<br>• If untreated, may lead to heart, kidney, liver, and lung diseases | • Can be transmitted during pregnancy, birth, or breastfeeding<br>• Developmental delays<br>• If untreated, will lead to death | No cure, but prescription medications can ease symptoms; medication may be prescribed during pregnancy to help manage risks to the unborn baby |
| **Genital herpes** | Caused by herpes simplex virus | • No noticeable symptoms<br>• Sores around the affected area with pain and itching | • Can be passed to baby during birth<br>• Respiratory issues, such as trouble breathing<br>• Bleeding<br>• Seizures | No cure, but prescribed medication can ease symptoms and control breakouts |
| **HPV** | A virus that exists in different forms; is the most common STI | • No noticeable symptoms<br>• Warts on genitals<br>• Painful urination<br>• Cervical and other types of cancer | • Premature delivery<br>• Low birthweight | No cure, but medications are available to ease symptoms |

*Goodheart-Willcox Publisher*

**4-5** (Continued.)

### Radiation, Lead, and Mercury Exposure

Radiation exposure can occur from X-rays and some other medical tests or treatments. Women should try to avoid getting any medical or dental X-rays while pregnant. Radiation occurs in higher doses in cancer treatments. Women should inform technicians of their pregnancy before receiving treatments of any kind. Both men and women exposed to too much radiation in hospital settings have shown higher risks of miscarriage for the pregnant woman.

Mercury exposure can occur from foods, such as mercury in some fish products. Because of this, women should try to limit their exposure to fish and shellfish containing mercury. Lead exposure can occur in the workplace or in the home. For example, old lead-based paint can still be found in some older apartments and homes.

## The Impact of Environmental Factors on Fetal Development

| Factor | Possible Effects |
|---|---|
| **Prenatal vitamins** | • Folic acid reduces brain/spinal cord defects<br>• Calcium builds strong bones and teeth<br>• Iron reduces chance of low birthweight |
| **Caffeine** | • Miscarriage |
| **Radiation, lead, or mercury** | • Miscarriage<br>• Congenital disorders |
| **Nicotine** | • Premature births<br>• Low birthweight<br>• Congenital disorders<br>• Cardiovascular disorders |
| **Marijuana** | • Premature births<br>• Low birthweight<br>• Neurological disorders<br>• Respiratory problems<br>• Slow weight gain<br>• SIDS |
| **Alcohol** | • Facial deformities<br>• Defective limbs<br>• Defective heart<br>• Below average intelligence<br>• Cognitive disabilities |
| **Cocaine** | • Low birthweight<br>• Shorter birth length<br>• Smaller head circumference<br>• Slower motor development through infancy<br>• Slower growth through age 10<br>• Excitability/irritability<br>• Neurological deficits<br>• Cognitive deficits<br>• Medical deficits<br>• Behavioral and attention issues |
| **Heroin** | • Behavioral and attention issues<br>• Withdrawal issues<br>• Excitability/irritability<br>• Excessive crying<br>• Disturbed sleep<br>• Slower motor development |
| **Methamphetamine** | • Low birthweight<br>• Higher infant mortality<br>• Neurological deficits<br>• Cognitive deficits<br>• Behavioral and attention issues |

*Goodheart-Willcox Publisher*

**4-6** Pregnant women should try to avoid as many risks as possible.

## Drug Use

Drugs are a major environmental risk for both mothers and their developing babies. Drug exposure can cause severe and long-term birth defects. These effects can be so long-term they affect the physical, cognitive, and socio-emotional development of a baby for his or her entire lifetime. Drugs include illegal drugs, prescription and over-the-counter drugs, alcohol, and nicotine. Drugs do not just include those that are swallowed or smoked. They can also have negative effects when in the environment. For example, secondhand smoke (smoke exhaled by someone else) can have negative effects. Drug use by fathers can also have an adverse effect on unborn, developing babies.

Major drugs that may cause birth defects are nicotine and alcohol, and illegal drugs such as marijuana, heroin, methadone, and cocaine. Prescription and over-the-counter drugs are also of concern, although many of their possible effects are not known.

Nicotine is a drug found in cigarettes and other tobacco products. Nicotine is a stimulant that is easily absorbed in an expectant mother's bloodstream. Once absorbed, nicotine travels from the mother to the developing baby. Because nicotine is a stimulant, the baby increases in activity just like the mother. Mothers who smoke are more likely to have premature, low birthweight babies who are at a higher risk of death than babies who are born full-term. Their babies are also more likely to have congenital abnormalities than babies born to mothers who do not smoke.

Alcohol is the drug that infants are most often exposed to prior to birth. Prenatal alcohol consumption is the leading cause of cognitive disabilities. Head and facial abnormalities along with heart, brain, and skeletal damage are common symptoms of **fetal alcohol syndrome (FAS)** or prenatal exposure to alcohol. Neither good nutrition before birth nor good health care after birth can change the effects of prenatal exposure to alcohol on the baby.

Marijuana is the most common (frequently used) illegal drug. Babies exposed to marijuana prenatally are often born early and are of low birthweight. They may also have neurological disorders, respiratory problems, and are slower

 **Health Connections**    **Fetal Alcohol Syndrome**

When any amount of alcohol is consumed during pregnancy, the environment of the unborn baby negatively changes. The baby becomes at risk for suffering fetal alcohol syndrome (FAS). The effects of FAS range from permanent physical and cognitive defects to death of the unborn child. The following are possible effects of FAS:

**Physical**

- low birthweight
- smaller head, eyes, and lips
- diminished muscle coordination
- poor vision and hearing
- problems with the heart, liver, bones, and central nervous system

**Cognitive**

- learning disabilities and possible retardation
- delays with speech development
- difficulties interacting in social situations
- hyperactive behavior

People with FAS require extra medical, educational, and therapeutic help. FAS, however, can be avoided altogether when no alcohol is consumed during pregnancy.

**Research Activity**

Research children born with FAS. What obstacles do they encounter in school and social situations?

to gain weight than their healthy counterparts. After birth, they are more likely to die from **sudden infant death syndrome (SIDS)**, which is an unexpected death for unknown reasons during the first year of life.

Other illegal drugs have the same devastating effects on infants—preterm births and low birthweights. Because they, too, are exposed to the drug, babies must go through drug withdrawals after birth when the exposure is stopped. This painful process involves excessive sweating, sneezing, yawning, tremors, and shaking. Babies exposed to illegal drugs have breathing and sucking or eating difficulties. They often cry incessantly, have trouble keeping food in their stomachs, have rigid bodies, and are hyperactive. In other words, their withdrawal experience is not different from adults. Those who survive the painful withdrawal process are more likely to die from SIDS or suffer lifelong consequences.

Although nicotine, alcohol, and illegal drugs are often the focus of prenatal development problems, legal drugs are a great concern, too. Prescription and over-the-counter drugs such as cold or cough medicines, aspirin, or other pain relievers should not be taken unless approved by a doctor who is aware of the pregnancy.

## Paternal Factors

The lifestyle of and environment surrounding women, both before and during pregnancy, is traditionally the focus of concern in prenatal development. Of course, this is because a woman carries the developing fetus within her body. The father may also affect conception and prenatal development, however.

Since a father's sperm is joined with the mother's egg at conception, quality of the sperm may have an impact on the results of the pregnancy. Lifestyle, health, and age all affect the quality of the sperm, **4-7**. A father's alcohol use before conception is an example of a lifestyle choice that may have an effect on a developing baby. The effect is difficult to measure precisely, but early studies suggest that such use may result in birth defects. Likewise, a father's drug use may also affect a developing baby in ways similar to a mother's use of drugs. When alcohol and drugs are used together, the effect of one over the other is difficult to determine.

After conception, if a father smokes, the secondhand smoke in the environment is inhaled by the mother and can have an effect similar to when a mother smokes. Fathers should try to never smoke around their baby's mother when she is pregnant or after birth in the child's presence.

*szefei/Shutterstock.com*

**4-7**  Factors such as a father's lifestyle, health, and age may affect the outcome of conception and the subsequent baby that develops.

## Checkpoint

1. What are genetic disorders and how can they affect pregnancy outcome?
2. How does a mother's age affect her pregnancy?
3. What is the difference between bacterial and viral STIs? Give two examples of each type of STI.
4. How can nicotine from a mother smoking or secondhand smoke affect her developing baby?
5. How can nicotine, alcohol, and illegal drugs affect a developing baby?
6. How might a father affect conception and prenatal development?

# Stages of Prenatal Development

A woman deals with many changes during the nine months of pregnancy. Learning about her pregnancy is the first. This news may cause stress. Even pregnancies that are planned can cause stress. The mother wonders about how her life will change. Is she ready to handle the additional responsibility? Are there adequate resources to care for the baby? How will her body change?

## First Trimester

The *first trimester* begins at conception and continues until about the twelfth week of pregnancy. A woman may not even realize she is pregnant during much of the first trimester. Especially if her periods are irregular (a missed period is often the first indicator that she is pregnant). There are other

## Health Connections    Physical Changes During Pregnancy

When a woman becomes pregnant, her body will go through many changes throughout the next nine months. For the first few weeks, a woman may be unaware that she is pregnant. As her body is preparing for the developing baby, she will begin to notice and display signs of pregnancy.

The first few bodily changes pregnant women experience are changes in menstruation, breast size, and stomach discomfort. Women do not continue to menstruate during pregnancy and a missed period is usually the first indicator of pregnancy. Pregnant women will also notice a slight increase in breast size and breast soreness. Since the body is producing breast milk for the baby, the breasts enlarge and become sore. Nausea, or "morning sickness," is another change some women experience while pregnant. Not all pregnant women experience nausea, but most do because of an increase in hormone levels.

As the uterus grows during pregnancy, many other physical changes also take place. The uterus expands to make room for the developing baby and pushes against the bladder, causing frequent urination. From all the bodily changes, pregnant women often feel fatigued. Weight gain, sore muscles, and changes to the skin are also common and normal changes pregnant women experience.

### Speaking Activity

Interview a mother who has recently given birth or who is expecting a child. Ask her about changes she is experiencing or has experienced. How did these changes affect her physically and socio-emotionally?

signs besides a missed period, however, including tiredness and mood changes. Although changes may not be as apparent from the outside, a tremendous amount of change is going on inside the mother's body.

The first trimester includes both the germinal and the embryonic periods of prenatal development. The **germinal period** extends from conception until about two weeks later when implantation in the uterus occurs. Here are the highlights. *Conception* occurs when a sperm penetrates the egg or ovum. The fertilized egg is now considered to be a **zygote**. Within hours, the zygote begins dividing first into two cells, then four. By the time five days have passed, the zygote is up to 64–128 cells and is now called a **blastocyst**. Within two weeks' span, the blastocyst will attach itself to the lining wall of the mother's uterus.

The next stage of the first trimester is called the **embryonic period**. From the second to the ninth week of pregnancy, astounding development occurs. At this stage, the developing baby is called an **embryo**. The embryo has three parts: the outermost layer (ectoderm), the middle layer (mesoderm), and the innermost layer (endoderm). These three layers are responsible for the formation of distinct parts, **4-8**.

Early in this stage, an umbilical cord, or life support line, develops between the embryo and the mother's uterine lining. The umbilical cord is attached to the *placenta*, a mass attached to the uterus that provides nutrients from the mother. The *umbilical cord* is the tube of veins that connects the placenta with the baby (at the site later called the belly button). This lifeline will provide oxygen, nutrients, and water through the mother's blood to the developing embryo. The embryo then floats free from the wall. Amniotic fluid will develop. This prevents the developing baby from shocks and movements and keeps the temperature constant as the mother carries on with life.

The development that occurs during the embryonic period is astonishing, **4-9**. The nervous system develops. The heart develops and begins to beat. Most body parts become identifiable. During this stage, the head is dominant.

The final stage of the first trimester begins the **fetal period**, which lasts until birth at the end of the third trimester. During this stage, the developing baby is called a **fetus**. All parts of the baby's body mature and overall size increases quickly.

| Parts of the Embryo | |
|---|---|
| **Part of Embryo** | **Parts of Body That Develop** |
| Ectoderm | Nervous system, ears, nose, eyes |
| Mesoderm | Bones, muscles, circulatory system, reproductive system |
| Endoderm | Digestive and respiratory systems |

*Goodheart-Willcox Publisher*

**4-8** Each part of the embryo is responsible for the development of different body parts and systems.

## An Overview of the Highlights in Prenatal Development*

### First Trimester

| First month | |
|---|---|

**First month**

- Conception: sperm and egg (ovum) unite
- Fertilized egg is considered to be a *zygote*
- Zygote divides up to 64–128 cells to create a *blastocyst*
- Blastocyst implants into uterus lining
- Nervous system (brain and spinal cord) begins to develop, continues throughout pregnancy
- Digestive system begins forming
- Heart begins to beat
- First signs of heart, face, arms, legs, and lungs show
- Tissue that will later form baby's backbone, skull, ribs, and muscles can be seen on ultrasound
- By end of the month, baby is called an *embryo* and is about ¼ inch long

**Second month**

- Head continues rapid growth appearing larger than rest of body
- Brain grows quickly and starts to direct baby's movements
- Liver and stomach begin working
- Legs and arms become longer and take shape
- Fingers and toes develop
- Ears, nose, and mouth take shape
- Eyes take on color and eyelids form
- By end of month, embryo is about 2 inches long and weighs about ⅓ ounce

**Third month**

- Baby is called a *fetus*
- Bones are growing
- Kidneys are working
- Fetus moves often, but cannot be felt by mother
- Toes are visible and elbows are identifiable
- Facial features are well-formed
- Fingerprints appear
- Fetus can open and close mouth and swallow
- May be possible to determine sex from genitals
- Head growth slows
- By end of month, baby is about 4 inches long and weighs about 1 ounce

*Images are not necessarily true-to-size.

*Goodheart-Willcox Publisher*

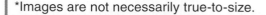

**4-9**   Many important changes occur during each of the stages in prenatal development.

(Continued on next page)

## An Overview of the Highlights in Prenatal Development*

### Second Trimester

| | |
|---|---|
| **Fourth month**<br>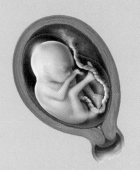 | • Umbilical cord grows and thickens to carry enough blood and nourishment to baby<br>• Placenta is now formed<br>• Airways develop, but are not yet in use<br>• Heartbeat is strong<br>• More muscles and bones develop<br>• Bones can be identified<br>• Fingernails appear<br>• Baby sleeps and wakes<br>• Limb movement becomes more coordinated<br>• Baby moves and kicks<br>• By end of month, baby is about 6 to 7 inches long and weighs about ½ pound |
| **Fifth month**<br>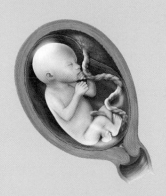 | • Baby's internal organs continue to grow<br>• Baby's movements increase and can be felt by mother<br>• Blood supply to lungs increases<br>• Heartbeat heard by stethoscope<br>• Eyebrows and eyelashes appear<br>• Scalp hair appears<br>• Sleeps and wakes in a pattern<br>• Silky body hair and a waxy coating protect baby's skin from watery surroundings<br>• By end of month, baby is about 9 inches long and weighs about 1 pound |
| **Sixth month**<br> | • Baby's growth speeds up<br>• Skin is red, wrinkled, and oily<br>• Fingernails identified<br>• Baby stretches, kicks, and sucks thumb<br>• Baby can open and close eyes and hear sounds<br>• By end of month, baby is about 12 inches long and weighs about 1½ pounds |

*Images are not necessarily true-to-size.

*Goodheart-Willcox Publisher*

4-9  (Continued.)

(Continued on next page)

## An Overview of the Highlights in Prenatal Development*

### Third Trimester

| | |
|---|---|
| **Seventh month**<br> | • Lungs are more mature and can support baby outside the uterus<br>• Brain and nervous system are much more mature<br>• Bones are more developed, but are still soft and flexible<br>• Skin is wrinkly and covered with a thick, white protective coating called *vernix*<br>• Fatty tissue begins developing under skin surface<br>• Baby kicks and stretches<br>• Outline of baby's fist, foot, or head may be seen outside mother's body when baby moves<br>• By end of month, baby is about 16 inches long and weighs about 3 pounds |
| **Eighth month**<br> | • Baby's growth continues<br>• Brain growth is rapid<br>• Skin is not wrinkled, and color is pink<br>• Baby kicks strongly, but has less room to move<br>• Baby may move into a head-down position in the uterus<br>• By end of month, baby is about 18 inches long and weighs about 5 pounds |
| **Ninth month**<br>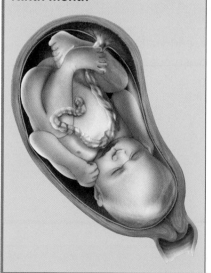 | • Baby gains about ½ pound weekly<br>• Lungs are mature<br>• Downy hair (laguno) that covers the skin disappears<br>• Baby positions itself into a head-down position to prepare for birth<br>• By birth, an average baby is about 20 inches long and weighs about 7 to 8 pounds |

*Images are not necessarily true-to-size.

Goodheart-Willcox Publisher

**4-9**   (Continued.)

## Second Trimester

By the beginning of the second trimester (13 to 24 weeks), one of the most important milestones for a pregnant woman is achieved. This is when she emotionally shifts from viewing pregnancy as a "state her body is in" to viewing her unborn child as a separate person from herself. During the second trimester, the mother's body is beginning to show the effects of pregnancy with an enlarged "belly," larger breasts, and expanding hips.

During the second trimester, body parts become more distinct including arms and legs, fingers and toes, and eyes and ears. Facial features become clear. When using ultrasound imaging, the bones of the developing baby can be seen. Movements of arms and legs become more coordinated and the baby's movements can be felt by the mother and sometimes by others. Even the sex of the baby can often be determined.

By the time the second trimester comes to an end, the developing fetus weighs 1–1½ pounds and may be 12–14 inches long. As the baby increases in size, so does the mother. Many women report that the best part of their pregnancy is during the second trimester as "morning sickness" is often over and the uncomfortable expanding body of the third trimester is yet to come.

## Third Trimester

If the baby is born as early as the beginning of the third trimester (24 to 40 weeks), there is a good chance of survival with proper medical care. In other words, all organs are developed and functioning. The last trimester is important for increased organ function, especially the lungs. Fatty tissue develops and the baby becomes both longer and heavier. By the end of the seventh month, the baby weighs about 3 pounds and is about 16 inches long. By birth at the end of the third trimester, an average baby weighs 7–8 pounds and is about 20 inches long.

**Health Connections**    **Music to the Womb**

Have you ever heard that playing music for an unborn child will stimulate and encourage intellectual development? Some pregnant women place headphones over the womb and play music to foster a stimulating environment for the fetus. The research on the effects of playing music in relation to intellectual development is inconclusive. Evidence does suggest, however, that the unborn baby will physically respond to music and sounds. The fetus begins to develop hearing during the 16th week. Studies have shown that when music is played over the womb after the 16th week, the fetus responds with increased or decreased heart rate depending on the music tempo.

Babies in the third trimester respond with physical movement. The amniotic fluid can amplify some pitch frequencies in the womb. Therefore, to protect the hearing development of the fetus, music should not be played too loudly.

### Research Activity

Most studies about the effects of music on the fetus use classical music as the sample. Do you think playing other types of music would have a different effect on the fetus? From journals, magazines, or other reliable sources, locate a reporting of one of the studies on music exposure to the fetus. Summarize your findings in a two-page report.

As the baby grows in size and weight, the mother's body prepares for the baby's birth. After nine months of preparation, the mother's body prepares for labor and delivery. The baby positions itself in a head-down position, **4-10**. As the baby's head moves into the pelvis, the mother often feels less pressure on her breathing and stomach. Sometimes women experience psychological changes. The most commonly mentioned is "nesting" or the desire to ready things for the upcoming new baby.

## Checkpoint

1. Describe what happens during the germinal period of prenatal development.
2. Describe what happens during the embryonic period of prenatal development.
3. Describe what happens during the fetal period of prenatal development.
4. Describe what happens during the third trimester.

## Birth

When a baby is full term (any time after 37 weeks), the mother is usually more than ready to meet her new son or daughter. By now, the baby should be in position and the mother begins to feel slight changes in her health. Mild cramps begin, which are **Braxton-Hicks contractions**. The mother may be slightly nauseous and may feel that something is about to change.

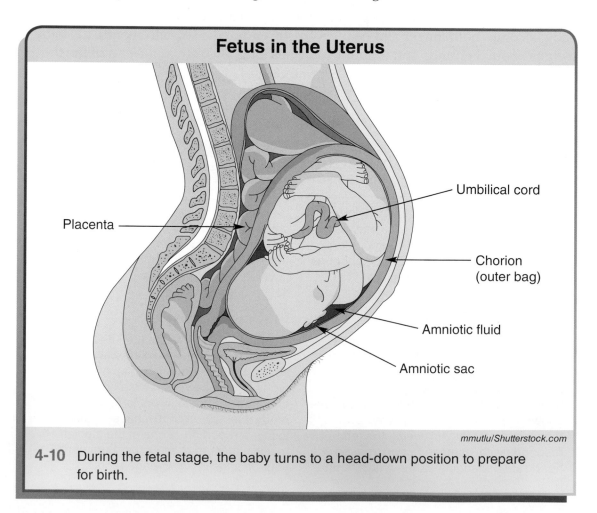

**Fetus in the Uterus**

Placenta

Umbilical cord

Chorion (outer bag)

Amniotic fluid

Amniotic sac

*mmutlu/Shutterstock.com*

**4-10**  During the fetal stage, the baby turns to a head-down position to prepare for birth.

## Stages of Labor

The first signs of real labor starting are felt and seen. Most mothers experience one or all of the following: blood or mucus when the mucous plug falls out of the cervix, her "water breaking" (passing of amniotic fluid), and the beginning of uncomfortable uterine contractions. These are called *contractions*. As labor progresses, these contractions become more intense and closer together. During birth, there are three stages that prepare the mother for delivery of her baby, **4-11**.

### Stage One—Dilation

The first stage is called the *dilation stage*. During this stage, the mother's cervix increases in diameter to allow for the baby to eventually pass through. The goal is 10 centimeters, or about 4 inches in diameter. This stage can last hours.

Fetal monitoring is often used during the labor or dilation stage. *Fetal monitors* are devices that track a baby's heart rate, the mother's contractions, and alert the medical staff to any signs of distress. Fetal monitoring is a good way to track the baby's stress through the labor and delivery process. Typically, one monitor is strapped around the top of the mother's stomach. The second monitor is inserted internally through the cervix and rests on top of the baby's head.

Some mothers choose natural childbirth. In **natural childbirth**, breathing and relaxation exercises are used to help the mother deal with pain. Often, a partner or coach is chosen to help the mother focus. One of the most well-known natural childbirth methods is called the **Lamaze method**. In this method, the partner helps the mother keep track of and time her contractions while providing emotional support. Natural childbirth can be used in hospitals, in birthing centers with a certified-nurse midwife, or at home with a **doula** (someone who is trained to provide emotional support during the birth process). Midwives and doulas usually work in close contact with medical professionals in case a complication arises.

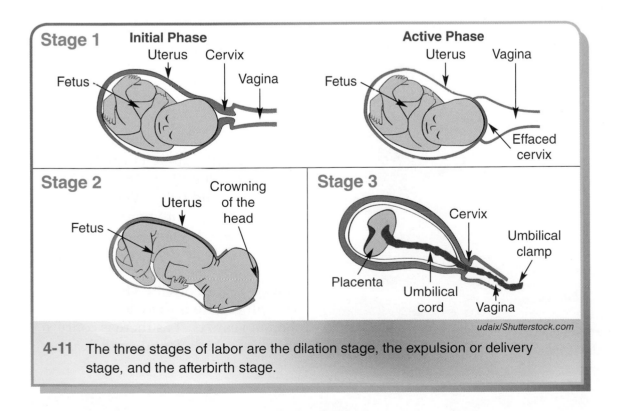

udaix/Shutterstock.com

**4-11**   The three stages of labor are the dilation stage, the expulsion or delivery stage, and the afterbirth stage.

## Cultural Connections    Birthing Practices Around the World

The cultural practices of birthing differ from country to country. Some countries and cultures encourage natural childbirths at home with a midwife present, some prefer hospital births, and some favor cesarean section births. In the Netherlands, natural childbirths at home are encouraged and more common than hospital births. A midwife is present to coach the mother during childbirth and to ensure the health and wellness of the mother and baby. A midwife will also return after childbirth to check on the mother and child, teach parenting skills, prepare meals, and help with housekeeping. In other countries, such as China and Paraguay, there is a growing preference toward C-sections. In China, nearly half of all childbirths are C-sections. Other than medical reasons, C-sections may be favored because of the choice of the baby's birth date, less time in labor, and the possibility for less pain.

### Discussion Activity

Discuss the possible advantages and disadvantages to natural, hospital, and cesarean-section births. Find current articles about changing trends in birthing practices around the globe to discuss with the class.

Most mothers choose to deliver their babies in hospitals, **4-12**. Again, natural childbirth can be used. Others choose to use medication to control pain. Local anesthetics, medications that numb the pain in a specific region of the body, are often used the most. Once the mother reaches full dilation, pain medications for contractions are usually not administered in a regular delivery.

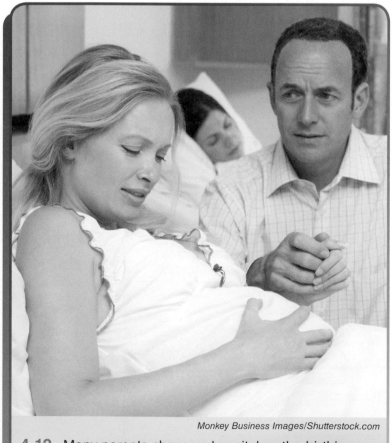

*Monkey Business Images/Shutterstock.com*

**4-12**  Many parents choose a hospital as the birthing place of their baby.

### Stage Two—Delivery

The second stage of labor is called the *expulsion stage* or delivery. Once the mother is fully dilated, the baby is ready to begin moving through the birth canal. Usually the baby's head appears first, quickly followed by the rest of the body. This stage is much shorter than the labor or dilation stage and only lasts about 1.5 hours for first time mothers and much shorter for those who have given birth before.

Sometimes the birth canal does not adequately stretch to allow the baby through without hurting both the mother and baby. When this is the case, an episiotomy procedure is done. An **episiotomy** is a surgical cut that allows the baby to pass through more easily. The surgical cut is quickly repaired with a few stitches. This procedure is done less routinely than in years past as there is concern about possible infection and healing afterward.

**Stage Three—Afterbirth**

The final stage of birth is called the *afterbirth stage*. During this final stage, the umbilical cord and the placenta are delivered. The stage does not last very long, only a few minutes to as long as an hour. The umbilical cord is cut and the new baby is now a separate, independent human being, **4-13**.

## Checkpoint

1. Define Braxton-Hicks contractions.
2. What are the three stages of labor?
3. Describe what happens during the first stage of labor.
4. Describe what happens during the second stage of labor.
5. Describe what happens during the third stage of labor.

# Birth Complications

The vast majority of births are "good" births. They go according to plan and result in a positive experience for both mother and baby. Once in awhile, however, complications occur. Some of these complications include unexpected preterm birth, the need for induced labor, and breech births. Some babies suffer from oxygen deprivation during birth. Others have Rh factor challenges. As mentioned earlier in the chapter, some babies are born using a surgical procedure rather than the usual method of labor and vaginal delivery. This procedure is called a *caesarian section* or *C-section*.

## Preterm Birth

Babies come earlier than expected (before full-term) for many reasons. Several of these reasons were previously discussed including the mother's age, health, and exposure to environmental toxins including smoking, alcohol, drugs, and other substances. Premature births may occur despite a mother's best efforts to provide the safest prenatal environment possible. Sometimes premature births are a result of too much crowding when twins or other multiple births struggle to share space inside the womb.

What happens if a baby comes earlier than expected? Babies who are born earlier are usually small in size having a low birthweight (less than 5.8 pounds). A **very low birthweight** baby weighs less than 3.5 pounds. These babies are at greater risks for many problems. The risk varies, however, depending on how early the baby arrives.

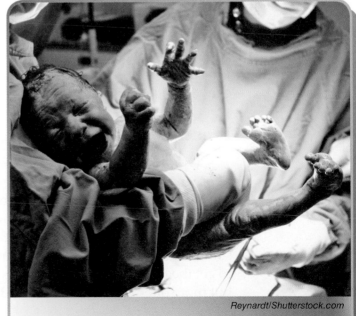

*Reynardt/Shutterstock.com*

**4-13**  After birth, the baby must adjust to life outside the mother's body.

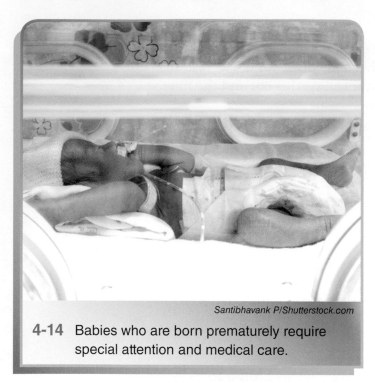

Santibhavank P/Shutterstock.com

**4-14** Babies who are born prematurely require special attention and medical care.

Babies born after 28 weeks have the best chance of survival among premature babies, **4-14**. By then, all organs are developed and functioning. Each day after week 28 adds to the baby's chances of good health and lessens the chance of developmental delays associated with early birth. For example, although the lungs are developed and functioning, each week after week 28 prepares the lungs for better functioning outside the womb.

Babies who are born early often face developmental challenges and require special care. They may grow slower, crawl later, and be delayed in other early milestones. Today, improvements in health care have greatly improved the chances of premature babies living a normal life. By the time most premature babies reach toddlerhood, they have often caught up with their full-term counterparts.

## Induced Labor

Sometimes, labor needs to start before the mother's body begins the birth process itself. **Induced labor** occurs when doctors use medication to initiate the birth process. Doctors may also break the amniotic sac, giving the mother's body a signal that labor is about to begin. Induced labor is not to be considered just out of convenience to the mother, but when there is risk to the mother or baby to prolong the waiting. For example, when a baby is well past the due date, he or she continues to grow and gain weight. Sometimes, the extra weight and size will be detrimental to the mother and baby if labor is not begun. Induced labor has some drawbacks. One is more intense labor contractions. These harder contractions are uncomfortable and painful for the mother, but may also create more stress for the baby. Two is the higher possibility that a C-section may be required from the more intense labor and stress on the baby. For example, when a baby's oxygen supply is compromised a quick decision must be made.

## Breech Birth

Typically, babies turn head down in a mother's pelvis during the last few weeks of pregnancy in preparation for their upcoming birth. Sometimes, however, they do not. A **breech birth** occurs when a baby does not "turn." Breech babies do not come through the birth canal in the typical head first fashion so careful guidance is needed by the birth attendant. Sometimes the baby comes feet first, sometimes crosswise, and sometimes buttocks first, **4-15**. Because this can be difficult, attempts are often made to get the baby to turn through massage and outside prodding. Sometimes this works, but more often, the breech baby is delivered by C-section.

## Oxygen Deprivation

Sometimes fetal monitoring determines that a baby is suffering from oxygen deprivation. **Oxygen deprivation** means that the baby's flow of oxygen is somehow interrupted. This can have grave consequences including damage to the brain or death. Sometimes, too much pressure on the baby's blood vessels during the birth process causes oxygen deprivation. Other times, an inadequate blood supply between the mother and baby causes oxygen deprivation. This insufficiency may be caused from problems with the placenta or umbilical cord. Whatever the reason, medical professionals must move quickly to deliver the baby safely.

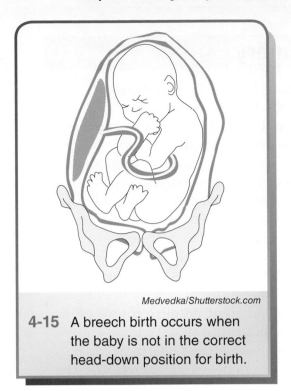

*Medvedka/Shutterstock.com*

**4-15** A breech birth occurs when the baby is not in the correct head-down position for birth.

## The Rh Factor

The **Rh factor** refers to the type of protein in red blood cells that does not match between the mother's and the baby's blood type. A mismatch between the mother and baby is of concern as incompatibility can cause miscarriage or infant death. In some cases, the baby may become anemic, or lacking in iron. In other cases, the baby experiences no harm. Results depend on the type and severity of the incompatibility.

Through routine blood tests during pregnancy, mismatches are detected. If the results are positive for the Rh factor, mothers can be treated and special care taken both during pregnancy and after delivery.

## Checkpoint

1. List five birth complications.
2. When can a baby viably survive outside the womb?
3. What kinds of problems might the preterm baby face?
4. What is induced labor? List two drawbacks of induced labor.
5. What is the Rh factor? What is the concern to mothers and their babies?

## Summary

Because babies are so dependent on their mother for food, oxygen, and protection, the mother must provide the healthiest and safest environment possible. Wellness, including nutrition, abstinence from drugs and other harmful substances, and a healthy lifestyle, is important before pregnancy as well as during pregnancy.

From conception to post-delivery, so much happens during these few months of life. After the mother's egg is fertilized with the father's sperm, development begins immediately. Within a couple of weeks, the brain and spinal cord begin to develop. Soon after, a heartbeat can be detected. Organ development follows. The fetus grows. Body parts become defined and functioning. By week 28 of pregnancy, the developing baby is capable of surviving outside the womb, with intensive medical care. In the last trimester, the baby gains significant weight, the lungs become better functioning, and the baby grows in length. These last few weeks of pregnancy are important to the baby's health and wellness. After 37 weeks, the baby is considered full-term.

The birth process begins with contractions and sometimes expulsion of the mucus plug and breakage of the amniotic sac. As labor continues, contractions become more intense and closer together. During labor, the cervix dilates to 10 centimeters. The head appears first, and intense pushing begins during the delivery stage. Once the baby is delivered, the placenta and umbilical cord follow during the afterbirth stage. The umbilical cord is cut and the baby is presented to the mother.

Pregnancy and birth are amazing life stages. They can be complicated by many factors. These include the mother's age and health status, the baby's reaction to the birth, exposure to alcohol and drugs, and blood incompatibility among other factors. Even so, the vast majority of pregnancies are uncomplicated resulting in the birth of a healthy baby.

## Vocabulary Activity

Read the text passages that contain each of the key terms. Then write the definitions of each term in your own words. Double-check your definitions by re-reading the text and using the text glossary.

## Critical Thinking

1. **Analyze.** Are pregnant women often shown in the most popular movies? Why or why not?
2. **Determine.** Describe nutritional needs before and during a pregnancy.
3. **Compare and contrast.** How might a pregnancy for a woman without medical care differ from one with medical care? Explain why medical care and good health are important before and during pregnancy.
4. **Assess.** What skills, resources, and experiences best prepare a woman for pregnancy?
5. **Identify.** Make a list of the top 10 items you think an expectant mother should know about her pregnancy.
6. **Evaluate.** If you could choose the perfect age to become a parent, what age would you choose?
7. **Determine.** Is teen pregnancy glamorized or "villainized" in society today?

8. **Cause and effect.** If a pregnant woman smoked a pack of cigarettes a day and ate the same unhealthy meal for lunch and dinner, how might this behavior affect her baby's development?

9. **Make inferences.** Using online sources, determine the top-selling pregnancy books today. What do these books have in common? What are the current "hot" topics?

10. **Predict.** At about how many weeks might a pregnant woman expect to feel her baby's legs and arms move for the first time?

11. **Draw conclusions.** How is childbirth depicted on situation comedy television shows? What might a person conclude about childbirth from these shows that might not be consistent with reality?

## Core Skills

12. **Reading.** Read a popular book or magazine about pregnancy or birth. What are the main topics covered?

13. **Writing.** Write a one-page letter that offers advice to a friend or family member who might be pregnant in the future.

14. **Speaking.** Form groups of three classmates. Have each person describe one of the trimesters of pregnancy.

15. **Listening.** Interview a woman who gave birth to a child in the past few years. Ask her to describe her experience.

16. **Math.** Make a shopping list of clothing items you might need if caring for a newborn baby. Total the price of these items. If possible, do comparison shopping.

17. **Writing.** In a short essay, describe environmental factors that can affect the development of a fetus.

18. **CTE Career Readiness Practice.** Use reliable Internet sources to investigate the changes that occur in a woman's body during pregnancy. Compare the changes of a 25-year-old pregnant woman with that of a 40-year-old pregnant woman.

## Research

19. Research the birth options available in your local community including hospitals, birthing centers, midwives, and doulas. Prepare a pamphlet of your findings.

20. Conduct Internet research to learn more about one of the birth complications discussed in this chapter. Write a one-page paper of your findings to present to the class.

## Event Prep

21. Select a topic from this chapter and create a lesson plan to teach the information to a grade level of your choice. In your lesson plan, include objectives, activities, and desired outcomes of the lesson. Arrange to present the lesson to an actual class of students. Ask the teacher of the class you taught to complete an evaluation of your performance. You may wish to expand your project by participating in an Educators Rising *Lesson Planning and Delivery Competition*. See your adviser for further information.

AISPIX by Image Source/Shutterstock.com

# FOCUS ON

## Unbiased Behavior

Throughout your life, you will interact with people at school, at work, and in your community. You may encounter people who categorize others using biased language. Offensive comments about age, gender, race, disability, or ethnicity used to describe someone are unethical and sometimes even illegal. Use bias-free language in all your communications, whether verbal or printed, to show respect for those with whom you come in contact. What could happen if someone in a helping or teaching role did not follow these practices with the people they meet on the job?

# Chapter 5 Infancy: Newborn to Age 1

Sergej Khakimullin/Shutterstock.com

## Objectives

After studying this chapter, you will be able to

- describe a newborn and his or her food, sleep, and other basic needs.
- analyze the physical development of babies in the first 12 months of life.
- analyze the cognitive development of babies in the first 12 months of life.
- analyze the socio-emotional development of babies in the first 12 months of life.
- compare and contrast various developmental theories relating to infants.
- identify developmental milestones infants achieve during the first 12 months of life.

## Reading Prep

Before reading, note the chapter objectives. Keep these in mind as you read, and focus on the structure of the author's writing. Was the information presented in a way that was clear and engaging?

## Key Terms

infancy
neonates
Apgar scale
Brazelton Neonatal Behavioral Assessment Scale
rooting reflex
bonding
postpartum period
postpartum depression

proximodistal development
cephalocaudal development
Shaken Baby Syndrome
crawling
creeping
Palmar grasp
pincer grasp
food intolerances
sensorimotor stage

object permanence
receptive language
trust versus mistrust
attachment
stranger anxiety
separation anxiety
unoccupied play
solitary play
temperament

### Visit the G-W Learning Companion Website to:

- **build** vocabulary with e-flash cards and interactive games;
- **assess** what you learn by completing self-assessment quizzes; and
- **expand** knowledge with activities that extend learning.

G-WLEARNING.com    www.g-wlearning.com/development/

Birth is the miracle of life. Since the beginning of humankind, babies survive the birth process in all sorts of conditions. People are often amazed by the ability of humans to procreate and the fragility and vulnerability of their young. Newborns, however, are quite adaptable and resilient. They are not "lumps" that only cry, eat, and need diaper changes. In fact, there is ample evidence that babies begin learning and adapting to their environment immediately after birth.

## Neonates

**Infancy** is the period from birth to the first birthday, **5-1**. Just after birth, babies are called **neonates**. This term refers to the time period from birth to age 1 month. In this section, you will learn more about the fascinating characteristics of these youngest human beings.

### Neonate Assessment

When you see a fictional birth on television or in the movies, both the mother and baby often look great. The birth process is short. The baby has great color, a nice round head, and the mother appears to be ready to throw a party. In actuality, mothers are often exhausted after giving birth, and the baby looks as if he or she just went through a brawl.

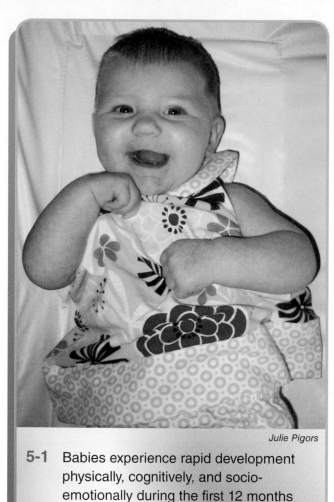

*Julie Pigors*

**5-1**   Babies experience rapid development physically, cognitively, and socio-emotionally during the first 12 months of life.

During a normal uncomplicated birth, a mother is usually able to hold her baby soon after birth. What will she see? Babies are covered in blood and a thin white coating called *vernix caseosa*. Their heads are temporarily misshapen as they go through the birth canal, often producing a cone-shaped head. They often look bluish in color for the first few seconds or minutes as their bodies adjust. The baby is quickly cleaned, and to the new parents, the child is exquisitely beautiful.

### Newborn Screening Tests

After birth, babies are tested to make sure they are healthy. The **Apgar scale** is administered at one minute and then again at five minutes after birth. The Apgar scale rates their heart and respiratory rates, muscle tone and body color, and reflex irritability. Babies can receive a score of 0, 1, or 2 in each of the areas with 10 being the highest possible total score, **5-2**. A score of 6 to 7 at one minute and then 8 to 10 at five minutes is a sign of a healthy baby. If the score is 7 or less at five minutes, then the baby will be tested again at ten minutes. Babies receiving low scores need special attention and medical care.

The **Brazelton Neonatal Behavioral Assessment Scale** is also given shortly after birth. This test measures a baby's reflexes and responses to light, sounds, and touch. The ability to catch the baby's attention and ability to be soothed are observed.

| The Apgar Scale | | | |
|---|---|---|---|
| **Sign** | **Scores** | | |
| | **0** | **1** | **2** |
| **Heart rate** | Absent | Slow; fewer than 100 beats per minute | Fast; more than 100 beats per minute |
| **Respiratory effort** | Absent | Irregular and slow; weak cry | Good; strong cry |
| **Muscle tone** | Limp | Weak; some flexing and bending of extremities | Strong; well-flexed |
| **Body color** | Blue and pale | Pink body, blue extremities | Completely pink |
| **Reflex irritability** | No response | Grimace | Crying, sneezing, and coughing |

*Goodheart-Willcox Publisher*

**5-2** The Apgar scale tests a newborn's physical condition immediately after birth.

## Reflexes

Babies are born with *reflexes*, the involuntary movements or actions that occur spontaneously. For example, newborns typically have the reflex to suck when something is placed on the roof of their mouth. They move toward a bottle or their mother's breast when the side of their mouth is stroked. This is called the **rooting reflex**. They can be startled, clasp an object placed in their hand, or even act as though they are walking or dancing when held upright. Some reflexes increase with age, but many diminish as a baby develops. Because these and other reflexes are considered normal for newborns, testing reflexes is often used to determine their health. Although babies have reflexes, they do not all exhibit them at the same level.

## Sensory

Can newborn babies hear, see, and smell like you do? Some senses are fully developed at birth, while others take a bit longer. Newborns can hear months before birth. They can sense, touch, and smell. Only their vision takes longer to develop, **5-3**. How do you know what babies can sense? Researchers conduct tests to see how neonates respond. For example, neonates respond with a grimace when a sour or bitter taste is put on their tongue. Their lips relax when given a sweet taste. Very young babies orient themselves toward the smell of their mothers or primary caregivers. They are drawn to breast milk over the smell of formula in their first few days (even breast milk that is not from their own mother). Around the world, swaddling (wrapping a baby snuggly in a blanket) is known to sooth neonates. This may be because the blanket simulates the tight womb from which they recently came.

*Flashon Studio/Shutterstock.com*

**5-3** An infant's eyes usually begin working together at about 6 months of age.

Even at birth, babies are able to see. Sight, however, is the least developed sense at birth as their visual abilities are not yet at an adult level. During the first year of life, their vision becomes more accurate as eyes continue to develop. This includes the connection between what the eye perceives and the message the brain receives.

## Care for Premature Babies

Although most babies leave the hospital and go home a day or two after birth, some are just not healthy enough to leave the hospital. Issues such as low birthweight, prematurity, and other birth or congenital complications may require special care. Specially trained medical professionals care for sick babies in intensive care nurseries (ICNs) and neonatal intensive care units (NICUs) located in larger hospitals. These specialized centers provide care for sick babies or babies failing to thrive.

## Bonding

Whether becoming a parent by birth or adoption, bonding is important, 5-4. **Bonding** is the emotional connection that a parent or caregiver develops with the baby. Bonding can occur throughout life, but is especially important during this stage. Bonding helps family members adjust to the transition. The feeling of bonding with the infant occurs immediately for some caregivers, but takes time for others. Bonding occurs when the caregiver spends time and builds confidence in forecasting and meeting the baby's needs.

*HannaMonika/Shutterstock.com*

**5-4** New parents are often concerned about bonding with their child.

## Bringing Baby Home

The trip home can be a significant event for babies born in hospitals or other birthing centers. Clothes are often specially chosen for this event. All of the necessary items are gathered including blankets, diapers, food, and an approved infant safety car seat. This is often the easy part, however. Once parents arrive home with their new baby, a time of adjustment awaits.

### Family Adjustments

A new family member certainly requires the adjustment of family members. Caregivers need time to adjust to the temperament, schedule, and needs of the new baby. Mothers who have just given birth need time for both physical and psychological adjustment. This period, called the **postpartum period**, usually lasts at least six weeks. Mothers live in anticipation of the birth of the babies they carry within their bodies. After birth, a huge hormonal shift occurs. Combined with sheer fatigue, stress from their new demanding role, and sometimes sadness from the "let down" after waiting, can all be overwhelming.

## Health Connections    Postpartum Care

Proper health for the mother is equally as important after childbirth as before and during pregnancy. Postpartum care usually lasts about six to eight weeks after childbirth. During this time, the mother's body is readjusting and recovering. Three key factors important during postpartum care are rest, nutrition, and physical activity.

- **Rest.** Rest is especially important for the mother during the first couple days after delivery. During this time, the mother's body needs to recuperate and revitalize. Once the newborn is home, getting adequate, uninterrupted sleep is difficult. This is because newborns do not yet sleep for more than about three hours at a time. Doctors recommend sleeping when the baby sleeps. During the first few weeks, new mothers should not overexert themselves. They may need help from family and possibly friends to complete everyday tasks.

- **Nutrition.** Proper nutritional care for the mother is important for her body to recover, whether breast-feeding or formula-feeding. Breast-feeding mothers will have slightly different nutritional needs. Mothers need to drink extra fluids and select water, milk, or juice instead of soda.

- **Physical Activity.** Activity is recommended in small amounts in the first few days after delivery. Increasing activity levels should be gradual. Becoming physically active will help the mother return to her pre-pregnancy weight, and will also benefit her mentally. The 2008 Physical Activity Guidelines for Americans recommends 150 minutes of physical activity per week, divided throughout the week, during the postpartum stage.

### Speaking Activity

Interview a mother to learn about her postpartum care. Prepare a list of questions prior to the interview.

---

When feelings of sadness, fatigue, and stress last more than a few weeks, a new mother may need to seek medical help. Somewhere between 10 and 20 percent of women experience **postpartum depression**, an intense sadness and oftentimes emotional withdrawal from others. Mothers who experience postpartum depression should find psychological and medical treatment as their babies can be adversely affected.

*Postpartum psychosis* is a rare, but very serious mental condition for a very small number of new mothers. Beyond feeling blue or suffering depression, mothers with postpartum psychosis suffer from delusions, hallucinations, hyperactivity, paranoia, and rapid mood swings. Immediate medical attention should be sought if postpartum psychosis is suspected.

Mothers are not the only ones to feel the need to adjust to a new baby. New fathers often report feelings of being overwhelmed with a new sense of responsibility. They are challenged by work and family balance issues. Role expectations often change. Responsibilities within the family often shift. The transition may be easier for parents who have children after they are already established in their careers. Fathers established in their careers prior to having children tend to be more involved in sharing household tasks during the transition.

### Single-Parent Families

Over one-third (some estimates say 40 percent) of neonates in America live in a single-parent home. Family adjustments with a new baby are hard in traditional families, but may be much harder for single-parent families unless adequate support is available. Friends, extended family, and community resources can provide some additional help in the overwhelming transition to parenthood. Additional sources of support can be few for many single parents. Both financial and social support may be inadequate. Being overwhelmed, combined with feelings of insecurity, can make bonding with the new baby difficult. Adjustments can be even more difficult if the single parent already has other children.

*joyfuldesigns/Shutterstock.com*

**5-5** Older children may enjoy helping care for a new sibling.

### Siblings and Extended Family Members

Parents are not the only ones adjusting to a new family member. Other children in the household, including siblings and stepsiblings, have an adjustment to make, **5-5**. Babies, especially neonates, take time to care for and nurture. Since this time is given by parents and caregivers, siblings can feel left out or cheated in what should be "their time." Younger children often struggle to understand that their new sibling is here to stay. Older siblings may resist accepting increased responsibilities. Siblings adjust best when their feelings are acknowledged and they are given time to interact with both their new family members and their parents.

Extended family members, including grandparents, aunts, uncles, and cousins must also adjust to the new, and very needy, family member. As family members adjust to their new roles and relationships within the family, the new member eventually becomes a welcomed part of the family.

## Checkpoint

1. What is a neonate?
2. Describe a neonate's physical characteristics.
3. How is the health and wellness of a newborn determined?
4. Describe newborns' reflexes and their abilities to hear, feel, touch, see, and taste.
5. What are some of the family adjustments that occur when a newborn comes home?

# Infants

Cuddly and cute. Fussy and demanding. Smiling and gurgling. Infants are all of these things. In the first 12 months of life, babies undergo tremendous changes. They are utterly dependent on their caregivers. They are learning how to survive in the world. Infants master an abundance of abilities and skills. They become attached to their caregivers and learn to recognize a stranger. In the following sections, you will become more familiar with how babies grow and change physically, learn, and relate to others and their environments.

## Physical Qualities and Changes

At birth, a baby's neck muscles are not strong enough to support the head. When holding a newborn, special care must be taken to support the baby's head and neck. Within weeks, the baby can support his or her own head. Within months, the baby can sit up, crawl, stand, climb, and eventually walk, **5-6**. The physical qualities and changes that occur are sequential and predictable.

*PondPond/Shutterstock.com*

**5-6**  Many babies learn to sit without support for short periods of time by 7 months of age.

Although babies develop at their own pace, there are some principles of development that will be discussed throughout this chapter. One principle of physical growth and change is the proximodistal pattern of development. Proximodistal development means that infants learn to control the muscles at the core of their bodies before the muscles further out from their abdominal center. For example, they can control their abdominal muscles allowing them to sit up before they can control their legs to walk. They can control their whole hands before they control their fingers to pick up bits of cereal or other small items.

## Bodily Proportions

At birth, a typical newborn weighs about 7.5 pounds and measures about 20 inches long. After birth, babies tend to lose approximately five percent of their weight. As they learn to suck, swallow, and digest their food, the weight comes back and they quickly grow. In the first 4 months, most babies double their birthweight. They grow about 1 inch per month in length or height. By the first birthday, the same baby might weigh 22 pounds and measure 30 inches long. The increase in body weight often makes an infant appear chubby, soft, and cuddly.

## Health Connections — Failure to Thrive

Infants grow rapidly, but sometimes experience *failure to thrive*, a stop in growth and weight gain. Usually, growth and weight gain are constant, when suddenly the infant seems to reach a growth peak.

Failure to thrive may indicate a medical problem. The infant may have a disease that prevents the body from properly absorbing and using nutrients. In these cases, the baby may be eating at a regular rate, but still cannot retain nutrients. The infant may have a condition that causes pain while eating. The baby may minimally eat or refuse to eat, regardless of how many feedings are offered. In other cases, caregivers may be ignoring, underfeeding, or unaware of the infant's needs.

If after 3 months the infant has not shown signs of growth, he or she should be taken to a doctor. With the help of a doctor, nutritionist, and attention from caregivers, failure to thrive can be remedied.

### Writing Activity

Create a Venn diagram of possible causes of failure to thrive. Label one circle *Internal* for causes that come from within the infant, such as a medical condition. Label the other circle *External* to record possible causes that come from the infant's environment. Are there causes that are both internal and external?

A baby's head is disproportionately large, about one-fourth of the total body length. This larger size relates to the process or sequencing of development. **Cephalocaudal development** is the way babies develop from the top of the head down to their extremities. Physical growth and changes occur at the top of the body first and work their way down. Babies can use their hands before they can crawl. They can crawl before they can walk. The brain grows faster than lower parts of the body. The cephalocaudal principle of development is not rigid and there can be exceptions. For example, some babies may learn to walk without crawling first.

*Jandrie Lombard/Shutterstock.com*

**5-7** The lower central incisors usually erupt first, quickly followed by the upper central incisors.

### Facial Features

"She has such a baby face!" What does that mean? Generally, this is a description meaning a person looks young, has a round-ish facial shape, soft features, large eyes, and soft skin. This description is common for infants.

Although their eyes are large in proportion to facial features, their noses are small. The timing of teeth eruption varies, but teeth typically appear in a predictable pattern, **5-7**. Many babies do not begin getting teeth until at least 6 months of age. A few babies may be born with one or more teeth. Other babies may not get their first tooth until they are more than a year old. Once this occurs, teeth eruption continues at a rapid pace. With more and more teeth breaking through their gums, many infants become fussy as they deal with the pain and soreness.

## Sensory Skills

As described earlier, newborns can hear, taste, and feel just like adults. They can see from birth, too, just not at an adult level. At birth, a baby might see an object placed 20 feet away just as clearly as an adult would see that object placed 600 feet away. In other words, objects in the distance are not seen as clearly during the first few months of life. By 1 year of age, the infant sees the distant object with the same clarity as a teen or an adult.

During the first month or two, babies do not see colors clearly as the color cones on their retinas (back of the eye that perceives color) are not yet fully formed. They do see high contrasts such as black and white, however. By 8 weeks of age, babies can discriminate between some colors.

When an infant views a human face, his or her eyes track around the perimeter or outer edges of the face. Within the first 2 months, their eyes begin to focus on the center of the face, between the eyes and nose. This focusing on the center of the face continues throughout life and is an important part of understanding communication.

## The Brain and Nervous System

The brain and nervous system begin to develop within days of conception. This growth and development continues throughout prenatal development and birth. Newborns' brains are perfect for what they need to do. That is, to learn about the world around them. Brain and nervous system development does not stop there, however. During infancy, both the brain and nervous system continue to develop at a rapid pace. Because of this, care must be taken to protect an infant from falls or other head injuries. A baby should never be shaken as the jostling of the brain from rapid movements can cause brain swelling and ultimate damage. **Shaken Baby Syndrome**, the tragic injuries that result from babies being shaken, should be avoided at all costs.

 **Health Connections**          **Shaken Baby Syndrome (SBS)**

An infant's brain is heavy in proportion to body size. When an infant is violently shaken, the brain hits the sides of the skull, and the infant does not have enough muscle strength to control the shaking. The impact of the shaking causes veins in the brain to break, resulting in internal bleeding, swelling, and loss of brain cells. The swelling causes pressure on the brain stem, which controls breathing and heart rate. In severe cases, brain swelling interferes with these vital functions and causes death.

For survivors of SBS, the effects to the brain are severe and can last a lifetime. Consequences include cognitive disabilities, visual impairments, hearing difficulties, speech problems, and behavioral disorders. Blindness, developmental delays, loss of hearing, and cerebral palsy are all possible outcomes of SBS. If you suspect a baby has been shaken, immediately alert a trusted adult.

### Research Activity

Infants, especially newborns, use crying as a method of communication. Babies frequently cry, often multiple times during the middle of the night. Research methods caregivers can use to cope with stressful moments when taking care of infants. Then, prepare a public health announcement using an electronic format to report your results to the class.

During infancy, there is dramatic growth in the brain. Pathways or synapses are formed, peaking at about 4 months of age. An infant's brain actually contains more brain cells, or neurons, than the adult brain. They are immersed in the moment, taking in everything around them. These are later pruned and trimmed back as brain pathways become more sophisticated throughout life.

Babies who engage in physical activity, are spoken to, and encouraged to verbalize for themselves (cooing, babbling) are more apt to develop strong brain pathways. Likewise, babies who are neglected fail to thrive both physically and cognitively.

### Motor Skills

Babies are fascinating to watch. They develop at their own pace and on a schedule that is normal for them. Over the course of the first 12 months, infants develop both their gross- and fine-motor skills at a rapid pace, **5-8**. This rapid development provides caregivers and parents with much to talk about and marvel over as babies master these new skills.

#### Gross-Motor Skills

Newborns cannot support their heads without help. By as early as 1 month of age, they begin to lift their heads slightly. By 4 months, they can hold their heads steady and by 6 months, they can balance their heads while in an upright position. During those same 6 months, they learn to roll over.

Crawling and creeping come next. **Crawling** is a type of dragging movement accomplished by the baby pulling forward by the arms and shoulders while lying on the stomach. (Also called *belly-crawling*.) **Creeping** is movement that occurs by using the hands and knees to pull the body forward while the stomach is raised off the ground. (Also called *knee-crawling*.) No two babies crawl or creep the same, and their unique efforts to move forward can be quite entertaining.

| Summary of Motor Skill Developmental Milestones | | |
|---|---|---|
| **Age** | **Gross-Motor Skill** | **Fine-Motor Skill** |
| **0–1 month** | Lift head when prone | Rooting reflex |
| **2–5 months** | Hold chest up, when prone<br>Rollover<br>Creeping | Grasp for objects<br>Bat at an object |
| **3–6 months** | Sit without support | Palmar grasp |
| **5–10 months** | Crawling<br>Stand while supported | Pincer grasp<br>Transfer object from hand to hand |
| **6–10 months** | Pull self up to stand | |
| **7–12 months** | Walk using a support | |
| **10–12 months** | Stand alone easily | Builds two block towers |

*Goodheart-Willcox Publisher*

**5-8**  Infant's gross- and fine-motor skills develop rapidly during the first 12 months of life.

At the same time, babies learn to sit without support. They are holding their heads steady and their abdominal muscles become stronger. Soon they will be able to support themselves when leaning against an object such as a piece of furniture. Before long, they are pulling themselves to a standing position and "walking" as they lean against a support. Next, a baby will stand without support, **5-9**. After a few tentative steps and much trial and error, the baby takes his or her first steps. This continues until the baby easily walks alone.

### Fine-Motor Skills

At birth, newborns' movements are reflexive. Infants first reach for people and objects, and then they grasp objects. Reaching and grasping attempts are significant because infants are actively interacting with the world around them.

Similar to gross-motor skills development, fine-motor skills development moves in sequential order. Infants first move their shoulders and elbows toward objects. Next, they move their hands by rotating their wrists. This is a common attempt for babies who are sitting and supporting themselves. They reach toward their caregivers, rotate their wrists and hands, and verbalize their desire for contact.

*Flashon Studio/Shutterstock.com*

**5-9**   Many infants learn to stand alone around 12 months of age.

Next, infants learn to coordinate their fingers and thumb. The thumb and forefinger coordinate first, followed by the use of all their fingers. Babies use the **Palmar grasp** to scrape up an object with their fingers into the palm of their hands. Imagine babies eating small food items off their high chair tray. Items are scooped into their fist. To get the items from them, you must uncurl their fingers. Babies next use the **pincer grasp**. When picking up small items such as bits of food on their high chair tray, they use their forefinger and thumb.

## Nutrition

Good nutrition is critical at any stage of development, but especially during infancy. Babies need well-balanced nutrition. Their needs are quite different from the nutritional needs of children or adults, however.

Because newborns are just learning to suck and swallow, their nutrition must come in liquid form. Breast milk is the ideal food for babies for at least the first 6 months of life. Mothers, for a variety of reasons, may be unable to breast-feed and choose to feed their babies formula. Adoption, health issues, and medication can keep a mother from breast-feeding. In these cases, careful selection of a nutritious formula can meet the nutritional needs of the infant.

*Teresa Kasprzycka/Shutterstock.com*

**5-10** Solids for infants are semiliquid, mushy foods such as commercially prepared baby foods or table foods that have been mashed, strained, or pureed.

Between 6 and 12 months, caregivers often start feeding infants solids, **5-10**. Caregivers are recommended to introduce new foods to babies one at a time, and in small amounts. They should also try to wait several days before adding another new food. This helps caregivers determine whether the baby has food intolerances. **Food intolerances** are reactions to foods that are unpleasant, such as digestive or behavioral problems.

## Sleeping

Newborn babies sleep most of the day and night. Typically, they sleep for about three hours and are awake for one, repeating the pattern around the clock. Eating and sleeping patterns are not always consistent, however, as babies adjust to changes in their health and environment. These patterns may work for the infants' needs, but are often hard on the caregivers.

Fortunately, babies' sleep needs change over the first few months of life. As babies grow, their stomachs are able to hold larger amounts for longer periods of time. They also adapt to the schedule of the household, following sleeping and waking patterns more closely. Throughout infancy, babies continue to need both a morning and afternoon nap and become quite cranky when naps are missed. Sleep is critically important to an infant's growth and development.

## *Safety* Connections     *Sudden Infant Death Syndrome (SIDS)*

SIDS can occur in infants under the age of 1. Before caregivers place the baby to sleep, the infant appears to be healthy and normal. When SIDS occurs, the death is unexpected and the cause of death is unknown.

New research indicates the cause of SIDS may be related to an irregularity in the sleep pattern of the infant, resulting in the inability to awake from sleep. Another possible cause is a buildup of carbon dioxide in the infant's bloodstream. Several other factors that may increase the potential of SIDS include the following:

- Exposure to tobacco, alcohol, or other drugs during the pregnancy.
- Exposure to secondhand smoke after birth.
- Lack of prenatal care.
- Teen pregnancy.
- Premature or multiple births.

The following precautions may help prevent SIDS:
- Do not allow infants to sleep on their stomachs.
- Ensure bedding is not too soft and pillows or stuffed animals are not in the crib.
- Do not allow infants to sleep with caregivers.
- Make sure the room is not too warm and infants do not feel hot.
- Allow the infant to sleep with a pacifier to keep airways open.

### Research Activity

Use reliable Internet resources to research risk factors, possible causes of, and prevention techniques for SIDS. Share your findings with the class.

Sudden infant death syndrome (SIDS) is a concern during the first year of life. SIDS most commonly occurs between 2 and 4 months of age and usually happens during the night for no apparent reason. To help prevent this untimely death, infants should be placed on their backs to sleep. Bedding, including crib bumpers and pillows, should be avoided because soft bedding can interfere with breathing. Prenatal drug use, including tobacco, may also increase the likelihood of SIDS.

## Signs of Cognitive Growth

Babies explore their world, learning more and more as they organize their experiences. They learn to coordinate what they sense (see, hear, feel, taste) with motor skills (actions). For example, babies love to put objects in their mouths, exploring the way they taste and feel. They touch, feel, and move objects around. With each new sensory exploration, cognitive development occurs.

### Piaget's Sensorimotor Stage

Piaget called this first stage of cognitive development the **sensorimotor stage**. In this stage, infants move from reflexes to interacting with the world around them using their ever-growing motor skills. Reaching, rolling, creeping, and crawling are all significant signs of cognitive growth, **5-11**. The sensorimotor stage continues throughout infancy until about age 2.

During the first few months of life, infants begin to understand object permanence. **Object permanence** is the understanding that people, places, or objects still exist even when they are out of sight or can no longer be heard or touched. For example, when a baby understands object permanence, a favorite toy may be covered with a blanket. The baby will yank the blanket off the toy, delighted and expecting to see the toy beneath. Piaget believed this is an important cognitive milestone.

*Mastering_Microstock/Shutterstock.com*

**5-11**  Physical, cognitive, and socio-emotional development occur together and are interdependent of one another.

### Skinner's Theory

Skinner theorized that one way infants learn is through operant conditioning. Using operant conditioning, a baby responds to a stimulus. Depending on the result, the baby will learn to repeat or stop the response. For example, imagine a father singing a happy little song to his son. The baby smiles and babbles in response. The father responds with a smile and words of praise to the baby. The baby learns that his own smile and response result in more positive interaction with his father.

zulufoto/Shutterstock.com

**5-12** Vygotsky believed that social interaction is critical to a baby's cognitive development.

## Vygotsky's Theory

The idea that the learning process is also a social process is not new. Vygotsky believed that children are social beings and develop their minds through interactions with caregivers and siblings, and others in close relationship, **5-12**. Through social interactions, infants learn not only by exploring their world through their senses, but by responding to and imitating others.

## Brain Development

Can babies remember? They can and do. Memory abilities develop over time, but babies begin to demonstrate familiarity or memory of certain objects or people. Their memories are not long lasting, but as they develop, these memories are retained longer. This explains why many teens and adults do not have memories of events much earlier than their third birthday. During infancy, the part of their brains where memory storage of events occurs is still immature.

## Language Development

As infants interact with others, they begin to associate symbols with their thoughts. These symbols are found in words or language. Language is a basic form of communication and as language ability is increased, deeper interaction occurs between the baby and caregivers, **5-13**.

## Cultural Connections    Language Learning

The process of learning a language is the same for all infants, regardless of language and culture. The language acquisition process begins in the womb. Even before a baby is born, he or she can recognize the voice of his or her mother. By the first month of life, newborns are very familiar with their caregiver's voice and show a preference for the language spoken. Even before infants' first words, they are able to distinguish the patterns of the language spoken in their environment and are aware when another language is spoken. The response of the infant to the caregiver's voice and

native language is a cognitive and emotional sign of development. The infant emotionally responds and has the intellectual understanding for which person in the room is the caregiver.

### Speaking Activity

Interview a caregiver of an infant to learn more about language development. Ask about signs the infant displays that reflect language development and understanding. Does the infant respond to the caregiver's voice? How? Write a summary of your interview and share your responses with the class.

How do infants learn language? First, babies must be biologically ready. Their brains must be at a certain development level to form words of a particular language. This includes both in terms of meaning and in terms of the physical ability to form certain sounds. Next, language is learned from interaction with others. Babies who do not have interaction do not learn a language. If a baby is not exposed to language during infancy when brain pathways are developing, then language is much harder to learn later in life. Lastly, babies understand language much before they can form words. This is termed **receptive language**. Most babies recognize their own name as young as 5 months of age. Therefore, talking to babies is critical to their language development and overall learning.

| Summary of Language Developmental Milestones ||
|---|---|
| **Age** | **Language** |
| **0–1 month** | Crying |
| **2–5 months** | Cooing |
| **5–10 months** | Babbling |
| **7–12 months** | Single words |

*Goodheart-Willcox Publisher*

**5-13** Infants learn to express themselves first by using sounds and then words.

Babies produce sounds from birth. Crying is the first step in language development as babies learn to cry differently based on their particular need. As parents and caregivers know, a hungry cry is different from a tired cry.

Language development continues to be social. Between 2 and 4 months of age, most infants begin to coo. This is a sound made at the back of the throat and most often in response to something pleasurable. By 6 months of age, babies babble, producing a string of consonants. The most common first babble is "ba, bab, ba…," a sound easily formed by the mouth. Imagine a grandparent responding to the babbling by talking to the baby. The baby will likely respond to the grandparent with another string of babble and so the interaction continues.

Between 8 and 12 months of age, many babies begin to communicate through gestures. Waving goodbye, blowing kisses, and shaking the head are common forms of communication that infants learn. This is a good time for infants to begin learning sign language as a form of communication.

## Health Connections    Baby Sign Language

Another way to communicate with infants is through baby sign language. Sign language can be a simple way of expression for an infant before speech has developed. Teaching baby sign language can also improve communication skills and be a form of bonding between caregivers and the infant.

To start, caregivers may use pre-established signs from American Sign Language or create their own symbols and meanings. Most caregivers begin by teaching symbols for everyday words, such as *mom*, *dad*, *milk*, or *book*. With encouragement, teaching simple words and symbols consistently and slowly increases the level of communication between infants and their caregivers.

**Speaking Activity**

With a partner, discuss the advantages and disadvantages to using American Sign Language versus creating your own unique symbols and meanings to teach baby sign language.

## Signs of Socio-emotional Growth

Physical and cognitive growth and development are highly related to socio-emotional growth. As discussed, babies develop their gross- and fine-motor skills through sensory input and social interaction. Learning and language development are dependent on social interaction. Even getting nutrition is a highly social endeavor.

According to Erikson's theory of psychosocial development, the stage for socio-emotional development during infancy is termed **trust versus mistrust**. During this stage, infants must learn to develop trust relationships with their caregivers. Developing trust, primarily through having their needs met, can have life-long effects on personal relationships with others. Trust can be learned at a later stage, but is optimally learned during infancy.

Caregivers and family members form the basis for learning trust. As needs are met, babies trust their caregivers. When babies cry, they learn that they will be comforted. As trust is learned, they are better able to learn self-care skills. Babies learn to comfort themselves when they wake up crying in the night. As caregivers respond with their presence and less with holding, babies learn to settle. This is only possible if they are not hungry, in pain, or uncomfortable.

### Relationship with Caregivers and Family

Infants have a special relationship with their caregivers and family members. As they develop trust, a special bond develops. Parents bond with their newborn babies. This relationship makes the caregiver want to nurture and care for the infant. During infancy, the child bonds with the caregiver. This is called *attachment*.

*Leonid and Anna Dedukh/Shutterstock.com*

**5-14** Forming a strong attachment with a caregiver early in infancy helps development.

**Attachment**, the emotional connection between the child and caregiver, occurs later in infancy. In attachment, the infant has preference for the caregiver or parents over others, **5-14**. They want that person to be in close proximity and are troubled when he or she is not. They become anxious when strangers approach. A stranger cannot replace the caregiver. At about 9 to 12 months of age, the distress of being left with a stranger peaks. This distress is called **stranger anxiety** and is considered an important developmental milestone.

Infants typically experience **separation anxiety** when their caregiver or parent leaves them in the care of a stranger. Although the experience can be stressful for all involved, showing distress is a sign that the child has attached to their parent or caregiver. Signs of separation anxiety include crying, screaming, and whining. Comfort from the stranger may not be readily accepted, but for most infants, distractions can divert their attention. Upon the parent's return, infants often cry again, but are easily comforted in the reunion. Separation anxiety usually begins at about 8 months of age and is considered another important developmental milestone in cognitive development.

During infancy, interaction with family members and caregivers is critical. At the same time, infants begin to learn how to engage in unoccupied play and eventually solitary play. **Unoccupied play** happens when a baby observes and focuses on an object or activity. For example, a 3-month-old may lie in a crib watching a toy mobile. **Solitary play** happens when an infant plays alone. A baby may sit and play with toy blocks without interacting with others. Both are milestones in socio-emotional development.

### Emotions and Temperament

Many relationships focus on sharing emotions. During infancy, emotions are imitated as babies learn how to express their emotions through observing others' reactions to events, **5-15**. As early as birth, some emotions such as pleasure or disgust are displayed. Within a few months, anger, wariness, and delight are shown. Shyness, fear, and anxiety come in the latter half of the first year.

Even at an early age, babies can show some control over their emotions. Control of emotions is learned gradually, but the foundation laid during infancy continues throughout the upcoming years.

**Temperament**, unique individual differences in the way people interact with the world, is persistent throughout life. A baby may be naturally shy or hesitant to experience something unfamiliar, or highly interactive. A baby's temperament has a large effect on how caregivers respond, especially if the baby's temperament is different from their own. As the baby gives clues to preferences, a caregiver responds in either an affirming or negative way. Of course, environment will shape and mold the baby's temperament over time. The tendency to approach the world in the same manner, however, remains constant.

*Ami Parikh/Shutterstock.com*

**5-15** During infancy, babies learn to express many emotions.

## Checkpoint

1. Name two general principles that describe the way infants develop.
2. How does vision change during infancy?
3. How can parents and caregivers encourage brain development during the first year?
4. What is the ideal food for infants? Why?
5. Describe gross- and fine-motor skill development in the first year of life.
6. Name and describe Piaget's cognitive stage of development in infancy.
7. Name and describe Erikson's stage for socio-emotional development during infancy.
8. Describe the infant's relationship with caregivers and family members during the first year of life.

## Special Needs

Some babies are born with genetic disorders that require special care. Many birth disorders, including fetal alcohol syndrome and Down syndrome, are known from birth. With proper medical care and intervention, caregivers can help infants reach their full potential and adapt to their environment. Others have special needs that develop or are recognized during infancy. Babies who are challenged with hearing impairment are usually not identified until they are several months old.

During infancy, some caregivers may begin to notice their children experiencing developmental delays or accelerations. A *developmental delay* means that a child's development lags behind the norms for other children the same age. A *developmental acceleration* means that a child's development exceeds the norms for other children the same age. Figure **5-16** shows some typical developmental milestones of infancy. When a child's development significantly lags behind the norms, caregivers should consult a doctor.

Facing the reality of a developmental challenge or delay is often difficult. When developmental challenges or delays are identified and acknowledged early, however, interventions can help tremendously. Interventions include medical care, special therapy, and resources. They also include social and emotional support for the parents.

### Recognizing Development Issues

Mica is the mother of 11-month-old Ari. Ari has always been a quiet baby and does not often cry, coo, or babble. Even when he is hungry, needs a diaper change, or is feeling tired, Ari seems to be content most of the time. Mica takes Ari to many public places, social gatherings, and family events. When being held by others, Ari is usually quiet and seems content, even if his mother is out of sight. Mica feels concerned that something is wrong with Ari.

Mica consulted her own mother, Orel, about this issue. Orel explains that Ari's temperament is naturally calm and there is no cause for concern. In fact, Mica should be happy that Ari is so quiet and calm. Orel says that soon enough, Ari will be talking and yelling and that Mica should enjoy the quiet while she can. Despite Orel's reassurance, Mica is still concerned.

- Do you think Mica is overreacting?
- How may Ari's minimal vocalizations be a sign of a developmental issue?
- Would your advice to Mica differ from Orel's? If so, what would you say to Mica?

### ✓ Checkpoint

1. What is the difference between a developmental delay and a developmental acceleration?
2. List six typical developmental milestones of infancy.
3. List three interventions that can help infants with special needs reach their full potential.

## Developmental Milestones: Newborn to Age 1

| Age | Physical | Cognitive | Socio-emotional |
|---|---|---|---|
| **Month 1** | • Focuses on objects in close range, about 8–12 inches from eyes<br>• Recognizes some sounds and voices<br>• Moves arms around in jumpy manner<br>• Lifts arms to mouth and eyes<br>• Can make a tightly closed fist<br>• Turns head to either side when laying on back<br>• Dislikes strong smells<br>• Prefers soft items and care that is gentle | • Responds to mother's voice<br>• Cries when assistance is needed | • Prefers the attention and faces of people over toys and other objects |
| **Month 3** | • Supports the upper body with arms when on stomach<br>• Kicks legs<br>• Uses leg muscles to resist flat surface at feet | • Follows objects in motion<br>• Responds to sounds | • Focuses on faces and watches closely<br>• Smiles<br>• Appears more expressive than in first month |
| **Months 4 to 7** | • Reaches for objects<br>• Can move object from one hand to the other<br>• Strengthens ability to follow objects in motion | • Recognizes his or her name<br>• Places objects in mouth to learn about them<br>• Shows interest in and responds to mirrors | • Is aware of differences in emotions through changes in voice<br>• Shows social comfort |
| **Months 8 to 12** | • Sits up without any help<br>• Can support body on hands and knees<br>• Can sit up and crawl<br>• Can walk with assistance<br>• Can stand<br>• Controls the release of an object from grasp<br>• Brings objects together<br>• Begins to self-feed using fingers | • Understands *no*<br>• Interacts with objects<br>• Communicates with gestures<br>• Imitates sounds such as tongue clicks | • Becomes shy around new people<br>• Demonstrates separation anxiety and shows preference for regular caregiver<br>• Shows disinterest in some objects and pushes away<br>• Enjoys "peek-a-boo" and similar games |

*Goodheart-Willcox Publisher*

**5-16**  Developmental milestones provide a general idea of when certain events will occur.

## Summary

Cute and cuddly, drooling and demanding, creeping and walking, infants spellbind caregivers with their rapid development. During infancy, infants grow and learn at a rapid pace. Babies grow significantly in both length and weight. There is speedy development in both gross- and fine-motor skills as babies depend less on reflexes and more on self-directed interactions with their environment.

During infancy, the brain develops neurons and pathways faster than in any other life stage. This peaks at about 4 months of age. From then on, the brain prunes away unneeded pathways, refining those that are needed. Because this is a critical time for brain development, social interaction and good nutrition are critical. Babies thrive on two-way interaction with their caregivers. Good nutrition, in the form of breast milk or high quality formula during the first 6 months, is vital.

Cognitive development during infancy is closely tied to socio-emotional development. Infants learn through social interaction with people and objects in the world around them. Development of trust in their caregivers is critical. An infant learns trust through a caregiver's attentiveness in meeting physical, cognitive, and socio-emotional needs.

Infancy sets the foundation for a lifetime of growing and learning. For optimum development, infants need to have their basic needs met. They need good health care. They need to be kept safe. Overall, infants need positive and loving relationships with their caregivers.

## Vocabulary Activity

On a separate sheet of paper, list words that relate to each of the terms. Then, work with a partner to explain how these words are related.

## Critical Thinking

1. **Compare and contrast.** How does the Apgar scale differ from the Brazelton Neonatal Behavioral Assessment Scale?

2. **Cause and effect.** If a mother has postpartum depression that goes untreated, what might happen to the family dynamic?

3. **Assess.** What reflexes are apparent during infancy? When do they typically first appear? Which reflexes disappear?

4. **Identify.** Use online or print sources to identify the advantages and disadvantages of breast-feeding versus formula-feeding.

5. **Determine.** Determine ways parents can get their baby on a sleeping and feeding schedule.

6. **Analyze.** Should people read to babies? If so, what kind of books should be read to them?

7. **Evaluate.** If an 8-month-old starts crying every time he or she is left with a babysitter, to what might you attribute this change of behavior?

8. **Draw conclusions.** What toys are currently the most popular for infants? Why do you think these toys are so popular?

9. **Predict.** If a baby is always shy and hesitant during infancy, how might the person's temperament be as an adult?

10. **Make inferences.** Observe print and television advertisements for baby products. Is there a common message about infant behavior that is inferred?

11. **Analyze.** Analyze the physical, emotional, social, and cognitive development of infants.

12. **Identify.** Summarize ways to promote the development of infants. How would these differ for infants with special needs?

13. **Analyze.** Discuss the influences of the family and society, such as caregivers and strangers, on infants.

14. **Determine.** List techniques for promoting the health and safety of infants. What types of safety and precautions are most important at this age?

# Core Skills

15. **Listening.** Interview a mother about her fears and concerns in bringing a newborn baby home. How prepared did she feel?

16. **Writing.** In a short essay, describe and analyze the developmental theories that apply to infancy.

17. **Math.** Babies require diapers. Calculate the cost of diapers over a 6-month period of time (on average 10 diapers per day) comparing a national brand to a generic or store brand.

18. **Reading.** Read a book about caring for infants. Use information from the book and from this chapter to complete the next activity.

19. **Writing.** Write a two-page "Tips for caring for a newborn baby" handout for babysitters. Include both bulleted points and explanations.

20. **Speaking.** Using the "Tips for caring for a newborn baby" handout, present a "newborn baby basics" speech for babysitters. Your speech should be less than 5 minutes.

21. **CTE Career Readiness Practice.** The ability to read and interpret information is an important workplace skill. Presume you work for ABC Toy Company who typically develops toys for infants. The company would like to create a new line of toys, but wants you to evaluate and interpret some research on the visual preferences of newborns. Locate three reliable sources of the latest information on the visual preferences of newborns. Read and interpret the information and determine how the visual preferences of newborns can be used to develop certain features for toys. Then write a report summarizing your findings.

# Research

22. Research when infants typically learn motor skills such as sitting up with support, sitting up without support, creeping, crawling, and walking. Create an electronic presentation to share your findings with the class.

23. Research brain development during infancy. What are the most important changes in the brain after birth? Write a two-page paper of your findings.

# Event Prep

24. What does it mean to nurture a child? Survey people in your school and ask them the question. Share your findings with the class. Then, research ways to nurture infants physically, cognitively, and socio-emotionally. Create a pamphlet outlining your findings. You may wish to expand your project by developing an FCCLA *Families Ties* project. Use the FCCLA *Planning Process* to guide your project planning. See your FCCLA adviser for further information.

# Chapter 6

# Toddlerhood: Ages 1 through 2

Felix Mizioznikov/Shutterstock.com

# Objectives

After studying this chapter, you will be able to

- analyze the physical development of toddlers.
- analyze the cognitive development of toddlers.
- analyze the socio-emotional development of toddlers.
- compare and contrast various developmental theories relating to toddlers.
- identify developmental milestones often achieved during the toddler years.

## Reading Prep

Recall all the information you already know about the development of toddlers. As you read the chapter, think of how the new information presented in the text matches or challenges your prior understanding of the topic. Think of direct connections you can make between the old material and the new material.

## Key Terms

toddlers

inoculations

scaffolding

zone of proximal development (ZPD)

holophrases

telegraphic speech

autonomy versus shame and doubt

temper tantrum

parallel play

### Visit the G-W Learning Companion Website to:

- **build** vocabulary with e-flash cards and interactive games;
- **assess** what you learn by completing self-assessment quizzes; and
- **expand** knowledge with activities that extend learning.

G-W LEARNING.com    www.g-wlearning.com/development/

Between the ages of 1 and 3 years, much growth and development occurs. Children's bodies mature as they develop physically. Gross- and fine-motor skills improve rapidly. Children learn how to feed themselves. They eagerly explore their environment and in the process learn many other new skills. Children also discover new ways to solve problems. They learn about themselves and others. In this chapter, typical markers of development for children ages 1 through 2 years will be discussed. Physical, cognitive, and socio-emotional developmental milestones will be highlighted.

## Physical Qualities and Changes

**Toddlers** are children between the ages of 1 and 3 years, **6-1**. They continue to grow physically, but the pace slows considerably. Bodily proportions change as the head decreases from one-fourth to one-fifth of the total body length by age 2 years. Children continue to be chubby, but they gradually lose their "baby fat" as their bodies lengthen. Arms, legs, hands, and feet also lengthen. By their second birthday, most toddlers weigh about 27 pounds and are about 3 feet tall (32 to 35 inches). At this point, they are about half of their final adult height. By their third birthday, toddlers often weigh about 32 pounds and their average height is about 38 inches.

*Mark and Jaye Warwick*

**6-1**  In their newfound independence, toddlers explore the world with much enthusiasm.

During the toddler years, more teeth develop. By the time toddlers reach their second birthday, most have all of their primary teeth with the exception of their second molars. This changes the look of their smile and facial features.

## Motor Skills

During the toddler years, children learn many new gross- and fine-motor skills. At the beginning of the toddler years, toddlers are often just learning how to take a few hesitant steps without support. Throughout the toddler years, they learn to walk quickly, **6-2**. Toddlers also learn to pull a toy on a string, run for short distances, kick, throw, walk backward, and climb stairs more easily. As toddlers explore their world, they move constantly. They fall and get back up many times an hour. Caregivers should provide a safe environment, but encourage this active exploration as much as possible.

*Monkey Business Images/Shutterstock.com*

**6-2**  The term *toddler* refers to the way children "toddle" as they walk during this stage.

# *Safety* Connections      *Childproofing*

Childproofing, or the process of ensuring a home is safe for children, is especially important for toddlers. During the toddler stage, toddlers are walking and exploring their world. They may grab on to furniture or loose items to help them balance. They are also curious and have enough fine- and gross-motor skills to open cabinets and get into bottles or liquids that may be harmful to the skin or even poisonous. Monitoring the movement of toddlers is always important and necessary. The following guidelines can help you childproof a home and make watching toddlers somewhat less stressful.

- Place sharp objects out of reach.
- Keep windows closed or open windows slightly and lock in place.
- Ensure medicine, kitchen, and other cabinets have childproof locks.
- Use outlet and power strip covers.
- Install child protection gates at tops and bottoms of staircases.
- Keep up-to-date on new safety regulations and product recalls for items such as cribs or certified child safety seats.

### Writing Activity

What other precautions could you take to ensure the safety of a toddler? Expand these guidelines by adding five more childproofing tips. Then inspect your home for child safety and write an action plan to address any safety concerns you noticed during your inspection.

Fine-motor skills also continue to develop. Once the pincer grasp is mastered, toddlers can feed themselves finger foods. They can hold a cup with handles. They can take off their own diapers and other items of clothing, even when their caregiver might think it inappropriate. Caregivers may occasionally walk in on just-wakened toddlers only to find them in their cribs with clothes and diapers removed and anything else within reach in their hands. During toddlerhood, caregivers must be careful to keep medications and other toxic substances out of reach. Because their fine-motor skills develop so quickly, toddlers often surprise their caregivers.

## Nutrition

During the toddler years, toddlers no longer require baby foods. They are learning to feed themselves and use a cup. Toddlers can also eat foods that are prepared for the family. They are able to pick up bite-sized foods, chew, and swallow various solid foods.

Toddlers' stomachs are small and they prefer to eat small portions many times during the day. Long periods between meals do not sustain them as their energy needs are high. Their taste buds are more sensitive than adults, and caregivers often interpret this as picky behavior. An assortment of flavors and textures can help toddlers enjoy a wider variety of foods.

To promote bone growth and strength, toddlers typically need to drink 2 cups of whole milk each day. Toddlers also need to eat a variety of nutritious foods including plenty of fruits and vegetables. Eating too many foods that are

## Health Connections    Preventing Feeding Problems

Toddlers are known for being picky eaters. They may dislike, refuse, or play with their foods. Although these are characteristics of the toddler during mealtime, these issues can be addressed with the patience of the caregiver. Following are tips to help prevent possible feeding issues:

- Serve foods in smaller portions. Too much food on a plate can be overwhelming.
- Use finger foods and avoid mixing foods together in dishes such as casseroles or salads. Toddlers prefer foods in separated forms.
- Avoid serving spicy foods.
- Introduce a new food by placing the food alongside favorite foods.
- Make sure the toddler is comfortable during mealtimes. Ensure the food is at a proper height, the plate is within reach, and the toddler's feet are flat on the floor.
- Provide toddler-friendly flatware, including larger, softer forks and spoons, and smaller, graspable cups.

- Make sure there are not too many distractions during mealtime. Toddlers are easily distracted by music or the television.
- Correct behavior when toddlers begin to play with food. Explain that the food is for eating and not for playing. When you see the toddler is finished eating, take the plate away before he or she begins to play with food.

Caregivers should try to maintain a positive attitude, model positive eating habits, and help the toddler when needed. If the toddler does not know how to self-feed, guide him or her to help with the feeding process.

### Writing Activity

Write a daily meal plan for a toddler using the tips provided in this feature. You may also use additional information obtained from a reliable source on the Internet.

high in calories and are low in nutritional value, such as junk foods, can cause toddlers to gain too much weight. Physicians can help determine toddlers' nutritional needs based on their height, weight, and physical activity level.

## Sleeping

Toddlers often need 10 to 15 hours of sleep each day. They have more regular sleep schedules than during infancy. Toddlers sleep for longer periods of time. They are often difficult to "put to bed" or transition from wake time to sleep time, however. Caregivers often need to help toddlers slow down and relax before sleep time. Evening rituals such as bath time or story times can help. Toddlers may become fearful and have nightmares. When this occurs, toddlers need comforting to feel safe and secure. Placing a night-light in the room or sleeping with a stuffed animal can often help toddlers feel safe, **6-3**.

At times, toddlers will get out of bed during the night to simply see what is happening. Caregivers often need to firmly, but calmly, prompt toddlers to return to bed so they can get the necessary sleep they need.

*kavring/Shutterstock.com*

**6-3**   Toddlers enjoy sleeping with their favorite stuffed animals for comfort.

## Toilet Learning

One of the most controversial topics in early childhood is when and how to teach toileting skills to children. Controversy surrounds both when to initiate and how to teach toilet learning. Many experts agree that toilet learning should not start until the young child is ready and able to exert bodily control.

How do caregivers know when children are ready to begin toilet learning? A common sign is the children's awareness of their need to "go." They may become more uncomfortable wearing diapers. They should be able to follow simple directions and show some bodily control. Usually this does not happen until a child is at least 18 months of age, and the process typically takes months to complete. Even after training is complete, accidents may occur for months or years before a young child can stay dry overnight. Many children can stay dry after age 5, but some, especially boys, lag.

## Medical and Dental Care

Regular medical care throughout the toddler years is important. The American Academy of Pediatrics recommends checkups at 12-, 18-, 24-, and 36-months to ensure toddlers are growing and thriving as they should. When visiting a health care professional, caregivers can ask questions about their toddler's development.

## Case Study ???

### Influenza Inoculations

Your older sister and brother-in-law have recently had a baby boy, Simon. Simon is 6 months old and is now old enough to receive the influenza inoculation. Your sister, Bianca, says that she never received the flu shot as a child and she turned out to be a healthy child and adult. On the other hand, your brother-in-law, Andy, is determined to get every possible immunization available for Simon to be precautious. Andy believes that inoculations are absolutely necessary, and received the flu shot annually throughout his childhood. The state that Bianca, Andy, and Simon live in recommends the flu shot, but does not require all children to receive the influenza inoculation. Andy and Bianca cannot seem to come to an agreement and have turned to you for advice.

- What other factors should Bianca and Andy take into consideration before deciding?
- What are the benefits to receiving the flu shot? Are there possible disadvantages?
- How would you advise Bianca and Andy?

Dental visits often begin by 2 years of age and then repeat every 6 months afterward. Dentists clean teeth and repair them when necessary. Dentists can also show caregivers how to properly care for toddlers' teeth. During the latter part of the toddler years, toddlers may "help" caregivers as a way to begin learning how to brush their own teeth.

Although controversial for some, most medical professionals encourage inoculations be given on a regular schedule throughout childhood. **Inoculations**, or vaccines, are substances that when given in shot form, produce or boost immunity to a specific disease such as measles or mumps, **6-4**.

## ✓ Checkpoint

1. What is the age range of toddlers?
2. Describe the gross- and fine-motor skills of toddlers.
3. How can caregivers promote bone growth in toddlers?
4. About how many hours of sleep do toddlers need each night?
5. What is an inoculation and what is its purpose?

## Signs of Cognitive Growth

Toddlers combine learned actions to reach more goals. Their thinking is organized through concepts. These concepts are simple at first, but then gradually change to more complex as the brain matures and experiences increase.

| Recommended Immunizations from Birth through Age 2 | | |
|---|---|---|
| **Immunization Name** | **Purpose** | **Month Inoculation Is Given** |
| **Hepatitis B** | Prevents a type of spreadable liver infection. | Three to four doses: at birth, within first 2 months, and between 6 to 18 months. |
| **Rotavirus** | Prevents a virus that causes diarrhea. Doses are swallowed, not injected. | Two to three doses: at months 2, 4, and 6 if necessary. |
| **Diphtheria, tetanus, and pertussis** | Prevents bacteria that causes diphtheria, a sickness that creates thick mucus in the back of the throat. Also prevents tetanus (lockjaw), and pertussis (whooping cough). | Five doses: at months 2, 4, and 6, and between months 15 through 18. The fourth dose may be administered at 12 months if 6 months has passed since the third dose. The fifth dose is administered between the ages of 4–6. |
| *Haemophilus influenzae* **type b** | Prevents bacteria that causes meningitis, pneumonia, interference with the respiration system, other infections, and death from these complications. | Three to four doses: at months 2, 4, and 6, and between months 12 and 15. A dose at month 6 may not be needed, which a doctor will help determine. |
| **Pneumococcal (pneumonia)** | Prevents bacteria that causes pneumonia, meningitis, and blood infections, which can all be fatal to infants and children. | Four doses: at months 2, 4, and 6, and between months 12 and 15. |
| **Inactivated poliovirus** | Prevents a virus that causes polio, which causes paralysis and stiff joints. Also prevents meningitis. | Four doses: at months 2, 4, and between months 6 through 18. A fourth dose is given between the ages of 4 to 6. |
| **Influenza inactivated** | Prevents the virus that causes the flu. | Dose at 6 months and yearly afterwards. |
| **Measles, mumps, and rubella** | Prevents the virus that causes<br>• measles—fever, rash, eye irritation, cough<br>• mumps—fever, swollen glands, muscle pain<br>• rubella—fever and rash | Two doses: between months 12 to 15, and again between the ages of 4 to 6. The second dose may be given earlier, if one month passes in between the first and second doses. |
| **Varicella (chicken pox)** | Prevents the chicken pox disease, which causes itching, rashes, and a fever. | Two doses: between months 12 and 15, and again between the ages of 4 to 6. |
| **Hepatitis A** | Prevents a type of spreadable liver disease. | Two doses: at month 12, and 6 to 18 months after the first dose. |
| **Meningococcal** | This vaccine is given in special circumstances to infants and toddlers living in countries with epidemics, who travel internationally, or those who have an improperly functioning spleen. | Dates given vary depending on the reason for this inoculation. |

Recommendations are reviewed and updated regularly. Check for updates at the American Academy of Pediatrics (**www.aap.org**).

*Goodheart-Willcox Publisher*

**6-4**   Immunizations help the body build a strong defense against certain diseases or illnesses.

Tom and Rachael Woznick

**6-5** Toddlers' thinking skills improve as they learn more about objects.

## Piaget's Sensorimotor Stage

According to Piaget's theory, toddlers are still in the sensorimotor stage. They put objects in their mouths and discover through their senses. Toddlers use discovery to solve problems such as building a tower out of blocks or running a toy car over a hurdle, **6-5**. Around 18 to 24 months of age, toddlers still figure things out using their senses, but they also start developing more sophisticated thought processes. For example, a toddler may stop to think about fitting a large object through a small opening rather than just physically testing to see if the object fits.

## Vygotsky's Theory

Caregivers are very instrumental in a toddler's learning as Vygotsky theorized. When caregivers and older peers or siblings help children at their level, they learn more. Helping a child is called **scaffolding**. For example, if an older sister is putting a puzzle together with a toddler, handing him pieces next to where they belong, the child will take the initiative to figure out the puzzle piece placement. Vygotsky called this interface of learning the **zone of proximal development (ZPD)**, or the level at which a child can learn with help.

Once a caregiver can find the child's ZPD, the child is more likely to learn new skills without feeling overwhelmed. Much scaffolding may be necessary, but as the child performs a task more, the scaffolding can be decreased and eventually removed. Then, a new ZPD is formed.

## Brain Development

During infancy, neurons in the brain grow and sprout branches or pathways. In fact, the brain makes more connections than it will ever need. During the toddler years, the neuron pathways continue to develop. Some are reinforced, while others are trimmed away. Just like pruning a rose bush, trimming away unnecessary branches helps to strengthen those that are needed most. This process will be described further in later chapters.

## Language Development

One of the most easily recognized signs of cognitive growth is the swift increase in language, both in understanding and using spoken words. Children's language skills increase significantly throughout the toddler years. At the beginning of the toddler years, children usually learn to say their first words, which are often *dada* and *mama* to identify their caregivers. By the end of the toddler years, children can usually say several hundred words.

## Cultural Connections — Bilingual Toddlers

Some families raise their children *bilingually*, or with the ability to speak two languages fluidly. There are many reasons caregivers decide to raise a child bilingually. Connecting to family heritage, enhancing cognitive ability, promoting multiculturalism, and providing an advantage in a global economy are all examples. Since the toddler is learning two languages at the same time, some caregivers become concerned that the toddler may confuse the languages.

Some caregivers report a delay in the toddler's ability to speak. Experts agree that this delay is temporary and not all children raised bilingually experience speech delays. Spoken communication may be slightly delayed, but is not an indicator that one language should be chosen over the other. Eventually, the child will be fluid in both languages.

Understanding a language is the foundation for the ability to speak the language. If a caregiver verbally names an object in either language and the toddler is able to identify the object, then bilingual education is successful.

### Speaking Activity

Interview the parent of a bilingual child. Ask the parent about the challenges and rewards of raising a child bilingually. Did the child experience a speech delay? Was the delay temporary? Then, interview a person who was raised bilingually. Compare the interview with the parent to the interview with the individual raised bilingually. Create a presentation and share your findings with the class.

---

Toddlers learn to use single words to communicate different objects or people. They name familiar items around them including animals, foods, toys, and people. They even learn to speak their own names and others, although often in delightfully unique ways. A toddler may call her brother Alex by the name *Ah Ah* later becoming *Ayicks*. This adaptation works until the toddler can pronounce the difficult letter *L* sound.

Toddlers often use one word to describe a whole group of items. A toddler may use the word *dog* to describe every animal at the zoo. These are called **holophrases**. These holophrases increase quickly. Dozens more are learned each month from about 18 months of age through much of early childhood.

Toddlers learn to combine words into two-word combinations. This is called **telegraphic speech**. A toddler might say "Daddy, up!" which means "Daddy, I want you to pick me up!" Although the use of telegraphic speech greatly improves communication, some toddlers struggle to express the idea of past or present tense.

## Reading

Social interaction has a huge impact on learning. Reading is one way to build this interaction. Toddlers love the cuddling and interaction that occurs when caregivers read a book to them. They like seeing colors and pictures, **6-6**. They like turning pages. They enjoy identifying objects and interacting with the reader. They do not, however, have patience or the mental ability to sit and listen to a story without visual and physical interaction. Books and reading are an excellent way to build bonds between the caregiver and wiggly toddler while encouraging the use of language.

*Supri Suharjoto/Shutterstock.com*

**6-6**  Toddlers love books for many reasons.

 **Checkpoint**

1. How do toddlers explore their environments?
2. Describe the zone of proximal development. Which theorist is known for ZPD?
3. Describe the language development of toddlers.
4. Define holophrases and give an example.

## Signs of Socio-emotional Growth

As you learned in Chapter 1, Maslow's *Theory of Human Needs* focuses on having basic needs met before other needs can be met. Babies must have their physical needs met in order to survive. They also need to be safe. They need to feel love and affection. All of these needs require social interaction.

Developmental theorists such as Piaget, Vygotsky, and Erikson all agree that children need a stimulating environment to promote learning, **6-7**. Toddlers are social people. Just as in any upcoming stage of life, toddlers have the need to be talked to, listened to, and interacted with on many levels. They need to be cared for and nurtured. As Erikson stated, children need to have their basic needs met, not neglected in order to develop trust.

Erikson described the next stage of socio-emotional development as **autonomy versus shame and doubt**. During this stage, young children begin to see themselves as separate from their caregivers, without feelings of embarrassment or uncertainty. This typically lasts throughout the toddler years.

| Summary of Major Developmental Theories from Birth through Age 2 | | | |
|---|---|---|---|
| **Type of Development** | **Age/Stage** | **Theory** | **Description** |
| **Cognitive** | Birth to 2 years | Piaget: Sensorimotor | Children begin to learn about the world through exploring with their mouths, grasping objects, and using other senses. Learning relies on reflexes, but moves to more sophisticated behaviors. |
| | Birth to 2 years | Skinner: Operant conditioning | As children respond to a stimulus, they will learn to repeat or stop their response. |
| **Language development** | Birth to 2 years | Vygotsky: Social interaction theory | Children develop their minds through interactions with caregivers, siblings, and others in close relationship. Through these interactions, children learn by responding to and imitating others. |
| **Socio-emotional** | Birth to 1 year | Erikson: Trust versus mistrust | Babies learn about trust from their caregivers who meet their needs including food, attention, physical contact, interaction, and safety. When needs are not met, babies do not learn to trust others and the world is perceived as unpredictable. |
| | 1 to 3 years | Erikson: Autonomy versus shame and doubt | Toddlers learn how to control their physical bodies by feeding, toileting, dressing and undressing, and making strides in physical development. As toddlers learn new skills, they become self-confident. A lack of control or independence can make them feel like failures and cause shame and doubt. |

Goodheart-Willcox Publisher

**6-7**   Theorists agree that toddlers learn by interacting with their environment.

During this time, toddlers say the word *no* frequently and with enthusiasm. To the despair of parents and caregivers, toddlers learn to separate themselves from others, with their own will and preferences.

## Relationships with Caregivers and Family

The trust babies develop for their caregivers helps them as they move into toddlerhood and are faced with the task of achieving *autonomy* (self-directing freedom) and independence. Relationships with others become much more reciprocal during the toddler years as more two-way interaction occurs. Caregivers direct toddlers' behavior more than when they were infants. Caregivers respond to toddlers' behaviors and attempt to shape future behaviors. "Don't touch," "Hot!" and "time for night-night" are common commands caregivers use when guiding toddlers. At the same time, toddlers are much less passive, reaching more toward independence.

*Aleksandr Markin/Shutterstock.com*

**6-8** Toddlers are active explorers with energy to carry out their goals.

As soon as they are mobile (crawling, walking, running), toddlers are on the move toward independence. Sitting on their caregiver's lap for long periods of time becomes much more difficult as toddlers want to explore their world, **6-8**. Singing songs, playing games, and practicing motor skills are all essential parts of family relationships.

## Emotions

Around age 2, toddlers become more emotionally sensitive than before. They react to many stimulating objects, people, and places in their environment. They become easily excited, upset, and scared. In addition to their own feelings, they are also sensitive to the feelings of others. Toddlers are aware of how adults are feeling, even when feelings are not verbalized. Toddlers are also aware of emotions in other toddlers and children and may adopt a similar emotional response. For example, if one toddler is crying, another toddler in the room may also begin to cry.

Toddlers are very affectionate to caregivers, family, friends, and pets. They are even affectionate to inanimate items, such as toys, blankets, or books. This affection translates into attachment to caregivers. When caregivers are leaving a room or are away, toddlers often demonstrate separation anxiety. This anxiety may continue into the preschool years.

The combination of heightened emotions and an active imagination can add to toddler anxiety. For example, if a toddler is afraid of the dark, his or her imagination may enhance or create negative images about the dark. The toddler may imagine monsters or scary shadows. Unlike infants, toddlers have more experience interacting with and observing the environment. They are more aware of situations, people, or stories that seem scary and therefore have more opportunities to be scared. Around age 2, these fears and anxieties may become nightmares.

When toddlers become upset, they often begin to express themselves physically and vocally. They may become upset because an activity ends, they did not get an item of interest, or they are simply not getting their way. In response, they may yell, cry, stomp their feet, or wave their arms. They may also lay on the floor, whether at home or in public. This emotional episode of upset behavior is called a **temper tantrum**. Temper tantrums are normal for this age group and can happen privately or publicly, **6-9**. These tantrums can be frustrating for both the toddler and caregivers.

## Developmentally Appropriate Guidance Techniques

Toddlers are aware of their surroundings and the people and events that occur around them. They want to participate. At the same time, they want to

Marina Dyakonova/Shutterstock.com

**6-9** Toddlers are very sensitive and may express their feelings through tantrums.

exert their autonomy and independence. Because of this, toddlers commonly say *no* in either word or action. Temper tantrums and resistance to situations and instructions are ways of expressing their desire to control their world. A good way for caregivers to respond is to first acknowledge their feelings. Toddlers may be frustrated with the situation. Knowing that caregivers understand their emotions can go a long way. Toddlers can learn to understand their own emotions as they mature into the preschool years.

Although having a rational discussion is not yet developmentally appropriate, acknowledging frustration can move toddlers toward understanding. An effective way to ward off many of these situations is to give toddlers choices. Ask the toddler "would you like to wear the blue shirt or the red shirt today?" By offering acceptable choices, the toddler experiences independence.

Giving toddlers early notice about upcoming events such as "grandma is coming over to visit" is also helpful. Because the concept of time is not understood, shorter lead times work best when letting the toddler know of upcoming events. Reminders for big events, such as birthdays, can be repeated over time. Lastly, a caregiver's response to situations should be as consistent as possible. Avoid getting caught up in your own emotions when responding to an emotional and seemingly irrational toddler.

## Play

Toddlers enjoy playing. They need to play. Physical coordination, cognitive development, and socio-emotional growth are all associated with play. During the toddler years, toddlers learn to parallel play. **Parallel play** involves playing alongside another, with little interaction. Toddlers may be next to each other, but their play remains in solitude, **6-10**. Caregivers may at times worry that their toddler is not social in parallel play, but this is completely normal. More interactive or group play is not typical until the preschool years.

rSnapshotPhotos/Shutterstock.com

**6-10** Toddlers may play with the same toy, but interact with each other minimally.

## Health Connections   Developmentally Appropriate Activities

When encouraging play with toddlers, select *developmentally appropriate activities*, or games and activities that encourage physical, cognitive, and socio-emotional development. Selecting play activities should incorporate the toddler's developmental level. For example, toddlers are very active and are still developing fine-motor skills. Therefore, large, soft items are often easier for them to grasp. Picture books with sounds stimulate the toddler's cognitive development, especially when the sound links to a picture.

Considering how activities will promote the developmental progress of the toddler is important when selecting activities and toys.

Following is a list of a few developmentally appropriate toys and activities for a toddler:
- plush dolls
- coloring books and picture books
- toys with music or animal sounds
- blocks and balls
- play dough
- singing activities

### Speaking Activity

Choose an item or activity that is not on the list above that would be developmentally appropriate for a toddler. Give a one-minute oral presentation to the class explaining the physical, cognitive, and socio-emotional benefits.

## Cultural and Societal Influences

Many parents have strong ideas about how their interactions with children should be and look. Toddlers often take more time and energy than parents realize. Many parents learn their parenting practices from their own experiences as a child, family members, and the larger culture.

The larger culture may include media influences. Much parenting information is available to parents including television and Internet resources. Parents and caregivers can easily and quickly access information about child development and typical behaviors. Forums for posting questions, social networking, and other resources can provide "new" ways of parenting that may be different from the way a parent was raised. Feeding, sleeping, and learning issues are often the focus.

Recently, a focus on making "baby geniuses" has been promoted. Studies show that many of these programs can have a negative effect on a young child's brain development. Videos and television provide a one-way interaction. Young children need two-way interactions with their caregivers to develop the necessary brain pathways. Current knowledge suggests that children should not be exposed to television and video until well after their second birthday.

There are a variety of ways to nurture young children. The most essential characteristics of caregivers and family members is to love and cherish their toddler. They should keep them safe. They should talk and interact with their toddlers about everything around them. By looking after toddlers' needs, they should be encouraged to explore their world and move toward independence.

## Checkpoint

1. Describe *autonomy versus shame and doubt* according to Erikson's theory.
2. How do relationships with caregivers change during the toddler years?
3. What is a temper tantrum? How can caregivers help reduce tantrums?
4. List three developmentally appropriate guidance techniques a caregiver can use to avoid causing frustration in toddlers.
5. What type of play do children typically engage in during the toddler years?
6. What are the most essential characteristics of caregivers and family members?

## Special Needs

Toddlers experience many new abilities and developmental milestones, **6-11**. Although everyone develops at slightly different rates, caregivers should note difficulties in reaching developmental milestones. If a developmental delay is evident, the toddler may be displaying signs of a special need.

| Developmental Milestones: Ages 1 through 2 | | | |
|---|---|---|---|
| **Age** | **Physical** | **Cognitive** | **Socio-emotional** |
| **12 months** | • Crawls on stomach<br>• Moves from sitting to crawling position<br>• Creeps up and down stairs<br>• Attempts to self-feed using spoon and cup | • Follows simple instructions<br>• Understands words have meanings<br>• Understands simple requests<br>• Shows interest in learning about objects and their names<br>• Enjoys music and attempts to sing | • Shows favoritism and attachment to toys or objects<br>• Begins responding with *no*<br>• Watches caregivers for responses to actions |
| **18 months** | • Walks without assistance<br>• Pushes or pulls objects while sitting<br>• Dances in standing position for short periods | • Understands the purpose of everyday items<br>• Identifies objects and body parts<br>• Refuses food or toys by shaking head or using hands to push food away<br>• Points to images or objects<br>• Understands object permanence<br>• Asks questions by raising voice at end of sentence | • Demonstrates desire to share object of interest with caregivers<br>• Exhibits temper tantrums<br>• Demonstrates comfort and affection toward familiar people |
| **24 months** | • Carries items while walking or pulls a toy behind<br>• Runs short distances<br>• Walks backward<br>• Kicks a ball<br>• Uses blocks to build<br>• Stands on toes<br>• Uses pincer grasp and a cup with handles to self-feed<br>• Undresses self | • Identifies objects when prompted by caregivers<br>• Tries to pronounce and repeat words in surrounding conversations<br>• Begins to organize objects by color or shape<br>• Uses discovery to solve problems | • Develops self-awareness<br>• Mimics behavior of others<br>• Shows interest in other children<br>• Engages in parallel play |

*Goodheart-Willcox Publisher*

**6-11**  Many physical, cognitive, and socio-emotional developmental milestones occur between the ages of 1 through 2.

One special need that may be detected is a loss of hearing. Hearing impairment can be present at birth or may develop from an illness, head injury, or other accident. Signs of hearing impairment include a lack of babbling, lack of attention to noise, and other language delays. In cases where loss of hearing is present at birth, the toddler may need to learn sign language, **6-12**.

*Susan Stevenson/Shutterstock.com*

**6-12**  Learning sign language as a form of communication can help meet special needs.

If the toddler has reduced hearing ability, hearing aids, surgery, and other therapy specialists are available to ease hearing ability.

Another physical and cognitive disability that may become apparent during the toddler years is cerebral palsy. This condition develops as a result of brain damage, which may have occurred during fetal development, birth, or shortly after birth. Cerebral palsy becomes noticeable as the child grows, but misses developmental milestones. Because brain damage affects motor skills and language development, signs of cerebral palsy may include significant delays or difficulties in sitting up, walking, swallowing, and using speech. Cerebral palsy is not curable, but can be treated with speech and physical therapy, medications, and specialized education.

 **Checkpoint**

1. How can a hearing impairment develop?
2. What are signs of a hearing impairment?
3. What is cerebral palsy?
4. How is cerebral palsy treated?

## Summary

Toddlers experience significant growth and development from infancy. Height, weight, limbs, and teeth continue to grow. Gross- and fine-motor skills continue to develop and toddlers are in constant motion. They walk, run, begin scribbling, and use the pincer grasp to self-feed. They have sensitive taste buds, small stomachs, and eat small portions throughout the day. They experience regular medical checkups and usually recommended inoculations. At night, they need about 10 to 15 hours of sleep.

Cognitively, toddlers' brains continue to grow and develop pathways. They are still in Piaget's sensorimotor stage and explore their environments by using their senses. According to Vygotsky, caregivers can enhance toddler's development by scaffolding and finding the ZPD. Language development increases as toddlers repeat single words and use telegraphic speech.

Toddlers need a stimulating environment to encourage learning and socio-emotional development. They are learning to be independent in Erikson's autonomy versus shame and doubt stage. Toddlers are highly sensitive and experience temper tantrums. Caregivers can use developmentally appropriate guidance techniques to help prevent tantrums. Play is important and toddlers engage in parallel play.

If developmental milestones are missed, a special need may be the underlying cause. A hearing impairment and cerebral palsy are examples of conditions that may be detected during the toddler years.

## Vocabulary Activity

For each of the key terms, identify a word or group of words describing a quality of the term—an *attribute*. Pair up with a classmate and discuss your list of attributes. Then, discuss your list of attributes with the whole class to increase understanding.

## Critical Thinking

1. **Identify.** Use online or print sources to identify foods that could pose potential safety risks for toddlers.
2. **Cause and effect.** What might happen if a child does not receive inoculations?
3. **Predict.** If a 2-year-old boy has two older brothers, how might this affect his development?
4. **Draw conclusions.** What might you assume about a toddler who talks a lot and has a large vocabulary?
5. **Determine.** How would you handle a toddler's temper tantrum?
6. **Assess.** Make a chart that shows developmentally appropriate guidance techniques for children during the toddler years.
7. **Evaluate.** Watch a toddler play for at least an hour. What types of activities does the toddler enjoy? How do these activities benefit the toddler's physical, cognitive, and socio-emotional development? Based on your observation, what other activities do you think would interest the toddler?
8. **Make inferences.** Make a photo picture collage of active toddlers. What activities are they performing? What types of learning are involved?

9. **Analyze.** Analyze the physical, emotional, social, and cognitive development of toddlers.

10. **Identify.** Summarize ways to promote the development of toddlers. How would these differ for toddlers with special needs?

11. **Analyze.** Discuss the influences of the family and society, such as caregivers and media influences, on toddlers.

12. **Determine.** List techniques for promoting the health and safety of toddlers. What types of safety and precautions are most important at this age?

13. **Draw conclusions.** Explain how appropriate medical and dental care impacts toddlers.

## Core Skills

14. **Math.** Lena is 2 years old and 33 inches tall. If Lena is half her final adult height, how tall will she be?

15. **Writing.** In a short essay, describe and analyze the developmental theories that apply to toddlerhood.

16. **Listening.** Listen to a toddler talk. What single words and word combinations does the toddler use? What vocabulary problems do you notice? How would you help the toddler correct these problems?

17. **Writing.** Write and illustrate a developmentally age-appropriate story for a toddler. If possible, read the story to a toddler or a group of toddlers. What did they like or dislike about the story?

18. **Speaking.** Working with a partner, role play various ways to positively handle a toddler's temper tantrum.

19. **CTE Career Readiness Practice.** Use Internet or print resources, or the help of a biology teacher, to examine how bones physically change and develop. Prepare a storyboard showing what happens as bones grow larger and denser through early years of the lifespan. Explain how good nutrition and physical activity impact bone development.

## Research

20. Search for several online videos that show toddlers interacting with others. Videos of twins are especially demonstrative. Use these video clips to show your classmates how language develops during the toddler years.

21. Use online or print sources to research videos, books, and games marketed toward toddlers. Choose three to evaluate. Are these toys and games developmentally appropriate activities for toddlers? Are they stimulating? Are they interactive? Do they promote social interaction with caregivers?

## Event Prep

22. Organize a project that will help address a current child development need in your community. For example, a local early childhood program may need help collecting donations of art supplies, books, or toys. Use the FCCLA *Planning Process* to guide your project planning. You may wish to use your project to participate in the *STAR Event Focus on Children*. See your FCCLA adviser for further information.

# Chapter 7

# Early Childhood: Ages 3 through 5

Rob Hainer/Shutterstock.com

# Objectives

After studying this chapter, you will be able to

- analyze the physical development of children ages 3 through 5.
- analyze the cognitive development of children ages 3 through 5.
- analyze the socio-emotional development of children ages 3 through 5.
- compare and contrast various developmental theories relating to preschoolers.
- identify developmentally appropriate guidance techniques for preschoolers.
- identify developmental milestones preschoolers achieve.

## Reading Prep

In preparation for reading this chapter, read the list of key terms. Which terms are already familiar to you? Which ones are not familiar at all? As you read, think about how your understanding of the meaning of a given term agrees with or is different from the text.

## Key Terms

preschoolers
postural control
hand and eye coordination
MyPlate
food allergies
allergy
asthma
preoperational stage
operations
intuition
centration
conservation
egocentrism

windows of opportunity
metacognition
metamemory
phonology
morphology
syntax
semantics
pragmatics
preconventional morality
initiative versus guilt
democratic parenting style
authoritarian parenting style
permissive parenting style

functional play
constructive play
associative play
cooperative play
gender identity
gender roles
attention deficit hyperactivity disorder (ADHD)
autism spectrum disorder (ASD)
Head Start

### Visit the G-W Learning Companion Website to:

- **build** vocabulary with e-flash cards and interactive games;
- **assess** what you learn by completing self-assessment quizzes; and
- **expand** knowledge with activities that extend learning.

G-WLEARNING.com   www.g-wlearning.com/development/

During early childhood, young children learn to run, hop, and skip. They learn to laugh, talk, joke, and sing. They become industrious and more independent. They are curious and want to please.

The development process during early childhood is gradual. Development does not happen in the same way, at the same time, for all children. Children will develop certain skills or abilities faster or slower than one another. Some children will talk early, while others will be delayed. Most children will become more independent. These differences are normal and expected.

## Physical Characteristics and Growth

**Preschoolers** are children between the ages of 3 through 5. During early childhood, children add about 2.5 to 3 inches in height and 3 to 5 pounds each year, **7-1**. Girls grow slightly slower than boys during this stage. Both boys and girls appear slimmer as the trunks of their bodies lengthen and body fat diminishes. Their legs and arms lengthen in comparison to their body height. Although their heads are still large in proportion to their bodies, children in this stage are not quite as top heavy. By the end of this stage, their body proportions are similar to those of an adult.

Individual differences in both height and weight become more apparent during early childhood. Sometimes these differences are due to heredity. A father who is short in stature may have a son who is also short in stature. Other times these differences are due to the environment. A child who does not have access to health care or nutritious food may fail to thrive and show below-average growth. Usually, differences are a combination of heredity and environment.

Facial features are also somewhat slimmer in early childhood when compared to the chubby faces of infants. With a full set of baby teeth, toothy smiles are common. As children reach the end of this stage, baby teeth fall out producing gaps in their smiles. Each missing tooth is seen as an achievement toward becoming a "big" girl or boy.

| Average Height and Weight for Ages 3 through 5 | | | | |
|---|---|---|---|---|
| Age (Years) | Height (in inches)* | | Weight (in pounds)* | |
| | Boys | Girls | Boys | Girls |
| 3 | 37½ | 37 | 31¾ | 31¾ |
| 3½ | 39¼ | 38½ | 34 | 34 |
| 4 | 40½ | 39¾ | 36½ | 34 |
| 4½ | 41¾ | 41¼ | 38½ | 37¾ |
| 5 | 43 | 42½ | 41¾ | 40 |
| 5½ | 44¼ | 43¾ | 43 | 42 |

*Height and weight measurements are averages. Each child develops at a slightly different rate.

*Goodheart-Willcox Publisher*

**7-1** Height and weight increases steadily during early childhood.

## Gross-Motor Skills

During early childhood, children are often in motion, **7-2**. In fact, they are as active as they may ever be in their lifetime. Motor skill development escalates at a rapid pace.

At age 2, most children are walking quickly. By the time they are 3 years of age, they are more confident in their abilities. They add simple movements such as jumping and twirling. Their bodies are more muscular and less rounded and chubby. Their bones are stronger. Bone sturdiness and muscular development enhances their abilities to throw or catch a ball, run and jump, climb a playground jungle gym, and other activities that require gross-motor skills.

Throughout early childhood, gross-motor skills are refined. This refinement of skills takes practice and balance and shows postural control. **Postural control** involves being able to achieve and maintain a state of balance while performing an activity. For example, preschoolers can demonstrate postural control by stabilizing themselves as they jump up and down or stand on one foot. By the time children reach the end of this stage, they are capable of learning many activities that require coordination. For example, they can learn to ride a bike, throw and catch a ball, shoot a basketball, or skate.

*Blend Images/Shutterstock.com*

**7-2** Running, skipping, jumping, and dancing are just some of the movements of young children.

## Fine-Motor Skills

Often, 3-year-olds can draw a circle, an X, or for some, form letters. They can color with crayons, hold a fork or spoon, and undo clothing. Putting simple puzzles together is a good activity for building **hand and eye coordination** (using visual input to guide a hand activity). They can even start learning to play a musical instrument. Although not yet learning to read music, children can hear music. Some believe that the sensory connection between the fine-motor skills and hearing create a perfect environment for learning a musical instrument.

By age 4, children can often copy alphabet letters, dress and undress, fold a piece of paper into triangles, and build a tower of blocks, **7-3**. By age 5, children can often write their name, string beads, use scissors, and hold a pencil or chopsticks correctly.

*anna karwowska/Shutterstock.com*

**7-3** Along with gross-motor skills, fine-motor skills rapidly develop during early childhood.

As young children develop their fine-motor skills, the preference for handedness (being left- or right-handed) becomes more apparent. Most young children show a strong preference, the majority being right-handed. Some, about 10 percent, show left-handed preference. Left-handedness is more common in boys than in girls.

## Nutrition

Because young children are so physically active, good nutrition, or fuel, is essential. Children learn what to eat, how to eat, and when to eat through instruction and by watching others. They learn to associate food with emotions. Food becomes a part of social interactions.

As young children become more independent, their food preferences are more pronounced. They are often picky about the food they eat. Part of children's perceived pickiness comes from their acute ability to taste. When compared to adolescents or adults, the taste buds on children's tongues rejuvenate at a much faster pace. In addition to taste, children may have preferences for textures, enjoying those that are most familiar.

Because early childhood is such an important time for exploration, introducing a variety of nutritional food choices can have lasting positive effects on children. Providing well-balanced meals is important during this critical time of growth. Young children typically eat smaller amounts due to their smaller stomach size. Therefore, healthy snacks between meals are often necessary.

The United States Department of Agriculture (USDA) created a food guidance system called **MyPlate** to help people ages 2 and older make healthful food choices. The MyPlate food guidance system divides foods into five groups. These are grains, vegetables, fruits, protein foods, and dairy. The website, Choose**MyPlate**.gov, offers daily checklists and tips to promote a healthful lifestyle. The checklists for preschoolers show how much children should eat from each group every day, **7-4**.

In early childhood, the eating habits of caregivers strongly influence the eating preferences of children. Eating meals on a regular schedule, decreasing distractions such as television, reducing stress from conflicts during meals, and offering healthy choices can have positive long-term effects. On the other hand, when meals are stressful or restrictive, the effects can be negative. For example,

## Cultural Connections    Media Influences

Through television, movies, computer usage, and video games, media can influence young children in a negative or positive way. While some advertisements promote *junk food*, or foods that are high in saturated fat and sugars, other organizations are using the same approach to counteract a potentially negative influence. These organizations create commercials that encourage proper nutrition and adequate physical activity.

To ensure a preschooler is meeting all his or her nutritional needs, follow the food serving suggestions of MyPlate. Limit the preschooler's screen time per day and encourage forms of physical activity. When children are watching TV, watch with them and get up during commercials to do some type of physical activity. This will also help avoid the advertisements.

### Research Activity

Record or watch a children's cartoon show or other program. During the commercial breaks, tally the number of food commercials. Of these commercials, how many advertisements are for healthful foods? Compare your findings with a classmate.

# MyPlate
# Daily Checklist

| GRAINS | VEGETABLES | FRUITS | DAIRY | PROTEIN FOODS |
|---|---|---|---|---|
| **5 ounces** | **1½ cups** | **1½ cups** | **2½ cups** | **4 ounces** |
| **Make half your grains whole grains** | **Vary your veggies** | **Focus on whole fruits** | **Move to low-fat or fat-free milk or yogurt** | **Vary your protein routine** |
| Find whole-grain foods by reading the Nutrition Facts label and ingredients list. | Choose a variety of colorful fresh, frozen, and canned vegetales – make sure to include dark green, red, and orange choices. | Focus on whole fruits that are fresh, frozen, canned, or dried. | Choose fat-free milk, yogurt, and soy beverages (soy milk) to cut back on your saturated fat. | Mix up your protein foods to include seafood, beans and peas, unsalted nuts and seeds, soy products, eggs, and lean meats and poultry. |

**Find your balance between food and physical activity**

Children 2 to 5 years old should play actively every day.

**Drink and eat less sodium, saturated fat, and added sugars. Limit:**
- Sodium to **1900 milligrams** a day.
- Saturated fat to **16 grams** a day.
- Added sugars to **35 grams** a day.

**Your results are based on a 1400 calorie pattern.**

*USDA*

**7-4** Following the MyPlate guidelines can help people plan nutritious meals.

restricting foods from a child's diet can lead to overeating when the food becomes available. The child may eat the food even when he or she feels full.

As children expand their food preferences, caregivers need to be concerned about food intolerances and allergies. As you learned earlier, *food intolerances* are reactions to foods that are unpleasant, such as digestive or behavioral problems. **Food allergies** occur when foods trigger a response by the body's immune system. Allergies can cause more severe reactions, including breathing problems or death. Simply being around the food can cause reactions in some children. The most common causes of allergies include milk, eggs, tree nuts, peanuts, soy, wheat, fish, and shellfish. Read food labels to avoid foods that may trigger intolerances or allergies and remove any offending foods from the diet.

## Safety Connections    *Safety During Playtime*

Play for preschoolers is an important part of their cognitive and socio-emotional development, as well as their physical growth and health. Preschooler play should be encouraged. Whether outside or inside, alone or with peers, preschoolers have the imagination to find or create an activity. Below are indoor and outdoor tips to ensure safety during playtime.

### Indoors

- Make sure play area is clear of harmful or poisonous substances and sharp objects
- Ensure there is plenty of space to move around without tripping or running into sharp edges
- Ensure outlets have protective covers

### Outdoors

- Make sure play area is clear of harmful or poisonous substances, broken glass, garden tools, or other dangerous items
- Inspect the play area for large holes or wells
- Ensure there are no poisonous plants or insects in play areas
- Check playground equipment to make sure there are no sharp edges or pieces missing
- Make sure preschoolers wear safety pads and a helmet when bicycling, roller skating, or other similar physical activities
- Always supervise swimming and water activities

### Discussion Activity

Compare and contrast play activities that involve physical activity and activities that are less physically active. How do both types of play affect the health and well-being of the preschooler?

## Physical Activity and Play

Young children love to play. Yet, most studies show that children today often do not get enough opportunity for physical play. Television watching, structured and scheduled activities, and parents' fear of children exploring in the outdoors can result in sedentary lifestyles for young children. When children play together without direct adult supervision, more physical activity often occurs. Family members modeling active behaviors can have a positive effect. Spending time outdoors in an unstructured environment can be helpful, too. Young children need supervision, but should also be able to structure free play themselves within social and safety limits.

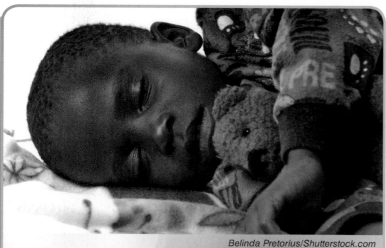

Belinda Pretorius/Shutterstock.com

**7-5**  Bedtimes and naps should be scheduled consistently during early childhood.

Physical activity and play are important to a child's physical, cognitive, and socio-emotional development. Some researchers say play is the main job of young children. Play is how preschoolers explore and learn about their world.

## Sleeping

On average, preschoolers need between 11 to 13 hours of sleep each night. Because preschoolers are very active, they also need about one nap per day. Establishing a healthy, regular sleep routine is important to ensure the preschooler is getting enough sleep, **7-5**. During this time, preschoolers may have trouble sleeping. They have vivid imaginations and may experience memorable dreams and nightmares. To feel comfortable and secure, preschoolers may wish to take a favorite stuffed animal to sleep.

## Toilet Learning

The progress of toilet learning varies among individual children. By age 3, preschoolers significantly improve their ability to control bathroom habits. They understand the need to use the bathroom and can communicate this to caregivers.

Although preschoolers usually make significant progress in toilet learning, they still have accidents. Difficulty in controlling bathroom habits overnight is called *enuresis*. Also known as "bed-wetting," enuresis is a common condition for preschoolers and improves with time. Overnight accidents may be caused by drinking too much liquid before bedtime, heavy sleep, fear of the dark, or a combination of factors.

Caregivers can help ease difficulties in the preschooler's toileting habits to help avoid accidents. Preschoolers often need to be reminded or asked if they need a trip to the bathroom before activities, car rides, going to a new place, or bedtime. They also need periodic reminders throughout the day. To help ease overnight accidents, limit liquids at night and create a dimly lit pathway to the bathroom. A night-light in a preschooler's room, dim hallways lights, and a light in the bathroom can create a friendly, safe trip at night. As preschoolers continue to grow and develop, they will be able to master toilet learning skills.

## Medical and Dental Care

By preschool, children have all of their baby teeth, or primary teeth. During the preschool years, primary teeth will loosen and fall out. This happens because permanent teeth are growing underneath and push out the primary teeth. Preschoolers feel the loose teeth and may try to wiggle or pull them. If teeth are pulled out too soon, the growth of surrounding teeth can be affected in how they grow into place. To ensure teeth are healthy and growing in properly, preschoolers usually visit the dentist twice per year. Caregivers can prevent dental issues by teaching preschoolers to brush their teeth twice a day using a fluoride paste.

# Case Study ???

### Toilet Learning

Zari and Erik have three children aged 3, 7, and 9. The couple's two older children were already well into the toilet learning process by age 3 and were nearing completion. Liam, who is 3-years-old and the youngest child, has not yet begun toilet learning. He is still in diapers. He does not seem to acknowledge when his diaper is wet or when he is excreting. Although the family has a child-sized toilet for learning, Liam does not show interest in using it. Liam's father, Erik, says Liam should begin toilet learning now. He argues that Liam should have begun the learning process at age 2 or sooner. He also notes Liam is behind in progress with toilet learning when compared to his siblings. Zari, Liam's mother, says Liam is not quite ready to begin toilet learning.

- Do you think Liam is ready to begin toilet learning?
- Is there a perfect age to begin toilet learning?
- Should Zari and Erik compare Liam's progress to his siblings' progress? Why or why not?
- How can stress affect Liam's toilet learning process?

As preschoolers are exposed to illnesses or different environments, they are more likely to become sick. This is because their immune systems are still developing and are not yet as strong as those of healthy adults. There are many illnesses common in childhood, **7-6**. Many children receive inoculations to help prevent these illnesses, but even with preventive care, they can still become sick.

| Common Childhood Illnesses | | | |
|---|---|---|---|
| **Illness** | **Cause** | **Symptoms** | **Treatment** |
| **Bronchitis** | Virus | Similar symptoms as the common cold, followed by a cough | Consult a physician to determine if antibiotics will help; over-the-counter medicines may help relieve symptoms |
| **Chicken pox (Varicella)** | Virus | Itching, rashes, scabs, fever | Prescribed medication; can be prevented by varicella vaccine |
| **Common cold** | Virus | Runny nose, sore throat, fever, dry cough, sneezing | Over-the-counter medications may help relieve symptoms; if symptoms persist, seek medical attention |
| **Ear infection** | Virus or bacteria | Pain in ear, muted hearing, ear drainage, mild fever | Treatment varies depending on the cause and seriousness of the ear infection |
| **Flu (Influenza)** | Virus | Fever, chills, lack of energy, cough | Seek early medical assistance |
| **German measles (Rubella)** | Virus | Fever and rash; may display no symptoms | Seek medical treatment; can be prevented with the measles, mumps, and rubella vaccine |
| **Measles** | Virus | Fever, rash, eye irritation, cough | Fluids, rest, and medicine to reduce fever; can be prevented with the measles, mumps, and rubella vaccine |
| **Meningitis** | Virus and bacteria | Inflammation in the brain and spinal cord that causes fatigue, fever, vomiting, headache, stiff neck, and possibly seizures | Emergency medical help is necessary; method of treatment varies depending on cause of illness |
| **Mumps** | Virus | Fever, swollen glands, muscle pain | Fluids, rest, and medicine to reduce fever; can be prevented with the measles, mumps, and rubella vaccine |
| **Pink eye (Conjunctivitis)** | Virus or bacteria | Inflammation of the eye, causing the eye to be pink with a thick pus discharge | Antibiotics administered with an eye dropper or an ointment; may disappear on its own |
| **Scarlet fever** | Bacteria | Sore throat, fever, headache, rash covering the torso, arms, and legs | Prescribed medication |
| **Strep throat** | Bacteria | Sore throat, coughing, swollen glands | Prescribed medication |
| **Whooping cough (Pertussis)** | Bacteria | Runny nose, heavy coughing, vomiting, and fatigue that can last for months | Medical treatment is needed; can be prevented by the diphtheria, tetanus, and pertussis vaccination |

*Goodheart-Willcox Publisher*

**7-6**    Many of these common childhood illnesses are communicable.

When a preschooler does become sick, medical attention may be necessary. Some illnesses, such as meningitis, require immediate medical care. Less serious illnesses, such as the common cold, may simply need time to heal. Because many illnesses are *communicable,* or spreadable, children should stay at home and not attend school until they are feeling better or have a doctor's release to return.

Preschoolers are not yet old enough to manage their own sickness, so caregivers need to help them stay on track for treating their illness. This includes taking them to the doctor and following directions for properly administering medications. Preschoolers also need extra care and attention to feel safe and comfortable. Caregivers might offer calm, quiet activities to allow sick children time to rest and still be entertained.

## Allergies and Asthma

Allergies and asthma are two other chronic conditions that are common in childhood. An **allergy** is a reaction that develops because of the immune system's overreaction to a normally harmless substance in the environment. The immune system perceives this substance, or *allergen,* to be harmful and the body reacts in a negative way when the allergen is present. There are many common types of allergies, including dander from pets, certain foods, insects, medication, fabrics and materials, or other airborne substances.

Symptoms from allergies can range from mild to severe. Mild reactions include itchy eyes, ears, or throat; red, puffy eyes; runny nose; sneezing; and small red patches called *hives.* Diarrhea, cramps, and vomiting can also be the result of an allergic reaction. A severe reaction to allergies is *anaphylaxis,* which causes the throat and tongue to swell. In a severe reaction, breathing becomes difficult and death can result.

The simplest way to treat allergies is to remove the source of the allergen from the child's environment whenever possible. If the allergen is a food source, ensure the child's food does not contain the allergen, **7-7**. Alert anyone who may have temporary care of the preschooler, such as teachers, family members, or babysitters. The preschooler may not understand that he or she is allergic to something and may try to eat the substance or be near the allergen, especially if other children are around the substance.

Children who suffer from allergies are also more likely to have asthma. **Asthma** is a disease that causes inflammation of the airways in the lungs. The cause of asthma is unknown, but research suggests it may be environmental or genetic. Similar to allergies, a person with asthma has certain substances that trigger an asthmatic reaction, also known as an *asthma attack.* During this attack, breathing becomes restricted along with wheezing and coughing episodes. Allergies, stress, smoke, physical activity, pollution, viruses, or other airborne chemicals can trigger asthma attacks.

Stephen Mcsweeny/Shutterstock.com

**7-7**  Foods containing peanuts and wheat commonly cause allergic reactions for many children.

Treatment for asthma is similar to treatment for allergies. Asthma is not curable, but needs to be managed. Children should be kept away from irritants as much as possible. Consult a doctor for prescribed medical treatment, which may include an inhaler.

## Preventive Care

Although some illnesses may be preventable, children as well as adults still become sick from time to time. Preventive health care can help reduce the risk of contracting illnesses. Optimizing the health of preschoolers includes ensuring preschoolers have sufficient nutrients to properly grow, develop, and strengthen their immune systems.

When there is a nutrient deficiency, the immune system weakens and has difficulty fighting illnesses and diseases. Following the food requirements from the five groups listed in MyPlate can help preschoolers meet their nutrient needs. Being physically active overall also improves health, **7-8**.

Scheduling regular health checkups in early childhood is also important. During the preschool years, an annual checkup is recommended to monitor growth and health. The doctor can discuss healthful lifestyle patterns involving nutrition, physical activity, and sleep.

*stefanolunardi/Shutterstock.com*

**7-8** Physical activity reduces the risk for certain types of diseases and illnesses during childhood and in the future.

## Health Connections    Poisonings

As children begin to explore their environments, they may unknowingly encounter toxic substances. There are many different types of poisonings, including those from plants and insects, food, carbon monoxide, lead, cleaning agents, hair products, and medications.

To treat an ingested poisoning, contact the Poison Control Center, a 24-hour hotline that can give first aid instructions depending on the type of poisoning. To prevent poisonings that occur within the home, make sure household items such as cleaning agents and medications are in a cabinet with safety locks to prevent a child from getting into them. If a poisoning occurs on an external body part, such as the eye or skin, remove clothing and flush the affected area with cool water.

Poison ivy or oak are outdoor plants that cause poisoning. These plants will cause a rash and itching on the surface of the skin. The skin's response to poison ivy occurs because of an allergic reaction to the plant's oil. Treat exposure to poison ivy by washing the affected area on the skin with soap and water for about 15 minutes to remove any lingering oil. Apply calamine lotion to reduce the rash and decrease itching. Teach children to identify poisonous plants so they can avoid them. Also, inspect the play area to ensure it is free of poisonous plants, substances, or other harmful items.

### Speaking Activity

Give a *Poisoning Prevention* presentation to a group of local preschoolers. Include information about how they could get poisoned and what to do if they think they got into a poison.

## Checkpoint

1. What bodily and facial changes can be expected in early childhood?
2. Describe typical gross- and fine-motor skills of children in early childhood.
3. Define postural controls and give an example.
4. What is the difference between a food intolerance and a food allergy?
5. List five common types of allergies.
6. What are three ways to optimize the health of preschoolers?

# Cognitive Characteristics and Growth

Young children are known for asking "why?" Why is the sky blue? Why are snowflakes white? What makes leaves fall off trees? Why is there a baby in her stomach? Why is he sick? Why do cats catch mice? Throughout early childhood, children seek rational answers to explain what they know through observation and experience.

### Piaget's Preoperational Stage

In early childhood, the world expands for children. They can walk and talk and explore new places. They can reason and think about the world in ways that were not possible in earlier stages. Piaget called this phase the **preoperational stage** of thinking. **Operations** refer to the formal or logical processes that are organized mental processes. Piaget referred to this stage as preoperational as it represents a time when children's use of symbolic and logical thinking grows. They use more reasoning and rational thought. This does not happen overnight, but is a process throughout early childhood.

In this stage, children continue to explore their world, learning more and more as they organize their experiences. They learn to use symbols, or language, as a way of understanding the world around them. Language may be spoken or an object or symbol for something else. For example, a child understands that a miniature toy cow represents a life-sized living cow when playing with a toy farm set. As young children enter the preoperational stage of thinking, they gradually move from using **intuition**, primitive reasoning based on feelings, to more rational and logical thinking.

The preoperational stage is marked by three characteristics. These include centration, lack of conservation, and egocentrism. **Centration** is the tendency to focus on just one aspect of something seen. **Conservation** refers to an ability to follow transformations of viewed objects.

In the preoperational stage, young children apply concentration to their difficulty in seeing transformations. Piaget showed this difficulty, or inability to follow transformations, when a short glass of water was poured into a taller, thinner glass. To young children, the second glass may appear to have more liquid, even when they observe the transformation, **7-9**. Piaget also showed children have difficulty understanding conservation or transformation with mass, numbers, length, weight, and area. A young child might observe the same 10 blocks taking up more space when separated over a larger area than when located close together. Piaget believed that children had difficulty seeing the steps in transformation.

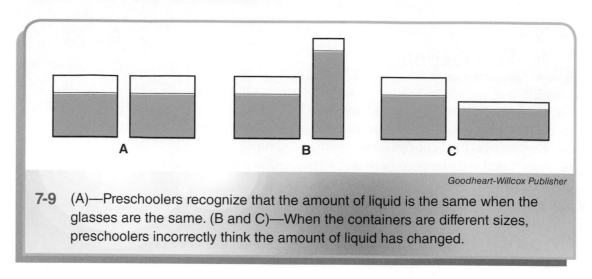

*Goodheart-Willcox Publisher*

**7-9**  (A)—Preschoolers recognize that the amount of liquid is the same when the glasses are the same. (B and C)—When the containers are different sizes, preschoolers incorrectly think the amount of liquid has changed.

Part of preoperational thought involves egocentrism. **Egocentrism** is an inability to take another person's perspective. This may come from the difficulty in perceiving transformations and understanding the thoughts and feelings of others. This is especially true if these thoughts are different from the preschoolers own thoughts or from what is displayed in facial expressions or behaviors.

Although much understanding about young children is based on Piaget's work, more recent research shows that conservation is understood earlier than before thought. The more children are exposed to transformations of objects, such as the same amount of clay being formed into different shapes, the more quickly they understand that things remain the same. As will be discussed later, children are also more capable of understanding other's thoughts and feelings than previously recognized.

## Vygotsky's Ideas

Fantasy stories, make-believe fairies, incredible superheroes, boogiemen, and monsters—the world of creative make-believe abounds in early childhood. Do you remember any favorite movies, television shows, or books that took you to another time and place as a young child? Did you play dress-up, act out stories, or insist on being called by another name to fit the character you played? This is so much a part of early childhood that movies abound about the fantasies and fears of this stage. Some young children even create fantasy playmates or invisible friends. These pretend peers can seem very real to young children as they carry on conversations and take care of their friends' needs.

Vygotsky believed that children learn what they know through social interaction. As brain pathways are pruned and refined, gross-motor skills develop. These increased skills allow young children to interact more freely with their world. Vygotsky theorized that as children play, the objects they use encourage imaginative thinking. Their concepts move from more realistic to abstract. Vygotsky saw children's imaginative play as a way to learn new skills.

Parents and caregivers should provide as many opportunities for creative and imaginative play as possible, **7-10**. Providing props such as dress-up clothes might spur the imagination. Sometimes, nothing is needed but free, uninhibited time and space. Parents and caregivers should let young children direct the play, allowing time to interact with others as well as time to play alone.

## Brain Development

By the time children reach age 3, they have about twice as many brain connections as adults. During the preschool years, neuron pathways continue to develop, some are reinforced, and others are trimmed away. As the brain develops, there are **windows of opportunity**, or time frames for optimizing the development of critical skills.

Windows of opportunity are ideal times because the child's brain is most receptive to learning. This is because specific neurological pathways are not yet complete. The lengths of time for physical, cognitive, and socio-emotional development windows vary. Some windows of opportunity are open from birth and continue throughout the childhood years into adulthood. Other windows of opportunity may only be open for a few months or years. If these windows are missed, it is difficult, but not impossible, for children to develop these abilities later. Providing children with rich experiences and activities throughout early childhood will stimulate brain growth and development.

*Warren Goldswain/Shutterstock.com*

**7-10**  Pretend play is a developmentally appropriate activity for preschoolers.

## Health Connections

### Environmental Influences Affect Brain Development

Factors in the environment can influence a child's brain development, whether positive or negative. Preschoolers are in constant motion and actively involved in learning about the world around them. They enjoy meeting new people, learning new concepts, and having new experiences. A loving, caring environment is scientifically proven to be a positive factor for stimulating brain development. Stress is proven to be a negative factor that interferes with the ability to complete the wiring of neuron pathways. The people within a child's environment are instrumental in helping the child learn and develop during windows of opportunity. To continue stimulating all types of development during windows of opportunity, caregivers, family members, and teachers should offer a variety of learning sources. Repetition in activities is also vital to solidify a developmental task.

### Writing Activity

Describe five activities that will stimulate a preschooler's physical, cognitive, and socio-emotional development.

## Language Development

Language is not only essential to communication, but is an important part of cognitive development in early childhood. Children first learn to communicate their needs to others. They learn to name people, animals, and colors. They learn simple counting. As this happens, children can focus on their inward thoughts. They think about what they are thinking, often referred to as **metacognition**. They think about what they remember, or **metamemory**. A common story instruction for verbal young children is "I was 'membering...."

Many young children have a unique way of speaking. Instead of saying "a couple of minutes ago," a child might instead say "a couple of whiles ago." These individual translations of language can be charming and fascinating to consider. Even so, learning a language usually occurs in a consistent order. Typically, young children learn phonology, followed by morphology, syntax, semantics, and then pragmatic use of language.

**Phonology** refers to the sounds that make up words. By the time children are 3 years of age, they can produce many of the sounds in language, although some of the consonant sounds may be delayed, **7-11**. After children have mastered the combination of sounds that make up words in a language, they move to morphology.

**Morphology** includes word structures and formations. For example, the verb *go* becomes *goes* in plural form. Where it becomes tricky is when words change form into something unrelated such as when *go* becomes *went* when used in the past tense. Learning morphology takes time, instruction, trial, and error. Young children should be encouraged in their attempts to use newly developing language skills.

| Sounds Preschoolers Master | | |
|---|---|---|
| **Age** | **Sound** | **Examples** |
| **3 years** | h | home, hug, doghouse |
| | m | man, hammer, hum |
| | n | now, penny, run |
| | p | play, hippo, pop |
| | w | with, water, wow |
| **4 years** | b | ball, baby, tub |
| | k | cat, chicken, kick |
| | f | fun, telephone, stuff |
| | g | girl, wagon, tag |
| **5 years** | d | dog, middle, hand |
| | ng | finger, sing |
| | y | yellow, onion, story |

*Goodheart-Willcox Publisher*

**7-11**   Many sounds preschoolers learn are found in the beginning, middle, and end of words.

**Syntax** refers to sentence structure, or when words are combined to form grammatical sentences. Preschoolers learn to lengthen their sentences by adding conjunctions, prepositions, and clauses. **Semantics** refers to the meaning of words, whereas **pragmatics** refers to using language properly.

Learning language is complex, but through experimentation, social interaction, and modeling, young children learn quickly. Some experts estimate that a child learns a new word during every waking hour resulting in a vocabulary of over 14,000 words at the end of early childhood. That is, just in time to enter school.

## Reading and Writing

One way that young children learn language and increase their vocabulary is by having adults and older children read books to them, **7-12**. Words used in children's books are often different from the everyday language used at home as imaginative creatures and talking animals are described. If the reader is engaged with the child, reading can be a positive social exchange. Reading to a child can provide a positive orientation for learning later in life if seen as a pleasant experience.

Most children recognize and identify some letters of the alphabet during early childhood. By the end of this stage, most can identify many if not all letters of the alphabet and can write their own name. Some can write their phone number or address, depending on the length. There is a rapid progression in a short amount of time from marking an $X$ to writing one's name or simple words. All of this occurs during the few short years of early childhood.

*Mitya/Shutterstock.com*

**7-12** Books provide a wonderful world of language for preschoolers.

## Humor

Humor can be used positively as a form of self-expression and language development. Preschoolers' imaginative conversations, fresh new observations about the world around them, and uninhibited reactions can be a source of much humor. Young children enjoy the humor in daily life events. In the earlier years of this stage, young children enjoy the funny sounds and faces made by others. Silly facial expressions, physical antics, or surprise movements such as hiding and being "found" can all cause peals of laughter.

As children near the end of early childhood, they become more interested in humor that centers on bodily functions and characteristics. They have mastered their own toileting and bodily functions. As a result, jokes about bodily mishaps can be humorous to them. As they are aware of the differences between boys and girls, a fascination and curiosity often takes the form of humor about these differences.

## Cultural Connections    Humor and Cognitive Development

Although styles of humor differ from culture to culture, studies confirm that humor is an indication of cognitive development. In a study conducted in China and Greece, two classes of children ages 4–5 were studied for humor recognition. The study found that the ability to find an image, object, or story as comical reflects intellectual growth. For example, an image of two mice dressed in human clothing pushing a stroller with a kitten as the passenger was shown to a classroom of 4- and 5-year-old children in China and Greece. Both Chinese and Greek children in the study found this image to be humorous. They recognized that cats and mice do not act or dress like humans, and also that cats and mice are natural enemies. To understand the humor of the image, the children must first have an understanding of the "normal" activities of both mice and cats. When the animals were behaving in another manner,

the children had the cognitive recognition that this is odd, and therefore silly, or humorous.

Researchers of this study also found the results to support Piaget's cognitive theory. The recognition of an animal acting in a nontraditional manner reflects the preoperational stage, when children begin to understand consistencies and inconsistencies in their environment. Although this image may not be universally comical to all preschoolers, the study found that overall, humor and cognitive development are positively related despite humor styles.

### Observation Activity

Observe a child between the ages of 3 and 5 to discover what he or she finds humorous. In order to find the object or action funny, what must the child first know to be able to recognize the humor?

Due to increased language skills, preschoolers are better able to manipulate language to achieve humorous results. In early childhood, humor that focuses on words used or spoken inappropriately is humorous. For example, a young child might find humor in an adult cartoon animal that speaks using baby talk.

Dave Clark Digital Photo/Shutterstock.com

7-13    In Kohlberg's stage of preconventional morality, young children may share toys with others based on possible rewards or punishment, not on "doing what is right."

## Kohlberg's Theory of Moral Development

Learning what is considered culturally right or wrong is a process. Younger children respond to rewards and punishments instead of making moral decisions, **7-13**. They are in Kohlberg's first level of moral development called **preconventional morality**. For example, a child may share toys with a playmate to avoid punishment, not because the child is motivated by a sense of caring for the playmate.

Over time, young children want to make a good impression on adults. Because of their increased cognitive skills, they are also capable of making up "tall tales" to avoid punishment. They are often concerned about what their parents think of them and whether they are labeled as "good" or "bad."

By the end of early childhood, young children can tell the difference between right and wrong. Although their judgment is still often based on potential rewards and punishments rather than universal moral truths or family values, they start to care more about doing what is right. For example, a 5-year-old may decide to do a task out of concern for helping a caregiver rather than fearing punishment.

## Checkpoint

1. Describe Piaget's preoperational stage of thinking.
2. Describe Vygotsky's ideas of how children learn new skills through play.
3. What are windows of opportunity?
4. Give two examples of how language develops in early childhood.
5. According to Kohlberg's theory, how do children in early childhood solve moral problems?

## Socio-emotional Characteristics and Growth

During early childhood, children are very busy. They love to dance, run, tell stories, share secrets, and explore their world. They have an abundance of energy. They are not very cautious, forget previous failures, and readily repeat their attempts at new activities. Children see themselves as their own person, separate from their parents and siblings. They can be exuberant and enthused about trying new activities. In their eagerness to do a task independently, they often fail. This failure can cause guilt, lowering their self-esteem. Erikson described the next stage of socio-emotional development as **initiative versus guilt**. (Figure **7-14** provides a summary of developmental theories as they relate to early childhood.)

| Summary of Major Developmental Theories Related to Early Childhood | | |
|---|---|---|
| **Type of Development** | **Theory** | **Description** |
| **Cognitive** | Piaget: Preoperational | Young children learn to communicate through language or other symbols. They do not make broad generalizations about things they learn, but learn specific knowledge. As they progress through this stage, they begin to understand concepts such as reversibility and consequences. |
| | Skinner: Operant conditioning | As a child responds to a stimulus such as a punishment or reward, the child will learn to repeat or stop the response. |
| **Socio-emotional development** | Erikson: Initiative versus guilt | Through discovery and exploration, young children learn about the world and their place in it. They learn what is real and what is imaginary. They learn to take initiative for their place in the world. Criticism and punishment can result in guilt for their own actions. |

*Goodheart-Willcox Publisher*

**7-14** Preschoolers' development builds on what they learned as infants and toddlers.

## Family Relationships

Young children need support, encouragement, and instruction to become independent. They need to try new tasks on their own even though they might fail. Family members can provide this support and encouragement. As young children become more independent, their sense of self and ultimately their confidence grows.

Transitioning from caring for children's needs to guiding their behavior requires an understanding of how young children see their world. In an attempt to allow more autonomy, parents can help children learn to make decisions themselves. It is always delightful seeing a young child, who obviously chose his or her own clothing, put together outfits in clashing colors or patterns, **7-15**.

## Parenting Relationships

The opportunity to make choices in inconsequential decisions can build confidence and a sense of self. Often, parents will ask a child to choose between two choices such as wearing the red or blue T-shirt. They may ask whether the child would like a banana cut in slices or peeled and eaten whole. Gradually, these choices are expanded into options that may include choices between two different options such as a banana or a peach. Some situations do not lend themselves toward child decision making and parents must make choices, especially when safety and health are involved.

*Nicki Hutter*

**7-15** What may seem mismatched fashion-wise may be functional for the preschooler.

Giving choices and encouraging children to practice decision making is a common practice for parents using the **democratic parenting style**. (Also called *authoritative parenting style*.) Parents who use this style offer support while setting clear limits. These limits or expectations may be strict, but they are set in a warm and responsive manner. Parents communicate their rationale for expectations in age-appropriate ways. A democratic parenting style can be used from early childhood through adolescence and into the transition years to young adulthood.

Other less effective types of parenting styles include authoritarian and permissive. An **authoritarian parenting style** tends to be controlling and corrective. These parents tend to be strict and expect obedience without discussion. Children with authoritarian parents may not understand why they are to behave a certain way.

A **permissive parenting style** tends to let children control situations, making the decisions with few limits or controls. Children who have few limits may have trouble getting along with others because they are only used to following their own rules.

### Sibling Relationships

Especially in the preschool years, frequent conflicts between siblings occur, **7-16**. Often, these conflicts center around sharing toys, food, playmates, or even their parents. New baby siblings can be a concern for many young children. Parents often work hard to prepare their young children for the new baby's arrival. Despite their best efforts, the reaction to the new sibling can best be described as unpredictable.

Some children welcome their baby sibling with open arms and a sense of nurturing. They see themselves as the older sibling and caretaker, separate from the needy infant. Other young children act out and regress in their behavior, vying for their parent's attention. If siblings have similar temperaments, there may be less conflict in the home. When personalities contrast, however, sibling conflicts often exist. This is not just true in early childhood, but throughout life.

*Kenishirotie/Shutterstock.com*

**7-16** If you have any brothers or sisters, you are well aware of the affect they have on your life.

Within the family, sibling conflicts are common. Young children are capable of settling these disagreements, but they often do not. Young children do not naturally apologize for their wrongdoing, but can learn to do so over time. They are more likely to resolve conflicts if a parent or other caregiver is present. Modeling problem solving and conflict resolution to young children is effective. So are warm responsive parental relationships.

## Developmentally Appropriate Guidance Techniques

Preschoolers have active imaginations and are constantly exploring their environment. They may test limits in unsafe or socially unacceptable ways. Guidance and discipline are used to redirect children into a safe or socially acceptable manner. The purpose of guidance and discipline is to help teach children self-control, independence, safety, and forms of socially acceptable actions and behavior, **7-17**. This includes calling attention to negative and positive behavior. *Punishment* is not the same as discipline, but rather a consequence for an unacceptable behavior. Three main types of discipline are power assertion, love withdrawal, and induction.

*Tom Prokop/Shutterstock.com*

**7-17** Caregivers use guidance and discipline to help children learn how to behave in socially acceptable ways.

### Power Assertion

Power assertion involves using physical means to punish or deny children privileges. Also known as *corporal punishment*, this form of discipline can physically and emotionally harm a child. Spanking falls within this category of discipline. Views on spanking vary widely, but most parenting experts advise against using spanking or power assertion as a form of discipline. Experts discourage power assertion mostly because it can be abusive. Power assertion also creates and relies on fear and demonstrates negative ways to handle emotions. Children who are disciplined with power assertion techniques are more likely to use power in their personal relationships, which creates a cycle of negativity.

### Love Withdrawal

Love withdrawal includes threatening to remove love, even temporarily, from the caregiver and child relationship. Examples of love withdrawal include threatening to send the child away, telling the child he or she is not wanted or favored, ignoring the child, or giving the child the "silent treatment." Experts consider love withdrawal to be emotionally damaging. According to Maslow's *Theory of Human Needs*, all people need to feel loved in order to reach optimal development and self-actualization. When caregivers threaten to take away love, they cause stress and instability within a child. Love withdrawal can send the wrong message that love is unsteady and can be used as a power tool.

### Induction

Induction is a form of discipline that uses logic and explanation to address a child's action or behavior. Induction involves listening to the child, understanding and acknowledging his or her emotions, and explaining the reasoning behind why an action or behavior is inappropriate or unacceptable. For example, if a child is hitting other children during playtime, the caregiver will first remove the child from the group. The caregiver will then acknowledge the child's feelings by saying statements such as, "I know you feel angry." Then the caregiver will explain why it is not acceptable to hit other children. Once the child understands why hitting is problematic and calms down, he or she can return to the play group.

Induction teaches children through logic and reasoning that actions have consequences. Induction also opens two-way communication between the caregiver and child. The caregiver explains consequences in a logical and calm manner. This sends the message to children that caregivers are approachable for discussing issues or problems in the future.

Induction as a form of guidance can be utilized when the child is old enough to understand reasoning. Induction is ineffective for the first year of a child's life. After the first year, induction becomes increasingly effective. By the preschool years, caregivers can begin a full conversation and use explanation techniques with the child.

## Emotions

Preschoolers experience a variety of emotions. They are not used to experiencing strong feelings and do not always control their emotions. Preschoolers often verbally and physically act out their emotions. The emotional development of the preschooler does change, however, from toddlerhood.

Preschoolers are easily pleased and like to please others. They seek emotional approval and attention from others, especially caregivers, siblings, and teachers, **7-18**. They often enjoy demonstrating what they know, but can be shy around strangers. They show attachment to caregivers and teachers and can experience stress when they are separated. Although the attachment is not as strong as in toddlerhood, preschoolers still prefer the care and company of certain adults.

forestpath/Shutterstock.com

**7-18**  Relationships with siblings are often more important to preschoolers than to toddlers.

Fears increase during the preschool years. They continue to fear the dark and unknown things or places. Similar to toddlerhood, preschoolers will imagine scary things and people. They have new fears of getting hurt. Visits to the doctor and dentist, being bitten by an insect or animal, and loud noises, such as thunderstorms are examples. They may also fear fire, large bodies of water, and other situations that may seem hurtful.

When preschoolers experience fear, anger, jealously, or sadness, they may express their emotions physically or verbally. Temper tantrums peak during ages 2 to 3, but can still occur in the preschool years. Preschoolers may yell and cry, but are less likely to bite, kick, or lay on the floor, as a toddler may do. Preschoolers have increased vocabularies and use words more often to express their feelings instead of temper tantrums.

Behind preschooler's actions are causes or issues provoking emotional responses. Family conflicts, relocating to a new area, and social problems are all examples of stressful events that could be triggering responses. Understanding the preschooler's concerns can help adults address the cause of the preschooler's emotions. Talking about preschooler's concerns and emotions can help soothe preschoolers while preparing them for interacting with other children.

## Friendships and Play

Ask 4-year-olds who their best friends are and they can most likely give you a ready answer. Friendships in early childhood provide much joy as children play together, share secrets, defend each other, and explore their world. Friends can enhance imaginary play as each takes on a role in their complex creative stories. Playing school, doctor, or acting out family roles are all part of early childhood.

Young children play differently with friends than they do with parents or other adults. Often, 3-year-olds use functional play. **Functional play** uses repetitive motions such as moving toy cars around or rocking a doll. By age 4, children begin more **constructive play** such as building with construction blocks, putting together puzzles, or creating a piece of art out of clay. They move from **associative play** (interacting while involved in parallel play) to cooperative play. In **cooperative play**, children build something together or make up elaborate rules to play.

## *Safety* Connections    *Recognizing Odd Behavior*

As children become more independent and play outdoors with less supervision, teaching preschoolers about safety involving unfamiliar people or even people the preschooler is familiar with becomes important. Children may have a preconceived notion of what a stranger is or how someone who is "bad" physically appears. Preschoolers may envision someone who is big, scary, and wearing ominous clothing. Inform preschoolers that even people who look harmless and seem friendly are not inherently safe. Similarly, not every unknown adult is "bad." Teach preschoolers to identify signs of odd behavior in adults, whether the adult is a stranger or a familiar acquaintance. This includes when an adult asks a child to

- do something or go somewhere without the caregiver's permission
- help a stranger with a task
- keep a secret
- ignore the caregiver's rules or directions

Caregivers should also instill confidence in preschoolers for how to respond in potentially dangerous situations. If preschoolers are able to recognize when a situation feels uncomfortable, they can be better equipped to respond. Teaching preschoolers to say *no* to adults and run for help might prevent a potentially dangerous situation.

### Speech Activity

Create a presentation for preschoolers about ways to identify potentially harmful strangers and situations. Include in the presentation tips the child can follow if a situation feels uncomfortable. Arrange to give your presentation to a class of preschoolers in a local school or day care.

Friendships help children learn how to interact socially, **7-19**. These interactions help children learn how to share and how to get along with others. Friendships provide support when feeling happy or sad. Friendships also help young children learn about people who are different from them. In recent years, researchers have gained an appreciation for the complexity of friendships in early childhood. In many ways, they are very similar to adult friendships.

*Randi Sokoloff/Shutterstock.com*

**7-19** Friendships are important in early childhood as they are in any stage of life.

Friendship skills are learned over time. Many 3-year-olds have difficulty understanding the concept of sharing. Sharing may still be difficult for a 5-year-old, but the concept is understood. Learning friendship skills helps young children better understand themselves, and is key to forming their own self-concept. The friendship skills in early childhood often carry forward through middle childhood and beyond.

## Cultural and Societal Influences

Very young children identify themselves as a girl or a boy. By 3 years of age, most children identify their gender. They have a sense about being a girl or a boy. This is called **gender identity**. During early childhood, children also learn the expectations that are associated with being a girl or a boy. They learn what is expected of them in how they should act, how they should feel, and what should be of interest to them. These are called **gender roles**. How does this happen? This topic goes back to the nature versus nurture debate. Some gender roles are based on biology. Much is based on what children are taught or how they are socialized.

Parents have the first, and one of the most impactful, early influences on gender expectations, **7-20**. These expectations may not be communicated in words, but are certainly communicated by actions. For example, parents may dress boys and girls differently or speak to them differently.

As children interact more with peers, this gives them a new source of information about gender. Peers tend to use forms of punishment and rewards for behaviors that are deemed gender appropriate according to the "rules" formed by different friendship groups. Often, these expectations are unspoken, but the reactions are easy to read. If a young boy chooses a princess costume for a party, the reaction of his peers may communicate to him that this is unacceptable.

StockLite/Shutterstock.com

**7-20**  Parents may treat girls and boys differently.

In addition to parents and peers, the larger culture also plays into how children view their gender and what this means. Children are motivated to fit in with others in society. They want to be included. Television, movies, music, advertisements, and toys are just some of the cultural influences that impact young children's views of themselves.

## Checkpoint

1. According to Erikson, what socio-emotional tasks do children in early childhood need to solve?
2. What are social relationships like in early childhood?
3. Describe the three main types of discipline.
4. Describe four types of play.
5. What is gender identity? Give an example of a gender role.

## Special Needs

During the preschool years, special needs become more evident. Just as in infancy and the toddler years, preschoolers have certain physical, cognitive, and socio-emotional developmental milestones they reach during early childhood, **7-21**.

Most elementary schools have screening tests for preschoolers to detect special needs. Screenings may detect physical, cognitive, or behavioral issues, and can also check for signs of giftedness. Although screening is usually a formal or standardized procedure, informal observation is equally important. The best person to informally observe a child is the caregiver. Since a caregiver spends the most time with the child, he or she may notice important details that a formal test may not be able to detect.

One behavioral disorder that can become evident during preschool is **attention deficit hyperactivity disorder (ADHD)**. ADHD affects an area in the brain and researchers believe the cause is genetic. ADHD begins to be detected when a child has difficulty paying attention or focusing on a task, is hyperactive, or impulsive both frequently and over time. Because these are common characteristics of young children, continued observation is often necessary to diagnose this special need. Other signs of ADHD that preschoolers may show include the following symptoms:

- difficulty focusing
- impulsive behavior
- hyperactivity (fidgets, has trouble waiting)
- eager to speak and shows little to no hesitation to speak
- lacks attention to detail
- does not listen when directly addressed

ADHD does not have a cure, but can be treated with therapy and medications. At the preschool age, therapy is chosen before medications. Physicians recommend medication as part of a treatment plan only if the condition severely affects the child's educational performance and social interaction. With proper treatment and management during childhood, children with ADHD can learn to manage symptoms on their own to prepare for adulthood.

| Developmental Milestones for Preschoolers | | | |
|---|---|---|---|
| **Age** | **Physical** | **Cognitive** | **Socio-emotional** |
| **3 years** | • Able to throw a ball overhand as hand and eye coordination increases<br>• Catches a ball by trapping it in arms<br>• Hops and jumps<br>• Pedals a tricycle<br>• Can draw a circle or an *X* | • Speaks in sentences between five and six words in length<br>• Begins to put puzzles with large pieces together<br>• Organizes items by color or shape<br>• Begins to count<br>• Follows more complex instructions | • Tells stories to others<br>• Shows interest in new people, objects, or experiences<br>• Shows affection for friends<br>• Tries to comfort other children when sad or hurt<br>• Engages in functional play<br>• Understands possession (*mine, hers, yours*) |
| **4 years** | • Draws shapes and letters<br>• Walks up and down stairs quickly<br>• Uses flatware, such as a fork and spoon<br>• Uses child scissors and follows cutting patterns<br>• Self-dresses | • Remembers portions of stories<br>• Identifies colors by name<br>• Uses intuition to solve problems<br>• Understands the concept of opposites<br>• Counts to 10 or higher<br>• Uses different tenses in language other than present tense<br>• Understands and interacts with programs or websites on a computer | • Engages in cooperative and constructive play<br>• Is increasingly self-aware of body, thoughts, emotions<br>• Can feel embarrassment<br>• May tell "tall tales" to protect self from consequences<br>• Begins to express anger by yelling |
| **5 years** | • Climbs<br>• Tumbles<br>• Runs<br>• Skips<br>• Learns to ride a bike with training wheels<br>• Controls toilet needs and is progressing in toilet learning | • Remembers his or her own name and address<br>• Writes his or her name<br>• Has a higher attention span<br>• Recognizes some written words | • Seeks approval from adults<br>• Is interested in other children and shows favoritism toward friends<br>• Engages in pretend play<br>• Desires to be like other children<br>• Is able to distinguish right from wrong<br>• Begins to understand the difference between reality and fantasy |

*Goodheart-Willcox Publisher*

**7-21** If these milestones are missed or delayed, there may be a greater issue preventing the preschooler from reaching the milestone.

Another common disability that is apparent by early childhood is autism. **Autism spectrum disorder (ASD)** is a broad term that describes complex developmental disabilities that lead to problems with social behaviors and communication. For example, a child with an ASD may have difficulty interacting socially with others, including close family members. The child may not be soothed from physical touch and may not attach well with a caregiver. Similar to ADHD, the child may be overstimulated by colors, sounds, or activities. The child may be averse to interacting with others including siblings or peers.

## Health Connections    Autism

Autism is a type of developmental disorder that can affect all areas of development. Only specialists can diagnose autism, but signs can be detected as early as age 1. Following are some of the signs of this disorder:

### Socio-emotional

- Lack of affection for caregiver.
- Does not smile at 6 months and little to no progress is made by 9 months.
- Shows no desire to share items of interest with caregiver.
- Is not interested in peers and has trouble interacting with other children.
- Does not make eye contact.

### Cognitive

- Does not babble at 12 months and does not speak at 16 months.
- Does not respond to or recognize name.

### Physical

- Strong preference for tasks with repetition.
- Arranges toys or items in a line in a therapeutic manner.
- Loss of normal developmental patterns between the ages of 3 and 4.
- Possible seizures.

### Research Activity

From reliable online or print resources, read more information about ASDs. What other disorders are classified as autistic?

Autism disorders often affect a child's ability to communicate, both verbally and nonverbally. This can be frustrating for all family members involved. Sometimes, the child may exhibit repetitive behaviors such as banging a spoon on the table, shaking his or her head, or throwing a toy.

ASD can range in severity, which explains the use of the term *spectrum*. ASD may be mild, moderate, or severe. Children with ASD can often attend school and interact with others at varying levels depending on the severity of the disorder.

The causes of ASDs are unknown, but something interferes with normal brain development before or after birth. At this time, there is no cure for ASDs, but behavioral and occupational therapies and medications may help treat some of the symptoms.

## Checkpoint

1. Which types of special needs typically surface during early childhood?
2. What is ADHD?
3. List five symptoms of ADHD.
4. What is autism spectrum disorder (ASD)?

## Development of School-Readiness Skills

The early childhood years are often described as the preschool years. That is, the years when children prepare to enter school. How is a child best prepared for school? Preparation for school takes more than learning colors, saying the alphabet, or writing a name correctly. Some children may already be developing basic reading skills. Age-appropriate cognitive skills are important. These are often measured by what a child knows.

In addition to cognitive skills, social and physical development readies a child for school. Learning to share, following simple instructions, verbalizing thoughts and needs, and interacting with other children are all important social skills that help a young child prepare for later school years, **7-22**. Likewise, appropriate physical development as seen in gross- and fine-motor skills is important.

*Pressmaster/Shutterstock.com*

**7-22** Social interactions can help young children prepare for the school years.

Gross-motor skills such as jumping, hopping, and balancing are related to social and cognitive abilities. Fine-motor skills such as holding eating utensils to feed one's self, holding a pencil or crayon, using scissors, and turning the pages in a book are important. Socially, motor skills help a child to fit in with his or her peers. Cognitively, motor development is related to learning. If a child is behind in his or her gross-motor skills, extra help can enhance cognitive skills.

All areas of development are important to a child's school readiness. Preschool programs are available to children who are at risk for not being ready for school. **Head Start** is a government preschool program that serves the needs of young children, especially those who are disadvantaged. By providing young children opportunities to learn school readiness skills, these programs prepare them for success in the next developmental stage, middle childhood.

## Checkpoint

1. List three important social skills that help a young child prepare for later school years.
2. How are motor skills related to social and cognitive abilities?
3. Describe the Head Start program.

## Summary

Children ages 3 through 5 undergo tremendous developmental changes. Although children develop in similar ways, each child is an individual. Each represents a different timeline for running, talking, toilet learning, and other developmental milestones.

Young children are eager to learn and are often talkative, humorous, imaginative, and love to play. Their vocabulary grows rapidly as they communicate with family and peers. They are gradually moving to more rational and logical thinking.

Young children are working toward autonomy. They become less dependent and begin to exert their will. Authoritative parents are most effective in guiding and supporting their child in decision making using firm expectations.

In early childhood, more special needs become apparent than during infancy. These include Autism Spectrum Disorders, Attention Deficit Hyperactivity Disorder, and other behavioral and learning disorders. Early intervention can help children learn and live to their full potential.

Each stage in life is a time of growth. As children grow and change, their experiences prepare them for the next stage of life. Each stage builds upon the previous one. Early childhood prepares children for the school years of middle childhood.

## Vocabulary Activity

Working in small teams, locate a small image online that visually describes or explains each of the key terms. To create flash cards, write each term on a note card and paste the image that describes or explains the term on the opposite side.

## Critical Thinking

1. **Predict.** How might lack of physical activity in the early childhood years affect quality of life in the future?

2. **Determine.** Observe a group of young children playing at a day care or on a playground. Which types of play are the children demonstrating?

3. **Draw conclusions.** Think about your favorite toys as a child. Why did these toys appeal to you? What do these choices say about you as a young child versus who you are today? Would these still be your favorite toys?

4. **Compare and contrast.** Do children need more free play or should adults direct more of their play experiences? What are the benefits of each? Why?

5. **Assess.** Think about your early childhood fears. What frightened you? What might cause these fears? How were you comforted?

6. **Cause and effect.** Watch a few hours of children's television programming. Pay attention to the commercials. What types of products are being marketed? How might this type of advertising influence young children?

7. **Identify.** How could you be a good friend to someone with a cognitive disability? How might you need to adjust your typical behaviors?

8. **Make inferences.** Imagine you are to babysit a young child with autism for an afternoon. How might you best plan your interactions and activities with the child?

9. **Analyze.** Analyze the physical, emotional, social, and cognitive development of preschoolers.

10. **Identify.** Summarize ways to promote the development of preschoolers. How would these differ for preschoolers with special needs?

11. **Analyze.** Discuss the influences of the family and society, including cultural influences, on preschoolers.

12. **Determine.** List techniques for promoting the health and safety of preschoolers. What types of safety and precautions are most important at this age?

13. **Determine.** Create a chart that shows developmentally appropriate guidance techniques for preschoolers.

14. **Draw conclusions.** Explain how appropriate medical and dental care impacts preschoolers.

## Core Skills

15. **Writing.** In a short essay, describe and analyze the developmental theories that apply to early childhood.

16. **Writing.** Write a two-page paper about your earliest memories as a young child. Are your memories tied to emotional events (happiness, excitement, fear, sadness)? Are there people included in those memories? If so, who?

17. **Speaking.** In small groups, share your experiences of working with young children. What are the challenges? What are the joys? What are your funniest observations?

18. **Math.** Find a game that teaches math concepts and play it with a young child. Which math concept is the child learning? For example, a board game may teach counting spaces or rolling dice may teach addition.

19. **Listening.** Go to a park playground, children's library, mall play area, or another public area where you can listen to the interactions between parents and young children. Listen to the conversations. Are the conversations more two-way or one-way? Are topics discussed or are only instructions given? Report your findings to the class.

20. **Reading.** Choose an age-appropriate book for a preschooler. Arrange to read the book to a group of young children. How do the children respond to the story? What do they like or dislike?

21. **CTE Career Readiness Practice.** Exceeding expectations is a way to be successful at school and in your career. Make a list of five expectations you have for yourself on a daily basis. For example, you may expect to be on time for school or meetings, complete tasks as assigned, and be courteous to others. Think about these expectations you have for yourself. Write a journal entry describing what you could do to exceed your expectations. What effect do you think exceeding expectations has on your success?

## Research

22. Search online medical sources to find out which childhood illnesses are most common. Choose one and make a list of possible treatments. Share your findings with the class.

23. Search for online articles to learn more about how young children are preoperational in their understanding of conservation of volume, mass, and numbers.

## Event Prep

24. Identify ways a healthful lifestyle is important for physical, cognitive, and socio-emotional development. Choose a topic to research further and create a 3–5 minute presentation. As a class, organize a health fair to show the presentations. Use the FCCLA *Planning Process* to guide your project planning. You may wish to expand your project by developing an FCCLA *Student Body* project. See your FCCLA adviser for further information.

# Chapter **8** Middle Childhood: Ages 6 through 10

pixcub/Shutterstock.com

# Objectives

After studying this chapter, you will be able to

- analyze the physical development of children ages 6 through 10.
- analyze the cognitive development of children ages 6 through 10.
- analyze the socio-emotional development of children ages 6 through 10.
- compare and contrast various developmental theories relating to children in middle childhood.
- identify developmentally appropriate guidance techniques for children in middle childhood.
- identify developmental milestones children in middle childhood achieve.

## Key Terms

| | |
|---|---|
| nutrient-dense | executive strategies |
| body composition | conventional morality |
| overweight | industry versus inferiority |
| obesity | bullying |
| malnutrition | stress |
| centering | hyperopia |
| reversibility | myopia |
| concrete operational stage | dyslexia |
| learning diversity | mainstreaming |
| learning styles | |

## Reading Prep

Before reading this chapter, conduct some Internet research on the growth and development of children ages 6 through 10. Choose two articles to read on the topic. As you read this chapter, think about the similarities and differences between the online articles and the text. Compare the different approaches the authors take to the material.

### Visit the G-W Learning Companion Website to:

- **build** vocabulary with e-flash cards and interactive games;
- **assess** what you learn by completing self-assessment quizzes; and
- **expand** knowledge with activities that extend learning.

G-WLEARNING.com    www.g-wlearning.com/development/

In general, during middle childhood, children are talkative, humorous, imaginative, and great at exploration. They focus on the present rather than the future. They show their feelings through laughs, smiles, and tears. Adult approval is important to them. Children are eager to learn. They are sensitive to the needs and feelings of others and are capable of making good friends. Their friendships can be both cooperative and competitive.

Each child, however, is an individual with a wide range of personality attributes, interests, abilities, experiences, and developmental patterns. While some children are talkative and athletic, others are quiet and contemplative. Some children are comfortable with change, while others are fearful of new experiences or environments.

In previous chapters, you learned that the development process is gradual. You also learned that development does not happen in the same way, at the same time, for all people. Some people, especially during childhood, will develop certain skills or abilities faster or slower than others, **8-1**.

In this chapter, you will learn about typical markers of development during middle childhood. Physical, cognitive, and socio-emotional developmental milestones will be highlighted. Because most children entering the stage of middle childhood experience the start of school, this chapter will start there as well to help you understand this fascinating life stage.

iofoto/Shutterstock.com

**8-1**  Differences in skills and abilities are normal and expected since children do not develop at the same rate.

# The School Environment

Most children enter kindergarten between the ages of 5 and 6. This is no coincidence. By then, children's language is developed to the point that their words can convey thoughts and events. Children can organize their thoughts, memorize, and use symbols such as the alphabet to represent sounds. They can count, recognize colors, and take turns.

Children of this age need to hear praise. They need approval and encouragement. The demands of school and other new experiences heighten these needs. Children want to please others, especially their teachers. They are often proud of their good work and disappointed with poor performance.

Children in middle childhood can follow two-step directions building up to multistep directions usually by the time they complete second grade, **8-2**. A teacher may instruct students to "put away your paper and pencil." Later, the teacher may be able to effectively instruct the students to "put away your paper and pencil and line up at the door" and they will be able to remember those directions.

*Monkey Business Images/Shutterstock.com*

**8-2** By the end of second grade, children are often able to use a computer keyboard and other technological devices to perform simple tasks.

## Cultural Connections   Educational Technology

Technology is used more and more as an educational tool, both in the classroom and at home. Since many children today have been surrounded with and engaged in technology since infancy, using technology can be more natural to and easy for them. They may even learn how to use technology faster than some adults.

Teachers often encourage technological use because technology can help develop critical thinking, communication, creativity, and collaboration, among other skills. These skills are transferrable for social, educational, and eventually workplace settings. Children can also begin to develop positive study skills.

For some children, using technology to learn can be fun and exciting.

Technology can engage visual, audio, and touch senses. With these senses engaged, learning activities can become game-like. When teachers or caregivers direct children to an educational website, game, or app, children can learn age-appropriate content at their own pace. As caregivers monitor technological use, they can also discover the child's preferred method of learning.

### Speaking Activity

Interview a caregiver or teacher of a child between the ages of 6 and 10. Ask about how technology is involved in the child's education. Is the technology involved in other areas of the child's development? Which technological tools does the child prefer when learning, if any?

Memory abilities increase throughout middle childhood. Learning addition and subtraction, multiplication tables, spelling, and other memorization tasks are an important part of learning. Reading ability increases. There is a strong focus on comprehension and critical thinking.

During middle childhood, children generally get along with their teachers. Although they are usually eager learners, the increasing demands of school can change some children's attitudes toward school. Teachers often notice a "slump" in attitude and interest in learning around age 9 or 10.

By the latter years of middle childhood, children are capable of much more complex thought. They can better sequence and order items. As a result, higher level math skills are achieved. They move past simple memorization to more complex memorization such as state capitols. Their short-term memory grows and experiences make more lasting impressions. Children are psychologically better able to focus on their activities. They have an interest in numbers, times, and dates. They become much more skilled at *quantifying*, or measuring the quantity of items.

At the same time, school achievements or struggles can become major issues in the lives of students. Both home and classroom expectations often increase. By the end of middle childhood, children are usually in the latter years of elementary school or, in some schools, beginning middle school. Typically, they are in the fifth and sixth grades.

## Checkpoint

1. List three tasks children can usually do by the time they enter kindergarten.
2. What type of directions can children typically follow by the time they complete second grade?
3. Describe how memory abilities increase during middle childhood.
4. At what age do teachers often notice a "slump" in children's attitudes and interest in learning?
5. List three tasks children can usually do by the latter years of middle childhood.

## Physical Characteristics and Growth

During middle childhood, children undergo several changes. Typical growth in height averages between 2 and 3 inches per year. Although adequate nutrition affects growth, height is mostly influenced by heredity. Boys and girls are similar in size and shape.

Although their physical growth in height is slow and steady, they often start gaining weight faster, **8-3**. Their left- or right-hand dominance is well established. Their coordination and endurance increase. Hand and eye coordination increases and becomes apparent when hitting a ball, shooting a basket, or playing computer games.

Many boys and girls have inward signs of changes that can be noticed through increased perspiration or sweating. They often struggle with requests

| Average Height and Weight for Children Ages 6 through 10 | | | | |
|---|---|---|---|---|
| Age (Years) | Height (in inches)* | | Weight (in pounds)* | |
| | Boys | Girls | Boys | Girls |
| 6 | 45¾ | 45 | 45½ | 43 |
| 7 | 48 | 47½ | 50¼ | 48½ |
| 8 | 50 | 49¾ | 55¾ | 54¾ |
| 9 | 52 | 53 | 62 | 62¾ |
| 10 | 54¼ | 54½ | 69¼ | 71¾ |

*Height and weight measurements are averages. Each child develops at a slightly different rate.

Goodheart-Willcox Publisher

**8-3**  During middle childhood, children's height and weight increases steadily.

to give increased attention to hygiene such as wearing deodorant or bathing regularly. As a result, the body odor can be quite apparent in school classrooms, especially after recess.

## Facial Features

The toothless smile of a child is one of the happiest smiles to see. Around 6 or 7 years of age, children often start to lose their baby teeth, **8-4**. Approximately 32 permanent teeth replace the 20 baby teeth children gradually lose. Some of these new teeth are additional molars. When the permanent teeth replace the smaller baby teeth, they often look oversized for the child's facial proportions. As facial features gradually change, teeth become proportionate to the child's mouth and jaw. Developed fine-motor skills enable children to self-care for their new set of teeth.

During middle childhood, children's facial features mature and elongate. The baby face succumbs to a more grown-up look. The need for eyeglasses is often discovered as children spend more time in school reading, drawing, and following teachers' visual explanations on the board.

## Gross-Motor Skills

"Look at me!" Do you remember the satisfaction you gained from successfully throwing and catching a ball? Doing a somersault? Running a race? Each new physical achievement made you feel grown-up and independent. Gross-motor development changes rapidly during middle childhood due to the growth and strengthening of large muscles. Learning new gross-motor skills can happen quickly.

Jenni Allen/Shutterstock.com

**8-4**  Losing the two front teeth is one of the most memorable events for children.

Children in middle childhood enjoy activities such as running, jumping, climbing, and playing catch. They are able to do a series of motions in a row such as playing hopscotch or swimming laps. They have improved flexibility and can bend and stretch easily. Their strength and speed increase, too. They can dance and ride a bike or skateboard with ease. Many children choose a favorite sport or other physical activity as they gain more skill and aptitude, **8-5**. Children vary greatly in their muscle control and coordination. These differences become very apparent as children play team sports.

## Fine-Motor Skills

Children make tremendous strides in fine-motor development as they continue to gain more control over small muscles. The muscles in children's hands develop rapidly and as a result, holding paintbrushes, pencils, building blocks, or instruments becomes easier.

In the early years of middle childhood, children can eat with a knife and fork, use scissors to cut objects out of paper, and build elaborate structures with building blocks. They can button their buttons and tie their shoes. They can enjoy written games such as connecting dots and tic-tac-toe. They can type on a keyboard. Children can draw a wide range of recognizable everyday objects such as houses, people, animals, and cars. They can print letters and make words and simple sentences.

*Monkey Business Images/Shutterstock.com*

**8-5** During middle childhood, children often become more interested in social games such as soccer or basketball.

Overall, huge leaps in fine-motor skill abilities occur during middle childhood. Although changes do not happen overnight, one skill leads to another until children are proficient at many fine-motor tasks, **8-6**. As a result, by the latter years of this stage, children can write and draw with more detail and accuracy. They are able to complete art projects that require more fine-motor precision such as creating a clay sculpture. Likewise, activities that combine mental abilities and fine-motor skills, such as board games, become more appealing.

## Nutrition

Compared to early childhood, school-age children are less finicky about food. Their taste buds are not as sensitive and some children are willing to explore new foods. For other children, pickiness in food choices becomes habitual.

*wavebreakmedia/Shutterstock.com*

**8-6**  Many children learn to play a musical instrument as finger strength increases.

Due to fine-motor skill development, children in middle childhood are capable of feeding themselves. They may still need some assistance in cutting meats or other difficult foods during the earlier years. Children in this stage often have food on their faces while eating and need reminders to chew with their mouths closed. Their appetites increase throughout middle childhood. Since their bodies are growing, frequent and nutritious meals and snacks are best.

---

## Health Connections    MyPlate

Nutritional needs of children ages 6 through 10 vary slightly according to age, weight, size, and level of physical activity. Regardless of these variable factors, school-age children need a well-balanced diet to meet the daily needs for grains, vegetables, fruits, dairy, and protein foods. According to MyPlate, the food group needs gradually increase in amount from the ages of 6 to 10. Below are the recommended food amounts for females age 6, 8, and 10 of average weight and height, who are physically active for 30 to 60 minutes per day.

| Food Group | Age 6 | Age 8 | Age 10 |
|---|---|---|---|
| Grains | 5 oz | 5 oz | 6 oz |
| Vegetables | 1.5 cups | 2 cups | 2.5 cups |
| Fruits | 1.5 cups | 1.5 cups | 1.5 cups |
| Dairy | 2.5 cups | 2.5 cups | 3 cups |
| Protein foods | 4 oz | 5 oz | 5 oz |

Recognizing nutrient-dense foods can help meet food group and nutritional needs. Examples of nutrient-dense foods include fruits, vegetables, whole-grain foods, seafood, beans, peas, and nuts. Meats and poultry that are lean or do not have much fat are also nutrient-dense choices. Other less fatty foods can be identified on the food label with claims such as *fat free*, *low fat*, or *reduced fat*. Foods that are *fortified*, or have added vitamins and minerals, may also be nutrient-dense food choices.

### Research Activity

Visit Choose**MyPlate**.gov and research the nutritional needs for males ages 6, 8, and 10. Do the nutritional needs differ from males to females? Create a daily meal plan for both a male and a female age 6, 8, or 10. Make sure your plan includes foods children would eat that fit the nutritional criteria.

During middle childhood, children are often making more of their own food choices at home, at school, and away from home. Poor nutrition may become an issue. Children should avoid junk foods that are high in calories and low in nutrients such as cookies and cakes. Instead, they can make nutrient-dense food choices. **Nutrient-dense** foods are rich in vitamins and minerals and contain relatively few calories. When foods have added sugars and solid fats, they also have many added calories. The additional calories act to dilute the nutrient density of the foods. For example, peaches are a nutrient-dense food choice. Canned peaches in heavy syrup are not because of the sugar added to prepare the syrup. The nutrients provided by the peaches are diluted by the calories from the syrup.

Proper nutrition is essential to the growth and development of children. Proper nutrition affects their physical growth, behavior, brain development, school performance, and learning. A well-balanced diet is best for children and adults of all ages. Following the MyPlate guidelines can assist children in getting the essential nutrients they need each day.

### Childhood Obesity

What is a healthy weight for children during middle childhood? Weight is not always the best gauge for determining a person's health. In fact, the amount of body fat a person carries has a much greater impact on health than total weight. **Body composition** describes the proportion of body fat to lean mass (muscle, bone, and water) in a person's body.

**Overweight** is defined as a high amount of body fat in relation to lean body mass. **Obesity** is an excessive amount of body fat. For example, a child is considered overweight when he or she is above a healthy weight, which varies by height and gender. To maintain a healthy weight, regular physical activity and healthy eating behaviors are necessary.

*Elena Elisseeva/Shutterstock.com*

**8-7** Keeping nutritious, ready-to-eat foods such as cheese cubes and fresh fruits on hand can encourage children to eat more healthy snacks.

Unfortunately, the number of overweight and obese children in America has been increasing at an epidemic rate during recent decades. Children may lead sedentary lives when safety concerns exist for active play or spaces for play simply are not convenient. In many schools, recess and physical education are reduced or eliminated. Children may frequently eat junk food as a snack instead of fruits and vegetables, **8-7**. Families may offer large portions at mealtimes. Friends and the media can negatively influence food choices. In addition, researchers have found that genetics may also play a large part in overweight and obesity conditions.

The concern over obesity is not just about appearance and being accepted by others, but is a grave health concern for Americans. For example, overweight and obese individuals are at increased risk for physical ailments such as coronary heart disease, congestive heart failure, stroke, gallstones, and osteoarthritis among others. Children are of particular concern because excessive weight and obesity in childhood can lead to diseases throughout life. Some of the weight-induced health concerns include high blood pressure, high blood cholesterol, and type 2 diabetes.

Both obesity and being overweight are complex health issues and there is no one simple remedy. Physicians can help determine a child's healthy weight and recommend a weight management plan that involves adopting healthy eating and physical activity behaviors.

## Childhood Malnutrition

Whether in urban, suburban, or rural settings, childhood malnutrition is both a national and global issue. When the body does not receive sufficient amounts of nutrients, malnutrition occurs as a result. **Malnutrition** is a chronic problem caused by a significant lack of nutrients within a person's diet.

Since children are undergoing tremendous physical and cognitive growth, malnutrition puts them at risk for poor cognitive and physical development. Children's immune systems are still developing and a lack of nutrients weakens the child's ability to fight illnesses. Malnutrition also puts children at risk for increased incidence of disease. Additional symptoms of malnutrition include fatigue, dizziness, dental problems, and a bloated stomach. By including plenty of nutrient-dense foods in the diet, malnutrition is preventable and treatable.

## Cultural Connections      Family Food Culture

The food culture of a family is another factor affecting a child's eating habits and weight. Food, as a part of culture, can determine common meal types and attitudes toward eating in the home. For example, some children may be encouraged to finish every bite on their plate, even if they are no longer hungry. Caregivers may encourage this habit to avoid wasting food or to make sure the child is well fed. Caregivers may not realize the negative effects or habits the child is learning by eating beyond the point of feeling "full."

Children can also learn negative eating habits when food is used as a reward. For example, caregivers may offer candy or fast food to a child if he or she completes all the chores. Children may then associate these food choices as special, since they are used as a reward. Children may then favor and value foods high in saturated fats and sugars over healthful snacks.

Other non-nutrient-dense foods may be prepared as main meals at home for economic or convenience reasons. Many inexpensive foods are both convenient to make and high in saturated fats and sugars. Since these meal choices may save time for meal preparation and are easy on the family budget, caregivers may favor such meals. Health consequences may be unintentional, but can have long-lasting effects. By incorporating more fresh fruits, vegetables, and nutrient-dense foods, caregivers can help promote healthful eating habits.

### Speaking Activity

Create a survey or interview to find out more about the eating habits learned by your peers when they were younger. Which types of foods were favored in their households? How do the habits they learned as children affect their eating choices today? Write a brief report of your findings.

## Physical Activity and Play

Children in middle childhood love to play, **8-8**. Many children enjoy playing team or group sports such as soccer, baseball, or tag. Team sports are beneficial for children because they gain experience interacting with others in addition to improving motor skills.

According to the *Physical Activity Guidelines for Americans*, children in middle childhood should be physically active for one hour per day. Since children between the ages of 6 and 10 tend to enjoy physical activity most of the time, achieving this goal is very plausible.

The three types of activities that can strengthen physical growth and development are aerobic, muscle-strengthening, and bone-strengthening activities. Aerobic activities such as running and riding a bike promote cardiorespiratory health, which strengthen the heart and lungs. Muscle-strengthening activities such as push-ups or sit-ups improve both large and small muscles. Bone-strengthening activities such as jumping rope or playing basketball create stronger bones to avoid bone-related diseases in the future.

*Robert Pernell/Shutterstock.com*

**8-8**  Activities that involve gross- and fine-motor skills are important to promote development during this stage.

## Sleeping

Children in middle childhood are usually great sleepers. They require about 10 hours of sleep per night. Fewer hours may result in trouble staying awake in class, challenges in learning, and low energy levels. Difficulty falling asleep, common in early childhood, ceases. Children wake up less often during the night with fewer nightmares. Their improved sleep is probably because daytime naps are less common, especially after the kindergarten year.

## Medical and Dental Care

During middle childhood, children are generally healthy. They continue to attend annual health checkups where their physical growth and development is monitored. Annual dental exams and cleanings every 6 months are a normal part of teeth care. With increased fine-motor skill abilities, children are better able to brush and floss their own teeth. They often need reminders to do so, however.

With increasing involvement in physical activities, broken bones, scrapes, cuts, strains, and sprains become more common, **8-9**. Children between the ages of 6 and 10 will still need help taking care of themselves and treating injuries. Caregivers need to be prepared to administer first aid for common injuries and other injuries that may occur, such as burns, electric shock, dental injuries, and choking.

## Cuts and Scrapes

Minor cuts and scrapes are the most common injuries in childhood. The main objective in treating a cut or scrape is to keep the wound clean from infection. The first step is to wash the wound with clean, cold water. Then stop any bleeding. This can be done by applying a sterile gauze strip or pad to the wound with pressure for about five minutes. Place antibacterial ointment over the cut or scrape. In the following hours and days, monitor the wound to check for signs of infection. Seek immediate medical attention if the cut is deep or will not stop bleeding after applying pressure, or is the result of an animal bite. Certain wounds may require stitches or a tetanus shot.

Pressmaster/Shutterstock.com

**8-9** Taking safety precautions, such as wearing a helmet while riding a bike, can help prevent some injuries.

## Strains and Sprains

With high involvement in sports and active play, sprains and strains are also common injuries for children. A *strain* occurs when the muscles or tendons are overworked and become injured. A *sprain* happens when ligaments within the joints are torn. Strains and sprains can be treated with the R.I.C.E. treatment, or *rest*, *ice*, *compression*, and *elevation*. When a sprain or strain is first detected, rest the injured part of the body. Apply an icepack to the affected area to numb the pain and reduce swelling. Using compression, wrap the wounded area for a minimum of two days. Finally, elevate the injured area to reduce swelling.

---

## *Safety* Connections    ***Preventing Common Injuries***

Some minor injuries can be prevented by using a helmet, knee and elbow pads, or other safety gear. Children can still have accidents and fall down or sprain an area, but helmets and safety pads can reduce the impact of a crash and prevent scratches, scrapes, sprains, strains, and possible dental injuries. Other accidents, such as electrical shock and burns may be prevented by ensuring outlets are covered and handles on pots and pans are turned away from the stove. Because complete prevention may not be possible, being aware of first aid techniques can help prevent infection and further damage.

### Listening Activity

Invite your school nurse to speak to the class about preventing accidents and injuries and performing first aid. You may also choose to take a first aid training course at your local hospital, through Red Cross, or the American Heart Association.

## Burns

Minor burns affect only the top layer of the skin, but more severe burns also affect deeper layers of skin and tissue. Fire, scalding water, the sun, chemicals, and electric shock can cause burns. There are three different degrees of burns, **8-10**.

For minor burns, place the affected area under cold water (not ice water). If surrounding clothing is sticking to the burn area, do not peel the clothing. After cooling, place a sterile gauze strip or bandage over the burn area. Seek immediate medical attention for serious burns.

## Electric Shock

Electric shock can occur from outlets, cords, frayed or exposed wires, and appliances. Turn off the source of electricity by disconnecting the circuit or unplugging the appliance. Separate the child from the source of the current and immediately seek medical attention. To avoid electric shock, keep appliances in good condition and away from water, and never overload outlets.

## Dental Injuries

Children during middle childhood are losing baby teeth and growing permanent teeth. Losing teeth is normal during this time. When a permanent tooth becomes loose, broken, or knocked out from sports, crashes, or another reason, the caregiver should take immediate action. Pick up the broken tooth carefully without touching the root end. Fill a container with whole milk and place the tooth inside. Cover the container. To stop bleeding, rinse the mouth with warm water and place a sterile gauze pad or ball of cotton over the affected area. Have the child apply pressure to the area by biting down on the protective cushioning. Seek immediate medical attention.

## Choking

Children may choke from pieces of food or small inedible objects, **8-11**. Initial signs of choking include coughing and gagging. Observe the child as long as he or she is coughing and can still talk and breathe. The child may

| Types of Burns | |
|---|---|
| **First-degree burn** | This is the mildest type of burn. Redness, pain, and minor swelling may be visible. First-degree burns affect only the top layer of skin. |
| **Second-degree burn** | This type of burn affects several skin layers beneath the top layer. Second-degree burns are more serious and often result in blisters, severe pain, and redness. These burns may require treatment from a medical professional. |
| **Third-degree burn** | This is the most severe burn because it affects all skin layers, underlying tissues, and possibly the nerves. Burn areas may be charred, leathery, or waxy in appearance. The burn area may be numb because of nerve damage. These burns must be treated by a medical professional and may require hospitalization. |

*Goodheart-Willcox Publisher*

**8-10**   Treatment of a burn depends on the burn type, area affected, and cause of the burn.

be able to dislodge the object by coughing. If the child's face turns blue and he or she stops coughing and is struggling to breathe, a trained person can perform immediate emergency procedures.

Both the Red Cross and the American Heart Association teach emergency procedures to relieve choking. Their methods are slightly different, however. The Red Cross teaches a "five-and-five" technique, which involves delivering five back blows between the shoulder blades, followed by five abdominal thrusts. The American Heart Association teaches the use of the abdominal thrust procedure. These procedures are often successful in dislodging an object from the victim's throat or airway passage, but sometimes CPR is needed. Immediately call 911 for further medical help.

Before attempting to perform emergency procedures such as the five-and-five technique or the abdominal thrust, take a training course through the Red Cross or American Heart Association.

| **Common Choking Hazards for Children** | |
|---|---|
| **Foods** | **Objects** |
| • Carrots | • Balloons |
| • Celery | • Batteries |
| • Cherries | • Coins |
| • Cough drops | • Crayons |
| • Hard candies | • Earrings |
| • Hot dogs | • Game pieces |
| • Ice cubes | • Rings |
| • Nuts | • Safety pins |
| • Popcorn | • Screws |
| • Raisins | • Small stones |

*Goodheart-Willcox Publisher*

**8-11**   These foods and objects are common choking hazards for children.

## Checkpoint

1. What bodily and facial changes can be expected in middle childhood?
2. Describe typical gross- and fine-motor skills of children in middle childhood.
3. What are nutrient-dense foods? Give an example.
4. What is malnutrition?
5. List three common accidents or injuries that may occur during middle childhood and describe how to treat them.

## Cognitive Characteristics and Growth

Children in middle childhood are able to answer *who, what, when, where,* and *why* questions. They become more skilled at grouping objects that belong together. About the time children reach the first grade, they begin to lose touch with creative impulses and fantasy as they put more emphasis on friends and schoolwork, **8-12**. Increases in language skills, problem solving, planning, understanding humor, and the ability to make moral decisions become more apparent. The ability to think in logical, objective terms begins to surface. As a result, learning the fundamentals of reading, writing, and mathematics are essential.

Pressmaster/Shutterstock.com

**8-12** Children must adjust to different daily schedules, concepts, and people when they enter elementary school.

## Piaget's Concrete Operational Stage

At the beginning of middle childhood, many children tend to focus on only one part of a situation. Piaget referred to this way of thinking as **centering** in his *preoperational stage* of cognitive development. For example, a 5- or 6-year-old may believe that a tall, narrow bottle of milk contains more milk than a short, wide bottle even when both are holding the same volume of liquid. Children believe this because they are only centering or focusing on one aspect such as the height of the bottle.

As with centering, children sometimes struggle with the concept of **reversibility**, which means actions can be reversed. Using the previous example, children may have difficulty understanding that pouring the milk from the short, wide bottle into the tall, narrow bottle will regain the original properties.

Within just a couple of years, children consider multiple aspects of the bottle when solving the problem. They consider both height and width. They understand reversibility. They realize that liquid is just being poured, not added or removed, **8-13**. Children also understand the concepts of time such as today, tomorrow, and yesterday. Piaget called this stage the **concrete operational stage**. During this stage, children are able to think logically based on their past experiences. Although age ranges are assigned to each stage, the transition between the preoperational stage and concrete operational stage is very gradual.

## Vygotsky's Ideas

As you learned in previous chapters, Vygotsky believed that children learn best through social interaction. During middle childhood, children may learn about addition and subtraction while actively pretending to buy and sell in a classroom grocery store with pretend money. This is more appropriate and effective

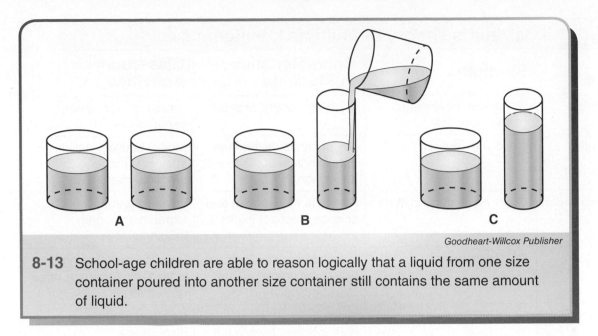

Goodheart-Willcox Publisher

**8-13** School-age children are able to reason logically that a liquid from one size container poured into another size container still contains the same amount of liquid.

than listening to their teacher lecture about money values. They learn from experiences such as riding a subway or city bus by watching their parents. Focusing on activities within the child's zone of proximal development (ZPD) will help promote the best learning opportunities during middle childhood.

## Brain Development

By the time children enter elementary school, their brains are almost at full adult size. Brain pathways become stronger. The frontal lobe part of the brain grows significantly, making it easier for children to complete increasingly difficult cognitive tasks.

The human brain is physically separated into two halves, or hemispheres, which are often called the *left brain* and the *right brain*. Each hemisphere controls different types of thinking. For example, left-brain thinking is often considered to be more logical and analytical. Right-brain thinking is often more intuitive and subjective. Because many children have strengths and weaknesses in both the left and right sides of the brain, there are different types of intelligence.

An authority on topics of intelligence is developmental psychologist Howard Gardner. His *Theory of Multiple Intelligences* proposes that people learn and process information in different ways. Gardner believes that in the process of learning, people use several types of intelligence, **8-14**. Where people differ is in the strengths of these intelligences and the ways in which they combine them to learn and carry out tasks. Understanding strengths and weaknesses in these areas can help children develop better ways to learn.

All children do not learn the same way or at the same pace. Differences in learning based on abilities or experiences are termed **learning diversity**. Do you know someone who was reading before kindergarten? Do you know someone who has a good memory, can solve complex problems, is extremely creative, but struggles to organize his or her thoughts or follow instructions? Perhaps a child has exceptional language skills. Do you know someone who shows dramatic talent? Making generalizations about intellectual ability is difficult because there are so many ways to measure ability. There is great diversity in learning.

| Gardner's Theory of Multiple Intelligences | | | |
|---|---|---|---|
| Type of Intelligence | Strengths | Characteristics in Students | Classroom Activities |
| Bodily-kinesthetic | Good with movement, hands, activities | Is athletic, crafty, or artistic | Drama, dance, crafts, experiments |
| Musical-rhythmic | Good with rhythm | Understands rhythm and tone, sings or hums to self, is emotional | Music, auditory activities, activities that require emotional sensitivity |
| Logical-mathematical | Good with logic and math | Performs well in math and science, abstract thinkers | Strategy games, experiments, math problems, logic exercises |
| Verbal-linguistic | Good with words | Is competent in written or oral communication, has large vocabulary | Reading, story telling, writing, crossword or other word puzzles |
| Interpersonal | Good with communication | Is communicative, demonstrates leadership skills, is sensitive to others | Group activities, discussions |
| Intrapersonal | Good analyzers | Is shy, reflective, goal-oriented | Journals, reflection exercises |
| Visual-spatial | Good with pictures | Has artistic skills, imaginative | Mazes, puzzles, drawing, daydreaming |
| Naturalistic | Good with recognizing and classifying living things such as plants and animals | Notices patterns and remembers things about the environment, has keen sensory skills, is interested in animals or plants, likes to be outside | Hands-on activities that are generally outdoors, field trips, journals |

*Goodheart-Willcox Publisher*

**8-14** According to developmental psychologist Howard Gardner, people possess multiple intelligences.

Learning styles are methods of taking in and processing information. Some people are visual learners. They learn by seeing information. Other people are auditory learners. They learn by hearing. Finally, some people are kinesthetic-tactile learners. They learn by experiencing and touching or doing. Figure **8-15** shows some possible classroom activities for each of these learning styles.

Most people are dominant in one learning style, but many are a combination of the three. Helping children to identify their own learning style is an important part of teaching and caregiving. Encouraging children to use all forms of learning enriches the learning process.

## Language Development

Language is composed of symbols that communicate meaning. Although children in early childhood make tremendous strides in verbal communication, children in middle childhood begin to use language to read and write. They can easily watch a television show or movie and immediately quote lines or sing lyrics they hear. The ability to memorize songs and poems comes quickly and easily for many children.

| Learning Styles and Possible Classroom Activities | | |
|---|---|---|
| **Visual Learners** | **Auditory Learners** | **Kinesthetic-Tactile Learners** |
| Displaying information on a whiteboard | Listening to lectures | Preparing demonstrations |
| Looking at photos | Listening to recordings | Doing experiments |
| Reading books | Listening to music | Dancing |
| Creating electronic presentations | Participating in discussions | Participating in drama |
| Viewing films | Viewing films | Playing games |
| Watching television | Watching television | Singing songs |
| Studying diagrams, charts, graphs | Reading out loud | Clapping hands |
| Using flip charts | Repeating information | Assembling objects with multiple parts |
| Creating timelines | Singing songs | Doing crafts |
| Using flashcards | Clapping hands | Creating projects |

*Goodheart-Willcox Publisher*

**8-15** Teaching students using a variety of methods is especially effective.

Children in middle childhood can be great storytellers. Often, their stories are quite complex and include concepts such as *before*, *why*, and *after*. By understanding more complicated concepts, children increase their vocabulary.

When children enter school, they often know over 2,000 words. For the next couple years, they will learn about 1,000 new words per year. By the latter years of middle childhood, vocabulary accelerates at great speed. By the fifth or sixth grade, children are learning about 20 new words a day and know about 40,000 words. They are capable of making quite long speeches about topics that interest them.

The sentences children speak and write start to become more complex in structure. They can understand syntax (sentence structure), grammar, and rules of writing. Multiple meanings of words are understood. Jokes and riddles are appreciated and more complex. Writing projects and reports are often assigned in fifth and sixth grade classes. These experiences are important for developing skills in later grades.

## Reading

Beginning with identification of alphabet letters followed by the recognition of letter combinations and the sounds they make, children begin to read whole words. Whole words are combined into sentences and paragraphs and before long, children are reading books. They understand the process of reading books from left to right and top to bottom.

*Monkey Business Images/Shutterstock.com*

**8-16** One of the most exciting milestones for children in kindergarten and first grade is learning to read.

Although some children learn to read before entering school, most begin the process during the kindergarten and first grade years, **8-16**. First and second graders typically make great strides in their reading ability. By the time they reach the end of their second grade year, many children are competent readers enjoying chapter books, although some may require extra assistance.

By the time children reach about 9 years of age, most can read. Some still struggle, while others are proficient. Readers are typically classified as emergent readers, developing readers, or independent readers. Emergent readers are just beginning to read. Many children begin this stage before or during the early years of elementary school. A few children, however, are still at this stage by the time they reach middle elementary school.

More children in these years are developing readers. They understand letters, sounds, and the meaning behind combinations of words. They may still be hesitant in reading alone or in front of others. Both emergent and developing readers can benefit from individualized instruction outside the classroom, **8-17**.

*Monkey Business Images/Shutterstock.com*

**8-17** Involvement in tutoring sessions or book clubs through the local library may help children improve reading skills.

Many children in the middle elementary school years are independent readers. They may be reading chapter books and enjoying complex stories. Book series are often popular with this age group. They enjoy reading stories about children their age or slightly older that play a part in adventures or fantasies. They also often enjoy reading stories about animals.

For many children, reading can be a creative experience that stimulates fantasies about becoming a crime solver, a scientist, or a mountain climber. Reading can take them into another world, another time, or another culture.

By the latter years of middle childhood, children are often proficient readers. Children may spend hours of free time pleasure reading. Reading competence is important in fifth and sixth grade as it forms the foundation for upper grades. Reading has a positive effect on all academic subjects. Instructions are better understood when reading ability and comprehension are high. Vocabulary increases when children read. Some children continue to struggle with reading, however. With assistance, children who are delayed can still become proficient readers.

## Writing

Writing goes hand-in-hand with learning to read. Children at the beginning of this stage typically know their full name, age, and address, and learn to write them accurately. As they learn to read words, they also learn to write.

Writing requires some skills that are different from reading skills, however. Fine-motor skills are required, **8-18**. Children in this stage may often write some letters backward or incorrectly, such as confusing the letters *d* and *b*. Typically, most children have mastered writing their letters correctly by the time they reach the end of second grade.

Throughout middle childhood, children become increasingly proficient at putting together thoughts into words and sentences. They begin to understand the structure of language, such as nouns and verbs. Capitalization, punctuation, and sentence structure are often learned in this stage.

## Humor

"Knock, knock. Who's there? Woo. Woo, who? Don't get so excited, it's just a joke." Children in middle childhood enjoy delivering the punch line. As cognitive skills become more sophisticated, children in this stage are able to mix words and logic, **8-19**. They enjoy rhymes and puns. Children who are not as comfortable using words for self-expression may use physical humor instead. Bathroom or off-color humor about body parts and body functions reaches its height during this stage. This may come from anxiety about controlling their bodily functions.

*Wilson Araujo/Shutterstock.com*

**8-18**  Writing skills improve throughout middle childhood as fine-motor skills increase.

Monkey Business Images/Shutterstock.com

**8-19** Humor can be used positively as a form of self-expression and as an aid to cognitive development.

Humor is also used as a coping mechanism, especially when children are uncomfortable. For example, when a classmate is reprimanded, onlooking classmates may laugh as a way of distancing themselves from the situation. Humor at the expense of others, however, is unkind and inappropriate.

## Executive Strategies

One of the most significant changes in the way children in the latter years of middle childhood think is the development of executive strategies. **Executive strategies** are skills used to solve problems. Executive strategies involve assessing problems, making goals, and developing plans to meet goals. They also involve implementing and evaluating solutions.

The ability to use executive strategies opens up a world of possibilities for classroom learning projects. Many children enjoy exploring using methods and materials for solving creative problems, **8-20**. Without guidance and encouragement, some children struggle with project completion. For example, homework may be finished, but never submitted. By the end of middle childhood, most will focus more on completion, however.

oliveromg/Shutterstock.com

**8-20** Working on projects can help children develop executive strategies.

## Kohlberg's Theory of Moral Development

Is cheating on a test wrong? Children in middle childhood are capable of making moral decisions. Some children may still be in Kohlberg's first level of moral development, or *preconventional morality*. If so, they may still use the possibility of rewards or punishment as a reason for making a decision. By cheating on a test, they might be rewarded with a higher grade or punished by being caught.

By the latter years of middle childhood, children often enter Kohlberg's second level of moral development, or **conventional morality**. In this level, children may make a moral decision based on the desire to be perceived as "good" or "bad." They may make their decision based on what laws and regulations state about cheating. School rules may forbid cheating. "Good" students do not cheat.

### Checkpoint

1. Describe Piaget's concrete operational stage of thinking.
2. What are three types of learning styles? Give an example of each.
3. How does language develop in middle childhood?
4. What are executive strategies? In what ways do they change how children in the latter years of middle childhood approach schoolwork?
5. Describe how children in Kohlberg's second level of moral development make moral decisions.

## Socio-emotional Characteristics and Growth

As Erikson described in his psychosocial stages of development, children in middle childhood are often in the stage of **industry versus inferiority**. Children are becoming more independent, and as a result, are learning more skills. Children have the opportunity to develop competencies both at school and at home. Through these activities, they develop a sense of self-confidence by becoming competent in the outside world. (Figure **8-21** provides a summary of developmental theories as they relate to middle childhood.)

Children in middle childhood like to feel grown-up and often boast about their abilities to younger children. If compared negatively to others, feelings of inferiority can surface. Adults, including parents and teachers, play a vital role in providing positive feedback to encourage children in their endeavors.

Children mature rapidly in several other ways, too. They can see their own successes and failures, as well as their strengths and weaknesses. They often tie their worth more closely with physical appearance. They start to believe that they are probably not good at everything, but have some abilities that are stronger than others. Likewise, they appreciate that others have strengths and weaknesses.

Children in this stage are often eager, friendly, and responsible. Having a job in the classroom or at home remains important. Although praise and encouragement continue to be important, children in this stage are sensitive to patronizing talk. They expect to be respected for their competence and ability and can respond well to rational explanations.

## Summary of Major Developmental Theories Related to Middle Childhood

| Type of Development | Theory | Description |
|---|---|---|
| **Cognitive** | Piaget: Concrete operational | Children in this stage can make generalizations and understand reversibility and consequences. They understand that an action or behavior can cause a chain of events resulting in a different result. They can group, subgroup, and make classification hierarchies. They become more logical during this stage. |
| | Skinner: Operant conditioning | As a child responds to a stimulus such as a punishment or reward, the child will learn to repeat or stop the response. |
| **Socio-emotional development** | Erikson: Industry versus inferiority | Children develop competencies both at school and at home. They develop a sense of self and confidence in becoming competent in the outside world. If they or others compare them negatively to others, feelings of inferiority can surface. |

*Goodheart-Willcox Publisher*

**8-21** This summary provides a review of developmental theories for children in middle childhood.

*Golden Pixels LLC/Shutterstock.com*

**8-22** Best friends often develop during middle childhood.

Socially, children in this stage want to be part of a group. They want to have friends and to be around other people, **8-22**. They want to do well. Children in middle childhood are better able to understand the feelings of others and be more compassionate. They can also show a lack of compassion and caring toward others. Their actions are not always malicious, but may be motivated by the realization that they can manipulate others.

The latter years of middle childhood can be a period of calm or a period of storm. As some fifth or sixth grade parents can tell you, the change in calm or storm of emotions can change by the minute or hour. Children often see themselves becoming "worldly" and independent. As a result, they test their knowledge by using "back talk" and rebellion. They can be eager to please or have a bad attitude, both in the same day. Adult relationships are important to them and they can develop strong bonds with their parents, teachers, coaches, or club leaders.

By the latter years of middle childhood, children tend to be very social. They like to be around other people. They enjoy being involved with groups and participating in activities such as team sports, scouts, clubs, or youth groups. Their feelings can be hurt easily by others and they often do not know how to deal with failure or rejection.

## Self-Concept

Children in middle childhood are quite industrious as they long to become more grown-up. By the time children reach this stage, most are differentiating themselves from their parents. They understand that they play a unique role and can make choices in life. One of the most common ways of defining self is to answer the question, "What do you want to be when you grow up?" In American culture, children usually respond by naming a profession such as an astronaut, veterinarian, firefighter, pop star, or race car driver. They often give creative answers such as a super hero with a special power or an inventor of gadgets for secret agents.

In middle childhood, boys and girls tend to see themselves as independent and believe they are able to function quite well on their own. They often define themselves and others in terms of their looks, material possessions, and activities.

By the latter years of middle childhood, children can be very industrious and interested in earning their own spending money, **8-23**. They tend to be self-confident in their abilities and in their strong bodies. They can also become self-conscious and feel as if everyone notices even small differences. For example, riding in a car that is not "cool" enough, getting a new haircut, wearing an item of clothing that is not in the newest fashion, or receiving an overly enthusiastic greeting in public from a parent can cause embarrassment.

Golden Pixels LLC/Shutterstock.com

**8-23** Some children perform jobs for pay such as dog walking.

---

## Cultural Connections  Positive Thoughts About the Future

During middle childhood, children begin to think about the future. They think about what they will do when they grow up and what their lives will be like. Encouraging a child to develop ideas about the future can be beneficial to his or her self-concept. With encouragement, children can see a positive future. They can feel a sense of belonging and purpose in the future. Positive thinking about the future can also affect the present. For example, if a child sets an achievable goal and takes steps toward meeting the goal in the present, he or she will begin to feel a sense of accomplishment, which is beneficial to self-esteem.

Different cultures have different ways of encouraging thoughts about the future. Many elementary and middle schools assign writing assignments asking students to visualize themselves in the future. Storybooks and role-playing may also be utilized to encourage future thoughts. Learning by observing adults nearby can also influence children's personal thoughts about the future. Other cultures may encourage plays, dancing, or another art form to encourage children to positively picture themselves in the future.

### Speaking Activity

Interview children between the ages of 6 and 10. Ask them what they want to be when they grow up and what they think their lives will be like. How can you encourage a child's future roles and build a positive future image?

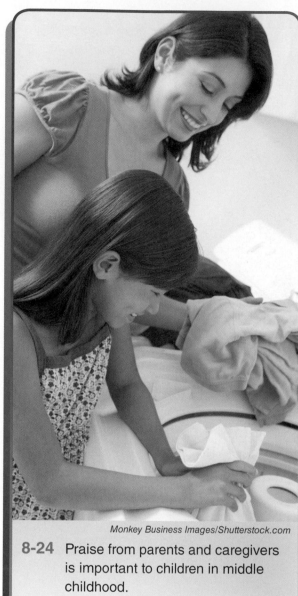

Monkey Business Images/Shutterstock.com

**8-24** Praise from parents and caregivers is important to children in middle childhood.

# Family Relationships

What are family relationships like in middle childhood? In general, children in this stage want to please others. They desire positive family relationships, especially with parents and other adults. They are eager to please. They respond well to established expectations and family rules. Children in middle childhood often tattle on others as a way to attract adult attention. When in the right mood, they are helpful with household chores. Given clear instructions, they are also very capable at completing tasks.

## Parenting Relationships

During middle childhood, children typically enjoy spending time with their families and this can be a relatively calm period in the family. They can play cards or board games, participate in recreational activities, or perform household chores alongside adult family members. Some children become interested in learning technical or mechanical skills at this age and enjoy learning from adult family members. They often enjoy their own space in the home and can care for their own belongings. They are still affectionate with both parents.

By the latter years of middle childhood, parents often notice their children's desire for increasing independence. At the same time, children need their parents or caregivers to reassure them and offer advice in difficult situations. They need their parents to spend time with them and talk to them, **8-24**. Keeping strong lines of communication open is also important. Teachers and other caregivers play an important part in this role, too.

## Sibling Relationships

Children in middle childhood can be caring toward siblings although they can also be mean at times. They can be sweet and helpful or argumentative. Sibling conflicts often increase during middle childhood. Children tend to be bossy and directive with younger siblings and annoying to older siblings. Sometimes these sibling conflicts arise because they desire to not be treated like a baby. Toward the end of middle childhood, moodiness increases and sibling relationships often become even more strained.

# Developmentally Appropriate Guidance Techniques

During middle childhood, children are becoming more independent, but still learning that actions have consequences. They need caregivers to listen to them, advise them, and set limits to ensure their safety. Using the induction form of discipline with positive reinforcement and role modeling can provide guidance to children in this stage.

As you learned in the previous chapter, using the induction form of discipline keeps the lines of communication open between caregivers and children. When a child demonstrates a negative action or behavior, the caregiver's response should relate to the misdeed of the child. Caregivers should keep the negative action separate from the child. The action may have been "bad," but the child should not feel as if he or she is a "bad person."

Caregivers should explain consequences to children in a calm, logical manner they can understand. Caregivers also need to listen to children. When caregivers listen to children's comments, they can better understand what children are thinking. This can help caregivers offer advice or explain matters further, if necessary.

Pointing out children's positive actions may also help children learn acceptable behaviors. Children are more likely to develop positive feelings about themselves when they receive praise from caregivers. This can help children build a healthy self-esteem.

Children in middle childhood are keen to imitate the behavior of adults in their lives, **8-25**. When adults respond negatively to such topics as nutrition, physical activity, education, or other people, children are also more likely to have a negative response. Children during middle childhood are establishing habits for the present and future. Role modeling positive behavior and actions can beneficially impact children in this age range.

*Rob Hainer/Shutterstock.com*

**8-25** Children pick up on the positive and negative habits of adults.

## Peer Relationships

As children move into the school environment, peers play a more important role in their lives. Best friends often occur, but may also often change. Sharing secrets, sticking up for each other, choosing partners, and play dates become a prominent part of their friendships. Birthday parties reach an all-time high. New social skills enable children to form close twosomes as well as friendship groups.

Although boys and girls comfortably play together in preschool, many children in early elementary school separate by gender. Girls play with girls and boys play with boys. These divisions can be strong and rather unfriendly at times. By the end of middle childhood, some children become interested in the opposite gender and classroom romances and crushes are common.

The opinions of peers are also valued highly, **8-26**. Fitting in becomes very important and is difficult for children who are labeled "different." Because children vary so widely in their rate of growth and development, they often stand out for being too tall, too short, too heavy, or too thin. They also stand out for not having the right clothes, living environment, activities, or skills.

Monkey Business Images/Shutterstock.com

**8-26** Peers are important for transmitting informal knowledge, fads, jokes, riddles, and other information.

Peer leaders often dominate in middle childhood. Children informally choose leaders of their peer group based on a number of criteria. Often, leaders are the children who have the new ideas or the newest toys. Attractiveness in physical appearance is prized. Outgoing children tend to be chosen as informal leaders. Children who mature early also tend to be chosen as social leaders during this stage. On a positive note, children who are kind and confident are often informal leaders. At the same time, those who fail to fit in are often not included. This is painful as children are reminded of their faults or differences.

By the latter years of middle childhood, children highly value friendships with peers. Friendships are often formed with other children from the same neighborhood or school. Although they may be more interested and aware of the opposite sex, friendships are still most commonly with the same gender.

# Case Study ???

## Single-Gender Classrooms

Kayley is looking forward to beginning third grade at a new school. After a rough second grade year, Kayley's parents decided to enroll her in an all-girls school in a nearby town. Why was second grade rough? Kayley had a hard time concentrating. The friendship "clubs" kept changing and she often came home distraught over whether she was "in or out" of the most popular recess club. A boy had been picking on her on the school bus despite efforts to have the bus driver oversee their interactions. Kayley's parents felt she would do better academically with less distractions and stress.

- Have you ever attended a single-gender school such as an all-girls or all-boys school? If so, describe the school.
- If given the opportunity, would you choose to attend a single-gender school? Why or why not? Does your reasoning lean more toward social or academic factors? What might your reasoning say about the culture in which you live?
- If not given the choice, how might your attendance at a single-gender school benefit you? How might it be detrimental to you?

## Bullying

By the time children reach this stage, they have become aware of the world around them. Unlike preschool children, they typically do not fear monsters and other imaginary creatures. Instead, they worry about school failures, unknown circumstances, death, and family problems. They may worry about world events and natural disasters. The terror of rejection is strong and motivates many of these fears. Socially, fear may be demonstrated in argumentative, aggressive, or apprehensive behaviors.

Sometimes their actions are malicious, however. Some children are more aggressive than others and if self-regulation has not been learned earlier in life, it comes out in more verbal and hostile ways during this stage.

**Bullying**, or the act of intimidating, threatening, or hurting someone else, often over a period of time, can be common during middle childhood. Verbal and physical bullying are often used. Name-calling, teasing, excluding others deliberately, laughing at someone and spreading rumors, pushing, hitting, and tripping are all forms of bullying. School personnel, parents, and other caregivers are taking bullying seriously as the effects are damaging and sometimes tragic. Building awareness through education can help.

## Play

Play is an important part of socio-emotional development in middle childhood. Group games and team sports become more appealing and popular. Children are capable of learning the basics of the game and its rules and enjoy the team effort. They are capable of organizing games that have rules and an objective and are able to wait for their turn when playing in a group or on teams. Although they understand how to take turns, they do not always want to comply. Still, they know how to share toys and often come up with rules for doing so.

At the beginning of this stage, children in middle childhood may not have the interactive skills needed to play in group games. By the time children reach the end of this stage, interactive skills have developed and teams and competition are common, **8-27**. Children do best when competition is downplayed and when they are not under pressure to perform. When competition is fierce, they may express anger and jealousy in physical ways. This is a sign that they are not emotionally ready for competition. Instead, organized sports at this age should involve fun and games.

---

## *Safety* Connections          *Stop Bullying*

Children need to be able to know what bullying is in order to better identify it. Then, children can learn ways to safely stand up to bullying and get help. Caregivers should encourage children to speak to a trusted adult if they are a victim of bullying, or if they are a witness to bullying. Adults can provide comfort and guidance to help children cope with the situation. Confidently saying "stop" might work. Other times, walking away when being bullied may be best. Friends can also offer safety and support just by being nearby. Do not encourage children to fight back, however. This might cause someone to get hurt, or get the child standing up to the bully in trouble.

### Listening Activity

Find some short online videos about bullying and after previewing to determine their suitability, watch them with a group of children ages 6 through 10. Ask children to discuss what they think about the videos.

Monkey Business Images/Shutterstock.com

**8-27** Team sports help children learn to work together with others to reach a common goal.

## Stress

In all stages of life, today's environment can promote stress. **Stress** is the body's response when faced with pressures and demands. Many people believe that childhood is the one time of life that is fairly stress-free as life seems pretty simple at home, school, and play. Children today, however, are living in a stressful world and they are feeling the effects. Typical stress inducers for children come from both inside and outside the home.

Inside the home, stress may come from changing family dynamics such as divorce, remarriage, and the subsequent changes in living conditions. Significant changes such as these may cause children to feel physical effects of stress. They may get headaches or stomach upsets. They may also feel emotional effects such as anger or sadness.

During middle childhood, children begin to focus outside their families for ideas and activities. They value the opinions of their peers. Fad toys and fashions become prominent. Popularity starts to become important as they feel the judgment of their peers and want to fit in with the crowd. School may become a source of stress. This is especially true for children who are academically struggling as well as those under unrealistic pressure to excel.

Caregivers should observe children and pay attention to signs that they might be going through a stressful situation. Children may need encouragement to talk about what is bothering them. They may not know how to deal with a situation. Sometimes just knowing that someone understands their feelings can be a big help. Children also need to be encouraged to get plenty of sleep and eat nutritious foods. Encouraging children to develop a hobby and get plenty of physical activity can also help them cope with stress.

## Cultural and Societal Influences

Reports vary on exactly how much time children spend watching television, texting, playing computer games, and surfing the Internet. There is general agreement, however, that the amount of time is significant.

Media can be educational and a positive form of communication between family members and peers. Children can use the Internet to research topics to complete schoolwork. They can learn about other cultures and customs. Children can also keep in touch with family members who live far away.

Media can also be negative. Media can eat up vast amounts of time that could be spent on more active pursuits. Media can also be used in place of face-to-face encounters that help children learn to communicate and interpret body language, facial expressions, and subtlety of language. When communication only occurs through media forms, these skills are not learned.

## Cultural Connections   Promoting Cultural Diversity

Cultural background influences the family unit, especially children within the unit. *Culture* includes holidays, food customs, religions, and traditions. A country's holidays can include all of these aspects and convey a value to children and the rest of society. For example, Thanksgiving in the United States is a family holiday where members share a meal, family time, and mention for what they are grateful. Other countries have holidays unique to their culture, which also communicate values. In Israel, students do not attend classes for Rosh Hashanah to celebrate the New Year. In Uruguay, Constitution Day is a national holiday celebrating the first constitution, which influences the government and people.

### Research Activity

Select three other countries and research one holiday from each country. Is there a U.S. holiday similar to this holiday? Which values are represented by each holiday?

Children can often be exposed to negative images and messages. Without more sophisticated problem-solving skills, children are vulnerable. Parents and caregivers should talk to children about the dangers and limit media exposure based on their personal values and standards. Parents may also preview movies, shows, or websites before their children watch or visit them to determine if the content is appropriate. Caregivers may also choose to watch shows with children or to monitor computer time. If any questionable topics come up or if children have questions, parents are there for a teachable moment.

## Checkpoint

1. According to Erikson, which socio-emotional tasks do children in middle childhood need to solve?
2. Describe relationships with family members during middle childhood.
3. Describe relationships with peers during middle childhood.
4. What is bullying? Give an example.
5. List three ways children might handle a stressful situation.

## Special Needs

Children between the ages of 6 through 10 continue to reach new physical, cognitive, and socio-emotional developmental milestones, **8-28**. During this time, special needs become more visible as milestones are either missed or delayed.

Many screenings are available during middle childhood. For example, hearing tests are usually administered at the ages of 6, 8, and 10 to detect hearing problems that may have developed after birth or early childhood. Vision and reading tests are other common screenings administered during this time.

Vision problems that often become more obvious during middle childhood may include hyperopia and myopia. **Hyperopia**, or farsightedness, is an eye condition that results in difficulty seeing objects that are near. **Myopia**, or nearsightedness, is a condition that results in difficulty seeing objects that are far away. Signs that a child may have a vision problem include holding a book too close or too far away, squinting, showing light sensitivity, or complaining of headaches and dizziness.

| Developmental Milestones: Ages 6 through 10 | | | |
|---|---|---|---|
| **Age** | **Physical** | **Cognitive** | **Socio-emotional** |
| 6–7 years | • Practices fine- and gross-motor skills to refine abilities<br>• Is active most of the time<br>• Jumps rope<br>• Rides a bike<br>• Dresses self<br>• Has improved hand and eye coordination and can draw more complex images<br>• Is able to tie own shoes | • Begins to understand the surrounding world through logic and learned experiences instead of accepting occurrences at face value<br>• Understands numeric values and can perform basic math<br>• Learns to tell time<br>• Improves reading skills<br>• Understands that objects have a specific use<br>• Understands the viewpoint of someone else<br>• Enjoys language humor<br>• Has increased ability to use technology and engage in computer games | • Follows rules in organized games<br>• Shares personal belongings<br>• Imitates adults<br>• Plays alone, but values friends<br>• Has increased ability to communicate with other children and adults |
| 8–9 years | • Has increased ability in strength<br>• Uses tools that require fine- and gross-motor skills<br>• Is capable of playing a musical instrument due to increased finger strength | • Understands concept of time, such as dates, months, and seasons<br>• Understands directions, such as left and right<br>• Has increased reading ability and enjoys reading for fun<br>• Thinks about self in the future<br>• Uses more involved computer software programs or interactive games | • Enjoys group games and activities, such as competitive games<br>• Plays with and becomes interested in members of the opposite sex<br>• Continues to show favoritism or preference for friends<br>• Begins to show more independence from caregivers<br>• Shows signs of worrying and stress |
| 10 plus years | • Growth of remaining permanent teeth occurs<br>• Has increased ability to use tools | • Has increased reading ability<br>• Has increased memory ability and can remember details<br>• Is able to write short stories and letters<br>• Begins to grasp the concept of abstract thinking<br>• Understands that questions may have more than one answer; not all answers are absolute<br>• Has increased attention span<br>• Is capable of using more advanced computer programs or applications | • Shows increasing interest in the opposite sex<br>• Values friendships with peers<br>• Is concerned about the opinions of peers regarding themselves<br>• Continues to develop and show independence<br>• Becomes more self-conscious and self-critical<br>• Is sensitive to criticism |

*Goodheart-Willcox Publisher*

**8-28** Children make significant strides in physical, cognitive, and socio-emotional development in middle childhood.

One learning disorder that may be discovered while trying to read is dyslexia (developmental reading disorder). **Dyslexia** is characterized by difficulty understanding and recognizing letters, symbols, and sentence meanings. This disorder causes reading to be very challenging and can also have an effect on verbal communication, **8-29**.

## Special Education

An intelligence test is often used to detect the extremes of special needs, which range from severe cognitive disabilities to giftedness and levels in between. Intelligence tests are controversial and numbers must be interpreted with caution. Using the *Intelligence Quotient (IQ)* rating system, a score of 70 indicates a cognitive disability and a score of 130 and above is an indicator of giftedness.

For students with special needs, the Individualized Education Program or Plan (IEP) describes the student's level of performance and how the child's special needs affect academic performance. Academic goals are determined within the program. The IEP describes specific accommodations or services the student may need to succeed in the classroom. This includes medical services. The goal of an IEP is to provide an optimum learning environment for the student to be successful in meeting his or her goals.

*Monkey Business Images/Shutterstock.com*

**8-29** With proper instruction, people with dyslexia can learn to read.

Special education provides adapted programs, extra help, specialized equipment, and materials to support students with special needs to participate in education. **Mainstreaming** is a term used to describe the placement of special needs students who show the ability to keep up with the curriculum into regular classrooms. *Inclusion* is a term used to describe the placement of special needs students into a regular classroom despite their inability to keep up academically. Inclusion focuses on the needs of the whole child.

No two children are exactly alike. The way they learn, their natural abilities, and experiences are unique. Parents, caregivers, and teachers play a critical role in helping children to use their abilities and skills to enhance learning. They also play a vital role in socializing children to accept and celebrate diversity in learning.

## Checkpoint

1. What is the difference between hyperopia and myopia?
2. What are some common characterizations of dyslexia?
3. Describe mainstreaming.
4. What is inclusion?

## Summary

During middle childhood, children undergo tremendous developmental changes. A major milestone is beginning school. Throughout middle childhood, children increase in language skills, problem solving, planning, understanding humor, and the ability to make moral decisions.

Throughout middle childhood, children's gross-motor skill development is rapid as coordination, aptitude, and balance increase. Children continue to gain more control over small muscles and fine-motor skills. They often enjoy participating in team sports. Children begin to make more of their own food choices during this stage and can better maintain a healthful weight by choosing nutrient-dense foods.

As school becomes a main focus of a child's life, it is important for parents, caregivers, and teachers to understand a diversity of learning styles in order to meet the needs of children in this stage. In the latter years of middle childhood, children are capable of much more complex thought. The ability to use executive strategies develops. The opinions of peers are also valued highly and fitting in becomes very important.

According to Erikson, children in middle childhood are often in the stage of industry versus inferiority. They are becoming more independent and learning more skills. Children have the opportunity to develop competencies both at school and at home. During this time, special needs become more visible as milestones are either missed or delayed.

## Vocabulary Activity

In teams, create categories for the terms and classify as many of the terms as possible. Then, share your ideas with the remainder of the class.

## Critical Thinking

1. **Analyze.** Analyze the physical, emotional, social, and cognitive development of children in middle childhood.

2. **Determine.** List techniques for promoting the health and safety of children in middle childhood. What types of safety and precautions are most important for this age?

3. **Identify.** Summarize ways to promote the development of children in middle childhood. How would these differ for children of this age with special needs?

4. **Analyze.** Discuss the influences of the family and society, including peers and cultural influences, on children in middle childhood.

5. **Determine.** Create a chart that shows developmentally appropriate guidance techniques for children in middle childhood.

6. **Draw conclusions.** Explain how appropriate medical and dental care impacts children in middle childhood.

7. **Make inferences.** Which gross- and fine-motor activities did you enjoy doing in middle childhood? Do you still enjoy doing these activities? Why or why not?

8. **Draw conclusions.** What factors in schools contribute to the rise in childhood obesity today?

9. **Assess.** What type of guidance techniques do you think were most effective when you were in middle childhood?

10. **Evaluate.** What are different ways that children might experience bullying?

11. **Predict.** How might communication technology be different for children today when they reach adulthood? How might they best prepare for their future?

12. **Compare and contrast.** How did you celebrate your birthday at age 7? How might you celebrate now? How do the differences reflect your development?

13. **Cause and effect.** Why do collectible toys appeal to children? How might collecting baseball cards or a series of dolls make a child feel about him or herself?

## Core Skills

14. **Writing.** In a short essay, describe and analyze the developmental theories that apply to middle childhood.

15. **Speaking.** Describe your biggest achievement in elementary school such as an art project, pet care, or sports accomplishment. Did you plan this achievement on your own or was someone else responsible?

16. **Reading.** Did you have a favorite book or book series in middle childhood? If so, reread this book or another newer book written for school-age children.

17. **Math.** Find a computer game, cards, or board game that teaches math concepts to children. Play the game with a school-age child.

18. **Listening.** Interview a school-age child about his or her friendships. Does the child most often cite same gender or opposite gender friendships? What does the child like most about his or her favorite friend? How does the child know that a friendship exists?

19. **CTE Career Readiness Practice.** Whether you see problems as challenges or opportunities, they often require creative thinking to solve them. Many new inventions come about from trying to solve a problem. Describe a situation in your life or in history where a problem led to the creation of a new way of doing things or a new invention.

## Research

20. Research childhood obesity causes, immediate and long-term effects on health and well-being, and prevention. Create an electronic presentation of your findings to share with the class.

21. Research extracurricular camps, sport activities, and arts available in your community. Which do you recommend for school-age children? Why?

## Event Prep

22. Divide the class into five groups. Each group should choose one of the following specific learning disabilities to research: dyslexia, dyscalculia, dysgraphia, dyspraxia, or dysphasia. Write a two-page paper that defines the disability, describes the effects of the disability, states how the disability is diagnosed, and identifies teaching strategies to help educate students with this disability. Create an electronic presentation of your findings to complement the research paper. You may wish to expand your project by participating in an Educators Rising *Researching Learning Challenges Competition.* See your adviser for further information.

# Chapter 9 Adolescence: Ages 11 through 19

Stephen Bonk/Shutterstock.com

## Objectives

After studying this chapter, you will be able to

- analyze the physical development of adolescents ages 11 through 19.
- analyze the cognitive development of adolescents ages 11 through 19.
- analyze the socio-emotional development of adolescents ages 11 through 19.
- compare and contrast various developmental theories relating to adolescents.
- identify developmentally appropriate guidance techniques for adolescents.
- examine factors contributing to independence.

## Reading Prep

Before reading the chapter, skim the photos and their captions. As you are reading, determine how these concepts contribute to the ideas presented in the text.

## Key Terms

| | | |
|---|---|---|
| adolescence | purging | identity versus identity confusion |
| puberty | binge-eating disorder | imaginary audience |
| pituitary gland | personal fable | peer pressure |
| asynchrony | invincible | cyberbullying |
| voice cracking | formal operations | substance abuse |
| energy balance | amygdala | extracurricular activities |
| eating disorder | prefrontal cortex | career and technical student organizations (CTSOs) |
| anorexia nervosa | metaphors | abstinence |
| bulimia nervosa | idiom | |
| bingeing | decision-making process | |

### Visit the G-W Learning Companion Website to:

- **build** vocabulary with e-flash cards and interactive games;
- **assess** what you learn by completing self-assessment quizzes; and
- **expand** knowledge with activities that extend learning.

**G-WLEARNING.com**   www.g-wlearning.com/development/

Many changes occur during the ages of 11 through 19. Students are now at the end of elementary school, in middle school, junior high, high school, or college. With the change in school settings, school expectations increase both scholastically and socially. Do you remember your first day of middle school or junior high? What about your first day of high school? You have probably changed considerably since those first days of school.

Physical changes are the most apparent during this stage of life. Cognitive and socio-emotional changes are significant, too. Older teens are in their last couple years of high school. They are facing graduation and preparing to further their education or enter the world of work. Some may join the military. With the anticipated changes that accompany graduation, expectations increase academically, vocationally, and socially.

Although these changes occur in a relatively short period of time, the makeover is gradual. Physical changes, however, can be more dramatic. In this chapter, typical markers of development will be discussed. Physical, cognitive, and socio-emotional developmental milestones will be highlighted.

## Physical Characteristics and Growth

**Adolescence** is the stage in life when humans go through the transforming process of changing from children to adults, **9-1**. Changes occur in height, weight, muscle development, and reproductive organs. The brain also changes in form and function. Although adolescents go through similar physical changes, no two have the same experiences or develop in the same way.

*Lisa F. Young/Shutterstock.com*

**9-1**    Except for infancy, the rate of physical growth and change during adolescence is unlike any other period in life.

# Puberty

**Puberty** is a period of development marked by growth spurts and sexual maturation. These changes are signaled by the body's pituitary gland. The **pituitary gland** is a small organ at the base of the brain that releases hormones that regulate growth and reproduction. *Hormones* are the chemicals that travel through the bloodstream and cause a change or development within the body.

The onset of puberty and the changes that occur during puberty happen at different times for everyone. These variations are normal and expected. The average age for the onset of puberty is 10–12 for females and 12–14 for males, but it may occur earlier or later.

## Growth Spurts

*Growth spurts* are rapid changes in both height and weight. During puberty, a person may grow as much as 3–4 inches in a single growth spurt which might last only a few months. Weight gain increases as fat tissue in females and muscle mass in males. Females increase in fat tissue at a younger age than males increase in muscle tissue.

During puberty, hands and feet grow to adult size. Since feet grow first and before the rest of the body, adolescents are often clumsy. Following the growth of hands and feet, the arms and legs increase in size. Because this growth often occurs at different rates, adolescents may appear to be "all arms and legs." This uneven timing of growth is called **asynchrony**.

## Health Connections — Changes in Skin

One common change that occurs during puberty is a noticeable difference in an adolescent's complexion or skin condition. When puberty begins, hormone levels are changing in the body. The changes in hormones cause a skin condition called *acne*, which is commonly known for the skin lesions it creates.

Acne occurs when the *sebaceous glands* (specialized structures in the pores of the skin) produce extra *sebum*, or oil. This excess production of sebum combines with dead skin cells and bacteria to clog the pores of the skin. When the pores become clogged, inflammation occurs. As a result, skin lesions such as blackheads, whiteheads, and pimples may form on the face, arms, shoulders, chest, and back.

A *blackhead* forms when inflammation occurs near the surface of the skin and pores that are partially clogged are exposed to air. The exposure to oxygen causes a reaction that changes the color of the surface to black. A *whitehead* forms when inflammation occurs near the skin's surface and the pores are completely clogged, which produces a raised white bump above the skin. Pimples are a result of the accumulation of dead skin cells, sebum, and bacteria becoming infected further below the skin's surface, which produces red bumps or pimples filled with *pus* (fluid related to the infection).

Acne can occur in mild or severe cases. Gently cleansing the affected areas and applying over-the-counter topical creams can often improve mild forms of acne. Some people may encourage "popping" the pimples to make them disappear, but this can scar and damage the skin and worsen the symptoms of acne. For more severe cases, adolescents may need to visit a *dermatologist*, or skin doctor. Dermatologists may prescribe a medication that can help relieve some symptoms of acne and offer advice on treatment methods.

### Research Activity

Create a survey for a group of adolescents to find out how they treat acne. What types of skin cleansing products and acne medications do they use? Tally the results of your survey and share your findings with the class.

There is a lag time between bone growth and muscle growth. Adolescents can go through phases when they lose relative strength in their limbs until their muscles catch up to bone growth. For example, ballet dancers may lose the ability to lift their legs high over their head. The loss of these abilities is usually short-lived.

By the latter years of adolescence, there are distinct gender differences in physical performance. Males are at a peak physical time for muscular and aerobic endurance. Females can reduce the physical performance differences they may experience with training.

## Physical Changes in Females

In addition to increases in height and weight, many other physical changes occur during puberty. In females, body fat develops around the hips, breasts, and thighs. The hips widen and the breasts enlarge. Hair grows on the body. Menstruation occurs. When menstrual cycles are just beginning, periods may be unpredictable. Eventually, many females experience regular cycles, and manage and adjust to new bodily functions.

Females increase in weight considerably during the early years of adolescence. As a result, some become overly sensitive about their weight gain. Many attempt to lose weight rather than accept the fact that their body changes are normal. This can lead to unhealthy eating behaviors, which can negatively affect growth and development and cause serious health problems.

Females often reach their full height during the middle years of adolescence. They stop growing around the age of 17. Their voices deepen into an adult voice. Older adolescents are usually more comfortable with their post-puberty bodies. Some, however, continue to be uncomfortable with how well their body meets perceived cultural expectations.

## Physical Changes in Males

Males typically do not experience a growth spurt until around the age of 14, **9-2**. On the outside, body changes and hair growth are usually covered and not visible to others. Internally, however, puberty has usually begun. The voice of a male changes during the early teen years and frequent **voice cracking**, or sporadic octave changes, occurs.

Most males are still growing in the middle years of adolescence. Although many achieve adult height around the age of 16, some continue to grow until about age 21. Males develop facial and body hair. Their voices are lower and no longer crack. Their shoulders broaden noticeably. They gain muscle mass and weight as they develop an adult male physique.

Sanmongkhol/Shutterstock.com

**9-2**  Males often do not appear physically different during the early years of adolescence.

## Cultural Connections  Body Image

"Am I normal?" is a question many adolescents often ask themselves. Adolescence can be confusing. Teens' bodies are changing at a faster rate than any time since infancy and they may not be physically developing at the same pace as their peers. New physical changes can be exciting. They can also be disconcerting for teens who believe their development is out of sync with their peers or does not meet a cultural standard. Females and males begin to feel self-conscious about their bodies.

*Body image* refers to the way people perceive their own physical appearance. Along with a personal body image, many people also have an *ideal* body type they aim to match. Teens are greatly influenced by the ideal body type most often seen in society. Many popular magazines, televisions shows, and movies feature thin women and muscular men. Teens compare their own body image to this "ideal" body image and then try to make physical adjustments. These comparisons are unrealistic and can negatively affect physical health and self-esteem.

### Research Activity

Research ways adolescents can improve body image during puberty. Create an electronic presentation of your findings to share with the class.

## Nutrition and Physical Activity

Adolescents are more responsible for their own food choices and consumption than in earlier stages of life. They learn food preparation skills and are often accountable for personal and family food shopping. Adolescents usually have very busy schedules, which may encourage unhealthy choices. They may skip important meals, such as breakfast. They may grab unhealthy items from a vending machine or fast-food restaurant. Snack choices may be high in fat and sugar, which do not provide the body with the essential nutrients needed to fuel growth.

Proper nutrition means eating all the nutrients needed through fruits, vegetables, grains, dairy, and protein foods. Eating regularly and following the recommendations from the USDA's **MyPlate** food guidance system can help adolescents maintain proper nutrition. Understanding how to manage physical activity levels also impacts weight management.

## Health Connections  Nutrient Needs for Physical Growth

During adolescence, the body is growing and changing significantly. Different nutrients are necessary to fuel growth and to strengthen and maintain cells and body tissues. Energy from foods supply and replenish the body's needs and enhance healthy growth. The three main energy sources for the body are from proteins, carbohydrates, and fats. In addition to being primary energy sources, the following are other functions and food sources of each nutrient:

- *Proteins* promote growth, maintenance, and repair of body organs. Common food sources include meats, fish, nuts, cheese, eggs, and dried beans.

- *Carbohydrates* build and repair muscles and other organs. Common food sources include pastas, whole-grain foods, sugars, and fresh fruits and vegetables.
- *Fats* produce hormones in the body. Common food sources include fish, avocados, and olives.

### Writing Activity

Keep a food log for a day to record foods you are eating. Does your daily meal plan reflect sources of proteins, carbohydrates, and fats? Write a journal entry describing ways you can incorporate more energy food sources in your diet.

The *Physical Activity Guidelines for Americans* suggest adolescents participate in 60 minutes of vigorous activity per day. Aerobic, bone-strengthening, and muscle-strengthening activities continue to be important for optimal development. Participating in activities such as team sports, dancing, or even walking can help meet these physical activity needs. Unplanned and unstructured activities, such as climbing stairs instead of taking an elevator, also count as meeting physical activity needs.

## Weight Management

*Weight management* is achieving and maintaining a healthy weight over time. Healthy body weight is determined by gender, height, and body frame. This means the weight amount will vary from person to person. Adolescents may wish to consult a doctor to determine their healthy body weight.

To maintain a healthy body weight, people must be in energy balance. To have **energy balance**, the intake of calories must equal the output of calories.

> **Energy Balance**
> Energy Intake = Energy Output

In other words, the calories gained through foods consumed should equal calories burned through everyday movements and physical activities. Energy intake involves foods consumed. Energy output involves physical activity levels. When either side of this energy equation is unbalanced, body weight is affected. For example, a person who regularly overeats and is physically inactive is likely to be overweight and at risk for obesity and other health problems. Ensuring the equation is balanced is a guide to maintaining healthy weight management.

Maintaining a healthy body weight through proper nutrition and physical activity positively affects physical and socio-emotional well-being, **9-3**. Adolescents are less likely to suffer from chronic, avoidable health problems or eating disorders. They also feel good about themselves, which helps to create a positive self-image.

## Eating Disorders

An **eating disorder** is a serious condition that involves abnormal eating patterns that can cause severe or life-threatening physical problems. Eating disorders can cause significant concerns both physically and emotionally. People who have eating disorders need professional help to treat the condition. Psychologists, nutritionists, and doctors can provide support. Early diagnosis and intervention can help enhance recovery.

*Rob Byron/Shutterstock.com*

**9-3** Health habits during adolescence impact health in adulthood.

## Safety Connections   *Avoid Fad Diets*

*Fad diets*, or popular diets promising quick and easy weight loss, are often promoted in commercials or other advertising. Fad diets appear popular, successful, and may even be endorsed by celebrities. They are termed *fad* diets because they often do not last.

Evaluating the healthfulness of a dieting plan is essential. Since fad diets often restrict eating a particular type of food, these dieting plans can be unsafe. Fad diets may especially be harmful to individuals with specific health needs. Fad diets may include pills, excluding a particular food group from the diet, or including only one food group in the diet. For example, a fad diet may claim a liquid-only diet can boost energy and promote rapid weight loss. An extreme dieting plan may involve fasting, or going lengthy periods without eating any meals.

The body requires essential nutrients to perform basic bodily functions, grow and develop, and maintain optimum health. To ensure all nutritional needs are met, people need a variety of foods to obtain sufficient amounts of each nutrient. When a diet excludes a food group or focuses on only one food group, the fad diet is likely unhealthy and should be avoided. Also, since these are short-term diets, they do nothing to promote long-term healthy eating habits needed for a lifetime of weight management.

### Reading Activity

Using magazines, books, or other reliable online sources, select one advertisement for a fad diet or dieting plan. How is the dieting plan marketed? List any claims in the advertisement for guaranteed weight loss. Then, read about the dieting plan and analyze the healthfulness of the plan. How do the suggested foods compare to USDA's **MyPlate** food guidelines?

### Anorexia Nervosa

**Anorexia nervosa**, the relentless pursuit of thinness through starvation, is one type of eating disorder. People who have anorexia have a fear of becoming overweight even though they are often underweight. Anorexia is more common in females than males, and typically develops in the early to mid-years of adolescence. Females who have anorexia are more likely to try to lose weight through self-starvation. Males, on the other hand, are more likely to try to lose weight through excessive exercising.

Anorexia can cause serious health problems, which can be life threatening. Anorexia involves self-starvation. Therefore, the body does not get the essential nutrients needed to grow, develop, and function. Body processes must slow down to conserve energy. Females typically stop menstruating because they have such a low amount of body fat. People who have anorexia also experience hair loss, fatigue, weakness, low blood pressure, and an abnormally slow heart rate. This increases the risk of heart failure.

Therapy or counseling from a professional who has experience with eating disorders is necessary to help people recover from anorexia nervosa. Nutritional counseling can help people learn ways to meet their nutritional needs.

### Bulimia Nervosa

**Bulimia nervosa** is an eating disorder that uses a bingeing and purging pattern. **Bingeing** involves consuming large amounts of food. **Purging** is a self-induced method of expelling food from the system by means such as vomiting or using laxatives. The majority of sufferers are females, often of normal weight. They are usually extremely concerned about their body weight and shape. People who have bulimia typically know their eating behaviors are abnormal and potentially harmful. Bulimia is linked to both depression and low self-esteem.

## Safety Connections — Preventing an Eating Disorder

Preventing an eating disorder is not as simple as telling someone to eat more or stop worrying about how they look. Eating disorders greatly affect physical and socio-emotional health. They develop from a combination of factors relating to self-esteem, personal body image, stress, and cultural views on the ideal body type. Since media influences of a thin body type for women and fit body type for men are nearly inescapable, these images may sneak into a person's subconscious. This means that people begin to compare their own bodies against the ideal body type most often seen in media outlets.

According to the National Eating Disorders Association, one way to prevent an eating disorder is to view television, movies, magazines, and online ads critically. Viewers are watching a crafted or photo-shopped image instead of an accurate portrayal of other people. Images and people in the media are casted by producers and executives. Individuals have the power to reject images that the media insists are popular. This is similar to songs played on the radio or other online sources. Just because a song is played constantly, that does not mean an individual must also like and accept the song. By not letting the media influence personal body image, individuals can maintain a better sense of self-esteem. Positive self-image, critical media viewing, and deemphasizing the importance of physical appearance are all ways to help prevent eating disorders.

### Writing Activity

Select one recent advertisement, television show, or movie emphasizing or favoring a certain body type. Write a letter to the producers or company that placed the advertisement expressing your view on physical appearances and why their product may be harmful or beneficial to viewers.

Bulimia nervosa can cause serious health problems because of the bingeing and purging cycle. The entire digestive system can become damaged. Chemical imbalances in the body can lead to heart failure. Damage to other organs can cause them to not function properly. As with anorexia nervosa, the most effective treatment for bulimia is therapy.

### Binge-Eating Disorder

**Binge-eating disorder** involves eating large amounts of food without taking any actions to reduce the amount of food intake. People with this disorder may be of average weight, but are often overweight because there is no purging of the excess food. Periods of bingeing are usually followed by feelings of shame or disgust and a lack of control over eating behaviors. People with this disorder are usually aware of their unhealthy eating habits, but feel they cannot or do not know how to break the negative pattern.

Health risks commonly associated with binge-eating disorder include high blood pressure, high cholesterol, diabetes, and heart disease. As with other eating disorders, the most effective treatment is therapy.

## Sleeping

Adolescents require plenty of sleep, especially during puberty. Physical changes require tremendous energy, and the body needs sleep to recover. Interestingly, hormonal changes often occur during sleep. Typically, adolescents need about 9–10 hours of sleep to feel rested.

## Health Connections — Getting Enough Sleep

Although lifestyles can be hectic during adolescence, some daily changes can help maintain regular sleeping hours. When possible, keeping a regular schedule can help save a set number of hours for sleeping. Setting a time limit for evening activities can also reduce the chances of an activity extending into sleeping hours.

The environment an adolescent sleeps in can affect the ease of sleeping. A dark, quiet room with a moderate temperature is ideal for many people. This is because a darker environment helps trigger the release of *melatonin*, a hormone that helps regulate the sleep cycle. Known as the *sleep hormone*, high levels of melatonin cause the feeling of sleepiness. At night, the pineal gland releases melatonin into the bloodstream, which helps put people to sleep. During daytime hours, melatonin is low, because bright lights interrupt melatonin levels. Therefore, falling asleep in a dark room can trigger melatonin.

Mealtimes scheduled right before bedtime can also interfere with sleep patterns. Scheduling meals earlier in the evening can reduce the impact food has on sleeping. Eating meals at an earlier time also gives the body time to digest.

### Research Activity

Some recent studies indicate that melatonin production may not begin for adolescents until later in the evening. This may be why some adolescents stay up late and have difficulty waking up early in the morning. Search online for articles about melatonin production in teens. Read the article that interests you the most and write a brief report of your findings to share with the class.

Just when adolescents require more sleep, however, there are often fewer sleep restrictions at home. Parents and caregivers often relax required bedtimes common in childhood. When adolescents do not get enough sleep, they may become irritable. They may also have more difficulty concentrating, which can negatively affect completion of schoolwork or other projects.

## Medical and Dental Care

As in early stages of childhood, adolescents continue to need to have annual health checkups. The type of exam depends on current health status and medical records from childhood. As part of a regular health exam, the doctor usually checks height, weight, and blood pressure. A doctor also inspects the body for sore, swollen areas, including tissues with lumps. A blood test may also be performed.

Beginning at age 11 or 12, a doctor may also recommend inoculations or vaccinations, **9-4**. The recommendations may differ for those who did not receive the recommended immunizations from birth through age 2.

Females and males often have their first genital exam during adolescence. Females schedule *gynecological* exams, while males schedule *testicular* exams. At gynecological exams, the doctor will conduct a Pap smear and pelvic examination. Both of these exams are to inspect for signs of abnormalities. At a testicular exam, the doctor inspects the genital area for signs of cancer or other abnormalities. Testicular cancer is the most common cancer in young men. Although these exams may seem uncomfortable and awkward, they are a normal, essential part in maintaining physical health.

## Recommended Immunizations in Adolescence*

| Immunization Name | Purpose | Age Inoculation Is Administered |
|---|---|---|
| Tdap | Protects against the bacteria that causes<br>• tetanus—muscle spasms and stiffness of the body; lockjaw<br>• diphtheria—thick mucus that forms in the back of the throat and causes difficulty breathing<br>• pertussis—whooping cough | One dose given once at age 11 or 12<br>Beginning at age 19, Td, a vaccine that protects against tetanus and diphtheria only, is recommended once every 10 years |
| Human papillomavirus (HPV) | Protects against HPV, which can cause different types of cancer, including cervical cancer for women | Three doses: one at age 11 or 12, the second dose 1–2 months after the first, and the third dose is administered 6 months after the first dose |
| Meningococcal | Protects against the bacteria that causes meningitis, an infection that causes inflammation around the brain and spinal cord | Two doses: one administered at age 11 or 12; booster dose is given at age 16 |
| Influenza | Protects against the influenza virus, which causes the flu | One dose recommended annually |

*Recommendations are reviewed and updated regularly. Check for updates at the American Academy of Pediatrics (www.aap.org).

Goodheart-Willcox Publisher

**9-4** Both males and females schedule doctor's visits to receive certain immunizations to prevent illnesses and diseases.

Galina Barskaya/Shutterstock.com

**9-5** The length of time each person wears braces varies.

Regular dental checkups are especially important during adolescence. Dentists recommend scheduling checkups every six months, with a cleaning once a year. Dentists inspect the mouth for *cavities*, or decay that causes holes in the teeth. At cleanings, dentists also check for and remove *plaque*, a sticky layer of bacteria that can appear at the base of teeth. When plaque hardens, it becomes *tartar*, which is more difficult to remove.

One common concern in adolescence is the smile structure. When teeth are crooked or interfere with speaking and eating habits, some preteens or teens opt to have braces. Braces are small devices placed over the teeth to help straighten and correct teeth alignment, **9-5**. Braces can improve speaking and eating habits and increase comfort when smiling.

The final teeth to grow in the mouth are wisdom teeth, which surface in late adolescence. Wisdom teeth are four teeth that surface in the back of the mouth, one in each corner of the mouth. Sometimes, wisdom teeth can push the surrounding teeth forward or sideways, causing pain and smile structure to change. To avoid these problems and others, dentists may remove wisdom teeth through a surgical procedure.

## Checkpoint

1. What is adolescence?
2. What key bodily changes can be expected during puberty?
3. Define *energy balance*. How does energy balance relate to managing healthy weight?
4. Describe three types of eating disorders.
5. What health exams are common during adolescence?
6. What are the final teeth to grow in the mouth? When do they typically surface?

## Cognitive Characteristics and Growth

Do adolescents think differently from children? They do in several ways. Adolescents think faster and can come up with multiple solutions to problems. They think creatively and abstractly about open-ended questions, such as "what would happen if...." They can connect how they feel to what they are thinking. Adolescents think about causes and change their behavior to adjust to what they believe, **9-6**.

*Larisa Lofitskaya/Shutterstock.com*

**9-6**   An adolescent may become a vegetarian as a result of a concern for animals.

Adolescents frequently resort to **personal fable**, a thinking pattern related to cognitive function. This means they distort and inflate the opinion of themselves and their own importance. They may believe they are on their way to becoming a pop star, a major league baseball player, or a real estate tycoon. Personal fable often leads to the dangerous belief of being **invincible**. Many adolescents believe that bad things will never happen to them because they are unique and special. In actuality, this way of thinking often causes adolescents to participate in high-risk behaviors that can be harmful and possibly result in death.

## Piaget's Cognitive Theory

Piaget described four stages of cognitive development. The **formal operations** stage is the fourth and final stage in his theory. He believed this stage starts at the beginning of adolescence.

The formal operations stage is different from the operational stage in middle childhood. During middle childhood, children tend to think in concrete terms. Their thoughts are based on what they experience in the material world. That is, those things they can feel, touch, and see.

Adolescents can reason abstractly. They use *metacognition*, which means to think about thinking. They formulate hypotheses. They think beyond the present and into the future. They can understand the structure of a math problem rather than just memorizing facts or performing basic calculations. Algebraic formulas are a good example of abstract thinking.

## Brain Development

The brain of an adolescent is both physically and functionally different from the brain of a child or an adult. By the early years of adolescence, the brain is full sized and larger than a child's brain. Gray matter, or the cells that actually make one think, have reached their peak. What changes are the connections between nerve cells. New pathways develop throughout adolescence and early adulthood. As this is happening, parts of the brain develop at different speeds.

The **amygdala**, which is the part of the brain responsible for emotional reactions such as anger, develops early. The prefrontal cortex develops later. The **prefrontal cortex** regulates emotions and impulse control. This part of the brain is still changing and maturing into early adulthood.

Because the amygdala develops more quickly than the prefrontal cortex, adolescents' brains function differently from adults, **9-7**. The actions of adolescents are guided more by emotions when making decisions or solving problems. They are more likely to act on impulse without thinking about possible consequences of their actions. They can easily become overly emotional. They are also more likely to engage in at-risk, dangerous behaviors.

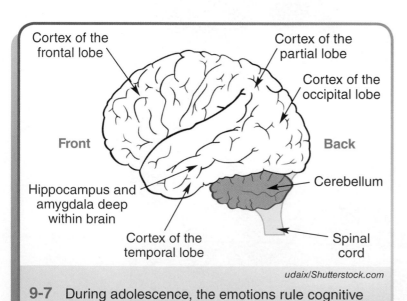

Cortex of the frontal lobe

Cortex of the partial lobe

Cortex of the occipital lobe

Front

Back

Cerebellum

Hippocampus and amygdala deep within brain

Cortex of the temporal lobe

Spinal cord

*udaix/Shutterstock.com*

**9-7**  During adolescence, the emotions rule cognitive reasoning as the prefrontal cortex continues to develop.

## Language Development

Language development continues to be important during adolescence. Following along with cognitive development, adolescents in formal operations use precise words to describe more complex, abstract thoughts. Complex thinking requires not only a larger vocabulary, but also more complex sentence structure in order to communicate these thoughts and ideas.

Adolescents differ from children in the way they can better understand and use metaphors and idioms. **Metaphors** connect two seemingly unlike objects or ideas that have something in common such as "my car is a lemon" to denote that a car has mechanical problems. An **idiom** is an expression that has cultural meaning, but does not necessarily make sense such as "a barn-burner day" to express a very busy day.

Adolescents also learn the social context of communication and can adapt their way of speaking to different situations. Communicating with a teacher should be different from communicating with peers or family members. Employees must learn how to communicate effectively with their employer. This includes not only overt communications, but also subtle messages such as when humor is appropriate or not. Learning pro-social language such as using *please* and *thank-you* are also important to being a socially competent communicator.

Since language includes more than spoken words, adolescents must learn to appropriately communicate nonverbally through their body language. The social aspect of communication is the most challenging for many adolescents.

## Cultural Connections — Slang and Pidgin Languages

In every generation, teens create new slang and phrases. Slang may include abbreviations, two or more words combined into one word, words that are shortened, or words that are entirely new. Slang may also include an already existing word, but the meaning has changed. Sometimes slang words become accepted by the greater society and can even be added into the dictionary. The process of creating slang is similar to how new languages develop and form.

Historically, when two or more cultures with different languages live in one location, a *pidgin language*, or one language that combines multiple languages, may form. The purpose of a pidgin language is to communicate with a neighboring culture who speaks a different language. Since the two cultures are living in the same area, they need to be able to communicate. Instead of picking only one language, the new language that develops combines both languages. This way, the two cultures compromise. For example, English and

Spanish combine into *Spanglish.* Speakers switch between speaking English and Spanish midsentence or story. The pidgin language has words, phrases, and grammatical structures from both languages.

In another example, Nigeria has many cultures and languages present in the country. English is the official language, but about 500 native languages are spoken throughout the country. Not everyone, however, speaks English or every native language. To ease the communication gap, a language informally called *Nigerian Pidgin* has formed. Nigerian Pidgin uses English and elements of the native language. This new language creates a common language for the entire country, which better enables communication, unity, and understanding.

### Research Activity

Historically, many pidgin languages have formed. Select one pidgin language and research the history of why the language formed.

*Giideon/Shutterstock.com*

**9-8**   Adolescents often enjoy book series that tell a story over time and in installments.

## The Decision-Making Process

**Step 1.** Decide which decisions need to be made

**Step 2.** Think through all possible alternatives

**Step 3.** Evaluate each alternative carefully

**Step 4.** Select the best alternative

**Step 5.** Act

**Step 6.** Evaluate the effectiveness of the decision

*Goodheart-Willcox Publisher*

**9-9**   Using the decision-making process is a good way to make important decisions.

### Reading and Writing

As language develops, so do reading and writing skills. Many popular book series that attract adolescents include science fiction, historical fiction, and teen or young adult novels, **9-8**. Many of these book series inspire movies or video games. To broaden students' academic knowledge base, assigned readings in high school often include classic stories.

Learning to write is a common task in elementary school. Learning to write complex thoughts is an important part of middle school and high school. Writing introductory, supporting, and summary paragraphs help adolescents organize their thoughts and ideas. Writing well is a skill that carries through life as adolescents move into adulthood and the working world.

## Decision Making

Adolescents are able to make many decisions on their own about opportunities presented to them. Their needs, wants, values, and goals all affect the decisions they make. Their brains are still developing, however, and they often make decisions impulsively. By understanding how to make decisions, adolescents can determine the best options for a given situation.

### The Decision-Making Process

The **decision-making process** is a series of steps that involves examining the issue, analyzing alternatives, and acting based on careful evaluation. There are six steps involved with the decision-making process, **9-9**.

1. **Decide which decision needs to be made.** Determine if the issue is a problem, opportunity, or goal.
2. **Think through all possible alternatives.** Usually, there is more than one possible way to address a decision.
3. **Evaluate each alternative carefully.** This may include thinking through the "best-case scenario" and "worst-case scenario."
4. **Select an alternative.** After careful evaluation of each alternative, make the choice that will be best for you.
5. **Act.** Carry through with the alternative selected.
6. **Evaluate the effectiveness of the decision.** Was this the best choice? Could the situation be handled differently next time?

### Setting Goals

The decision-making process can help in setting goals. Adolescence is a time to reflect on the present and develop ideas and desires for the future. Goals that are set and achieved during adolescence can help prepare for the future. Two types of goals are short- and long-term goals.

*Short-term goals* are goals that are achievable in the immediate to near future. For example, a student may set the goal to receive an "A" on the upcoming math test. Setting time aside to study several times throughout the week may be a necessary step to achieving this goal.

*Long-term goals* are major goals that may take months or even years to achieve. An example of a long-term goal may be to attend college or to reach a certain career standing. A series of goals may be necessary in order to reach long-term goals. For example, taking certain classes, getting good grades, and performing volunteer work may all be necessary goals that you need to accomplish in order to meet the long-term goal of attending college. Using the decision-making process and careful planning can help make these goals attainable.

### The FCCLA Planning Process

Similar to the decision-making process, the FCCLA planning process can also help identify, analyze, and execute a strategy to help set and meet a goal, **9-10**. There are five steps in the FCCLA planning process.

1. **Identify concerns.** Recognize the problem and review options.
2. **Set a goal.** Envision the goal and final outcome desired.
3. **Form a plan.** Decide the steps needed to reach the goal, answering such questions as *who, what, where, when, why,* and *how.*
4. **Act.** Carry through with the plan.
5. **Follow up.** Evaluate the success of the plan. Acknowledge and thank others for their help in meeting the goal.

---

## The Planning Process

⊙ **Identify concerns**
- Brainstorm for ideas
- Evaluate
- Narrow down

↑ **Set your goal**
- Be specific
- Consider resources

□ **Form a plan**
- Who
- What
- When
- Where
- How

□ **Act**
- Carry out plan

▦ **Follow up**
- Evaluate
- Publicize
- Recognize

**FCCLA** Family, Career and Community Leaders of America
The Ultimate Leadership Experience

*FCCLA*

**9-10** The FCCLA planning process can assist in decision making, problem solving, and goal achievement.

### Resource Management

To make decisions and reach goals, the management of resources, or items available to reach or achieve a goal, is crucial. There are many available resources. *Human resources* are resources that come from within yourself or from other people. Examples include knowledge, time, energy, and abilities. Friends and family are valuable human resources. *Nonhuman resources* include material items, such as money, books, and other objects. Amounts of nonhuman resources vary from person to person. *Community resources* are shared with others and may include such places as libraries, parks, stores, or museums.

### Accept Responsibility for Decisions

Accepting responsibility for decisions, whether they are positive or negative, is part of becoming independent. You may have heard the phrase, "people who are accountable." People who are accountable acknowledge, accept, and make decisions or actions in regard to themselves or a given topic. When a negative outcome occurs, they create a new plan to fix or better address the issue. They accept that their actions affect others and act accordingly for the best outcome.

## Kohlberg's Theory of Moral Development

Many adolescents are in Kohlberg's second level of moral development, or *conventional morality*. They are making moral decisions based on how others perceive them, **9-11**. Adolescents are also making moral decisions based

*michaeljung/Shutterstock.com*

**9-11** Adolescents seek the approval of their parents and other adults close to them, and often adopt their moral values.

## Health Connections    Time Management

Time, like other resources, is limited. Time management involves using time in a responsible way in order to meet needs, deadlines, and goals. Effectively managing time can reduce stress, which can improve well-being. Teens often have hectic, demanding schedules. Keeping a schedule can help evaluate where there may be extra time throughout the day.

One effective way to manage time is to create a priority list. A *priority list* is a list of activities a person must do or would like to do for a given time. Different factors can determine the order of a priority list. For example, a priority list may be in chronological order, which lists activities by due date. This format may be helpful for arranging school projects, assignments, and essays. Values may also determine the order of priorities. A priority list guided by values may be helpful when scheduling social activities, such as family and friend time, team practices, or time spent alone. A priority list may be guided by values, goals, and due dates.

Multitasking is another time management strategy. *Multitasking*, or dovetailing, means doing more than one thing at a time. For example, if you are doing a load of laundry while you are studying, you are multitasking.

### Writing Activity

Create a schedule for the rest of the week, including due dates and dates with friends and family. Then, create a priority list of all your assignments and activities. Try to follow your priority list, but be flexible. At the end of the week, evaluate your schedule and priority list. Was your time effectively managed?

---

on respect for laws and regulations. They think about society as a whole and respect authority. When faced with growing independence, they try out new ideas and values. They have a greater ability to express their feelings and often embrace moral or global issues with conviction. They are often idealistic and concerned about their personal impact on the world. They often think in all-or-nothing terms and tend to take a strong stance about an issue with no room for variances or exceptions.

## Checkpoint

1. Describe how adolescents frequently resort to personal fable. What is the danger of resorting to personal fable?
2. According to Piaget, what is the formal operations stage of cognitive development?
3. How is the brain development of an adolescent unique from a child or an adult?
4. What are the six steps of the decision-making process?
5. How can the decision-making process and FCCLA planning process help meet short- and long-term goals?
6. According to Kohlberg's theory, how do adolescents make moral decisions?

# Socio-emotional Characteristics and Growth

As adolescents traverse the unparalleled changes of puberty, emotions ride up and down. Hormones contribute to the emotional rollercoaster, but the developing brain also plays a part. Their focus is on establishing an identity and becoming more independent. Relationships within the family change and peers are extremely important. Adolescents want to fit in with the crowd and to be accepted. They can get involved in risky activities without thinking about consequences. Developing refusal skills is important to avoid potentially dangerous and harmful situations.

## Self-Identity

According to the theorist Erikson, the most important task of adolescence is the quest to establish identity and life roles, **9-12**. He termed this stage **identity versus identity confusion**. Adolescents subconsciously ask the questions, "Who am I?" and "What role do I play?" They experiment with different roles and integrate opinions of others to formulate a sense of self. The adolescent years are the prime time for experimentation with likes and dislikes, values and beliefs, educational and occupational goals, and role expectations. Adolescents explore what makes them unique from others.

During this time, adolescents see themselves as the main player on the stage of life. They believe that everyone is watching them. This is called **imaginary audience**. Why? With so many changes occurring, everything from entering a new school to developing a new and unfamiliar body, adolescents can be overwhelmed. They assume that everyone is watching.

Adolescents often express concern about how they look and are sensitive about their appearance, **9-13**. Self-esteem becomes closely associated with feelings about their bodies. Do they look right? Are they dressed right? Are they saying the right things? Since adolescents are experiencing rapid physical changes, they may feel awkward and gangly. Adolescents sometimes spend considerable time on their outward appearance, including grooming and experimenting with new styles in hair or makeup.

| Summary of Major Developmental Theories Related to Adolescents | | |
|---|---|---|
| **Type of Development** | **Theory** | **Description** |
| **Cognitive** | Piaget: Formal operations | Individuals become more logical and can process abstract thoughts during this stage. They can make predictions about cause and effect, use analogies and metaphors, and entertain "what if" questions. Objects do not need to be seen to be considered. |
| **Socio-emotional development** | Erikson: Identity versus identity confusion | Adolescents begin to understand and experiment with a number of different roles. A task during this stage is to integrate multiple roles such as sister, daughter, student, athlete, friend, or employee into one consistent role. If a central or core identity is not established, role confusion exists. |

*Goodheart-Willcox Publisher*

**9-12**   This figure provides a summary of developmental theories as they relate to adolescents.

How can adolescents develop positive self-esteem? Adults play an important part in helping them to better understand themselves. Providing information about changes that are occurring along with helping them learn social skills to cope with the changes is critical.

As they near the end of this stage, adolescents are often more self-assured and have fewer self-doubts. They have a better understanding of who they are and what roles they play. They do not completely achieve a sense of self-identity in adolescence, however. Most continue to define themselves well into early adulthood.

## Family Relationships

As adolescents become more interested in the opinions and friendship of others, they often formulate their own ideas and values. This process is a necessary part of becoming independent and developing self-identity. In early adolescence, however, this process is just beginning and the transition can be difficult for family members.

An adolescent's need for privacy can also affect family members. Adolescents often need to sort through the challenges and new ideas that confront them during this stage. Combined with their changing bodies, they need time alone. This sudden need for privacy can feel like a rejection to parents and siblings, especially when communication slows between family members.

Adolescents often become awkward around the demonstration of physical affection with family members. Sometimes they feel embarrassed when seen in public with parents. At the same time, they start to see parents as people. Moodiness is also a challenge for families with adolescents, **9-14**.

At the same time, adolescents can contribute greatly to the family. They are strong and capable of performing household chores including housecleaning, yard work, and child care. They are often hired for their services and can earn, save, and spend their own money.

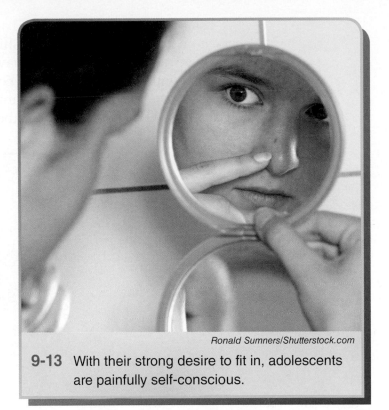

*Ronald Sumners/Shutterstock.com*

**9-13** With their strong desire to fit in, adolescents are painfully self-conscious.

*littleny/Shutterstock.com*

**9-14** During adolescence, moodiness often relates to hormonal changes, brain development, rapid growth, sexual maturation, and a growing desire to be independent.

Establishing independence and autonomy from others, especially family members, is an important part of establishing identity. Adolescents, especially during the middle years of this stage, tend to have the most conflict with parents and other adult authority figures. They also tend to confide less with their parents. This does not mean that they sever relationships with family members. Instead, adolescents develop personal and social skills to eventually become self-sufficient adults.

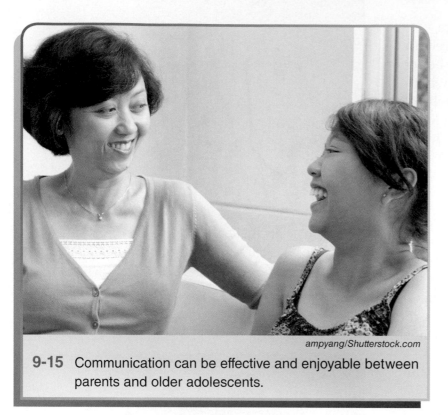

ampyang/Shutterstock.com

**9-15** Communication can be effective and enjoyable between parents and older adolescents.

By the end of this stage, adolescents often have busy schedules and are more independent. They usually spend less time with their families. When not working or going to school, they may prefer to spend more time with friends or alone. This is an important part of establishing identity outside the family.

When mutual respect is perceived, family relationships between older adolescents and adult family members can be very positive, **9-15**. Older adolescents often respect the opinions of adult family members and ask for advice. Adult family members often appreciate a new perspective on current issues. Problems may arise if family expectations and responsibilities do not change with the maturing adolescent.

## Developmentally Appropriate Guidance Techniques

During adolescence, relationships with family members may become strained. Adolescents are establishing their self-identity and gaining independence. They attempt to solve problems independently without as much parental input as in childhood. Parents often struggle with the parenting process during adolescence. Interactions with adolescents are different from those during childhood. Parents may have difficulty accepting that their child is gaining independence and maturing beyond childhood.

Easing family strains requires effort from parents and adolescents. Expressing feelings openly and without placing blame can promote effective communication. Taking the time to understand the other's point of view can ease stress for both parties.

Common types of messages involved in parent-adolescent communication are you-messages, I-messages, and we-messages, **9-16**. *You-messages*, or messages beginning with "you," can be negative and are often accusatory. You-messages focus on the other person and call attention to perceived misdeeds or missteps. *I-messages* are statements beginning with "I" that allow speakers to take responsibility for their feelings or actions. I-messages avoid placing blame on others.

*We-messages* are statements acknowledging that parents and adolescents need to work together to solve an issue. We-messages indicate teamwork and

| Message Types | |
| --- | --- |
| **Scenario** | Ben has spilled milk on the carpet. |
| **You-message** | "You spilled milk all over the carpet. You're clumsy." |
| **I-message** | "I shouldn't have placed the glass of milk so close to the edge of the table." |
| **We-message** | "We can both help clean the spill." |

*Goodheart-Willcox Publisher*

**9-16** When communicating with family members, I-messages and we-messages are more likely to bring about positive feelings.

cooperation. These types of statements can ease open communication and develop interpersonal skills. Good communication and interpersonal skills are helpful in all aspects of life, especially in school, the workplace, and social situations.

## Peer Relationships

Relationships with peers continue to be important during the adolescent years. Learning to socialize in group settings requires skills that are different from those learned in childhood. Adolescents are learning to feel at ease with the opposite gender through social group activities. They develop more mature friendship skills and become comfortable with simply talking in addition to doing activities together. Texting, phone calls, and other electronic mediums are important forms of communication.

During the adolescent years, popularity and the opinions of peers are very important. Adolescents rely on peers for advice about fashion, music, slang language, and other cultural topics. Because adolescents tend to view themselves as the center of attention, the perceived opinions of peers can have devastating effects.

## Cultural Connections   Diverse Friendships

Although building friendships with people your own age is important, establishing friendships with people of different ages can be beneficial, too. Every person can offer different information and relate unique experiences. Developing friendships with people in your neighborhood, including children, younger adults, and older adults, can help both parties develop socio-emotionally and cognitively. Speaking with people outside of your age group can expand your thought process and be socially engaging.

Developing diverse friendships is a way to learn about the experiences of people in other stages in the lifespan. You may be surprised to learn that connecting to other people of different ages is not difficult. When speaking with children, you may remember being a child yourself. When speaking to older adults, you may be surprised to find out they experienced situations similar to ones you are currently experiencing. In either direction of the lifespan, you can learn and develop your own communication and interpersonal skills by fostering diverse friendships of differing ages.

### Speaking Activity

Interview an older adult about major events that occurred when he or she was your age. Then, interview a child about the important people in his or her life. Write a brief summary about the ease or difficulty you found in relating to people of differing ages and how you relate to both people you interviewed.

## Peer Pressure

**Peer pressure** is the influence a group of people has on an individual in the same age group. Activities, styles, and peer mannerisms influence the individual. Peer pressure can be subtle or forceful. The individual may feel pressure to adopt similar habits of other classmates or the larger group, **9-17**. Peer pressure is often thought of as negative, but can also be positive.

Peer pressure is negative when an individual's physical, social, or emotional well-being is compromised, or negatively impacted. During the adolescent years, negative peer pressure and influence increases. Adolescents are more likely to engage in high-risk behaviors in response to peer pressure. At-risk behaviors may include using tobacco, alcohol, and other drugs.

Negative peer pressure also includes forms of bullying, which can occur in person or through electronic means. **Cyberbullying** is the harassment of others through a digital medium. Cyberbullying includes cruel and hurtful messages. In severe cases, legal action may be taken against the violator.

Peer pressure is positive when the comments, actions, or styles affect the individual in a positive manner. For example, encouraging a friend to study more often or offering to study with him or her to prepare for an exam is a way of exhibiting positive peer pressure.

### Substance Abuse and At-Risk Behavior

At times, adolescents may face negative pressure from peers to use tobacco, alcohol, and other drugs. Some adolescents may give in to the pressure to fit in with their peers. These behaviors are dangerous and can have harmful effects physically, socially, and emotionally.

*Pressmaster/Shutterstock.com*

**9-17** Teens often have a deep desire to fit in and to feel a sense of belonging with their peers.

## *Safety* Connections    *Inhalant Abuse*

Another form of substance abuse involves inhalants. *Inhalants* are drugs introduced to the bloodstream by sniffing, snorting, or otherwise inhaling a toxic substance to create a "high." Types of inhalants include common household items, such as cleaning, cooking, or cosmetic products. Markers, hairspray, glue, nail polish remover, gasoline, and paints are among the most common forms of inhalant abuse.

The chemicals in each product used as inhalants are harmful to the body and can cause severe damage. When a product's fumes are inhaled, the toxic chemicals travel from the lungs into the bloodstream and then to the brain. These chemicals can damage or kill brain cells. There are many risks involved with using inhalants. Short-term effects include headaches, dizziness, delayed or slurred speech, hallucinations, difficulty walking, vomiting, and fainting. Users can also develop a psychological dependency. Long-term effects include

- damage to the nose and throat
- damage to the lungs, heart, kidneys, and other muscles
- permanent loss of smell and hearing
- difficulty concentrating
- memory loss
- depression
- brain damage
- death

When inhalants are used, the heartbeat increases to a dangerous level. The heart can suddenly stop, causing cardiac arrest and death.

### Writing Activity

Create a body diagram highlighting the possible affected areas of using inhalants. Next to each body part, write the effect of the inhalant to the body. Drawings may be created by hand or electronically.

---

**Substance abuse** is the misuse of drugs to a toxic, dangerous level. Many drugs, such as nicotine, alcohol, and other substances are addictive and can cause dependencies. A *physical dependency* develops when the body becomes reliant on the presence of a drug in the system to properly function. A *psychological dependency* develops when a person uses a drug for the feeling it causes. He or she may feel the drug is needed to be "normal."

Tobacco, which includes cigarettes, chewing tobacco, and snuff, contains *nicotine*, an addictive substance. Health risks associated with nicotine include lung diseases, respiratory cancers, emphysema, and strokes. The use of nicotine can also cause complications for the throat, tongue, and teeth.

Alcohol is another commonly abused drug. Alcohol is a *depressant*, which causes the body to have delayed reactions in the nervous system. Depressants interfere with the cognitive process, affecting speech, judgment, vision, coordination, and mobility. Health risks include liver disease and cancer, heart problems, and alcoholism.

Other commonly abused substances include marijuana, cocaine, heroin, PCP, LSD, and other hallucinogens. Even legal drugs, such as prescribed and over-the-counter medications can be misused, **9-18**. These types of drugs pose great risks to health, including

- cancer
- heart, lung, and blood vessel damage
- memory loss and other brain damage
- delusional behavior
- violence
- death

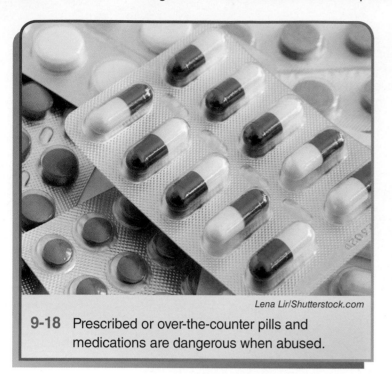

Lena Lir/Shutterstock.com

**9-18** Prescribed or over-the-counter pills and medications are dangerous when abused.

There are resources to help those with nicotine, alcohol, and other drug addictions. School guidance counselors, therapists, health clinics, hotlines, support groups, and community services often have programs to help cope with addictions and substance abuse. There are also many local and national campaigns that offer resources for recognizing and treating drug-related problems.

## Handling Peer Pressure

In childhood, children are often told what to do and how to act by their parents, teachers, and caregivers. They often hear the word *no*. "Don't touch that," "don't talk like that," and "do as I say" are common retorts. Although parents and teachers may still do a lot of directing, adolescents must learn the skills to direct their own behaviors. This often requires developing refusal skills.

Turning down unwanted sexual advances, bullying, experimenting with drugs and alcohol, or participation in criminal or illegal activities are some of the challenges adolescents face. Refusal skills include the ability to turn down an offer from another whether it is an invitation to be involved in an activity or to speak or act a certain way. Refusal skills take practice to learn.

Effectively using refusal skills requires confidence, especially when peer pressure encourages an adolescent to accept the invitation, **9-19**. Adolescents

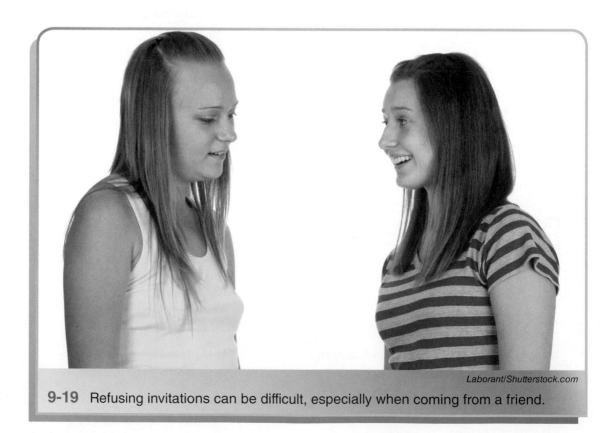

Laborant/Shutterstock.com

**9-19** Refusing invitations can be difficult, especially when coming from a friend.

benefit when they have support from friends, parents, or other adults with similar values. Sharing the challenges may result in encouragement from others to make good choices. For some adolescents, encouragement may be hard to find within their close circle of friends or even in their family. In these cases, teachers, coaches, and community leaders can lend support.

## Extracurricular Activities

Fitting in and belonging to a group are very important in adolescence. **Extracurricular activities** (those before or after school) promote group interactions and have a positive effect on social skills. Group activities, teams, and clubs provide an opportunity for adolescents to feel social acceptance. Many extracurricular activities are available to adolescents such as math clubs, scout and youth programs, sports teams, hobby groups, and classes that teach skills. **Career and technical student organizations (CTSOs)** provide students with opportunities to demonstrate social skills such as loyalty, responsibility, and leadership, **9-20**. Extracurricular activities also provide a way for adolescents to use positive peer pressure to support group members.

| Career and Technical Student Organizations (CTSOs) | | |
|---|---|---|
| **CTSO** | **Description** | **Website** |
| **Business Professionals of America (BPA)** | BPA prepares students for business and related fields by developing problem-solving, teamwork, and leadership skills. | www.bpa.org |
| **DECA** | DECA helps students develop leadership skills with a focus on marketing, business, hospitality services, finance, and entrepreneurship. | www.deca.org |
| **Educators Rising** | Educators Rising encourages leadership skills for students interested in education and related careers. | www.educatorsrising.org |
| **Family, Career and Community Leaders of America (FCCLA)** | FCCLA encourages personal development, leadership, and teamwork skills, while focusing on family, community, and career topics. | www.fccla.com |
| **Future Business Leaders of America (FBLA)** | FBLA helps students develop leadership skills with a focus on business, management, and related career fields. | www.fbla.org |
| **Health Occupation Students of America (HOSA)** | Supported by the U.S. Department of Education, HOSA helps prepare students for the health care industry with technical and interpersonal skills. | www.hosa.org |
| **National FFA Organization** | FFA prepares students for studies and careers in agriculture science, such as farming, food science, veterinarian studies, and engineering. | www.ffa.org |
| **SkillsUSA** | SkillsUSA helps students develop technical workplace skills to transition from high school to college. | www.skillsusa.org |
| **Technology Student Association (TSA)** | TSA focuses on using technology to develop leadership and teamwork skills for several career fields. | www.tsaweb.org |

*Goodheart-Willcox Publisher*

**9-20** Joining a CTSO can help develop personal, social, and workplace skills.

## Dating

During the adolescent years, dating becomes a fascinating, relevant topic. Comfort with the idea of dating is gradual. Dating readiness will occur at different ages. During the early years of adolescence, interest in the opposite gender often develops and crushes are common for both males and females. Others may still be somewhat unresponsive to dating and romantic notions. Some may not feel ready to date until early adulthood. All of these responses are normal as attitudes toward dating vary amongst individuals and cultures.

Although dating practices and customs differ, dating commonly happens in stages. The first stage is *group dating,* where peers attend or schedule activities in a mixed group setting. Groups may attend a school event or schedule an activity, such as bowling. Events may also be unplanned. Group dating provides less pressure on individuals within the group and allows friendships to develop before a romantic relationship.

The next stage of dating is *casual dating,* which involves two people spending time together in order to get to know each other. Casual dating is a way to explore the comfort level with dating and discover desirable traits in a partner. Also known as *random dating,* casual dating is not a committed, serious relationship. Individuals in the pair may be casually dating other people.

*Steady dating* occurs when the couple is exclusive and commit to each other. This stage of dating is more serious. A friendship exists in addition to a romantic relationship, **9-21**. Steady dating is more likely to occur later in this stage when adolescents are more mature and comfortable with themselves.

Some adolescents will begin to express romantic feelings in a physical manner. Engaging in sexual activity, however, can result in teen pregnancy and contracting sexually transmitted infections. Contrary to what some may believe, a girl can get pregnant the first time she has sexual intercourse. To avoid pregnancy and STIs, the

## Health Connections    Recognizing Healthy and Unhealthy Relationships

Dating relationships can be healthy and beneficial to individuals. They can also be unhealthy and destructive. Personal traits can influence the relationship. Recognizing signs of both a healthy and an unhealthy relationship is important for health and safety.

In a healthy relationship, both individuals feel comfortable around each other. They trust and support each other. Partners encourage each other to reach their maximum potential. They also challenge and learn from each other. Partners treat each other with respect, care, and consideration.

In an unhealthy relationship, a partner may try to pressure the other person to do or say something he or she is unwilling or not ready to do. Partners may have communication problems.

Other signs of a negative relationship include
- dishonesty
- jealousy
- fear and discomfort
- lack of respect and controlling behaviors

Sometimes, romantic feelings can be *unrequited,* or one-sided. Although one person may have strong feelings, the other may not share these same feelings. To be a healthy, positive relationship, feelings should be mutual.

### Speaking Activity

Interview a therapist to learn more about recognizing signs that a relationship is unhealthy and should end. Find out ways a person can end an unhealthy relationship as carefully and quickly as possible. Share your findings with the class.

bikeriderlondon/Shutterstock.com

**9-21** When both partners care for and respect each other and themselves, steady relationships can be positive and healthy.

only form of contraception that is 100 percent effective is abstinence. **Abstinence** means choosing not to engage in sexual activity. There are many nonphysical ways to show care and affection for a dating partner.

## Cultural and Societal Influences

Adolescents are surrounded by the media. With constant use of digital technology, including smartphones, the Internet, television shows, and movies, the media is a major part of daily life. Media influences may be direct or indirect. For example, movies, television shows, and available information can have an indirect influence. Issues such as the "ideal" body type, latest fashions, teen relationships, and family issues are addressed in the media. Other forms of media allow adolescents to instantly access information or to connect with others. Text and instant messaging lets friends and family communicate with each other more frequently. These types of media are more personal and can directly affect adolescents.

Social networking sites are also prominent and can be highly influential. This modern cultural trend can evoke positive and negative reactions, **9-22**. Social networking sites can be beneficial for keeping in contact with friends and family that live far away. Stories and images can be shared to reduce the feeling of physical distance and to maintain a sense of involvement.

Social networking sites can also affect self-identity. By developing a personal profile, adolescents can shape and visually see who they are and who they might like to become. Profiles can also positively affirm identity and goals. Adolescents can explore and share interests, while developing goals and ideas for the future.

Social networking sites can also negatively influence self-identity. With so many pictures, online friends, and interests displayed, adolescents may feel they are not living up to perceived standards. They may feel excluded from social activities. With instances of cyberbullying, social networking sites can create a negative effect on self-identity and may cause feelings of depression.

*Darko Zelijkovic/Shutterstock.com*

**9-22** Digital trends can evoke a variety of emotional responses, which can affect well-being.

## Case Study ???

### The Influence of Texting

Regina, a 16-year-old junior in high school, has just received a new smartphone for her birthday. Her old phone was slow and not easy to use, so she did not often use the phone. Regina is excited about her new phone's many capabilities, and is happy that she is now technologically up-to-date with her friends.

Unlike Regina's old phone, the new smartphone has unlimited texting. Her younger brother, Shaun, notices that Regina is texting all the time. In fact, she seems to be addicted to texting. Regina sends text messages at dinner, during homework, while watching movies, and even at school. Regina just earned her license and usually drives Shaun to school. Shaun is noticing that Regina has even started to read, type, and send text messages while driving. Shaun feels uncomfortable when Regina drives. When Regina is looking down at her phone, no one seems to be driving the car. Shaun is unsure of how to communicate his concerns to Regina.

- Can people become addicted to texting?
- How do Regina's texting habits while driving demonstrate personal fable and invincibility?
- How is Regina endangering herself, Shaun, and the lives of others?
- Is peer pressure a factor in Regina's texting decisions?
- How should Shaun handle the situation?

When using the Internet, it is important to remember that posting pictures and information can also have negative consequences. Once pictures and information are posted online, they are out of the control of the person who posted them. Another person can repost them without the original person's consent or knowledge. Individuals should avoid posting images or content that has the potential of causing professional or legal consequences or personal embarrassment for themselves or others.

## Depression and Suicide

Depression and suicide are prevalent in the adolescent years. Many factors contribute to depression in adolescence. A lack of friends can promote feelings of isolation. Feelings of rejection from peers, both friendships and romantic pairings, can be overwhelming. Financial problems, school struggles, being a victim of bullying, or a perceived lack of parent support can all play a part in depression for adolescents.

Adolescent females may be twice as likely to experience depression as adolescent males. Why? Some researchers believe that females focus on their feelings more often than males. Culturally, females tend to see more media images that focus on unrealistic and unattainable body images and fashions. In the early years of adolescence, females notice body changes earlier than males. When combined with school, peer, and family changes, adolescents can become overwhelmed, **9-23**.

Exposure to media or peers who focus on suicide can also impact an adolescent's likelihood of attempting suicide. Alcohol use and a family background of suicide or suicide attempts can further influence thoughts of suicide.

With depression, strong, negative feelings from inside can develop and are not easy to ignore. Loneliness, stress, or feelings of failure or inadequacy are factors. Those who are depressed often feel as though there are little to no positive things in their life. They feel a sense of hopelessness about the present and future.

Depression may lead to suicide or the decision for a person to end his or her own life. Suicide is rarely a concern in childhood. In adolescence, suicide attempts and successes are much more common. Suicide threats and attempts should always be taken seriously, as they are a symptom of much deeper issues. When hearing an adolescent share suicidal thoughts or plans with peers, never dismiss this as "idle talk." Report the information, even if told in confidence, to a trusted adult such as a parent, teacher, or school guidance counselor. Suicide is too serious and devastating to keep such secrets.

Speaking with a school guidance counselor, therapist, family member, or friend can make a difference for struggling adolescents. Community support programs including substance abuse education may help. When adolescents who are struggling are identified early, intervention can help them cope with their problems.

*Francis Wong Chee Yen/Shutterstock.com*

**9-23**  Feelings of depression can be common in adolescence.

## Health Connections    Depression Versus Sadness

Sadness and depression are two words that may be used interchangeably, but are different in meaning and severity. Sadness is a temporary state, whereas depression cannot be easily overcome. Sadness is a normal emotion that people of all ages experience from time to time. Depression, however, is more serious and does not disappear in a few days.

*Clinical depression* is a severe case of depression often caused by a combination of genetic and environmental influences. Signs of sadness and clinical depression can overlap, so it is important to distinguish the differences between these two conditions. The following are symptoms and indicators of clinical depression, which are more severe than feelings of sadness:

- changes in eating habits (consuming less or more than usual)
- weight loss or gain
- insomnia or oversleeping accompanied by fatigue
- loss of focus
- feelings of futility about the present and future
- suicidal thoughts

Periodic changes in the lifespan may trigger the effects of depression, but the person may not be clinically depressed. For example, the loss of a family member or friend can cause symptoms of depression for days, weeks, or months. If in doubt about whether symptoms indicate sadness or depression, talking about concerns with a friend, family member, or school psychologist may help. Professional counselors can help determine the stressors, treatment, and help relieve symptoms.

### Writing Activity

What are possible coping strategies for dealing with depression and sadness? Write an article outlining positive coping mechanisms for handling feelings of sadness and depression.

## Checkpoint

1. According to Erikson, what factors contribute to defining self-identity?
2. What methods can be used to improve the parent-teen relationship?
3. How do social relationships change during adolescence?
4. Describe the different stages of dating.
5. List six possible health risks involved with substance abuse.
6. List three factors that may contribute to depression in adolescence.

## Special Needs

While some adolescents are preparing for independence and adulthood, others may need extra help and support. Problems discovered during adolescence are likely to continue into adulthood. Other special needs may develop throughout the lifespan. Car accidents, sports injuries, natural disasters, or severe illnesses may occur and cause a person to become disabled. Physical disabilities may include the inability to walk, see, or hear. In these cases, cognitive ability may not be affected. Although a physical disability may be present, intellectual ability may be the same or greater than peers.

Recovery from physical disabilities requires therapy. Depending on the injury type, those who sustained an injury may need to regain strength or learn to use other muscles to accomplish the same tasks. Physical therapy offers treatment to an area through physical or mechanical strategies, such as physical activities, massages, or water or heat therapy. Occupational therapy involves recovering or building strength by practicing everyday activities, such as holding an eating utensil or self-dressing. Both types of therapy aim to prepare the person for independent living.

In combination with physical or occupational therapy, recreational and psychological therapy may also be prescribed. Recreational therapy involves recuperation through sports, dance, music, or arts and crafts activities. Recreational therapy focuses on physical and socio-emotional health. Psychological therapy can also help a person emotionally and mentally adjust to the new challenges and life changes they may be facing.

People with physical disabilities will need to adjust to new lifestyles. Special equipment such as wheelchairs, walking aids, or other aids may be needed, **9-24**. Depending on the type of accident, a person with a physical disability may also need new house accommodations to make maneuverability less challenging. With therapy and support from family and friends, people with physical disabilities can learn to live independent lives.

Teens with cognitive disabilities also begin to plan for the transitioning phase from school to adulthood. According to the Individuals with Disabilities Education Act (IDEA), the teen's parents, teachers, and other professionals examine and develop a plan for the teen's transition to adulthood by age 16. This Individualized Education Plan (IEP) outlines steps for the teen to pursue goals after high school, including postsecondary education, occupational studies, employment, or independent living.

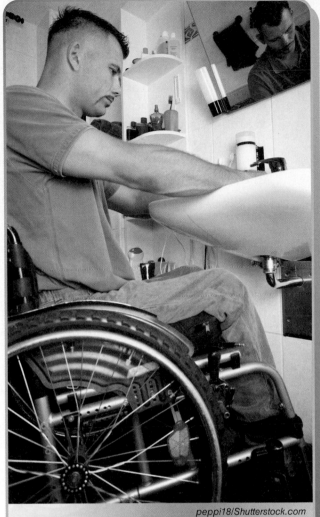

peppi18/Shutterstock.com

**9-24** Some equipment, such as wheelchairs, can help people with disabilities meet physical needs.

Some cognitive disabilities may not allow for independent living. Individuals with severe cognitive disabilities may still need the aid of family members and other support for everyday living. After students with special needs graduate high school, they may transition into an adult care facility.

 **Checkpoint**

1. How might a person obtain a physical disability that was not present in childhood?
2. How do different types of therapy help a person recover from a serious accident or injury?
3. What steps are outlined in a teen's Individualized Education Plan?

## Summary

Adolescence is the transitional stage from childhood to adulthood. Puberty causes physical and chemical changes within the body. All adolescents go through the same physical changes based on gender, but the onset of puberty and rate of development vary. Nutritional needs change from childhood and caloric intake increases.

As the body changes, so does the brain. Because the amygdala develops before the prefrontal cortex, adolescents often make emotional decisions without always thinking about consequences. Adolescents are able to make independent decisions using decision-making and planning methods.

Self-identity and peers are important socio-emotional factors to adolescents. They are often in the stage of *identity versus identity confusion*, as recognized by Erikson. Family relationships remain important, but peers can be a priority. Peers and peer pressure may influence an individual's decisions.

Special needs may develop from accidents or illnesses. Special care and equipment is needed to adjust to a new lifestyle with a disability.

## Vocabulary Activity

With a partner, choose two words from the terms list to compare. Create a Venn diagram to compare your words and identify differences. Write one term under the left circle and the other term under the right. Where the circles overlap, write two characteristics the terms have in common. For each term, write a difference of the term for each characteristic in its respective outer circle.

## Critical Thinking

1. **Analyze.** Analyze the biological, emotional, social, and cognitive development of adolescents.

2. **Analyze.** Discuss the influences of the family and society, including peers and cultural influences, on adolescents.

3. **Compare and contrast.** Interview a middle-aged adult about what his or her life was like in high school. Compare and contrast your life today with the activities, cares, and concerns of his or her day. What are the similarities and differences?

4. **Assess.** How have your interactions with parents or caregivers changed since you were a child? Do you have more responsibilities? Are there higher expectations?

5. **Evaluate.** What are the most common sources of conflict between you and your parents or caregivers? How and why will these conflicts change?

6. **Draw conclusions.** What is the hottest trend in back-to-school fashion this year? Who or what might have influenced this trend?

7. **Determine.** Think about a situation in which you experienced peer pressure. How well did you handle the situation? What refusal skills do you need to develop to better handle situations of this type?

8. **Cause and effect.** If a person is abusing drugs, what legal problems can result?

9. **Analyze.** Listen to the lyrics from several songs of a popular teen pop star. What are the themes of the lyrics? How do these lyrics relate to the concerns of adolescents?

10. **Predict.** How will social networking affect this generation of adolescents as they become adults and technology continues to advance?

11. **Determine.** List techniques for promoting the health and safety of adolescents. What types of safety and precautions are most important for adolescents?

12. **Determine.** Create a chart that shows developmentally appropriate guidance techniques for adolescents.

13. **Identify.** Summarize ways to promote the development of adolescents. How would these differ for adolescents with special needs?

14. **Draw conclusions.** Explain how appropriate medical and dental care impacts adolescents.

15. **Identify.** What are the concerns among your friends right now? How are they dealing with these concerns or fears? Are these healthy actions?

16. **Make inferences.** If you were to grow up in a culture very different from your own, how might you be different? If you immigrated to your current culture as an adolescent, how might your view of the world be affected?

## Core Skills

17. **Writing.** Write a two-page letter to a young adolescent who will soon be experiencing puberty.

18. **Speaking.** Working in pairs, share with a classmate what your first day of middle school, junior high, or another new experience was like.

19. **Listening.** Listen to a conversation between young adolescents. What subjects are covered? Do they use unique words or slang?

20. **Math.** Some adolescents have access to a car. Given your mileage specifics, determine the cost of gas to drive to school (and work and/or sports activities) each day based on today's average price of gas.

21. **Writing.** In a short essay, describe and analyze the developmental theories that apply to the growth and development of adolescence.

22. **CTE Career Readiness Practice.** You will have a number of options to consider when thinking about future career plans. Approaching the different options available to you in a logical way can help in the decision-making process. Create a chart showing the pros and cons of pursuing a career that requires additional schooling after high school. List all the positives on the left under the *Pros* heading and any negatives on the right under the *Cons* heading. Reflect on the items. Has the list helped you come to a decision? Why or why not?

## Research

23. Research colleges and universities that interest you. Make a list of attributes that attract you most.

24. Using a data collection method of your choice, conduct a research experiment in your school to determine how many students have ever texted while driving. Compile the data and create a presentation about texting and driving to share with the student body.

## Event Prep

25. Choose one of the topics from this chapter, such as body image, weight management, handling peer pressure, or dating, to research further. Create a three to five minute oral presentation on your topic. Be sure to practice your speech until you feel comfortable and confident communicating all the information you are presenting. You may wish to expand your project by participating in an Educators Rising *Public Speaking Competition*. See your adviser for further information.

Katrina Brown/Shutterstock.com

# Objectives

After studying this chapter, you will be able to

- describe events that commonly occur during the transitional stage of young adulthood.
- analyze the physical development of young adults ages 20 through 39.
- analyze the cognitive development of young adults ages 20 through 39.
- analyze the socio-emotional development of young adults ages 20 through 39.
- summarize how young adults form attachments and establish committed relationships.
- identify special needs that people may develop or acquire during early adulthood.

## Reading Prep

As you read this chapter, determine the purpose or point of view of the author. What aspects of the text help to establish this purpose or point of view?

## Key Terms

| | | |
|---|---|---|
| social clock | postconventional morality | affectionate love |
| insomnia | intimacy versus isolation | romantic love |
| binge drinking | intimacy | consummate love |
| alcoholism | secure attachment style | infatuation |
| fluid intelligence | avoidant attachment style | compromise |
| crystallized intelligence | anxious attachment style | unconditional love |
| postformal stage | | |

### Visit the G-W Learning Companion Website to:

- **build** vocabulary with e-flash cards and interactive games;
- **assess** what you learn by completing self-assessment quizzes; and
- **expand** knowledge with activities that extend learning.

G-WLEARNING.com   www.g-wlearning.com/development/

In this chapter, you will learn about physical qualities and changes that occur during early adulthood between the ages of 20 through 39. Brain and subsequent cognitive changes along with socio-emotional changes will also be discussed. Note that this sphere of development focuses more on personal decisions and lifestyle changes than on growth and development characteristics. Family is a critical issue during this stage of life. Much emphasis is on relationships, and the importance of such decisions as marriage and parenting. Because people entering this stage are establishing their self-identity as adults, this chapter will start there as well.

## Becoming an Adult

In the U.S., the law often treats teens as adults when they become 18 years of age. They reach important milestones such as being eligible to vote. They can also be tried as adults in a court of law. Upon reaching their eighteenth birthday, however, teens do not suddenly become self-dependent adults. The transition from teen to independent adult varies for everyone. This is the *transitional stage of young adulthood*, which typically occurs between ages 19 through 26.

For many people, self-definition of adulthood does not happen until they meet certain social roles and expectations. Social expectations of adulthood vary by culture and are often tied to social clock expectations. **Social clock** refers to cultural expectations of when major life milestones should occur. These expectations may include completing an education, living on their own, establishing a career, marrying, or having children. Family members often reinforce these expectations.

Despite family and cultural expectations, there comes a time when young adults must claim responsibility for their own well-being. Many young adults leave their parental home and establish their own independent lifestyle. Making good decisions and taking care of one's needs and the needs of others become more evident.

## Cultural Connections    Coming of Age

Each culture defines *adult* differently and symbolizes the start of adulthood in different ways. Some cultures have certain ages that determine adulthood and others decide adulthood by events. The following are traditions and ceremonies that mark the beginning of adulthood.

- **Bar and bat mitzvahs.** In Jewish tradition, when adolescents reach age 13, they celebrate their entrance into adulthood by holding a religious ceremony. Boys become *bar mitzvahs* and girls become *bat mitzvahs*. These ceremonies also signify continuing religious education and upholding traditions.
- **Quinceañera.** In Latin American cultures, a quinceañera is held as a celebration when a girl reaches age 15. The first part of the quinceañera focuses on religion. The second

part of the ceremony is celebrated with a festive gathering. Family and friends celebrate as the girl is introduced to society as a young woman.

- **The Debut.** In Filipino culture, when a female reaches 18 years of age, a grand celebration, or debut, is held for her. The celebration announces the debutante to society as an adult. The *cotillion* is an elaborate dance with frequent changing of partners that is a traditional part of the debut celebration.

### Research Activity

Select one culture and research the coming-of-age traditions. Create a pamphlet or electronic presentation displaying your research to share with the class.

## Transitioning from High School

As people transition out of high school, they often become more responsible for making decisions that can affect their lifestyle for years to come. There are many *postsecondary options* or choices available after the completion of high school. Some people may decide to continue with education and attend a college or university. Others may pursue a career option immediately after high school. Joining the military or traveling abroad are still other options. (You will learn more about career preparation and opportunities later in this text.)

Early adulthood is often a time of experimentation. Young adults continue to develop interests and abilities and pursue a postsecondary option. Sometimes, young adults must adjust their initial plans. For example, after getting a first job, a young adult may decide he or she does not actually enjoy working in that field, **10-1**.

Since young adults are dealing with many new transitions, they may experience new emotions. These changes can be challenging. Leaving a well-known environment for an entirely new location with new people can be intimidating and stressful. Young adults may feel fear, anxiety, and depression. Adjusting may be difficult. On the other hand, transitioning from high school can be highly exciting as people are able to establish their adult identities and manage their own lives. They gain new friends, experiences, and knowledge. Feeling a range of emotions is common and normal during this time, especially when new environments and living situations change.

## Testing Living Situations

In many cultures such as in the United States, leaving the family home is a mark of independence and adulthood. As young adults establish their self-dependence, living situations often change. Staying in college dorms, renting an apartment, having a roommate, or buying a house are significant transitions in the life of a young adult.

The idea of moving out of the family home may seem exciting. However, the stark reality of paying the bills, purchasing and preparing food, doing laundry, and maintaining the living space can be a difficult transition. Over time, these responsibilities become second nature as young adults transition into being more comfortable with the responsibility of caring for themselves and others.

*George Dolgikh/Shutterstock.com*

**10-1**  Young adults typically change jobs more often than at any other time in adulthood.

## Health Connections    Stress

During early adulthood, many aspects of life are changing and evolving. Selecting a postsecondary option, living in a new environment, and experiencing a change in relationships are examples of psychosocial changes. These natural, cultural changes can be a cause of stress, called *stressors*. Stress can negatively or positively impact wellness. Following are physical and psychological effects of stress:

### Physical

- sweaty palms
- increased heart rate
- headaches
- stomachaches
- fatigue
- weakening of the immune system
- worsening of preexisting health conditions

### Psychological

- anger
- irritability
- loss of focus
- withdrawal
- feelings of depression

An individual's reaction to stress depends on the stressor and how long the stressor may be an issue. For example, a short-term stressor may involve conducting an interview for a class assignment. Before the interview, you may feel some physical symptoms. These symptoms, however, will most likely alleviate once the interview is complete. This type of stress can positively impact wellness because even though you were stressed, you were able to try something new and difficult.

Effects of stress may be long lasting if the situation is long-term, such as dealing with a friend's addiction or the illness of a family member. In these cases, the stress can negatively impact wellness as the effects of stress can weaken the immune system and physically age a person when the stressor is ongoing.

According to the American Psychological Association, there are methods to manage stress and reduce effects on the body. Identifying the stressor, spending time alone to reflect and relax, getting adequate sleep, and not expecting perfection can help you reduce and cope with stress levels.

### Research Activity

Research other methods and techniques for relieving stress. Which methods are most useful to you? Create a list of five stress-relieving techniques that you find most helpful.

## Checkpoint

1. In the United States, at what age does the law often treat teens as adults?
2. What does the term *social clock* mean? List two common social clock expectations.
3. List three postsecondary options often available after the completion of high school.
4. Give an example of how young adults may test living situations.

## Physical Qualities and Changes

During young adulthood, adults no longer grow physically. Young adults are stronger and faster, have more muscle tissue, better eyesight and hearing, more lung capacity, and a better immune system than middle age or older adults. By the age of 30, physical abilities often start to decline. Both women and men commonly experience weight gains during early adulthood.

Hearing, vision, smell, and taste all reach their crest during adolescence and early adulthood. Around the age of 30, hearing starts to decline. Changes in eyesight, especially the ability to see up close, often become apparent toward the end of this life stage.

## Optimum Physical Functioning

Young adulthood is the time for strong physical performance, especially before the age of 30. Speed, strength, agility, and balance all reach their peak during this time. Athletes and non-athletes can jump higher, swing harder, lift more weight, and swim faster during the late teens and early adult years than any other time, **10-2**.

Part of the peak performance of this stage relates to skeletal maturity. Bones finally reach their full size. During the twenties, bones are at a higher calcium level than any other stage of life. Thus bones are strong. Muscles are also at their highest performance level. During the twenties, young adults have more muscle mass than at any other time throughout adulthood.

After the age of 30, physical performance and athletic ability begin to decline for the first time in life. During early adulthood, people see both the peak and the beginning of the gradual decline of physical performance. Women often gain weight, increasing their body fat tissue. Men increase their weight in both muscle and fat tissue. Starting in the latter twenties, fat tissue increases while muscle strength decreases for both men and women.

*Andresr/Shutterstock.com*

**10-2**  After a hard workout or physical activity, young adults often recover quickly.

## Nutrition

Throughout early adulthood, energy needs decrease. Reducing food intake from the amounts consumed during adolescence is often necessary to avoid unhealthy weight gains. Being overweight or obese can increase the risk for chronic diseases such as type 2 diabetes, high cholesterol, and high blood pressure. Making nutrient-dense food choices and avoiding foods high in cholesterol, sodium, and fat are important for optimum health.

Some nutrient needs increase during early adulthood. Calcium, iron, potassium, zinc, vitamin D, and the B vitamins are nutrients that are often lacking during this life stage. Therefore, nutrient-dense food choices are important. Eating a variety of healthful foods such as fruits, vegetables, seafood, whole grains, and low-fat dairy can help meet nutritional needs.

Culturally, dining at restaurants can be a main social activity during early adulthood, **10-3**. When selecting from the menu, identify items that are low in fat, not fried, and have less sugar and salt. Selecting smaller portion sizes and food items with more fruits and vegetables can also help.

*Diego Cervo/Shutterstock.com*

**10-3** Selecting healthful foods while dining out can be challenging.

Eating habits in adolescence and early adulthood have far-reaching effects. Being at an unhealthy weight or having an eating disorder in adolescence is likely to be a health issue in adulthood. Likewise, healthful eating habits are also likely to continue.

As in other life stages, nutrition needs vary depending on height, weight, and level of physical activity. The MyPlate food guidance system can help determine nutrition needs throughout early adulthood.

## Physical Activity

The *Physical Activity Guidelines for Americans* recommend adults participate in 150 minutes of moderate or 75 minutes of vigorous physical activity per week. As in other stages of life, adults may choose to divide this time for physical activities throughout the week.

 **Health Connections    Diabetes**

*Diabetes* describes the body's inability to produce or properly process insulin. The body uses insulin to help process sugars and starches from food. Insulin transfers them from the bloodstream to cells to provide energy to the body. When the body produces little or no insulin, sugars or *glucose* can buildup in the bloodstream, which can be dangerous. There are three different types of diabetes.

- **Type 1**—The body does not produce insulin. This type is usually detected in childhood.
- **Type 2**—The body does not produce enough insulin or has trouble processing insulin levels. This type is usually detected in older adulthood.
- **Gestational diabetes**—Diabetes that develops only during pregnancy.

Type 2 diabetes is most common. There are many factors that increase an individual's likelihood of being diagnosed with diabetes. Following are high-risk factors:

- genetics
- ethnicity—African, Asian, Latino, and Native Americans
- age—most common in older adulthood, but can be diagnosed in early adulthood

- being overweight and obese
- poor diet
- lack of physical activity

Symptoms from diabetes vary. Symptoms of type 2 diabetes include frequent urination, slow-healing infections, vision problems, significant thirst, rapid weight loss, numbness in hands and/or feet, or no symptoms. Blood tests can detect the body's glucose levels and determine if levels are regular. *Prediabetes* describes glucose levels that are high, but not high enough to diagnosis diabetes. Changes to lifestyle can help lower the risk for diabetes.

Although diabetes is not curable, there are treatment options. Insulin injections and other medications may be prescribed. Changes in dieting and physical activity can also help manage diabetes.

**Research Activity**

Visit the American Diabetes Association website at www.diabetes.org to discover how lifestyle changes in early adulthood can decrease the risk for type 2 diabetes. Create an electronic presentation to share your findings with the class.

Aerobic and muscle-strengthening activities are important for maintaining physical health. Aerobic activities exercise larger muscles and include activities such as walking, biking, and swimming. Muscle-strengthening activities help maintain a balanced weight and can also benefit the health of bones. These activities include weight lifting, push-ups, and sit-ups. Flexibility is another important health aspect, which includes activities that stretch the muscles and enhance movement. Dancing is an example of a flexibility activity.

Physical activity promotes individual health and can also be a social activity. Taking an aerobics class, visiting the local health club, walking with a friend, or playing a team sport are all social activities. Building or maintaining physical activity habits can positively impact a person's health in the future. Physical activity also helps to maintain a healthy body weight, lower stress, and reduce the occurrence of anxiety and depression.

## Sleeping

On average, adults need 7–9 hours of sleep per night. Some people may function well on 7 hours, while others may need a full 9 hours of sleep and no less, **10-4**. The body needs sleep to relax and revitalize in preparation for the next day. A lack of sleep interferes with energy levels, which affect multiple aspects of well-being.

*leungchopan/Shutterstock.com*

**10-4** The number of necessary hours needed for sleep differs among individuals.

## Health Connections    Types of Sleep

While sleeping, the body experiences two different types of sleep: non-rapid eye movement (NREM) and rapid eye movement (REM). NREM accounts for about 75 percent of all sleep. NREM begins as a person closes his or her eyes to sleep. The body transitions into a resting period and heart rate, blood pressure, and body temperature slightly decrease. During NREM, the body will also repair tissues and reenergize.

When not in the NREM stage, the body experiences REM. This type of sleep accounts for about 25 percent of total sleep. The eyes move back and forth, which occurs about every hour and a half while sleeping. Further energy is gained for the body and the brain recharges as well. During REM, dreaming occurs. The amount of REM sleep experienced affects the ability to remember and process information the next day. Getting the right amount of sleep is important to maintaining a healthy lifestyle and optimum functioning.

### Research Activity

Research the effects a lack of sleep can have on a person. From a reliable journal, magazine, or online source, find a brief article discussing a lack of sleep. Summarize your findings and report your article to the class.

During early adulthood, people may experience insomnia. **Insomnia** is the inability to fall asleep or to sleep more than a few hours at a time. Any of the following factors or a combination of factors can cause insomnia:

- stress
- anxiety
- depression
- caffeine, nicotine, and alcohol
- medications
- medical conditions
- change in work schedule
- irregular sleep schedules or uncomfortable sleep environment

Treatment options vary depending on the severity of insomnia, but may include lifestyle adjustments, therapy, or medications. Getting the necessary hours of sleep each night is important to maintaining health.

## Medical and Dental Care

Young adults have fewer chronic diseases, colds, flu, or respiratory problems than children. This does not necessarily mean they are healthier, but they are more immune due to past exposure.

Medical and dental exams continue to be important during early adulthood. Annual health exams promote good health and can be a way to check for potential health issues. Height, weight, and blood pressure are checked. Any symptoms or concerns should be discussed. Family medical history is also important to review with the doctor. This can help determine which diseases or illnesses a person may be more likely to encounter. Depending on information presented, the doctor may request additional tests or exams for such issues as cholesterol, diabetes, STIs, or cancers.

## Health Connections    Family Medical History

Knowing family medical history is especially important during young adulthood. Understanding illnesses and diseases of parents, grandparents, aunts, uncles, and siblings are directly relevant to an individual.

When family medical history is known, individuals can determine which health issues they may be at risk of developing. They can begin planning and taking preventive health measures to decrease their health risk. Lifestyle habits established in early adulthood can have positive impacts on future health. Individuals can be proactive in adjusting nutrition and physical activity habits to help counter health risks that run in their family. For example, if high cholesterol is common in the family, an individual may choose to alter dieting plans and make healthful food choices.

Many physicians recommend specific health screenings based on family medical history and age of the patient. These health screenings can identify early signs of a disease. The individual can then take measures to fight against the illness at an earlier stage instead of a more advanced stage.

### Listening Activity

Interview your parents and grandparents to learn about your family medical history. Which types of illnesses and diseases are prevalent in your family? Ask family members about the age the illness was first detected. What preventive measures can you take to help decrease your own risk of fighting this disease?

Annual dental exams can identify oral issues such as cavities, gingivitis, and gum disease, **10-5**. Catching these problems early can prevent the conditions from worsening and causing discomfort in the future. Brushing and flossing after meals and receiving teeth cleanings every six months can help promote oral health.

Healthful lifestyle choices during early adulthood can act as preventive health measures for the future. Preventive health includes maintaining regular sleep, eating, and physical activity habits. Maintaining oral care and hygiene are daily preventive tasks. Preventive health also includes monitoring lifestyle choices, such as avoiding high-risk behaviors. Specific preventive care varies depending on family medical history and the environment. Optimizing health patterns in early adulthood builds positive health patterns for middle and older adulthood.

## Effects of Alcohol Abuse

As young adults reach the legal age to buy and consume alcohol, experimentation with alcohol and binge drinking is often more prevalent. **Binge drinking** is the heavy consumption of alcohol over a short period of time. Binge drinking is especially common during the transitional years and can lead to **alcoholism**, or the addiction to alcohol. *Alcoholics*, those who suffer from alcoholism, may have a psychological and physical dependence on alcohol.

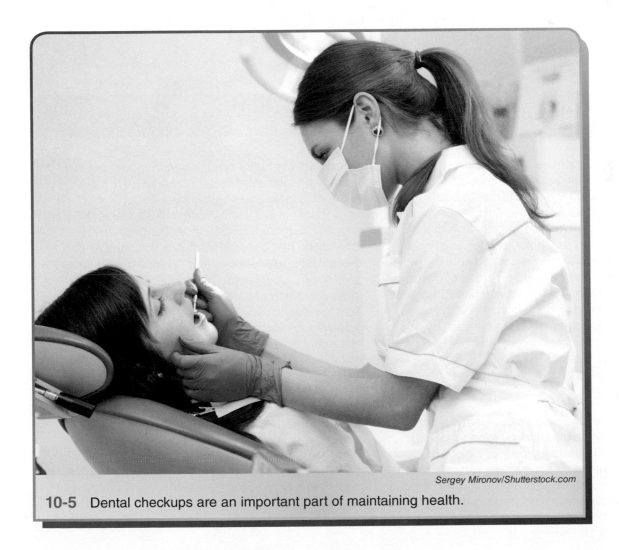

*Sergey Mironov/Shutterstock.com*

**10-5**   Dental checkups are an important part of maintaining health.

Binge drinking has many negative health effects. Oftentimes, people who binge drink do not know when to stop drinking. They may drink dangerous levels of alcohol and suffer from alcohol poisoning. *Alcohol poisoning* is the result of an overconsumption of alcohol, which the body cannot process or has significant trouble processing. Effects of alcohol poisoning include low blood pressure, low body temperature, loss of control over the nervous system, loss of consciousness, trouble breathing, and possibly even death.

Alcohol is a toxin and impairs the body's ability to physically and mentally function. Judgment is quickly impaired and causes many accidents and poor choices. Some accidents and choices may be fatal. Over a long period of time, alcoholism can cause kidney and liver damage, various types of cancers, heart and nerve problems, and death.

Alcoholism also affects personal relationships and work performance. Friendships, family relationships, and personal relationships are all negatively affected by alcoholism. Surrounding family members are also affected when an individual suffers from alcoholism. These problems can also transition into the workplace, which can lead to increased absences, tardiness, workplace accidents, illnesses, and lower productivity.

There are many resources available to help someone struggling with an addiction to alcohol. Support groups, such as Alcoholics Anonymous, can help teach coping methods and healthful strategies. Hotlines, pamphlets, and therapy sessions can also help a person struggling with an addiction. For others, programs such as rehabilitation, or rehab, may be a necessary intervention.

## Health Connections    Nicotine Use

Tobacco and nicotine are common substances that are abused during early adulthood. Habits formed during this stage are difficult to break and often last throughout a lifetime. This is because nicotine is an addictive substance, which can cause both a physical and psychological dependency.

Nicotine has many physical and social consequences. Physically, many areas of the body are negatively impacted by nicotine use. Smokers are at a higher risk for the following health issues:
- mouth, esophagus, and lung cancers
- bladder, kidney, cervix, and other various types of cancers
- chronic bronchitis and other lung diseases
- heart disease
- stroke

Socially, tobacco users cause individuals surrounding them to inhale *secondhand smoke* or smoke from cigarettes, pipes, or cigars. Secondhand smoke can negatively affect individuals surrounding a person who is smoking, even though secondhand smokers are not directly using tobacco.

Health effects for inhaling secondhand smoke include an increased risk for respiratory irritation, heart diseases, and lung cancer.

Smoking is the most controllable cause of cancer. As more information on the health hazards of nicotine has become available, the number of people who use tobacco and nicotine has decreased over the last few years. To maintain the optimum physical health of early adulthood, eliminating the use of nicotine maintains a healthy body. For those addicted to nicotine, quitting may be difficult. There are many available treatments and support groups to help reduce the use of tobacco.

### Research Activity

Research the history of nicotine use in the United States. As more information has become available, how have social views changed on nicotine use? Using reliable sources, create a pamphlet or electronic presentation explaining the history of nicotine use. Share your presentation with the class.

## Checkpoint

1. Describe common physical qualities and capabilities that can be expected in young adulthood.
2. Which nutrient needs increase during young adulthood?
3. List four factors that can contribute to insomnia.
4. How can young adults make healthful lifestyle choices to act as preventive health measures for the future?
5. Define the terms *binge drinking* and *alcoholism*.
6. What types of resources are available to help alcoholics?

# Signs of Cognitive Change

Early adulthood is a time of high intellectual functioning. **Fluid intelligence**, the ability to reason abstractly, is at a peak in young adulthood. Calculating mathematical problems with speed or learning things quickly is a part of fluid intelligence.

Young adults can also focus on topics that interest them at a high level. Choosing a career, area of study, or a hobby are some examples of this focus. **Crystallized intelligence**, which includes judgment, knowledge, and skills needed in life and work, is the focus of much of this stage. Young adults learn this type of intelligence through both experience and education.

Many inventions, social movements, and new ways of approaching life have come from young adults. Young adults often learn quickly and have good memories for data and experiences. Although creativity continues throughout adulthood, the younger years are a time of great innovative energy, **10-6**.

*Vadym Drobot/Shutterstock.com*

**10-6**   Young adults are known for their creativity.

## Piaget's Cognitive Theory

As you learned through earlier chapters, Piaget identified four stages of cognitive development. The final stage is *formal operations*. He identified this stage as emerging in adolescence and continuing throughout adulthood. As you may recall, rational thought, abstract thinking, and complex problem solving characterize the formal operations stage.

In the years after Piaget's formal theorizing about how people think, some researchers have proposed that much cognitive development happens after adolescence. Some theorists term this the **postformal stage** of cognitive development. During this stage, adults appear to be better at dealing with complex questions they may never fully answer. They more readily accept the reality of seemingly "fuzzy" problems. They understand that a solution may be appropriate in one context, but inappropriate in another. Young adults tend to be less concerned with finding the one right answer and more concerned with practical results.

## Brain Development

When a teen enters the twenties, the brain does not suddenly change. Brain changes happen gradually. By adolescence, gray matter or the cells that actually make a person think have reached their peak and connections between nerve cells form new pathways. As this is happening, parts of the brain develop at different speeds.

The prefrontal cortex, which regulates emotions and impulse control, is not fully developed until about age 26. After this age, young adults rely less on emotions in their cognitive reasoning. Their cognitive functioning is very efficient. They are often able to solve complex and abstract problems more easily. They are able to think deeply and more realistically about many issues.

## Language Development

An important aspect of transition from adolescence to early adulthood is communication style. There are differences between informal, social discussions and entry into the world of business communications. Teens are often more comfortable with shorthand text messages and instant messaging. In adulthood, the expectations for professional conversation and written skills can be a very big change. Excellent writing skills are often necessary when preparing documents and sending messages in the workplace.

## Cultural Connections    Body Language

*Nonverbal communication*, or sending messages without using words, is another common form of communication. Nonverbal communication can be a less clear form of communicating, since direct communication is not used. *Body language* is a form of nonverbal communication that involves using facial expressions, appearance, posture, and gestures to send messages. Body language may be conscious or unconscious. For example, if a student is slouching in class, the teacher may interpret the slouching as disinterest in the subject. The student, however, may not be aware of his or her posture and may simply be tired.

Body language meanings and practices differ among cultures and can sometimes result in unclear messages or misunderstandings. For example, in some Latin American and Asian cultures, holding direct eye contact is considered disrespectful. In some Middle Eastern cultures, holding eye contact can be a sign of flirtation. In U.S. culture, eye contact is usually considered to be a sign of listening, understanding, honesty, or confidence. When interacting cross culturally, miscommunications can easily be made. Being aware of customs in other cultures can help prevent misunderstandings.

### Listening Activity

Without any volume or subtitles, watch a portion of a film or television show. Analyze the body language of the characters. Through watching the characters' bodies and interaction, can you guess the type of scene happening in the plot line? Then, rewind the clip to view with sound. How accurate was your assessment based on body language?

In addition to written language, verbal and nonverbal communication skills are important. Being able to listen attentively and provide feedback to supervisors and coworkers are essential skills. Nonverbal skills include many facets of presence such as manner of dress and grooming, eye contact, and something as simple as a firm handshake. Someone mumbling and looking down at his or her shoes does not make a great impression with anyone, **10-7**. Appearance, speech, vocabulary, posture, and many other nonverbal signals become much more important forms of communication in adult life.

### Kohlberg's Theory of Moral Development

Kohlberg's final stage of moral development is **postconventional morality**. During this stage, adults begin to care about the local community, environment, and society. Values and ethics become factors in making decisions, especially for those impacting many people. The abilities to respect others and feel compassion usually fully develop during this stage. Human rights, voting, and environmental conditions are examples of adult concerns during this stage of moral development. This moral stage is less egocentric and therefore differs from earlier stages.

*Stephen Coburn/Shutterstock.com*

**10-7** The saying "you only have one chance to make a good first impression" is very applicable to meeting someone in a business setting.

## Checkpoint

1. What is the difference between fluid and crystallized intelligence?
2. How do young adult cognitive skills differ from adolescent cognitive skills?
3. Define *postformal stage*.
4. What are the two types of communication?
5. What is Kohlberg's final stage of moral development? How does this moral stage differ from earlier stages?

## Signs of Socio-emotional Change

A 20-year-old may be very different from a 39-year-old, but in many ways they are the same. Young adults are establishing their identity and leaving their families. They are setting themselves up for years ahead, and making family and career decisions. They are taking responsibility for themselves and others. Young adults are forming social alliances and support outside of and beyond their childhood family.

Erikson captured early adulthood as the stage when faced with making social decisions. He referred to this stage of socio-emotional development as the **intimacy versus isolation** phase. **Intimacy** refers to the self-disclosure and sharing of private thoughts and emotions. This includes relationships with family, friends, and even coworkers. Erikson theorized that if people do not establish intimate relationships during young adulthood, they risk isolation from others.

## Family Relationships

During the transition to adulthood, young adults alter their relationships with family members, **10-8**. Although the parent-teen relationship is often challenging and can be conflict-ridden, the parent to adult-child relationship is less stressful. Parents can offer advice and be a source of emotional support while young adults establish their independence. Parents may also continue to be a source of financial support until young adults gain financial independence. When this occurs, parents oftentimes expect their adult children to follow their rules. This can be a source of conflict, and family members need to work together and communicate openly to resolve issues with each other.

Sibling relationships also change as people enter adulthood, sometimes becoming less contentious or conflict-ridden. Sibling relationships may grow stronger in adulthood. Other times relationships grow apart as siblings no longer live with each other. To maintain or strengthen sibling relationships, siblings need to share their thoughts and concerns with each other and try to understand each other's feelings. As with any other relationship, open communication is important.

*szefei/Shutterstock.com*

**10-8** The relationship between a parent and an adult child is different from the relationship between a parent and a child or a teen.

## Friendships

Friendships are an important aspect of young adulthood. Friends offer emotional support and care. They can provide an emotional outlet for the stressors of life by providing entertainment and companionship. Some friendships form quickly, while others develop over time with repeated interaction.

Friendships in early adulthood differ from earlier stages in life. Although friendships may continue from adolescence or childhood, the dynamic of the friendships may change. For the first time, distance may separate friends. Depending on the postsecondary option chosen, friends may have less contact with each other. As individuals develop their adult lives, daily schedules change and usually differ from other friends. Friendships do not necessarily end, but are likely to change, **10-9**.

*Blend Images/Shutterstock.com*

**10-9** With continued communication, care, and consideration, friendships can grow and develop with individuals throughout the lifespan.

In addition to changing relationships, entirely new friendships form from new environments. Classes, work, and other activities may be sources of new friendships. These friendships are completely new, as individuals will not know each other's background. People may become acquaintances, develop friendships based on activities, or become close friends. New friendships may also develop into romantic relationships.

## Intimacy

Intimacy can occur in friendships, family relationships, and romantic relationships. When forming new relationships, intimacy gradually develops as trust is established. In relationships between acquaintances, intimacy may never develop. According to Erikson, developing trusting and intimate relationships is a key task during early adulthood.

Many young adults choose to establish their own relationships and create their own families. In relationships, there are different types of *attachment styles*, which refer to the level of intimacy shared with another person. Young adults who show a **secure attachment style** perceive relationships positively and often establish relationships smoothly and naturally, **10-10**.

Other attachment styles may resist intimacy, closeness, or confidence in another partner. Some young adults exhibit an **avoidant attachment style**. These adults tend to avoid "getting too close" to others or avoid commitment. Those who show an avoidant style may often have multiple, short-lived relationships. Others show an **anxious attachment style**. They are often anxious, possessive, demanding, and tend to lack trust in relationship partners.

William Perugini/Shutterstock.com

**10-10** Many young adults develop secure attachments.

## Love

Although there is only one word for *love* in English, there are many different types of love people experience in relationships. Love for a family member differs from love for a friend, pet, or romantic partner. *Friendly love*, or the care, consideration, and intimacy felt for another person, can be at the base of many types of relationships.

A romantic relationship may begin with friendly love and become affectionate love. **Affectionate love** involves romantic ways of expressing love for each other, which are not necessarily sexual. **Romantic love** develops from the combination of friendly love and affectionate love. Romantic love creates the feelings of security in the relationship and care and appreciation for each other. This type of love can further evolve into consummate love. **Consummate love** is the combination of affectionate love and a desire to commit to the relationship through good times and challenges. For many, consummate love results in marriage. Young adults can relate to many developmental theories, including the different types of love, **10-11**.

Feelings of love can easily be confused with infatuation. **Infatuation** is an obsession with someone based on appearance or ability. People who experience feelings of infatuation are usually attracted to and impressed with another person, but do not know the person well. Infatuation can be a powerful and overwhelming emotion. Love differs from infatuation in that love is mutual, respectful, and enriching.

## Mate Selection

One of the main purposes of dating is to determine whether a dating partner is a good match for a lifetime. Dating allows a person to determine desirable traits and characteristics in a spouse. During the steady dating stage, a couple may decide to become engaged. The couple discusses important values, lifestyles, and family choices. This ongoing conversation evolves as the couple learns more about each other's expectations, desires, and goals. The following are important topics to discuss to determine marriage readiness:

- **Finances.** Finances are one of the most common arguments between spouses. Financial management affects the standard of living. The couple should discuss the lifestyle they envision for the future. Will a financial struggle be evident? This discussion can prevent future arguments from developing.

## Summary of Major Developmental Theories Related to Young Adults

| Type of Development | Theory | Description |
|---|---|---|
| Cognitive | LaBouvie-Vief: Postformal operations | Individuals are logical, and can process abstract thoughts during this stage. They can make predictions about cause and effect, use analogies and metaphors, and entertain "what if" questions. |
| Moral | Kohlberg: Postconventional morality | Young adults begin to make decisions in consideration for the surrounding environment. The local community, society, and global issues become concerns. |
| Socio-emotional development | Erikson: Intimacy versus isolation | Young adults establish relationships for support outside of their family of origin (parents and siblings) to create intimacy and avoid isolation from others. These relationships include friendships and marriage. |
| | Sternberg's Triangle of love | Romantic, affectionate, and consummate love. Consummate love occurs when romantic love is combined with a desire to commit to the relationship through good times and challenges. |
| | John Bowlby and Mary Ainsworth: Attachment styles | Young adults forming new relationships exhibit three different types of attachment styles. People with secure attachment perceive relationships positively. People with avoidant attachment styles avoid "getting too close" to others or avoid commitment. Those with anxious attachment styles are possessive and demanding. They tend to lack trust in a relationship. |

*Goodheart-Willcox Publisher*

**10-11** During young adulthood, theories place much emphasis on relationships.

- **Career paths.** Career choices significantly impact well-being for the individual as well as the family unit. Partners should discuss goals for the future, as well as how career choices may impact a family and lifestyle.

- **Living situation.** A major issue couples should discuss is where they want to live. Factors include type of home, location, climate, cost, and local resources available. For example, living in an apartment in a city or a house in a rural area are two different lifestyles. Similarly, couples must decide if other family members will live with them. How might their choice of living situations affect a future family?

- **The decision to parent.** Discussing future children is an important conversation to have before getting married. Partners need to know about each other's family expectations. Does he or she envision many, few, or no children? If the couple decides to become parents, when? How will they raise the child or children?

- **Family expansion.** When a couple marries, each partner gains the family members of his or her spouse. Relationships with in-laws can be positive and supporting. They can also be challenging. Partners need to consider relationships with in-laws as well as the spouse. Similarly, if one partner already has a child, the other person must consider becoming a stepparent and providing for the needs of the child.

# Engagement and Marriage

Engagement is an exciting, happy time for the couple. They announce their commitment to family, friends, and society. During this time, the couple continues to discuss upcoming issues, plan for the wedding ceremony, and make plans for the future.

Couples may often spend thousands of dollars and months or years planning their wedding. A bridal gown, wedding rings, flowers, food, and a reception are all part of the wedding ritual. Depending on the preferences of the bride and groom, the wedding ceremony may be large, small, or include only the couple.

The excitement from the engagement period and wedding can cause views and expectations to shift once a couple is married. To achieve and maintain a positive, healthy marriage, couples must remember to use open communication. Being able to comfortably discuss issues together can help resolve problems in a calm, efficient manner. Trust, consideration, a sense of humor, and appreciation can also help.

Early in marriage, partners often have to adjust to new lifestyle changes. Ideally, the marriage will be without conflict. This vision, however, is unrealistic. The reality is that marriage takes hard work and effort to maintain a relationship, through good times and bad. All relationships experience conflict, which is a healthy, normal part of relationships. Successful marriage partners value and care for each other, support each other, and solve problems together.

When making decisions or arguing, spouses need to learn to compromise. To **compromise** means to reach an agreement by incorporating each partner's goals and ideas into one solution. Each person accepts a part of the other person's idea to reach a middle ground. Compromising is usually the most fair, since each person reaches a conclusion that includes some original preferences. Open communication is key to reaching a decision based on compromise. With communication, compromise, consideration, trust, honesty, and a sense of humor, marriages can remain successful.

## Cultural Connections — International Wedding Traditions and Customs

Marriage traditions and customs vary from culture to culture. For many cultures, weddings are a highly celebrated time for the bride, groom, and their families. Traditions are based on regional culture, religion, and family traditions. Following is a sample of international wedding traditions:

- **India.** Traditionally, weddings take place for one week, including rituals prior to the ceremony. Before the ceremony, the bride and groom's feet are washed in water and oil. The bride's hands and feet are then intricately decorated with designs in henna. At the ceremony, the bride wears a red, yellow, or white *sari* with gold and silver adornments. The groom wears an ivory or cream colored *dhoti* and may also wear a turban with white flowers. The marriage becomes official when the groom ties a thread from himself to the bride to symbolize unity and a life connection.

- **Iran.** Iranian weddings are based in Persian culture. Weddings may last for 3 to 7 days and include flowers, fire and light, spices, and a mirror. At the ceremony, candles are placed near the mirror to symbolize fate, energy, and a bright future. The bride and groom are married underneath a special scarf held by family members. Sugar is placed over the scarf to symbolize reigning sweetness and happiness.

### Research Activity

Research other international wedding traditions. How do they vary from culture to culture? What do the traditions have in common? Report your findings to the class.

## Cultural Connections   Marriage Laws

In addition to the engagement period and wedding ceremony, there are also legal procedures the couple takes to legitimize the marriage. When a couple decides to marry, they must fill out legal paperwork and obtain a marriage license. The marriage license has many purposes, including adjusting Social Security benefits. To obtain a license, individuals must have proof of identity, be of a certain age, and be of sound mind. Laws and requirements will vary from state to state.

Another legal consideration is the decision to sign a *prenuptial agreement*. This optional agreement determines how finances and material items would be divided in the case of a divorce. Each partner consults attorneys, who are also present to witness the signing. This contract is completed and signed by both partners prior to the wedding ceremony.

Traditionally, when a couple decides to marry, the female changes her last name to her spouse's last name. This is not a legal requirement. If a name change is made, she will need to register the change, which has legal implications.

### Speaking Activity

Do you think a bride should change her last name when getting married? Why or why not? With a partner, discuss and debate your points.

## The Decision to Parent

Some young couples approach parenthood with planning and foresight. They assess their economic situation. They discuss roles and expectations. Others approach parenthood with romantic ideals of blissful moments and strengthened relationships. Some couples are surprised to learn of their pregnancy and impending parenthood. However parenthood is approached, it usually involves a mixture of emotions from excitement and joy to worry and anxiety over upcoming responsibilities. Often, couples report that becoming a parent is their most significant and life changing experience.

Choosing to become a parent is a permanent decision, and should take careful consideration. Since young adults are in optimum physical conditioning, many decide to become parents during early adulthood, **10-12**. The decision to have, or not have, children, however, is a personal choice that couples should make together. The following are just a few questions to take into consideration before having a child:

- How do both partners feel about children? Do they like children?
- Will each partner have enough love and patience to care for a child?
- Does the couple have the financial resources to support a child?
- Can a stable, healthy environment be provided for the child?

*Andy Dean Photography/Shutterstock.com*

**10-12**   Becoming a parent is a reality for many married couples.

There are many challenges, rewards, and responsibilities of parenting. Challenges are ongoing and will change as the child grows and develops. Similarly, the roles and rewards will change as the children grow and develop.

## Roles and Responsibilities

Parenting carries with it certain roles and responsibilities. Raising a child is a major life task that involves tremendous emotional, physical, mental, and financial resources. Parents also gain new roles. In addition to roles they currently have, such as son or daughter, aunt or uncle, friend, and coworker, parents must accept their new titles, *Mom* and *Dad*. Parents play many roles, each changing as their children mature. Parents are nurturers, managers, and advisors. They may act as mediators, especially in sibling disputes. Sometimes they act as social initiators, encouraging their children to build friendships. Parents are mentors and economic supporters.

Parents assume these roles in order to help provide for the needs of their children. Meeting children's needs is the most important function of parenting. This includes physical needs, such as food, water, shelter, and clothing. It also includes meeting cognitive needs to encourage and develop a child's learning. Parents spend time with children to ensure they understand new challenges and concepts. If a child is experiencing a developmental delay, parents must meet a child's special needs to reach optimum development.

Parents also need to meet socio-emotional needs for their children. Parents often have **unconditional love**, or love without limits or exceptions, for their children, **10-13**. In addition to providing a loving, nurturing environment, parents also help children develop healthy emotions and appropriate ways to express them. Parents help guide children's social interactions and act as role models to show appropriate behavior. These skills help children function socially without supervision.

The ability to meet some of a child's needs is related to the family's financial ability. A significant amount of money is needed to raise a child to adulthood. Clothes, food, housing, medical expenses, education, child care, toys, and extracurricular activities are just some examples of parenting costs. Parenting is costly and has great financial impact on families. Parents must be able to financially provide for the costs of raising children.

## Challenges and Rewards

Meeting all of a child's needs is challenging. In order to meet the physical, cognitive, and socio-emotional needs of children, parents make personal sacrifices and adjustments to their lives. Parents refocus their attention on a child and focus less attention on themselves. Parents may have less or no time for their personal hobbies and interests. They may have less time for social outings.

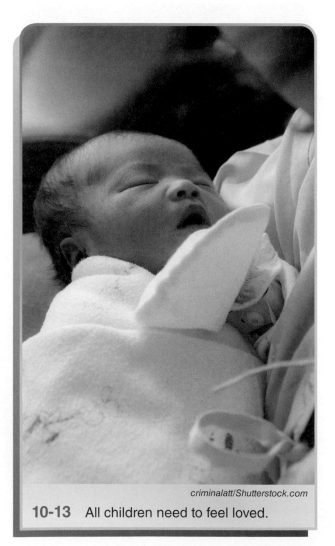

criminalatt/Shutterstock.com

**10-13** All children need to feel loved.

Parenting costs a considerable amount of time and energy. Children need constant care and attention. Especially with newborns, parents sacrifice their own sleep to feed, change, or comfort the baby during the night. At the same time, they must have the energy to help the child optimally develop. The decision to raise a child can also affect career opportunities and relationships.

Even with all the responsibilities and challenges of raising a child, the great majority of teens and young adults report they would like to be a parent someday. Parents often report their children are their greatest joy in life, more so than their friends, hobbies, or even careers. Many people choose to parent to experience the excitement and humorous moments with a child, **10-14**. For many, the ability to love a child and to be loved by a child are heavy factors. Whether a child is biological, adopted, or being fostered, all children can offer tremendous, unique rewards.

## Resolving Relationship Issues

When conflicts arise, open communication can help resolve an issue and relieve tension and stress. I-messages can help communicate a partner's thoughts and emotions clearly. Avoid you-messages, or statements that place blame and resort to name-calling. We-messages can be used to jointly share effort in resolving the conflict.

*Mark and Jaye Warwick*

**10-14**   The rewards of parenting are endless and can occur on a daily basis.

The environment of a discussion can influence the outcome of the issue. A quiet environment without distractions and noise can allow for more open communication. Similarly, an environment without friends or family members may be best. Both partners should feel comfortable to openly discuss their concerns.

The mood of each partner before a discussion can also influence the resolution. If either partner is feeling stressed, irritated, or angry, postponing a discussion may be best. Discussing a conflict should not, however, be postponed or avoided for too long. When couples do not discuss issues, the problem can grow worse. Tension and possibly feelings of resentment can increase between both people.

One method to help a couple resolve conflicts is attending counseling. Counseling can create a hospitable environment for both partners with the help of a professional. In couples or marriage counseling, a therapist will encourage partners to discuss issues and understand the other person's position, **10-15**. The counselor will also help guide the couple to a compromise or solution.

mangostock/Shutterstock.com

10-15    Counseling sessions can ease negative feelings, while proactively addressing issues.

## Breakups, Divorce, and Remarriage

Sometimes, even with counseling and effort from both partners, the relationship is still dysfunctional. The couple may experience conflicts that are more difficult to resolve or cannot be resolved. They may no longer get along with and understand each other. Instances of mistrust can arise. Partners in the relationship may need to evaluate the relationship as a whole and decide to end the relationship.

Breakups, separation, and divorce can feel tragic to those involved. The impact of ending a relationship differs depending on the length of a relationship. Individuals may develop negative thoughts or self-concepts. The success of a relationship should not, however, reflect self-worth. A healing process will follow and individuals can gradually move forward. Individuals may also feel relieved that a stressful or uncomfortable relationship has ended.

Relationships may end during the dating or engagement stages. When discussing marriage readiness during the engagement period, the couple may decide they are less compatible than previously thought. Their differences may be too great and would inevitably introduce more problems in the future. This breakup is painful, but prevents future issues and conflicts.

Divorce after marriage has higher stakes than dating relationship breakups, **10-16**. Both partners must readjust to life separately. Children especially feel the impact of divorce. New issues of living situations and the frequency of visitation from either parent can be confusing and painful for children.

About half of divorced adults remarry. When children are involved, stepfamilies form upon remarriage. Stepfamilies present their own unique challenges in family relationships. Time, communication, and patience are required for effective family functioning.

## Cultural and Societal Influences

Individuals in early adulthood face many cultural influences and expectations. With social clock expectations, young adults feel pressure for how to make decisions about new life choices. Often, advice is given for which postsecondary option to choose, how to manage personal relationships, and when to have children. Some advice comes directly from family or friends. Advice may also be indirect and come from films, books, magazines, television, the Internet, or other sources of media. Images constantly displayed may subconsciously influence an individual's ideas on when and how to make decisions.

*iofoto/Shutterstock.com*

**10-16**  Divorce impacts all family members.

## Case Study ???

### Selecting a Postsecondary Option

Abbas is an excellent student who excels in the area of arts. He is currently in his first year of study at a local college. He is taking general classes and has not decided which area of study to pursue. In high school, Abbas was the president of the school's art club. He also volunteered to teach art classes to older adults at the library and donated art to the community center to place throughout the community. Although Abbas enjoys the arts, he is uncertain about pursuing arts as a professional area of study.

Abbas's family has a history of medical professions, such as dentists, pediatricians, and medical researchers. If Abbas pursues the arts, he is concerned he will not have the support of his parents and family. Instead of studying arts, Abbas is considering selecting a premedical route of study. He believes this will make his parents proud. He reasons that his math and science skills are decent, but could probably be improved with time and devotion. Abbas is concerned both studies will have difficulties. Lately, he has been feeling overwhelmed and stressed about making a decision.

- What factors are influencing Abbas's decision to select a field of study?
- What are the advantages and disadvantages of selecting medicine as a field of study?
- How can Abbas reduce his stress relating to this decision?
- What advice would you offer Abbas?

mangostock/Shutterstock.com

**10-17** Many singles make their career or other pursuits their top priority.

For young adults choosing post-secondary options, family members and culture may influence decisions. For various reasons, some families and cultures view certain postsecondary options as more desirable than others. These familial and cultural views can contribute to the stress of an individual, especially if he or she does not prefer a given option.

Sometimes, individuals deviate from expected timelines or choose not to follow expectations. For example, a common question posed to newlyweds is when the couple expects children. This is often interpreted as pressure to enter the childbearing stage in the family life cycle. The decision to have children depends on the couple and their readiness and ability to parent. The couple may also decide not to have children.

One growing trend in U.S. culture is singlehood. Some people choose singlehood because it allows for great flexibility and time to dedicate to personal interests, **10-17**. Singles may not desire to enter a romantic relationship, but often have many friends, family members, and lead active lifestyles. Single people may have a background of romantic relationships or marriage, but find they are much happier single.

## Checkpoint

1. Define *social clock*.
2. What is the primary socio-emotional task of early adulthood?
3. How do relationships with parents change in early adulthood?
4. Name the different kinds of love.
5. List five important topics couples discuss to help determine marriage readiness.
6. What is the most important function of parenting?
7. What are some of the pressures young adults feel from cultural influences?

## Special Needs

By early adulthood, most special needs have been identified at earlier stages in the life cycle. The individual has more experience with and knowledge about the special need and can more easily manage. For some, however, special needs are acquired or discovered in early adulthood. These recently identified special needs present new challenges to daily living.

One cognitive disorder detected in the latter teen years or early adulthood is bipolar disorder. Bipolar disorder affects socio-emotional health and is characterized by severe mood swings that range from manic to depressive. During manic phases, a person may exhibit high energy, irritability, and impulsive behavior. Depressive phases include fatigue, loss of interest in favored activities, and changes in eating or sleeping habits, **10-18**. There is no cure for bipolar disorder, but treatment of symptoms may include medication and therapy. A support system is also important to the individual's well-being.

Whereas bipolar disorder is detected, other disorders can be acquired. One disorder that can be acquired in early adulthood is post traumatic stress disorder (PTSD). PTSD is a condition that results when an individual experiences a dangerous, horrific situation. PTSD effects socio-emotional and physical well-being. Victims of this disorder frequently relive the memory, which triggers feelings of anxiety, anger, and fear. Difficulty sleeping, nightmares, tenseness, or feeling a loss of emotions are other symptoms of PTSD. Although war veterans are most often associated with PTSD, victims of assault and those who experience death can also suffer from PTSD. With therapy and sometimes medication, symptoms can be relieved and PTSD can be managed.

*indianstockimages/Shutterstock.com*

**10-18**   Feelings of despair are common for people with bipolar disorder.

For adults with more severe cognitive disorders that impair the ability to perform everyday tasks, individuals may need frequent help from caregivers. They may not be able to live independently. For these individuals, mental health adult living facilities can offer a transition from home and assistance and supervision with daily living.

## Checkpoint

1. Describe characteristics of bipolar disorder.
2. What is PTSD? What are some of the effects of PTSD?
3. What are mental health adult living facilities?

## Summary

Physically, young adults are at optimal functioning. Bones are at their full maturity and muscles are at peak performance. Speed, strength, and agility are at their highest and begin to gradually decline.

Cognitively, young adults are in the postformal stage and are able to assess abstract concepts. The prefrontal cortex area of the brain reaches full maturity. Young adults use judgment, knowledge, and skills to solve problems and rely less on emotional responses.

Socio-emotional changes occur as young adults experience new life changes and environments. Relationships with parents and siblings change. Most young adults form new close, intimate relationships. Young adults consider the decision to marry and parent. Others elect to stay single. Breakups, separation, and divorce may happen as relationships change.

Young adults with special needs gain experience and confidence in managing their lives. Other adults acquire special needs and readjust their lives accordingly.

Overall, young adulthood is a time of tremendous intellectual, social, and emotional growth and change. The many changes in early adulthood affect the remaining stages of life.

## Vocabulary Activity

Review the terms and identify any that can be divided into smaller parts, having *roots* and *suffixes* or *prefixes*. Write these terms on a sheet of paper. Beside each term, list the root word and prefix or suffix. How do root words help you understand meaning? suffixes and prefixes?

## Critical Thinking

1. **Analyze.** Discuss cultural and societal influences on people in early adulthood.
2. **Analyze.** Explain why social interaction and relationships with family and peers are important for early adults.
3. **Identify.** Make a list of your hopes and dreams after high school.
4. **Assess.** Why do you think binge drinking is a serious health issue among young adults? Ask some young and middle age adults why this might be.
5. **Determine.** What talents, skills, and interests do you have now that will help you move into young adulthood? Which skills do you still need to develop? How will you do this?
6. **Evaluate.** What effect might the experience of post-high school job training have on a young adult? How might these experiences impact a person beyond gaining "book knowledge"?
7. **Predict.** How do you expect your life to be different in five years? ten years? Do you expect your goals to change or remain the same?
8. **Draw conclusions.** When you think about well-known celebrities today who are in young adulthood, which ones do you believe are making the best life choices? What experiences, resources, or knowledge likely motivated them to make good choices?
9. **Analyze.** What skills and resources would best prepare a person to become a first-time mother or father?
10. **Compare and contrast.** Visit a restaurant or store and compare a young adult versus a middle age adult server or cashier. Are there any differences or similarities observed? Are your conclusions based on stereotypes or facts?
11. **Make inferences.** Why do like-age adult groups tend to gather together?

If a cross-generation group is gathered together, what assumptions might you make about their relationships?

12. **Cause and effect.** Young adults are not required to attend counseling or relationship classes in order to get a marriage license. Should premarital counseling be required? Might doing so have any effect on the current divorce rate?

## Core Skills

13. **Writing.** In a short essay, describe and analyze the developmental theories that apply to early adulthood, including biological, cognitive, emotional, moral, and psychosocial development.

14. **Speaking.** What do you look forward to the most about becoming an adult? Share your thoughts with your classmates.

15. **Writing.** Write a two-page fictional journal entry about your feelings on the day before a big life event such as starting a new job, graduating from college, getting married, or having a baby.

16. **Listening.** Interview a classmate who has an older sibling in young adulthood, specifically the transitional stage. What types of challenges is the sibling facing? How is this sibling's relationship different with parents or caregivers when compared to your classmate?

17. **Reading.** Read a book about choosing a career. Write a two-page summary of the book to share with the class.

18. **Math.** Make a list of items you would need to live in an apartment including kitchen equipment or furniture. Look through ads to find as many sale items as possible. Estimate the cost of outfitting a small apartment.

19. **CTE Career Readiness Practice.** As a person who navigates life by firmly adhering to a strong code of ethics, you find yourself facing an ethical dilemma. A friend from work confides in you about her struggle with alcohol and makes you promise not to tell anyone. You have noticed that your friend is absent frequently. When she is at work, her productivity is low and she does not look well. You have concerns about her health and life. You wonder if you should share your observations with your friend's family or her work supervisor. What should you do? What is the best way to practice integrity in this situation? What decision is best for your friend and those she interacts with daily?

## Research

20. Search online for information about brain development in early adulthood. Write a one-page article of your findings. Be sure to use reliable sources and cite them in your paper.

21. Research substance abuse issues common in early adulthood. Design a poster or webpage that informs your classmates about one health challenge including symptoms, long-term effects, and possible treatments.

## Event Prep

22. You have 10 minutes to prepare a two-minute oral speech on a topic assigned by your instructor that is related to a current educational issue. You may use one index card for taking notes, which you can refer to during the presentation. Have someone be a timekeeper as you give your speech in class. You may wish to expand your project by participating in an Educators Rising *Impromptu Speaking Competition*. See your adviser for further information.

Monkey Business Images/Shutterstock.com

# Objectives

After studying this chapter, you will be able to

- analyze physical changes that occur in middle-aged adults.
- analyze cognitive changes that occur in middle-aged adults.
- analyze socio-emotional changes that occur in middle-aged adults.
- summarize how middle-aged adults express generativity rather than stagnation.
- identify how supportive relationships impact physical, cognitive, and socio-emotional well-being.
- give an example of how becoming an adult during a specific period of time in history impacts a person's life.

## Reading Prep

As you read this chapter, stop at the checkpoints and take time to answer the questions. Were you able to answer these questions without referring to the chapter content?

## Key Terms

| | | |
|---|---|---|
| climacteric | benign | maturity |
| testosterone | malignant | generativity versus stagnation |
| estrogen | chemotherapy | biological generativity |
| progesterone | cardiovascular disease | parental generativity |
| perimenopause | atherosclerosis | work generativity |
| menopause | plaque | cultural generativity |
| visual acuity | inductive reasoning | sandwich generation |
| presbyopia | deductive reasoning | universal design |
| sarcopenia | episodic memories | |
| osteoporosis | semantic memories | |

### Visit the G-W Learning Companion Website to:

- **build** vocabulary with e-flash cards and interactive games;
- **assess** what you learn by completing self-assessment quizzes; and
- **expand** knowledge with activities that extend learning.

G-WLEARNING.com    www.g-wlearning.com/development/

There are developmental milestones that remain the same for everyone as they pass through the middle age stage of life. Although health care may extend life, historical events may alter experiences, and personal experiences may change a person, some things remain the same. Just as in earlier stages of life, physical, cognitive, and socio-emotional characteristics are similar of people in middle age.

# Physical Qualities and Changes

Middle adulthood typically refers to the time period from ages 40 through 65 years. As the physical body ages, several visible signs indicate that things are not quite the same. These changes happen slowly and over time. The skin wrinkles and sometimes age spots appear. Hair thins and turns gray. Nails thicken and are more brittle. Teeth may become more yellow. These physical changes happen at different rates and individuals may experience changes to different degrees. Most changes are gradual, including those affecting the reproductive system, sensory skills, muscle mass and bone density, and physical ability.

## Climacteric and Menopause

During the middle adult years, reproductive capacity declines or is lost for both men and women. This is called **climacteric**. For men, this decline happens slowly and many men can continue to father children well into older adulthood. Even so, a decrease does occur as the male hormone **testosterone** declines. During climacteric, men may experience changes in moods and emotions.

Women experience a decrease in **estrogen** and **progesterone** (hormones that are found in higher levels in females than males). Over time, these decreases in hormones cause irregular menstrual periods. This first stage of reduced fertility is called **perimenopause**. Perimenopause can last several years and is often accompanied by *hot flashes*, or feelings of being very warm. Sometimes these hot flashes can cause sleeplessness resulting in mood changes and forgetfulness. When periods cease for a year or more, women officially reach **menopause** and can no longer reproduce.

## Cultural Connections   Global Views on Aging

U.S. views on aging tend to be negative. Much emphasis is placed on the value of youth, especially physical appearance. Aging, however, is not globally perceived as negative. In many cultures, the more a person ages, the more a person is respected and valued in society.

A recent cross-cultural study posted by the U.S. National Library of Medicine surveyed young adults on their views of aging adults. Participants from China, India, Malaysia, New Zealand, and Russia generally reported increasingly positive views the older the adult becomes. Areas surveyed included knowledge, respect, and standard of living.

This means young adults believed knowledge, respect, and standard of living increase with age in their societies. Although some aspects of aging were negative across all countries surveyed, the overall views in many eastern countries remained positive.

### Research Activity

Create a brief survey to discover other people's views on aging. How do your peers view aging? Create a graph displaying the results. Then interview two middle-aged adults to ask how they feel about the changes of aging.

## Changes in Sensory Skills

One of the first observed sensory changes in middle adulthood is diminished hearing. Even before middle age, young adults may have difficulty hearing very high and very low frequencies. This slow change is usually not noticed at the beginning of middle age. Toward the end of middle adulthood, the pace of hearing loss quickens. Adults who live or work in noisy environments or listen to loud music may notice accelerated loss.

The loss of **visual acuity**, or vision sharpness, is more noticeable. By the mid-forties, the lens of the eye starts to thicken and slightly pigmented layers of color form on the eye lens. The condition of **presbyopia** is also common due to loss of elasticity of the lens of the eye, which results in a slow decrease in the ability to focus on nearby objects. Many adults hold objects further away, such as at arm's length, in order to better focus their eye lens, **11-1**.

*wavebreakmedia/Shutterstock.com*

**11-1**   Presbyopia causes many middle-aged adults to wear reading glasses.

## Changes in Muscle Mass and Bone Density

During middle adulthood, **sarcopenia**, the loss of muscle mass and strength, occurs. At the same time, fat tissue increases. Many middle-aged adults notice that where the fat is deposited on their body changes as well. During middle adulthood, accumulation of fat tissue around the stomach or belly is common for both men and women. Women also tend to see more fat tissue around their hips and thighs than during earlier adulthood years.

At the same time, many adults may feel stiffness in their bones. As the cushions between bones become less efficient, movement becomes more difficult. Progressively, bone loss occurs. Calcium deficiency causes bones to become brittle and less dense, which may result in a condition called **osteoporosis**. Because bone loss is linked to estrogen and progesterone, bone loss is more pronounced in women, especially after the age of 50. People are not all the same, however, and the amount of bone loss varies by person.

As muscle mass and bone density decrease, so does muscle strength. The good news is that physical activity can slow or reverse many of these changes. To counteract the potential bone loss, taking calcium supplements and participating in muscle strengthening activities such as push-ups or sit-ups is recommended, especially for women. Physical activity can slow the loss of muscle tissue and the increase in fat tissue for both men and women. Getting plenty of physical activity can also stimulate the immune system to counteract potential risks of disease while promoting good health.

## Nutrition and Physical Activity

As physical abilities decline, good nutrition and regular physical activity are even more important to maintain in this stage of life. Maintaining a healthy weight helps to counteract many health problems. Physical activity helps people control weight and maintain muscle strength. Without some change in diet and activity level, the average person will gain 10 to 20 pounds throughout middle age.

In middle adulthood, people commonly gain one to two pounds per year. Excessive weight can increase the risk of diabetes, heart disease, and osteoporosis. Carrying extra weight can be hard on body joints such as the knees. Knee joints may need to be replaced with artificial joints through surgical procedures. The risk of developing several different types of cancer also increases.

Reducing calorie intake by just 100 calories a day and taking a daily walk can decrease the tendency for gradual weight increase over the years. Following the MyPlate guidelines and the *Physical Activity Guidelines for Americans* can help adults meet nutritional needs and maintain physical health.

## Sleeping

Middle-aged adults continue to need between 7–9 hours of sleep each night for optimal functioning. Since adults in this stage tend to have many caretaking responsibilities, busy lifestyles can interfere with sleep schedules. Balancing family responsibilities, work, and social relationships can be demanding and adults may lose some hours of sleep. A consistent lack of sleep can result in both short- and long-term effects. Symptoms from inadequate sleep may include the reduced ability to concentrate, solve problems, and be productive. Other symptoms may include irritability, depression, and weight gain.

## Health Connections    Avoid a Sedentary Lifestyle

Middle adulthood is a busy time for juggling responsibilities. As work and family responsibilities increase, people tend to sit and drive more. They stand and walk less. Fewer sports activities fill leisure time. Computer desk time and conferences or meetings increase at work. Watching television while sitting on the couch may increase. Adults may adapt to a *sedentary lifestyle*. That is, one that involves a lot of sitting and resting with very little physical activity.

With the added tendency to gain weight during middle adulthood, physical activity is crucial. The signs of aging occur at a much faster rate for those who lead a sedentary lifestyle without physical activity. Depression and anxiety are more common for inactive individuals. Activity lowers stress and tends to increase overall energy level. Physical activity increases a person's self-esteem.

The good news is that physical activity can be initiated at any age during middle adulthood. People can achieve the same positive health effects as if physical activity were started earlier in life.

### Speaking Activity

What advice could you offer a middle-aged adult to begin participating in physical activities? With a partner, list the benefits of physical activity. Then create a list of suggested activities to reintroduce middle-aged adults to physical activity.

Some women in the perimenopause or menopause stage experience trouble with sleeping. They report insomnia, which affects the mood and level of productivity for the next day. Hot flashes that occur during perimenopause and menopause can also occur during periods of sleep. The sensation of being overheated and sweaty can awaken a person from sleep and make returning to sleep difficult. Although hot flashes may not last long, they can disturb the overall sleep pattern.

## Medical and Dental Care

During middle adulthood, scheduling regular health checkups remains important, **11-2**. Doctors can detect signs of a health issue and assure good health. The number of recommended checkups varies. Some health screenings are recommended at a certain age. Other health screenings may be recommended sooner based on family medical history. Medical professionals may suggest screenings depending on individual symptoms.

Wellness and eye exams are two common recommended exams during middle adulthood. Doctors recommend scheduling regular or annual wellness exams. At these exams, physicians measure height and weight and discuss lifestyle choices. Optometrists, or eye doctors, recommend scheduling exams at least every two years or sooner if adults notice a decrease in visual acuity. Adults with a history of vision problems, diabetes, or other concerns may schedule annual eye exams.

For middle-aged adults, dentists recommend scheduling visits once a year and cleanings every six months. Brushing twice a day, flossing, and using mouth wash continue to be preventive care for dental health, **11-3**. Adults can still develop cavities, just as in adolescence. Dental exams can detect cavities, early signs of gingivitis, gum disease, and other oral issues.

*Stuart Jenner/Shutterstock.com*

**11-2**  Even when no symptoms of an illness are present, medical professionals recommend scheduling visits.

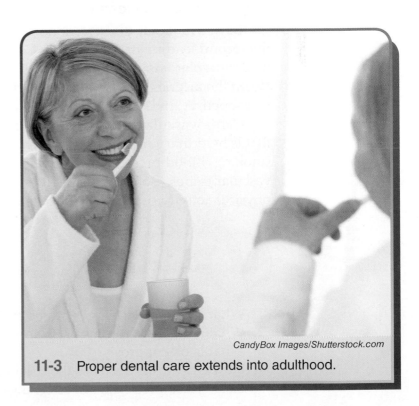

*CandyBox Images/Shutterstock.com*

**11-3**  Proper dental care extends into adulthood.

## Health and Disease

In middle adulthood, chronic diseases (those that persist for a long time) overtake accidents as the leading cause of death. Chronic diseases usually start slowly and last for years, if not a lifetime. Diabetes and arthritis are common examples of chronic diseases. They are less common in early adulthood, but increase during middle age. Some chronic diseases lead to diminished quality of life whereas others lead to premature death. Cancer is the leading cause of death.

### Cancer

Cancer is the abnormal growth and division of cells in the body. This can result in invasive *tumors* or growths in the body. A **benign** tumor is noncancerous. **Malignant** is the term used to describe tumors that are cancerous. Cancer can occur in any part of the body such as the lungs, brain, bones, or stomach. Cancers are treated in various ways including **chemotherapy** (the use of cancer-killing chemicals or drugs), radiation, and surgical removal. Most cancers are caused by a combination of genetic and environmental factors. Environmental causes can be reduced through lifestyle choices. Great strides continue to occur in cancer prevention and treatment. Medical screenings, education, and advances in treatments reduce the number of deaths from many cancers.

Starting at age 40, doctors recommend women schedule a mammogram to screen for breast cancer. A *mammogram* is an X-ray of the breasts that checks for unusual tissue growth. Mammograms can identify early signs of breast cancer, which can lead to preventive care and treatment if necessary. After age 40, doctors often recommend scheduling a mammogram every year.

Men in middle adulthood are at a higher risk for prostate cancer. Prostate cancer is an abnormal growth of cells in the prostate, a gland that is part of the male reproductive system. A doctor will help determine the necessity of screening early for prostate cancer.

### Cardiovascular Disease

**Cardiovascular disease**, abnormal function of the heart or blood vessels, is the second leading cause of death. Cardiovascular disease is caused by the process of **atherosclerosis**, or the clogging of arteries with a **plaque** (a fatty substance). When the arteries are completely blocked, a *heart attack* occurs if the heart function is stopped. A *stroke* occurs if the blockage is in the brain.

Cardiovascular disease is not a normal part of aging, but rather a disease that is hereditary or a result of unhealthful lifestyle choices such as a poor diet or smoking. Blood pressure levels are important to monitor, which relate to cardiovascular issues. Good health habits such as proper nutrition, stress management, physical activity, and preventive health care may reduce risks.

## Checkpoint

1. What key bodily changes can be expected in middle adulthood?
2. What are the symptoms of menopause?
3. What is osteoporosis?
4. How can adults decrease the risk of gradual weight gain?
5. List at least three exams or screenings doctors recommend for middle-aged adults.

## Health Connections — Cholesterol

The body naturally produces *cholesterol*, a fatlike substance found in cells of the human body. Cholesterol is a normal part of everyday body regulation. Because the body produces cholesterol, people do not need to seek extra cholesterol from their diets. Many foods in the diet, such as animal products, contain cholesterol. When a person ingests too much cholesterol, he or she is at a higher risk of developing heart-related problems.

The following are "bad" and "good" types of cholesterol that doctors routinely monitor as part of health exams:

- **Low-density lipoprotein (LDL)**—known as "bad" cholesterol, this type can cause buildup and clog the arteries when too much is present in the bloodstream.

- **High-density lipoprotein (HDL)**—referred to as "good" cholesterol, higher amounts of HDL can reduce the risk of heart-related problems.

Foods containing higher amounts of saturated fat, such as eggs, bacon, and other animal products can increase levels of LDL. Although family medical history is a contributing factor, maintaining a healthful diet that includes fruits, vegetables, and whole grains can help reduce LDL levels. Maintaining physical activity and practicing weight management can also keep levels of LDL to a minimum.

### Research Activity

Research food sources of HDL. With a partner, work together to create a one-day menu plan for someone with high cholesterol. Compare your dieting plan with MyPlate to ensure all food groups are still incorporated in the diet.

## Signs of Cognitive Change

In middle adulthood, cognitive changes occur. Some cognitive functions improve while others decline. Fluid intelligence, or the ability to reason abstractly, often peaks in early adulthood, but may start to decline in middle adulthood. Crystallized intelligence, which includes judgment and accumulated knowledge, often increases in middle adulthood, **11-4**.

The ability to reason peaks during middle adulthood. Adults use inductive and deductive reasoning skills. Both types of reasoning involve logic. **Inductive reasoning** involves making conclusions by moving from detailed facts to general theory. Inductive reasoning begins with a detailed, zoomed-in view and then zooms out to make a conclusion. For example, if each bite of chocolate cake served at one restaurant is sweet, an individual may conclude that all chocolate cake is sweet. Adults are also able to use deductive reasoning to reach conclusions. **Deductive reasoning** uses general observation or theory to reach a detailed conclusion. Deductive reasoning looks at the larger picture and zooms in to a focal point. For example, if all chocolate cake is sweet, an adult can assume the chocolate cake offered at a new restaurant will be sweet, too.

*Yuri Arcurs/Shutterstock.com*

**11-4**  Middle-aged adults use their experiences to apply information to their daily lives.

## The Middle-Aged Brain

Middle-aged adults often demonstrate expertise knowledge or skills. Information may be processed more automatically and efficiently than in early adulthood. Middle-aged adults may have better strategies for solving problems. They develop creative shortcuts and are more flexible in coming up with possible solutions. Part of this creative flexibility comes through experience.

People in young adulthood tend to be better at remembering episodic memories than those in middle adulthood. **Episodic memories** are those that include personal experiences or events such as remembering where you left your car keys. **Semantic memories**, on the other hand, focus on knowledge such as how to change a flat tire on a car. Middle-aged adults tend to remember semantic memories as experience gives them time and practice.

Cognitive decline varies by individual. Mental exercises such as solving problems, memorizing facts or numbers, and keeping up on news help the brain function efficiently, **11-5**. Poor health can negatively affect cognitive abilities. Medications can cause confusion or memory loss.

## Language Changes

Adults in middle adulthood generally continue to improve their language skills. They have more experience with and exposure to a diverse vocabulary. As a result, adults have a large vocabulary database. Since middle-aged adults are often experts and professionals in their field, they may have their own content-specific language, known as *jargon*.

*Blend Images/Shutterstock.com*

**11-5** Reading the newspaper and doing puzzles are stimulating experiences that can keep brain functioning sharp.

Although most adults in middle age are no longer in school, they can continue to improve their language, memory, and reasoning skills. Reading books can strengthen vocabulary. Activities such as crossword puzzles, word searches, and trivia games help keep cognitive skills sharp. Crosswords puzzles and other word games can help adults learn more *synonyms*, or different words with the same meanings. These types of games can also improve semantic memory skills.

## Moral Development

According to Kohlberg's theory of moral development, middle age adults are in the final stage of moral development, which is *postconventional morality*. During middle adulthood, adults continue to care about their community, environment, and society as a whole. They are able to respect others and be compassionate. Middle-aged adults often become more secure in their decisions and beliefs.

Spiritual beliefs and religion may become more important when compared to young adulthood. Middle-aged adults may be drawn to spirituality and religion as they are more often personally faced with death. The death of parents, friends, and colleagues becomes more common than in earlier stages of life. Middle-aged adults start to ask questions about what they hope to leave as a legacy. They become more interested in establishing and living by their personal values rather than those of others.

## Checkpoint

1. How do middle-aged adult cognitive skills differ from younger adults?
2. What is the difference between inductive and deductive reasoning?
3. How do language skills change in middle adulthood?
4. Middle-aged adults are in which stage of Kohlberg's moral development theory?

## Cultural Connections — Balancing Work, Family, and Community Responsibilities

As adults are in Kohlberg's postconventional stage of morality, many adults value the importance of helping others. Offering support or help to others includes helping local, national, and international communities. Many adults spend extra time or schedule time to volunteer. Adults may lead donation drives, participate in walks or runs for charity, and volunteer in soup kitchens. They may also offer their personal resources, such as finances, knowledge, or emotional support. The volunteering opportunities are limitless.

Balancing volunteering with work and family responsibilities can be challenging. Sometimes, these obligations can overlap. For example, a middle-aged adult can add a volunteering opportunity to family time. This way, other family members can help the volunteering cause while spending time together. The workplace may also schedule or offer volunteering or charity opportunities outside of working hours. These activities are usually family friendly. Work, family, and community responsibilities are all addressed in these activities. As parents experience an empty nest when their children are grown, volunteer opportunities may increase as more free time may become available.

### Community Activity

Research local volunteering opportunities in your community. Create a list and add two suggestions of volunteering possibilities. Then share your list with the class.

# Signs of Socio-emotional Change

In middle adulthood, people tend to look both backward to their youth and forward in expectation of the remaining years of their lives. Throughout middle adulthood, changes continue to occur. Children are born, grow up, and leave home. Relationships grow, change, and sometimes dissolve. New jobs begin, while unemployment is a reality for others. People get sick, some get well, and some die. Changes are a reality in life. By the time people reach middle age, most have lived through many life changes. **Maturity** is the ability to adapt to the inevitable changes that happen in life.

Erikson captured middle adulthood as the stage when people are faced with coming to terms with choices made in adolescence and young adulthood. Middle adulthood is a time for figuring out how to leave legacies of one's self to the next generation. Erikson called this stage of socio-emotional development the **generativity versus stagnation** phase. *Generativity* refers to giving back to future generations. *Stagnation* centers around living for oneself without consideration for the potential impact on the next generation. (See **11-6** for a summary of theories relating to middle adulthood.)

Generativity takes many forms. **Biological generativity** involves raising children. This is a form of giving back to the next generation, especially when relationships are positive. Raising a child through adolescence and into adulthood can positively affect the future. A person does not have to be a biological or adoptive parent to affect the next generation, however. Being involved in children's lives through volunteer or paid work can have a great impact. Relationships within extended family, such as a cousin, niece, or nephew can be positive, too. This is called **parental generativity**.

| Summary of Major Developmental Theories Related to Middle Adulthood | | |
|---|---|---|
| **Type of Development** | **Theory** | **Description** |
| **Cognitive** | Fluid and crystallized intelligence | Crystallized intelligence begins to peak whereas fluid intelligence tends to decline. |
| | Inductive reasoning | Individuals use detailed facts to form a general theory. |
| | Deductive reasoning | Individuals use general observation or theory to reach a detailed conclusion. |
| | LaBouvie-Vief: Postformal operations | Individuals are logical, concrete, and can process abstract thoughts during this stage. They can make predictions about cause and effect, use analogies and metaphors, and entertain "what if" questions. Objects do not need to be seen to be considered. |
| **Socio-emotional development** | Erikson: Generativity versus stagnation | The socio-emotional stage in middle adulthood when adults begin either to leave legacies of one's self to the next generation or to live solely for themselves. |

*Goodheart-Willcox Publisher*

**11-6** During middle adulthood, people continue to experience developmental changes.

## Cultural Connections — Self-Identity in Middle Adulthood

Many middle-aged adults are very confident with their self-identities. By middle adulthood, the concept of self-identity has grown and evolved. Self-identity is solid and adults are more secure in who they are.

In a cross-sectional study published by the American Psychological Association, researchers found that the confidence in self-esteem peaks around age 60. This means adults feel better about themselves at age 60 than they did during their teens, twenties, thirties, etc. Researchers suggest many lifetime milestones are associated with the latter years of middle adulthood. Having a successful career, family members and friends, and a healthful lifestyle all contribute to positive views on self-esteem.

Some adults experience a period of self-reevaluation in middle adulthood. Commonly called a *midlife crisis*, middle age adults may pause to reflect on accomplishments, changes, and missed goals throughout their lives. The media often identifies midlife crises with buying a new car or adopting a new, younger look. Midlife crises, however, may be more internal for adults and less drastic. Adults may be learning to accept their current age and beginning to plan for their future years as an older adult.

### Writing Activity

In a journal, write a reflection of how you envision yourself at age 60. What goals do you expect to accomplish by this time? Keep this journal entry for future reflection.

---

Generativity can also be found in the workplace. Adults who give to the next generation through mentoring, training or teaching job skills, or communicating workplace cultural values are participating in **work generativity**. Likewise, communicating cultural values and traditions in the larger society is called **cultural generativity**. Teaching the younger generation about food habits, language, manners, or social expectations falls within this type of generativity.

## Family Relationships

Part of the balancing act of middle age is playing the role of both a child to aging parents and a parent to increasingly independent children. For many adults, they find themselves providing escalating care for their aging parents who need more help with decision making and daily tasks. Sometimes they may need help with health issues. At the same time, these caregivers may be providing assistance to their teens or young adult children. As many middle-aged adults welcome grandchildren, their responsibilities are multiplied even further. The balancing act of providing care between generations creates a group called the **sandwich generation**.

Caring for aging parents requires time and patience. These challenges can affect physical and socio-emotional health. Adults living in the sandwich generation often emotionally struggle with declining health and new demands of their parents. At the same time, they must continue to parent their own children. Schedules can become overly busy. For many, the demands of children, household responsibilities, work, and caring for parents create stress and role overload.

## Cultural Connections — Sandwich Generation Coping Strategies and Rewards

Members of the sandwich generation may be overwhelmed with changes to family structure and new living situations. Before adult parents move into the house, holding a family conversation can help answer other family member's questions and expectations. Explaining why grandparents may need to move into the house can reduce feelings of confusion or resentment. Open communication can also create an environment of understanding and sympathy.

With intergenerational living, lifestyle changes may need to be made. Finances may be tight and financial planning may be necessary. Creating a family spending plan can limit expenses and help prevent financial stress. In addition to a financial plan, a family schedule can help determine the needs of all family members and help manage time and common resources.

Another coping strategy for sandwich generation members includes creating time alone and maintaining other relationships. Since adults are playing multiple roles, having time alone can help with socio-emotional health. Friends can also be a strong source of support.

Although providing care for parents and children is challenging, living in a three-generational household can be rewarding. With aging parents nearby, the sandwich generation can ensure the health and well-being of their parents. Family members can offer one another companionship, which can create a positive shift in the parent-adult child relationship. Similarly, grandparents and the youngest generation can develop a closer relationship.

### Speaking Activity

In groups, create and then role-play a scenario in which a family is living in an intergenerational household. Include possible challenges, rewards, and coping skills in each scenario. Share performances with the class.

## The Empty Nest

Although some adults become new parents during middle adulthood, many adults welcome their first child during early adulthood. Those who become parents during the earlier adulthood stage are parenting teens and young adults when they reach middle adulthood. As their adult children leave home, one by one the household shrinks. When the last child leaves home, the term *empty nest* is often used.

Facing an empty nest can provide both benefits and challenges. The newfound freedom from caretaking responsibilities opens up opportunities to pursue interests such as hobbies, travel, education, or employment changes. The empty nest can also cause grieving for a life chapter that is over. Whether seen as a benefit or a challenge, most parents adapt gradually to their new life roles.

Sometimes adult children return home after having formerly left. For various reasons including job loss, completing an education, divorce, or health issues, adult children move back into the family home. Refilling the empty nest is not uncommon today.

## Becoming a Grandparent

Parents often become grandparents during their middle adult years. Some new grandparents have great difficulty in defining themselves as "grandpa" or "grandma." They may choose alternate names to avoid the perceived aging label. Many, however, describe the experience with enthusiasm and delight.

Why do some view becoming a grandparent as such an enjoyable experience? Many adults enjoy spending time with and loving a child without the hassles of daily care and discipline, **11-7**. Rather than carrying the load and responsibility for the children's growth and development, grandparents can play the role of companion and supporter. Sometimes, grandparents may find themselves in the role of parenting their children's children. This increased responsibility for daily care causes the grandparenting role to become more similar to a parenting role. As with any role transition, adjustment often takes time.

*Monkey Business Images/Shutterstock.com*

**11-7**   Many people report how much more relaxing grandparenting is as opposed to parenting a child.

## Case Study ???

### Refilling the Empty Nest

Both Emily and Ty left their family home right after high school graduation. Emily moved into a college dorm. A couple of years later, Ty moved into an apartment with friends. Recently, changes in roommate situations have motivated them both to move back into their family home. The problem is things have changed.

Emily and Ty's father lost his job during an economic downturn. Their mother increased her work hours to cover expenses. Their daily schedules are less traditional and their father, who had never participated much in household duties, now performs most of them. Finances are tighter than they used to be, but their parents seem to be enjoying their new lifestyle. They are very interested in physical fitness and maintain a healthy living environment. Emily and Ty are both used to their independence, but have agreed to realign their lifestyle while living in their parent's home.

- In what ways do adult children benefit from returning to the family home? In what ways do parents benefit?
- What are other reasons young adults move back into the family home?
- What are some of the challenges Emily, Ty, and their parents may encounter?
- Are there negative stigmas attached to young adults returning to live in the family home? If so, what are they and why do they exist?

## Marital Adjustments

Once children leave the house to pursue postsecondary options, parents experience a shift in living arrangements and emotions. The home may seem quieter since the children are no longer there. If children were the focus of the marriage, communication between spouses may become a struggle.

During this time, couples may need to reestablish their relationship. Couples often rediscover each other as middle-aged adults. The couple may relocate, travel, pursue education, or try new activities together. The marriage improves as the couple enters a new stage in the family life cycle together.

Other marriages may have different outcomes. Some marriages may falter and dissolve. Entering the dating scene after having been away can be quite challenging. Many people who experience divorce, however, also choose to remarry. Many of these remarriages are between two people who have both been married before and often have children. This results in blended families and more family adjustments.

# Supportive Relationships

People are social beings and need to have other people surrounding them. Having supportive relationships is important in any stage of life. Positive relationships contribute to physical, cognitive, social, and emotional well-being. Having supportive relationships can also help reduce stress by alleviating the feeling of being alone. Support may come from family members, friends, neighbors, or coworkers.

Supportive relationships are healthy relationships that include give-and-take between those involved. When dealing with new changes, adults may feel reluctant to ask for help. Other family members or friends, however, can offer

## *Safety* Connections

### The Impact of Positive Relationships

Relationships with family and friends can often be a source of emotional support, especially in challenging times or crises. Family and friends can offer differing points of view and may be able to make suggestions for alleviating some stressors.

If family and friends are not available or are not reliable sources of emotional support, however, resources are available to help adults cope with changes. Whether issues involve unemployment, changes in family structure, substance abuse, illness, or death, many resources can offer support and advice. There are many organizations for specific matters that can offer professional advice and contribute to well-being. Hotlines, counselors, and group meetings can offer emotional and sometimes social support for specific issues. For example, if a family member is experiencing cancer, support groups are available to help people experiencing

similar struggles with cancer cope together. Experiences, coping strategies, challenges, and rewards may be discussed, which support group members may benefit from while helping others.

Different people have different coping strategies and handle situations uniquely. Help from friends, family, or another source of emotional support can help individuals prevent stress, depression, and even suicide. Since crises can affect all aspects of well-being, ensuring others feel supported can be a preventive measure in health and safety.

### Writing Activity

Think of a struggle you have experienced in your life. How might you offer advice to a friend, family member, or acquaintance experiencing a similar problem today? Write a one-page reflection paper offering support and advice.

support or reassurance and advice. Accepting help and support is important to well-being. Communicating with people who are supportive can create an understanding of new changes adults are experiencing. Middle-aged adults may be able to offer advice and support on another topic in return. The give-and-take relationship creates a balance between those involved in the relationship.

## Work and Career Roles

As adults face midlife, they often question whether their chosen career is the one they wish to continue for the rest of their working life. They may have reached the height of success or perhaps face disappointment they did not go as far as desired. Others face involuntary job loss and unemployment through lay-offs or firing. As with any unexpected transition, the risk for anxiety, depression, and physical illness is increased when change is out of one's control. Middle-aged adults often have these feelings more acutely as their sense of responsibility to others is strong. Some adults decide that midlife is the perfect time to make changes. They may choose to change jobs, obtain additional training, seek further education, or start their own business, **11-8**.

## Learning How to Enjoy Leisure Time

After working hard for many years, people in middle adulthood often have to learn how to relax and enjoy leisure time. They may often blame mounting responsibilities for their inability to take time to pursue interests and activities of their own choosing. Learning to relax, however, is essential to physical, social, and emotional health.

*Monkey Business Images/Shutterstock.com*

**11-8** Midlife adult learners are a common sight in colleges and universities today.

Taking advantage of leisure opportunities is especially important in middle adulthood. When children leave home, health fails, responsibilities increase at work, or parents need more help, taking time for personal pursuits can be essential in relieving stress. Lowering stress improves quality of life. Leisure activities help to define self-identity outside of career or family identity. These new interests can also help adults transition into future retirement.

### Preparing for Retirement

Retirement is often on the minds of middle-aged adults as they mentally and financially prepare for the future when employment income ceases, **11-9**. Just as in any major decision, individuals approach upcoming changes in different ways. Some plan and save. They may dream of new hobbies, travel, and experiences. Others work to avoid the topic. For some, the thought of retirement causes stress and worry. For others, they cannot imagine giving up employment. Much depends on a person's ability to cope with change.

*Monkey Business Images/Shutterstock.com*

**11-9**  Although some people retire from their jobs during middle adulthood, most wait until older adulthood.

## Cultural and Societal Influences

Becoming an adult during a specific period of time in history impacts your life. The significant social, political, and economic events during this "coming of age" period of life influence a generation. Living through an economic recession, a political election, a significant natural disaster, or a war tends to change people. Not only do the large events impact a generation, but the personal, individual ones do as well. Getting married, losing a job, being injured in a car accident, and having a child are all personal events that mold a person for life.

As adults move into middle age, they often think of themselves as younger than their actual age. They see more differences between themselves and their own interests and those of people in younger adulthood. Sometimes these interest differences are based on generational experiences in adolescence and younger adulthood. Those who are born in a similar time in history are called *generational cohorts*. Current middle age and younger adults fall into three generational cohorts including the Baby Boomer Generation, Generation X, and the Millennial Generation.

### The Baby Boomer Generation

In the United States following World War II, approximately 77 million babies were born between the years of 1946 and 1964. This generation is known as the *Baby Boomer Generation*, **11-10**. Today, those who make up this generation are simply called *Baby Boomers* or even just *Boomers*.

Monkey Business Images/Shutterstock.com

**11-10**   Members of the *Baby Boomers Generation* are squarely in the middle age stage of life with many moving into older adulthood.

Baby Boomers have influenced American trends from a very early age. During infancy and childhood, increased attention was placed on parenting, nutrition, and education. Later, when this generation entered adolescence and early adulthood, their ideas, opinions, and politics forever changed American society. Corporate America, government, and the educational system are currently led by this generation. The oldest of this generation began turning 65 years of age in 2011. Currently, their life expectancy is 83 years of age. With improved health care and healthy lifestyles, however, many will probably live well into their 90s or even over 100.

What impact will the aging Baby Boomer Generation have on American society? They have already redefined the expectations of middle adulthood. Many people believe they will redefine the meaning and purpose of older adulthood, too. They want to remain active and continue to participate in society. They want to be financially secure and maintain strong physical, emotional, and social health. How do these goals change expectations? Health care, independent living, workforce participation and retirement, and marriage and family trends in aging are hot topics as Baby Boomers age.

### Generation X

*Generation X* followed the Baby Boomer Generation. Born between 1965 and 1979, this generation of Americans experienced huge social changes including increased rights for minorities and women. The Vietnam War was raging and many lost family members. A sharp increase in the divorce rate meant an increase in single-parent families. Some of these children were products of the Boomer Generation, but many of their parents were born prior. They were significantly fewer in number, but have made large contributions as adults.

## Cultural Connections    Changes in Technology

Technology is a major part of everyday living. Digital products are found at home, shopping centers, the workplace, and everywhere in between. Developments in technology are rapid and quickly change. Unlike the Millennial Generation, middle-aged adults did not grow up with technology surrounding them. This can mean that learning about technology may take a bit more time. Some middle-aged adults may struggle to keep up with technological advancements.

Many classes offer help for adults on how to become more comfortable in using new technology and software programs. Community libraries often offer free classes for how to use common computer software programs. Classes can also include how to use social networking sites, e-readers, and smartphone technology. Having a good understanding of technology can positively impact professional and social communication.

### Writing Activity

Interview a middle-aged adult comparing technology he or she used during adolescence to technology now. How have technological trends changed since he or she was younger? Summarize your interview in a *feature article*, a magazine-style article featuring the person you interviewed. Then submit the article to the school newspaper or website for possible publication.

Sometimes members of Generation X are called the *Digital Generation* as they were children and teens when the first personal computer was introduced. They saw the introduction of the fax machine and Internet. As young adults, they were responsible for the technological products people know and use today. Their approach to work has changed business environments to include such programs and policies as flexible hours and casual business dress. They are bordering on the end of young adulthood and the beginning of middle age.

### The Millennial Generation

Although the focus in the past half century has been on the huge population of the Baby Boomers, they do have competition. The large Baby Boomer Generation produced another large generation—their children and grandchildren—that are often referred to as the Echo Boomers or more commonly, the *Millennial Generation*. This generation was born between 1980 and 1995. Although not quite as large as the Baby Boomer Generation, the Millennial Generation is already making a huge impact on society. Currently, the Millennial Generation is either entering or entrenched in young adulthood.

## Checkpoint

1. According to Erikson, which stage of socio-emotional development are middle-aged adults experiencing? What is the struggle in this stage?
2. What is the *sandwich generation*? List some of the challenges this generation faces.
3. Describe a supportive relationship.
4. Why is taking advantage of leisure opportunities especially important in middle adulthood?
5. How does the generation people are born in impact an individual's life?

**Cultural Connections** Generation Naming

How do the names of each generation form? The answer varies. Mostly, generational group names are formed by society as a whole. A generational name is suggested through a book, article, movie, or other form of media. Then, the larger society either accepts or rejects the name. Some generational names form as the generation ages or after a generation has passed. Generations may also have multiple names.

Usually, each generation is named after a significant factor or attribute that describes the generational cohort. For example, the term *Baby Boomers* describes the significantly large increase in birth rates after WWII. The term *Millennials* describes a generation coming of age and continuing to age during the 2000s.

Other times, a placeholder name is used until the generation ages and additional characteristics become known. For example, those born between 1980–1995 were first known as *Generation Y*. Today, they are commonly referred to as the *Millennial Generation*. The next generation, those born after 1995, describes *Generation Z*. As this group continues to age, the name may change.

**Speaking Activity**

What do you think *Generation Z* should be called? Research other names that may replace *Generation Z*. Then, create a survey asking your peers their opinions. Create a graph to display your results.

## Special Needs

During middle adulthood, special needs can develop as a result of aging. These changes may be challenging, but are not uncommon. Sometimes, changes to the structure of a home need to be made to accommodate special needs.

**Universal design** is housing design that meets the physical needs of people of all ages and abilities. Universal design includes adjusting countertop height, creating a wheelchair accessible ramp, and widening the hallways for adults in wheelchairs. Features are also added, such as handrails for safety and convenience, wooden floors for wheelchairs and walking aids, and waterproof seats in the shower. Universal design can also apply to children's needs. The main purposes of universal design are safety, convenience, and accessibility.

## Checkpoint

1. What is universal design?
2. List two examples of universal design features.
3. What are the main purposes of universal design?

## Summary

During middle adulthood, sensory changes happen gradually. Muscle mass and strength decline, while fat tissue increases. Chronic disease is much more common than in earlier years. Genetics, lifestyle, and preventive health care all play a part in controlling the onset and progression of disease.

In middle adulthood, some cognitive functions improve while others decline. Crystallized intelligence peaks and adults use inductive and deductive reasoning to solve problems. Middle-aged adults are better at recalling semantic memories than episodic memories.

The major socio-emotional task during middle adulthood is deciding how to leave a legacy to younger generations. Erikson called this task *generativity versus stagnation*. Generativity can be achieved through giving back to children, coworkers, or lending cultural competence or expertise.

Middle-aged adults may find themselves a part of the *sandwich generation* as they care for their aging parents as well as adolescent or adult children. They may also experience the *empty nest* as children grow up and leave the home. Grandchildren may be born. At the same time, work continues to be important. Many plan for retirement. As in any other life stage, some people have special needs that may require additional attention.

## Vocabulary Activity

Play vocabulary bingo with the terms for the chapter. Create your own bingo cards by placing chapter terms randomly on the card in bingo format. Take turns reading the definitions of the terms. As you locate terms on your card, place a checkmark in the box. Shout out bingo when you fill a row across, down, or diagonally.

## Critical Thinking

1. **Predict.** Observe the physical features of an older family member you resemble. What might you expect in physical appearance changes as you age?

2. **Draw conclusions.** Look at clothing for teens, young adults, and middle age adults. How does the clothing compare in style including modesty, coverage, and fit? What does this experience tell you about typical body and image differences between these age groups?

3. **Determine.** Do you agree with the statement "age 60 is the new age 40"? Why or why not?

4. **Analyze.** Watch a television talk show that features people sharing their problems with viewers. Determine the approximate ages of the show's guests. Does the way in which the person tells his or her story reflect what you have learned about young adults versus middle-aged adults? How do stress and reflective thinking play a part?

5. **Identify.** Identify a "generativity" activity of a middle age adult you know. Describe how this person is "giving back" rather than remaining stagnant.

6. **Evaluate.** Imagine a day overscheduled with too many tasks and responsibilities, all of which are important. How might your solution to solving scheduling problems differ from a middle-aged adult's solution? How might these differences reflect fluid versus crystallized intelligence?

7. **Assess.** What are the roles a middle-aged adult in your family plays in life (brother, wife, mother, friend, coworker, boss, caretaker, volunteer, etc.)? How might these roles be in conflict?

8. **Compare and contrast.** Read a magazine intended for teens and a magazine intended for middle-aged adults. What products are being advertised? How are they the same or different? What does this tell you about how people change from adolescence to middle adulthood?

9. **Make inferences.** Read a local daily newspaper. Most newspapers target middle age adults. What conclusions can you gain from reading the news as presented?

10. **Cause and effect.** Role-play a conversation between a teen having a difficult time getting up for school and a parent in middle age who cannot be late for work, but needs to drive his or her child to school.

11. **Analyze.** Discuss cultural and societal influences on people in middle adulthood.

12. **Analyze.** Explain why social interaction and relationships with family and peers are important for middle adults.

## Core Skills

13. **Listening.** Interview two middle-aged adults. Ask them what sensory changes they have noticed since young adulthood.

14. **Math.** Plan and cook a meal for a family. Prepare items that require measuring ingredients, combining, and cooking or baking.

15. **Writing.** In a short essay, describe and analyze the developmental theories that apply to middle adulthood, including biological, cognitive, emotional, moral, and psychosocial development.

16. **Speaking.** Working in groups with your classmates, talk about what your 30-year high school reunion might be like. How might you change? How might you be the same?

17. **Reading.** Read a biography of a person in middle age who you admire.

18. **CTE Career Readiness Practice.** Presume you are a dietitian. Your interpersonal skills—your ability to listen, speak, and empathize—are a great asset in working with clients. Lilly is your latest client. She was recently diagnosed with osteoporosis. In addition to the medicine her doctor prescribed, Lilly was instructed to seek nutrition counseling about ways to increase the calcium in her diet. What calcium-rich foods would you recommend to Lilly? Why? How much should she have daily?

## Research

19. Research calcium needs throughout the lifespan. How can people get more calcium at a younger age? Write a one-page paper of your findings.

20. Research one chronic illness that is more common in middle adulthood than earlier in life. Design a poster or webpage that informs your classmates about this health challenge including symptoms and possible treatments.

## Event Prep

21. Identify organizations in your community that provide volunteer opportunities that interest you. Select one of the organizations to visit to learn more about ways you could help meet a need, such as volunteering your time or arranging for donations. You may wish to expand your project by participating in the FCCLA *Leadership Service in Action Program*. Use the FCCLA *Planning Process* to guide your *leadership* service project planning. See your FCCLA adviser for further information.

# Chapter 12 Older Adulthood: Age 66 Plus

Noam Armonn/Shutterstock.com

# Objectives

After studying this chapter, you will be able to

- analyze physical changes that occur in older adults.
- analyze cognitive changes that occur in older adults.
- analyze socio-emotional changes that occur in older adults.
- summarize how older adults might express integrity rather than despair.
- identify how supportive relationships impact physical, cognitive, and socio-emotional well-being in older adulthood.
- compare and contrast the stages of dying and the stages of grief.

## Reading Prep

Before reading this chapter, go to the end of the chapter and read the summary. The chapter summary highlights important information that was presented in the chapter. Did this help you prepare to understand the content?

## Key Terms

| | | |
|---|---|---|
| centenarian | sleep apnea | hospice care |
| liver spots | dentures | Last Will and Testament |
| incontinence | Medicare | beneficiaries |
| cataracts | Social Security | living will |
| glaucoma | integrity versus despair | intestate |
| macular degeneration | matriarch | widow |
| periphery | patriarch | widower |
| diabetic retinopathy | ageism | bereavement |
| presbycusis | dementia | grief |
| tinnitus | Alzheimer's disease | mourning |

**Visit the G-W Learning Companion Website to:**

- **build** vocabulary with e-flash cards and interactive games;
- **assess** what you learn by completing self-assessment quizzes; and
- **expand** knowledge with activities that extend learning.

www.g-wlearning.com/development/

Individuals in the older adulthood stage of the life cycle experience aging differently and at varying rates. Some older adults may be physically and mentally active, travelling, and very social. In the beginning years of this stage, adults may be retiring, are often welcoming grandchildren, and may be experiencing new social roles. Others may be experiencing new physical limitations, which can impact daily activities.

Throughout older adulthood, people begin to "slow down." Chronic illnesses may flair up, and health may decline dramatically. Some older adults may need help with daily care. As for cognitive changes, forgetfulness and confusion may occur. Other older adults, however, remain just as active and alert as they were in previous years.

Even with good health, aging is inevitable and life is finite. In the United States, the typical lifespan is 78 years of age. Women most commonly have a life expectancy of 81 years. Men live to age 76 on average. As in each stage of life, physical, cognitive, and socio-emotional changes occur gradually over a range of years.

## Physical Qualities and Changes

Older adulthood typically refers to the stage when people are age 66 and above. This spans a wide range of ages. Those entering older adulthood are just starting to see perceptual declines when compared to people ages 85 years and older. **Centenarian** refers to a person age 100 or older. A 66-year-old is much different from an 85-year-old or a 100-year-old.

Changes in physical appearance and functioning are common for many older adults. People expect to become more wrinkled as they age. Skin becomes less elastic. Age spots occur. These harmless age spots, known as **liver spots**, are flat gray, brown, or black. They vary in size and may appear on the face, hands, shoulders, and arms. Older adults become shorter in stature or height as they experience cartilage loss in their vertebrae. Muscle tissue and body weight decreases. Muscles give body firmness, and as muscle loss occurs, older bodies

### Cultural Connections — Global Life Expectancies

The life expectancies differ for men and women around the world. Some countries have higher life expectancies, while others have lower expectancies. Following is a sample of various global life expectancies:

| Country | Average | Men | Women |
|---------|---------|-----|-------|
| Japan | 83 | 80 | 87 |
| Canada | 81 | 78 | 84 |
| China | 74 | 72 | 77 |
| Brazil | 72 | 69 | 76 |
| Iran | 70 | 68 | 71 |
| India | 67 | 66 | 68 |

| Country | Average | Men | Women |
|---------|---------|-----|-------|
| Russia | 66 | 60 | 73 |
| Haiti | 62 | 61 | 63 |
| Ethiopia | 56 | 53 | 59 |
| Chad | 48 | 47 | 49 |

**Research Activity**

Select one country from the list or another country of your choice. Using reliable resources, research possible causes for the life expectancy in that country. Summarize your findings in a two-page informative essay.

often sag. Muscle loss also affects range of motion, and movements become slower. Physical activities such as strengthening exercises can slow this process, improving both physical appearance and abilities.

Other signs of aging cannot be seen externally. Internal body organs age and lose some efficiency of their function. The brain shrinks and pulls away from the skull. Blood flow to the brain decreases. As the heart's capacity decreases and blood vessels harden, the heart might have to pump harder to get blood to other organs. Lungs have a lower air capacity. The digestive system slows, often resulting in constipation. Incontinence, which is involuntary urination or defecation, may occur as health problems increase. Although these changes are normal, some happen faster for those who live sedentary lifestyles.

## Changes in Sensory Skills

Sensory changes from middle adulthood continue throughout older adulthood, **12-1**. *Presbyopia*, a slow decrease in the ability to focus on nearby objects, progressively worsens. The ability to adjust from light to darkness, from low glare to high glare, and to see objects in the side view becomes more challenging. Other vision conditions often develop. Eye doctors recommend scheduling visits at least every 1–2 years, but sooner if changes in visual acuity are noted. Doctors recommend having hearing tested annually to help detect changes in hearing.

### Vision Conditions

The most common vision conditions in older adulthood are cataracts, glaucoma, macular degeneration, and diabetic retinopathy. As people age, the lens of the eye thickens causing cloudy or distorted vision. This condition is known as cataracts. Colors are not as bright, and details become blurry. For a while, eyeglasses can help clarify vision. As the disease progresses, however, surgery is necessary. A simple laser surgical procedure can restore the lens to clearer vision.

## Health Connections    Biological Theories on Aging

In addition to biological changes that adults experience as they age, such as physical decline, there are also theories on aging. These theories offer explanations as to why the body deteriorates or functions differently from younger adulthood. Following are three of the most common biological theories on aging:

- **Cellular clock theory**—Cells need to divide to rejuvenate and to perform effectively in body functions. Cells can only divide about 75–80 times throughout life. When cells have trouble dividing, the body cannot perform optimally. Leonard Hayflick theorized that since cells have a time limit in dividing, the maximum age of life expectancy is between 120–125 years.
- **Free-radical theory**—Cells metabolize and produce byproducts, or free radicals.

*Free radicals* are unstable oxygen particles that damage other cells and interfere with regular body functions. Free radicals damage DNA, which can lead to many diseases and disorders.

- **Hormonal stress theory**—The body's reaction to stress changes as the body ages. Instead of reacting quickly to stress, the body remains in a state of stress longer than in previous stages of the life cycle. As a result, the body's immune system weakens, which leads to higher risks for illnesses and diseases.

### Speaking Activity

With a partner, discuss the three biological theories on aging. Of the three, does one sound more likely than another? Do you have another theory for why aging occurs?

bikeriderlondon/Shutterstock.com

**12-1** Both vision and hearing declines are gradual throughout older adulthood.

**Glaucoma** is an eye condition that involves damage to the optic nerve. This damage is caused by fluid buildup that puts pressure on the nerve. Glaucoma is far less common than cataracts. Typical treatment often includes eyedrops that help reduce pressure in the eye. If left untreated, glaucoma can cause irreversible blindness.

**Macular degeneration** is an eye disease that causes people to have difficulty seeing objects inside the center of the field of vision. Objects in the **periphery**, the outer edges of the center view, are clearly visible. Objects directly in the center of the field of vision, however, become more difficult to see. Macular degeneration occurs when the *retina*, the light-sensitive tissue at the back of the eye, deteriorates. The worsening retina is difficult to treat. Macular degeneration is the leading cause of blindness in older adults.

**Diabetic retinopathy** is an eye disease that involves damage to the blood vessels in the retina. The blood vessels become blocked and leak fluid into the eye. This causes blurred vision and then blindness if left untreated. Diabetic retinopathy is the most common diabetic eye disease that can affect people with either type 1 or type 2 diabetes, **12-2**. People who have diabetes should have a dilated eye exam annually and try to control blood sugar levels, blood cholesterol, and blood pressure. Laser surgery is often a necessary treatment once the disease progresses.

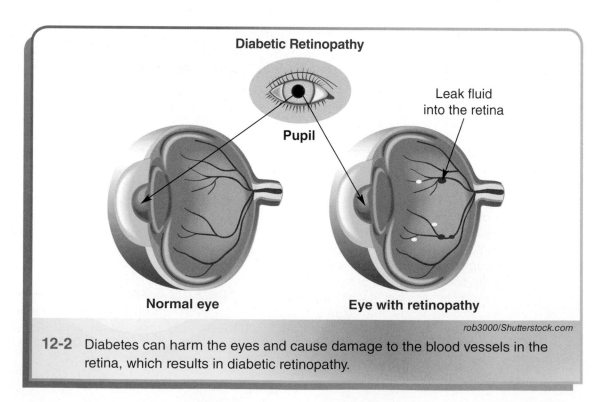

rob3000/Shutterstock.com

**12-2** Diabetes can harm the eyes and cause damage to the blood vessels in the retina, which results in diabetic retinopathy.

## Hearing Loss

With age, hearing loss typically occurs. Hearing loss can happen for a variety of reasons, including genetics, illness, exposure to loud sounds, and damage to the inner or middle ear. Hearing loss associated with age is called **presbycusis**, which is most often caused from damage to the inner ear. Many older adults complain of hearing a ringing sound in their ears, called **tinnitus**. Hearing changes can make communication difficult as listening and deciphering messages from others becomes problematic. Hearing loss can also lead to increased feelings of isolation from family and friends, which may then lead to depression. *Hearing aids*, assistive devices that amplify sound, can help older adults cope with hearing loss.

## Other Sensory Changes

Other sensory changes include a decrease in the sense of taste and smell along with less sensitivity to pain and touch. Both of these sensory changes can affect quality of life. When food smells and tastes become less pronounced, many older adults lose interest in preparing or eating appealing meals. In addition to a decrease in taste and smell, older adults may experience decreased sensations in touch. Older adults are often less sensitive to heat and cold temperature changes. Extremities such as hands and feet often feel cold despite warm gloves or socks. Older adults can be burned by hot water more than others as pain sensitivity does not register as quickly.

# Changes in Body Composition and Strength

Many of the physical changes affecting body composition and strength that occur in middle adulthood continue through older adulthood. *Sarcopenia*, the loss of muscle mass and strength, continues to increase. Fat tissue increases, and fat deposits continue to change as well. Joints often ache. Many adults feel more stiffness in their bones along with muscle aches and pains.

---

## *Safety* Connections          *Coping with Sensory Changes*

Experiencing sensory changes in older adulthood can interfere with simple tasks in everyday living. At times, losing sensory abilities can also interfere with an individual's safety. For example, the abilities to smell and taste inform a person whether or not food is still fresh and acceptable to eat. A sense of touch can let an individual know a surface is too hot and to quickly remove his or her hand. When these senses are diminishing, older adults may use other means to prevent safety hazards.

- **Vision.** Increase the number of lights and make sure lighting covers the home evenly. This may reduce glare, thereby improving ease of vision.
- **Taste.** Use herbs for cooking and seasoning instead of salt or sugar when foods taste bland. The ability to taste salt and sugar are usually the first two taste senses affected. Adding more salt to an already salted dish will increase sodium levels, which can negatively impact cardiovascular health.
- **Touch.** Set the thermostat on a water heater to 120°F (48.9°C) to avoid scalding water for showers or baths. This temperature is also safe for children.

### Listening Activity

Obtain a pair of thick gloves and earplugs to simulate the experience of losing sensory abilities. Working with a partner, have one person wear earplugs, while the other gives instructions. Instructions may include how to fold paper in a certain shape, spell a name, or arrive at a local store. Then, have the partner who was giving instructions put on the thick gloves and try to pick up a thin piece of paper or tie his or her shoes. As a class, discuss how the earplugs and gloves affected sensory abilities.

Conditions affecting the bones, such as osteoporosis, continue to cause brittle, less dense bones. Osteoporosis causes some adults to stand hunched over, and standing up straight is difficult, **12-3**. Bones break more easily. Despite the bodily declines, nutrition and fitness remain important for promoting good health and slowing progression of muscle and bone strength loss.

## Nutrition and Physical Activity

As in any other stage of life, proper nutrition is vital to maintain health. Although nutritional needs change in older adulthood, adults still need to consume a variety of foods from the fruits, vegetables, grains, dairy, and protein food groups.

The body's ability to absorb certain nutrients decreases in older adulthood. Older adults may need to take dietary supplements to ensure they are meeting nutritional needs. The needs for calcium and vitamin D increase to help promote bone strength. Vitamin B$_{12}$ and potassium needs also increase. By increasing fiber and water intake, older adults may prevent constipation. Sources for these additional nutritional needs include milk, bananas, whole-grain foods, fortified foods, and dietary supplements.

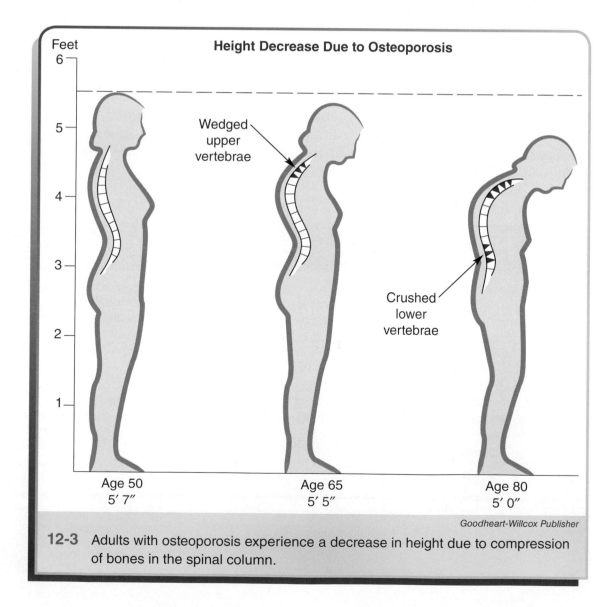

Goodheart-Willcox Publisher

**12-3**  Adults with osteoporosis experience a decrease in height due to compression of bones in the spinal column.

Caloric needs vary depending on age, weight, height, and level of physical activity. Medications and state of health can have an effect on nutritional needs. Older adults may need to consult a nutritionist or dietitian to create a dietary plan. Calories consumed should come from nutrient-dense, well-balanced sources that include protein, vitamins, and minerals, **12-4**. Weight and chronic health issues such as kidney disease, high cholesterol, and hypertension may be controlled by healthful changes in the diet.

Physical fitness achieved through activity is also important to maintain health in any stage of life. Physical activity recommendations for older adults vary depending on ability and condition of health. The *Physical Activity Guidelines for Americans* recommend 150 minutes of physical activity per week for older adults in good health. Adults with health conditions and chronic illnesses may engage in physical activity as ability and comfort allow. Aerobic activities, such as walking, swimming, or bicycling can benefit the heart and other muscles. Muscle-strengthening activities, such as lifting everyday items, and some stretching exercises can also improve health.

*Monkey Business Images/Shutterstock.com*

**12-4** Well-being may improve by the monitoring of food intake.

## Sleeping

"Early to bed and early to rise makes a man healthy, wealthy, and wise!" is a proverb from the 1735 edition of *Poor Richard's Almanack*, published by Benjamin Franklin. Many older adults literally follow this saying, **12-5**. Throughout older adulthood, adults continue to need 7–9 hours of sleep. As adults age, they may experience more trouble falling and staying asleep. Although they might spend 7–9 hours in bed, frequent waking can disrupt sleep. As a result, older adults may take frequent naps.

Sleeping becomes a safety issue for some people. **Sleep apnea** is a condition in which the airway collapses or becomes blocked and causes a person to have pauses in breathing while sleeping. These pauses can last from several seconds to a few minutes. Breathing then resumes, often with a loud snort or choking sound. This change in sleep pattern often results in a poor sleep quality, which leaves a person feeling tired during the day.

For those who experience the onset of diseases in older age, the progression is quicker. Since the body's immune system becomes less effective in fighting illness, diseases can progress more rapidly. Older adults are more likely to catch common colds and flu, which many times may develop into conditions that are more serious.

### Health Care

A growing older adult population can be seen around the world. This is partly due to better health care resulting in a longer life expectancy. In fact, the reduction in deaths due to heart disease is one of the largest contributing factors toward increased life expectancy. Increasing the quality and years of healthy life and eliminating health disparities are concerns of older adults. Many diseases can be prevented or at least symptoms can be relieved with proper nutrition, physical activity, food availability, weight management, oral health, vision, and hearing care.

With many conditions, illnesses, and diseases, care from doctors and medicine becomes necessary. In older adulthood, this often translates into a greater need for expensive medical care. Medical care includes doctor visits, hospitalization, rehabilitation, and prescription drugs.

In the United States, Medicare and Social Security have been offered to older Americans for many decades—some in the form of aid, some in the form of prepaid care. **Medicare**, a government health insurance program, helps older adults pay for medical costs. **Social Security**, a government retirement fund, provides supplemental income to Americans who are at least 62 years of age and who have met employment contribution eligibility standards. Other assistance programs are available for special needs populations.

## Cultural Connections   U.S. Life Expectancy

In the United States, the life expectancy has steadily increased throughout the years for men and women. Currently, the average life expectancy is 78 years. In 1900, the average life expectancy was only 47 years. Life expectancy for women was 48 years and men 46 years. Improvements in medicine, technology, and culture have contributed to increased life expectancy. Research has led to new medicines, which have made some illnesses or infections curable. Illnesses considered fatal in a previous decade or century are now treatable and no longer life threatening.

Changes in societal attitudes toward health have also shifted. For example, smoking cigarettes used to be a common activity. Today, people have more knowledge of the negative health effects of nicotine and can make more informed choices. More nutrition information is available to help people make healthful choices. Technology has also made significant contributions to the medical field. Life expectancy has improved due to other avenues, such as increased communication and other developments.

### Research Activity

Research three inventions or discoveries that have contributed to an improved life expectancy for men and women since 1900. Inventions or discoveries may be medical, technological, or societal. Create an electronic presentation and share your research with the class.

## Checkpoint

1. What age range does older adulthood typically include? What is a centenarian?
2. List three common changes older adults may experience in body composition and strength.
3. Describe common sensory changes in older adulthood.
4. Explain the increase for nutritional needs in older adults.
5. Describe sleep apnea.
6. Compare and contrast Medicare and Social Security.

# Signs of Cognitive Change

As in any stage of life, aging affects cognitive changes and development. In older adulthood, cognitive abilities may decline. For many active, healthy adults, this decline is slow and may not be very noticeable. For others, especially those suffering from depression or related health issues, the decline may be more pronounced. Some slowing of processing skills and forgetfulness does occur. Aging brains are resilient, however, and they respond to stimulating experiences. How aging affects each person's cognitive abilities will of course vary among individuals.

## Brain Functioning

Since the brain is shrinking in older adulthood, brain processing is impacted. As a result, older adults may have more trouble processing new information, recalling memories, and concentrating. Adults may also have more trouble moving from one task to the next. The ability to learn can be affected by a decline in cognitive abilities. The rate of cognitive decline, however, is much slower and less dramatic than previously thought, especially for active and healthy adults. With a slower learning pace and much repetition, older adults can learn as effectively as younger ones.

## Case Study ???

### Driving in Older Adulthood

Jody's dad, Earl, is 94-years-old. He has driven most of his life and has been a very good driver. He has never caused an accident and has only gotten two tickets—one for speeding and one for rolling through a stop sign. Earl's last driving infraction was 10 years ago.

Last week, Earl renewed his driver's license. The process to renew his license required an eye exam, but did not require retaking either the written or the driving test. Although Earl is doing fine now, Jody worries what will happen in the next few years. She is aware that older adults are much more likely to be in traffic accidents than the majority of the population, especially when health and cognitive challenges are present.

- Should Jody be concerned? Why or why not?
- If older adults, such as Earl, have proven to be good drivers, should there be an age limit on the right to have a driver's license? If so, what should the age limit be? If not, when or why should a driver's license be revoked?
- Why might driving privileges and age concerns cause conflicts among family members?

### Memory

During older adulthood, people expect some memory loss. An often-heard refrain from older adults is "my memory is just not what it used to be." Because memory affects so much of daily life, losing memory abilities can prove to be challenging.

Older adults may remember some details easier than others. For example, they may search for a word that is "on the tip of their tongue," but can easily remember very specific details of a childhood experience. Why does this happen? One theory claims memory loss comes from having too much information compiled over time. In other words, the brain can only hold so much information and may be experiencing data overload. Another theory states that memory decline occurs as brain functioning decreases. Most likely, memory loss occurs because of a combination of both theories. Memory games and exercises can help retain short-term recall.

Monkey Business Images/Shutterstock.com

**12-6**  Memories based on past education and experience, including years of practicing vocabulary, are retained as long-term verbal skills.

### Language Changes

Although memory decreases and learning methods may change, verbal ability remains stable and may actually increase slightly during older adulthood. This may seem contradictory. How can a person still search for a word, yet have better verbal ability? All memory abilities do not decrease at the same rate. Short-term memories are harder for older adults to retrieve than long-term memories. Because verbal ability is built on long-term memory, older adults often have a larger and more sophisticated vocabulary than younger adults, **12-6**.

## Health Connections     Using Technology to Improve Memory Skills

There are many benefits of using technology to improve memory and cognitive ability. Many forms of technology, such as computers, tablets, e-readers, and smartphones, can offer adults activities and games to help improve memory. Crossword activities, puzzles, trivia games, and other word and memory games are some examples that focus on improving short-term memory and cognitive ability. Since older adults struggle with short-term memory, engaging in these types of games and activities can help sharpen and improve cognitive skills.

For adults who are uncomfortable with using new technology, many classes are offered through libraries, community colleges, or other outlets. Learning how to use technology in a classroom setting teaches adults new skills in a social environment. Keeping up-to-date with technology may also allow older adults to bond with younger family members in person or through social networking sites.

#### Speaking Activity

Interview an older adult about the use of technology in his or her life. How comfortable with technology is this person? Does the person enjoy technology? If not, what types of activities does the person engage in to maintain memory ability? Write a brief report of your findings and present your information to the class.

## Moral Development

Older adults remain in Kohlberg's postconventional morality stage of moral development. Traits of this stage include valuing society as a whole and successfully contributing to the well-being of others. Older adults have a lifetime of experiences to form their moral decisions. For many, morality is based on collective wisdom, traditions, or common ways of doing things in the larger society. Morality may also include spiritual beliefs and religion.

## Checkpoint

1. How do older adult cognitive skills change?
2. Compare and contrast two theories that explain memory loss in older adults.
3. How do long-term memories influence older adult's language abilities?
4. Older adults are in which stage of Kohlberg's moral development theory?

## Signs of Socio-emotional Change

People are social beings. The need to be connected with others does not diminish in older adulthood, although social roles may change. Older adults move out of parenting roles. Taking care of grandchildren or great-grandchildren may occur less often as physical abilities diminish. Work and career roles change, **12-7**. At the beginning of older adulthood, many people retire.

StockLite/Shutterstock.com

**12-7**  Some employers value the experience and integrity of older workers who are able to meet the physical demands of a job.

How do older adults cope? Why are some more resilient to these changes than others? Erikson theorized that older adults experience a period of reviewing their life and accepting or struggling with experiences and decisions. This stage of Erikson's psychosocial development theory is called **integrity versus despair**. *Integrity* involves accepting one's life choices, including successes and failures. *Despair* refers to dissatisfaction with life choices. Erikson asserted that this final stage begins around 60 years of age and involves evaluating integrity in one's life versus despair over reaching the end of life.

Erikson theorized that older adults who face changing roles with optimism and enthusiasm are more likely to feel integrity. They do not despair over what did not happen and what they cannot change. They acknowledge and accept what has been and who they are today, including achievements, career choices, and relationships. (See **12-8** for a summary of theories relating to older adulthood.)

## Family Relationships

Family relationships remain important in older adulthood. As adults continue through the aging stage, family size and structure commonly change. Grandchildren, in-laws, and extended family members are added to the family. Some older adults may meet great-grandchildren or great-nieces and nephews. Social roles change as new relationships develop and new bonds form.

The relationship between aging parents and adult children may also change. Older adults may require more help and support from their adult children. Older adults may also struggle with accepting help. They may see acceptance of help

| Summary of Major Developmental Theories Related to Older Adulthood | | |
|---|---|---|
| **Type of Development** | **Theory** | **Description** |
| **Cognitive** | Fluid and crystallized intelligence | Crystallized intelligence continues to dominate as fluid intelligence continues to decrease. |
| **Socio-emotional development** | Erikson: Integrity versus despair | The final socio-emotional stage in older adulthood in which adults come to terms with their life review rather than despairing over what did not happen and what they cannot change. |
| | Activity theory | The more active and involved older adults are, the more satisfied they are with life. |
| | Kubler-Ross: Stages of dying | The five mental and emotional stages of facing death: denial, anger, bargaining, depression, and acceptance. |

*Goodheart-Willcox Publisher*

**12-8** Erikson described the final socio-emotional stage as a reflective, retrospective viewing of one's life.

as a sign of losing independence. As aging parents learn to accept help, they can continue to offer advice to their adult children who are also experiencing another stage of the aging process.

Other relationships with immediate family members, such as siblings, also continue to develop. The importance of these relationships may increase as personal and family changes occur. Sibling relationships can strengthen as siblings experience similar changes, rewards, and losses, **12-9**.

Many older adult siblings face the passing of their parents and other siblings. These transition periods are significant as remaining siblings take on new roles. If there is a surviving parent, the siblings often help the remaining parent adjust. The oldest remaining sibling may take on the role of becoming the oldest adult in the family. A woman may become the **matriarch**, the oldest influential female family member. A man may become the **patriarch**, or the oldest influential male family member.

*Yuri Arcurs/Shutterstock.com*

**12-9** From shared experiences, siblings can bond in new ways and offer each other support and understanding.

### Marriages

As marriages continue into older adulthood, partners can experience changes together and offer support to each other. Partners may also practice generativity by passing stories, knowledge, and traditions to younger generations.

New romantic relationships may also develop during older adulthood. As many older adults lose spouses and partners through death or divorce, new relationships form. Older adults may fall in love. They may choose to commit to marriage. The vast majority of these marriages are not first marriages, but remarriages following the loss of a spouse.

These marriages are not unlike those of earlier years. New relationships start with attraction followed by friendly love, romantic love, and then commitment. The motivation for remarriage does not differ greatly from young adulthood. Many older adults simply desire companionship.

## Importance of Social Interaction

The need for love, acceptance, and companionship extend into older adulthood. Maintaining relationships that include friends and community members is critical for older adults. Social relationships can help reduce feelings of depression, sadness, or loneliness.

As in other life stages, relationships with friends in older adulthood can have a positive impact on health and well-being. Friends can provide help and support when needed. They may relate to major life events. New grandchildren, the death of loved ones, and retirement are examples of changes friends may also be experiencing.

## Cultural Connections   Social Groups for Older Adults

Many communities offer socializing groups specifically for older adults. Similar to clubs for adolescents or younger adults, older adult groups may be based on common interests, religion, or culture. Groups may focus on hobbies, such as reading, knitting, or painting. They may also organize physical activities, such as group walking or swimming. Joining a social group can be a way for older adults to remain physically active, social, and engaged. Libraries, gyms, and other community centers are all common places that organize socializing groups for older adults.

### Writing Activity

What are the benefits of social groups for older adults? With a partner, write a list of benefits involved when older adults join a social group. How does the social group improve physical, cognitive, and socio-emotional well-being? What activities might you want to be involved in when you are an older adult? In what ways do they differ from your interests today?

Community relationships and activities also contribute to the personal satisfaction and well-being of older adults. Socializing, volunteering, joining a group at the library, taking classes, and gardening all contribute to well-being and society. In accordance with Kohlberg's postconventional morality stage, older adults have a need to contribute to society. Since many older adults will be transitioning or have already transitioned into retirement, social interaction may decrease. Establishing community relationships helps fulfill societal and social needs.

## Workforce Participation and Retirement

In some occupations, such as airline pilots, there is a mandatory retirement age. For most, there is not. Making the decision to retire is a major life decision that involves the loss of an important social role or identity, **12-10**. Deciding when to retire is also a major financial decision.

*Blend Images/Shutterstock.com*

**12-10**   Most working adults retire from paid full-time employment sometime during older adulthood.

Some people look forward to retiring with great anticipation. Others approach retirement with concern. Retirement affects not only the worker, but also his or her spouse. Older adults today are more likely to continue working longer than previous generations in the last century. Reasons for extending work may include continuing financial benefits, staying active, and maintaining regular social interaction.

There are many options available to people after they retire. Many people choose to travel or participate in hobbies or spend more time with family and friends. Some people choose to get a part-time job. Others choose to volunteer in meaningful activities in their community or place of worship. As workforce participation decreases, so does the identifying of oneself based on a role performed at work. Being known as a doctor, teacher, or plumber becomes something of the past rather than the present. As more time passes, career identity becomes less of a self-identity.

## Emotional Changes

Are older adults less happy than younger adults? Most studies indicate that despite physical and social role changes, many older adults report a higher level of happiness than younger adults. Older adults may actually be more optimistic, or focus on positive memories and upcoming events. For some, negative self-identity and depression can develop as aging progresses.

Depression is common in older adulthood as work and family roles change and physical abilities decrease. These changes may be seen as losses. Intense sadness, pessimism, and hopelessness may follow. Loss of friends and family members increase these feelings. Feelings of depression can also increase if independence and control are lost, if financial resources are scarce, or familial and social interaction are reduced.

Due to a growing number of physical ailments, many older adults take multiple medications and supplements to relieve pain and other symptoms. Many of these medications have side effects that cause depression, especially when adults take more than one prescription, **12-11**.

How do older adults positively respond to diminishing social and economic roles? Several factors are associated with a positive attitude toward an older adult's emerging identity. Maintaining social relationships with old and new friends and spending time participating in club or community events positively affect self-esteem. Following the news, reading, and completing mental exercises keep the mind active and connected with the world, which also positively affect self-esteem.

*Supri Suharjoto/Shutterstock.com*

**12-11**  Prescribed medications can contribute to feelings of depression.

## Cultural and Societal Influences

There are many myths that surround aging and older adulthood. Myths on aging come from societal sharing of false or inaccurate beliefs. Bias against, or unfair treatment of, older adults is termed **ageism**. One myth about aging is that older adults are rigid and inflexible. They do not like new ideas or ways of doing things. They become crabby and impatient with younger people. In reality, older adults have a lot to offer society. Although people often remain true to their temperament or personality, most tend to mellow with age. They are often more accepting of differences in others than they may have been in middle age. Older adults are the carriers of cultural traditions. They have lived life and have wisdom or expert knowledge in practical issues.

## Checkpoint

1. According to Erikson, what is the primary socio-emotional task of older adulthood?
2. List three examples of how social roles change during older adulthood.
3. Why is social interaction important in older adulthood?
4. Why may older adults view retiring as challenging?
5. Describe *ageism* and give an example.

Jack Q/Shutterstock.com

**12-12**  Mental exercises can slow the effects of dementia.

## Special Needs

Special needs in older adulthood vary. Many special needs are related to physical ailments, as the body is declining in ability. In addition to medications, adults may need to make other lifestyle adjustments to accommodate for changes. For example, adults with osteoporosis may need a walking aid. Cognitive changes require other treatments.

In older adulthood, dementia is common, **12-12**. **Dementia** is a term used to describe cognitive declines and memory loss, which are caused by damage to the brain. Dementia impairs a person's ability to perform everyday tasks, such as self-dressing, cleaning, eating, and remembering where items are placed. Not all older adults, however, suffer from dementia.

Memory loss for those with dementia differs from normal forgetfulness. An example of a dementia concern would be noted when an adult asks the same question repeatedly, without realizing they already asked the question. Dementia can also affect language ability. Older adults can confuse words and meanings, which interferes with communication. As dementia continues, older adults can become frustrated. They may display irritability and even personality changes.

Treatment for dementia depends on the severity of symptoms. Dementia does not have a cure, but with some medications, symptoms may significantly improve. A caregiver may need to help with daily functions and make changes to a living environment to improve safety.

Whereas dementia is a slow decline in abilities, **Alzheimer's disease** is a progressive brain disorder that includes not only memory loss, but also progressively severe confusion. People with Alzheimer's disease may not be able to recall past life events. They may also forget where they are, how they got there, and how to leave. Eventually, they have trouble speaking or recognizing family and friends. They may also suffer from hallucinations and depression. Similar to dementia, there is no current cure. Treatment options include therapy, medications, help from a caregiver, and adjustments to housing. Researchers are currently working to develop a cure for Alzheimer's disease.

## Housing Options

With decreasing physical abilities, many older adults have difficulty caring for themselves. Daily tasks such as grooming, meal preparation, and household chores can be difficult. Medical issues may limit walking or lifting. Cognitive or mental health issues may impair judgment. The time may come when alternative living arrangements must be made, especially when safety becomes an issue.

**Health Connections**    **Coping with Alzheimer's Disease**

Adults suffering from Alzheimer's disease may eventually reach a point in their illness when they no longer remember their own family members. To any family member of an Alzheimer's patient, watching the decline of memory loss can be emotionally challenging. Feelings of anger and sadness can surface when a family member with Alzheimer's forgets another's name or who they are. Watching him or her struggle with language can also be frustrating.

Understanding and patience can be effective traits to successful caregiving. Learning about the disease and the effects can help ease caregiver frustration. Forgetting names, language, and everyday tasks is unintentional. Older adults may be aware of their own confusion and display signs of anger, irritability, or depression. Responding with patience can help improve the relationship between the caregiver and adult with Alzheimer's.

Show signs of emotional support to make the older adult feel more at ease. A simple gesture such as smiling can improve the mood and tone. Also, continue to speak positively and respectfully to an adult with Alzheimer's. Creating a positive atmosphere and personal interaction can have a lasting effect, even if the affected person does not remember.

### Research Activity

There are many resources available explaining Alzheimer's disease. From a reliable book, magazine, journal, or online resource, find an article relating to Alzheimer's disease. This may include information for the patient, caregiver, or family members of an adult with Alzheimer's disease. What are other areas of life this disease may impact? Write a brief summary of your research.

## Transitioning from Independent to Family Living

Just as in other stages of life, many older adults value independence. Many fear the loss of independence and an inability to no longer care for themselves. Older adults, however, are a diverse group and a significant number still live independently. Many older adults want to grow old in their own homes. They may not want to move in with other family members or into new living arrangements. They may measure their quality of life by the amount of independence they perceive in their living conditions. With housing modifications, proper care, and safety precautions, they may be able to live independently. They may have a home health care worker, often a nurse, who can check on them periodically. Older adults may try to live independently as long as possible.

Some older adults are not able to live independently because of poor health. In many cultures, older adults often live with family members or friends. Having older adults move into an adult child's house may be expected by all family members. Sometimes others need to make housing decisions for older adults if their mental or cognitive status is impaired. Older people requiring assistance from caregivers are often dependent for their physical, psychological, social, and sometimes economic needs.

Moving from independence to increasing dependence is a major family-life transition. Older adults adjust to new roles while dealing with issues related to aging and mortality. When older adults move in with adult children, middle-aged adults become members of the sandwich generation. Caregivers can become emotionally drained, and physically exhausted.

## Living in New Communities

During older adulthood, abilities often decline and older adults may need help with daily tasks or require new living arrangements. Although some may still live independently, with a spouse, or other family members, other older adults may move into new living communities. New living arrangements can be an option to provide more care as needed.

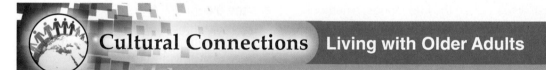

## Cultural Connections    Living with Older Adults

In many cultures, moving older adults into the main family house is part of the culture and tradition. For example, in India, younger family members, especially males, provide care for older family members in one home. These living arrangements create a pattern of intergenerational living. Inviting older adults to move into the family home is much more common than alternative arrangements for older adults. Although the number of adult living facilities is slowly growing in India, there are very few available. This reflects the view of the larger culture, which accepts living with aging parents as normal and expected. Other adults may also live independently, but living with family is the most common.

### Speaking Activity

Interview a grandparent or older adult to understand his or her views on living facilities. Does he or she favor one living arrangement over another? Why? Write a brief summary of your report and share your findings with the class.

Three main types of living communities offer different levels of support. *Independent living communities* provide housing for older adults who can care for themselves, but desire the community support of those of similar age. *Assisted living housing* environments provide gradually expanded oversight and help with daily activities, **12-13**. Medical care can be provided when necessary. *Retirement homes* provide more intense nursing care for residents, usually with a medical staff that provides oversight as needed.

Although some older adults are optimistic about new living arrangements, others struggle with the new transition. They may be resentful of losing the independence they had when living alone or with a loved one. Like any major transition, change can be emotionally difficult. If the move requires parting with some possessions, older adults may feel additional loss for objects representing a past stage in life.

## Hospice Care

Caring for a loved one who is terminally ill is beyond what many people are capable of handling physically, emotionally, and financially. **Hospice care**, a form of care given by trained medical professionals, focuses on making a person comfortable in his or her last days and hours of life. Caregivers attempt to control their patient's pain while serving emotional and sometimes spiritual needs. Care can be provided either in the patient's home or in a hospice living center. Hospice caregivers not only focus on the patient, but the needs of the family and loved ones as well.

*Monkey Business Images/Shutterstock.com*

**12-13**  Assisted living housing environments often provide meals and social activities.

## Checkpoint

1. What is dementia? How does dementia differ from normal memory loss?
2. Define *Alzheimer's disease*. What are treatment options available for Alzheimer's disease?
3. Why may living arrangements need to change as an adult ages?
4. What are three main types of living communities available for older adults?
5. Explain hospice care and the needs it serves.

# Death and Grief

Just as birth marks the beginning of life, death marks the end. Facing death is one of the most significant life events one experiences. When people face their own death, they reflect on their own life and accept that death is a part of their life. Facing another person's death means understanding that the person will no longer be there. Death can mean that one period in life may end, while a new one is beginning. Memorials, including written tributes, gatherings of friends and family, photo albums, and electronic journals of memories, are ways people typically remember and honor those who have died, **12-14**.

## Outlook on Death

As adults progress through older adulthood, they become aware of impending death, especially as many of their friends and loved ones pass away. People may come to a point in their life when they do not fear death, but instead, they

*Yuri Arcurs/Shutterstock.com*

**12-14**  How does a person cope with the loss of a loved one?

see this event as a reality in the relatively near future. When older adults speak about death, younger people may feel uncomfortable as they are not yet ready to think of their own *mortality* (eventual death).

Older adults will often plan for their inevitable passing in a rational and organized way. People may arrange their own funeral or memorial services in advance. They may seek burial plots or cremation holdings. They may prepare a **Last Will and Testament**, or will, which is a legally binding document that gives directions on how to divide financial assets. Those who receive the financial assets are called **beneficiaries**. Many also have a living will. A **living will** is a legal document that informs family and medical workers of preferences for being kept alive by artificial means, or allows the decision to let them pass, when there is no chance of recovery. Creating these legal documents eases the process of dying for the individual, family, and friends.

Some older adults do not make any advance preparations. Dying **intestate** means to die without a will. This can cause problems for remaining loved ones. When there is no will, state laws determine the division of assets among remaining family members. Estate taxes are often much higher and family members often incur additional expenses such as court costs and attorney fees.

## The Stages of Dying

Accepting the reality of one's own impending death is difficult. People often move through a process of acceptance as they face their own mortality. Learning to accept death is not an easy process. Many times, the rate of acceptance depends on the length of time people have left and the sense of control they feel.

Typically, there are five common stages people experience when learning to cope with their own death, **12-15**. Each person is different and will not experience these stages in the same way. For some, one of these stages may last longer than another stage. The levels of severity can differ, too.

---

### The Stages of Dying

1. **Denial.** In this first stage, individuals who learn they are terminally ill reject the idea of dying. They may ignore the concept of their own death and decide not to acknowledge it. They cannot believe that this could be happening to them.
2. **Anger.** During the second stage, feelings of negativity and resentment develop. Individuals may be angry at the illness or disease. They may be angry that they will experience death and possible pain, while others are still going to be alive and healthy.
3. **Bargaining.** In this stage, individuals realize their own death, but wish for more time. They may propose deals or exchanges in order to preserve their own life. Bargaining may be with doctors, family, friends, or a higher power. For example, an individual may offer to become a "better person" if his or her life is extended.
4. **Depression.** In the fourth stage, individuals struggle with the loss of life. They may think about people, activities, and events they will miss. They may become sad, withdrawn, and lose interest in activities. They may be afraid or feel they are not ready.
5. **Acceptance.** In the final stage, individuals understand and accept that the reality of their own death is near. They may no longer be afraid or resentful. This stage is usually calm, which can transition into a peaceful passing.

*Goodheart-Willcox Publisher*

**12-15**  Some people experience the stages of dying in order, some experience them out of order, while others may skip stages altogether.

### Importance of Support and Care

The process of dying is difficult for everyone involved, especially if the dying process is extended over time due to illness or disability. Having support and care from family, friends, and health care professionals is important to the well-being of the adult coping with dying. When an individual has a support group, he or she can more easily process and deal with the stages of dying than if facing these challenges alone. Accepting the process of dying also allows friends and family members to say goodbye, resolve any past conflicts, and organize personal and financial matters. Loved ones can care for the dying family member or friend while learning to cope with and acknowledge the death of the loved one.

### Widowhood

One of the most difficult losses for older adults is losing a spouse through death. For those who have spent time as a couple for many years, they may feel like a part of themselves is gone forever. In a marriage, when the husband passes away, the wife becomes a **widow**, the female surviving spouse. If the wife dies, the surviving husband becomes a **widower**.

**Bereavement** is a term used to describe the state of losing a loved one through death. **Grief** describes the mental anguish or sadness that accompanies bereavement. Great distress and sorrow are often part of grieving. **Mourning** includes the period when family members and friends remember and grieve for the loss of a beloved one. The length of mourning varies per individual. Different cultures may have different customs involved with mourning, **12-16**.

Losses of friends and loved ones bring a variety of responses. Closeness in the relationship, proximity, dependence, and cause of death, such as a sudden or unexpected loss all influence the grieving process.

*Ashley Whitworth/Shutterstock.com*

**12-16** Mourning may include wearing black or the shedding of tears.

## Stages of Grieving

Losing a friend or loved one can cause strong emotional reactions. Sadness, disbelief, numbness, anxiety, loneliness, and despair are common. Losing a friend or family member can be traumatic, even when it is believed to be the "right time." Coping with the death of someone else is termed *grieving.* Grieving is complex and is experienced differently by different people. Similar to the stages of dying, there are also five stages of grieving.

1. **Denial.** Survivors of the loved one may not believe or fully understand that the loved one passed away. They may ignore the death and continue in daily activities as if it did not happen.
2. **Anger.** After denial, feelings of anger may arise. The individual may be angry that he or she is left to deal with many new issues and possibly new roles. The individual may also be angry toward other family members, friends, and coworkers in the belief that others do not understand.

**Cultural Connections**   Grieving Customs

Different cultures have different customs when grieving for the loss of a loved one. Some cultures have a certain amount of days the grieving period is observed. Others have particular housing modifications that are made. The following is a sample of global grieving practices:

- **Israel.** In Jewish tradition, mourners practice sitting *shiva*, a period of seven days when family members gather to mourn the loss of a loved one. During this time, mourners do not participate in work or leisure activities. Candles are placed in the house of mourning. Mirrors may also be covered to turn attention away from individuals and toward the person who has just passed away. Stories about the deceased individual are shared and encouraged.

- **Greece.** Traditionally, the mourning period lasts for 40 days, but may last longer. Immediate family members wear black during this period and do not attend social or leisure activities. Adult males may wear a black armband to commemorate a loss.

### Research Activity

Imagine a friend has recently lost a loved one and is going through the five stages of grieving. Create a pamphlet or electronic presentation that lists suggested healthful tips or activities to help him or her through the grieving process. Then, share your presentation with the class.

3. **Bargaining.** This stage occurs before the loved one dies. The individual may try to offer a deal or exchange in order to extend the life of a loved one.
4. **Depression.** Feelings of sadness, despair, withdrawal, and possibly loneliness may dominate now that the survivor understands the loved one will no longer be alive.
5. **Acceptance.** In the final stage, individuals begin to accept or feel comfortable with the loss of the loved one. They recognize that death is a normal part of the lifespan. They are able to move forward, without forgetting the loved one's death.

Experiencing grief is normal and healthy. As in the stages of dying, individuals may not experience these stages in order. They may skip stages or spend more time in one stage than another. There is no right or wrong amount of time to spend grieving. After experiencing a death, the survivor may continue to grieve for weeks, months, or years after the death. A family's culture may influence the grieving process.

Friends and family can help individuals cope with the natural grieving process. This is especially important in helping older adults who have lost a life partner. Celebrating the life, unique contributions, and personality of the one lost through death may ease the feeling of loss. Death is inevitable, and although is not always easy to accept, is the final chapter of life.

## Checkpoint

1. Compare and contrast the difference between a Last Will and Testament and a living will.
2. List and explain the five stages of dying.
3. Differentiate between the terms *bereavement*, *grief*, and *mourning*.
4. How do the five stages of dying differ from the five stages of grieving?

## Summary

Older adulthood includes adults age 66 and above. During older adulthood, vision, hearing, and sensory changes may decline. Muscle mass, bone density, and strength also continue to decline. Arthritis, hypertension, and sleep apnea can also challenge older adults. Physical activity and meeting nutritional needs can help adults stay healthy and active.

Cognitive abilities may decline and memory loss may also occur. As the brain is shrinking, brain processing slows. Language abilities remain stable as older adults can more easily access long-term memories. Morally, older adults are in Kohlberg's postconventional stage.

The major socio-emotional task according to Erikson's psychosocial theory is *integrity versus despair*. Integrity can be achieved by reflecting on one's life and accepting both successes and failures. Older adults learn to accept changing roles, involving family, friends, and retirement. Many lose their partners to death and become widows or widowers.

As adults continue to age and decline, they may need help with daily living tasks. They may seek alternate living arrangements. Eventually, older adults face their own mortality. They commonly experience the five stages of dying and grieving. Family, friends, and those who are medically trained can help the dying face the final stage with dignity and care.

## Vocabulary Activity

On a separate sheet of paper, list words that relate to each of the key terms. Then, work with a partner to explain how these words are related.

## Critical Thinking

1. **Predict.** What do you believe will be the average life expectancy for your generation? How long do you hope to live? What factors will affect the average life expectancy for your generation?

2. **Cause and effect.** The average life expectancy in Japan is several years longer than the United States. Why might this be? What issues might this cause for national governments?

3. **Analyze.** Discuss cultural and societal influences on people in late adulthood.

4. **Analyze.** Do you interact with older adults on a daily basis? If so, who and when? If not, why not? What might your answer say about cross-generational interactions in your culture?

5. **Identify.** Find newspaper articles about aging or events facing older adults. Cut the articles out and, together with your classmates, create a bulletin board that summarizes these news events.

6. **Draw conclusions.** If the older adult generation is the fastest growing segment of society, how might this affect the way people live, government spending, consumer products, and health care?

7. **Evaluate.** Find a popular film that features at least one older adult. Is the person portrayed in a positive light? What ideas about aging are communicated in the film?

8. **Assess.** Older adults are often employed as greeters in retail stores or as ushers in sports arenas or performance halls. Why might some employers prefer older adults for these positions?

9. **Compare and contrast.** Interview a family member or friend who is over age 66. Ask him or her about physical, cognitive, and socio-emotional changes experienced since high school.

10. **Make inferences.** Conduct research about the decade of time when a 60-, 70-, 80-, or 90-year-old attended high school. Describe how the historical events of the decade may have affected the values, motivations, fears, and worldview of this person today.

11. **Analyze.** Explain why social interaction and relationships with family and peers are important for people in late adulthood.

## Core Skills

12. **Speaking.** Report on an interaction you have had with an older adult. This interaction could be a face-to-face conversation, e-mail exchange, letter, or other form of communication. Report on any differences seen in how the two of you communicated.

13. **Writing.** Write a two-page fictional story about an older adult living with integrity versus despair.

14. **Reading.** Find a copy of the American Association of Retired Persons (AARP) magazine at a local library or online. Read at least five articles.

15. **Math.** For the next two weeks, inquire about a discount for older adults at every store, restaurant, or other service you and your family use or visit. Calculate how much you could save on your spending if you were eligible for this discount.

16. **Listening.** Interview an adolescent, a young adult, a middle-aged adult, and an older adult and ask them to answer the following question: How do you feel about death? Record your responses and share them with the class.

17. **Writing.** In a short essay, describe and analyze the developmental theories that apply to older adulthood, including biological, cognitive, emotional, moral, and psychosocial development.

18. **CTE Career Readiness Practice.** Complete an oral history by interviewing a person who is retired. If you are unable to interview someone, read one or more case studies about retirement from reliable Internet or library resources. How does the information you learned from the interview or reading compare to information presented by the author of your text? Write a detailed summary of your interview or reading, describing how retirement affected the person's life.

## Research

19. Research one of the more common eye ailments in older adulthood. Design a poster or webpage that informs your classmates about this health challenge including symptoms and possible treatments.

20. Research living options available in your local community for older adults. Include independent living communities, assisted living housing, and retirement homes. Make a chart or graph comparing the costs and attributes of each.

## Event Prep

21. As a class, identify leadership opportunities at various stages throughout the lifespan. For example, becoming involved in a student organization in high school can offer leadership opportunities. Involvement in a work committee or community action group promotes leadership throughout adulthood. Identify ways in which you can become a lifelong leader and create a plan of action. You may wish to expand your project by developing an FCCLA *Leadership Service in Action* project. Use the FCCLA *Planning Process* to guide your project planning. See your FCCLA adviser for further information.

# Part 3

## Strategies Promoting Lifetime Human Development

Monkey Business Images/Shutterstock.com

## FOCUS ON

## Truthful Communcation

Ethical communications are very important in both personal and business life. Distorting information for personal gain is an unethical practice. An ethical communicator depends on honesty, accuracy, and truthfulness to guide all communications. Communication must be honest and presented in an unbiased manner. Facts should be given without distortion, and if the information is an opinion, label it as such. Do not take credit for ideas that belong to someone else—always identify your sources. What do you think would happen if someone in a helping or teaching role did not follow these practices with the people they meet on the job?

# Chapter 13

## Child and Adult Care Resources for Families

Zurijeta/Shutterstock.com

# Objectives

After studying this chapter, you will be able to

- analyze four main types of child care programs families often use.
- compare and contrast family child care and center-based child care.
- analyze various methods parents and caregivers use for selecting quality child care.
- differentiate between developmentally appropriate practices and developmentally inappropriate practices.
- compare and contrast different types of older adult care available to families.

## Reading Prep

Before reading this chapter, read the feature on the part-opening page. How does this feature relate to what is being presented in the content?

## Key Terms

nannies

au pairs

playgroups

family child care centers

day care centers

preschool programs

children in self-care

school-age child care programs

accredited

child–caregiver ratio

developmentally appropriate practices (DAPs)

developmentally inappropriate practices (DIPs)

adult day care

## Visit the G-W Learning Companion Website to:

- **build** vocabulary with e-flash cards and interactive games;
- **assess** what you learn by completing self-assessment quizzes; and
- **expand** knowledge with activities that extend learning.

G-WLEARNING.com www.g-wlearning.com/development/

Children need care. Sometimes older adults do, too. Caring for children and older family members takes time, energy, and financial resources. Managing all three can be challenging to families as obtaining financial resources, such as holding a job, takes time and energy away from spending time with those needing extra care. As a result, children and older adults may need care provided by nonfamily members.

Families need to be prepared to make informed decisions about child and adult care. The process starts by understanding the needs of the child or older adult. Making these decisions requires listening, as well as asking questions. Families also need to be aware of available resources. Ideally, planning for the future can occur while older family members are able to express their desires and make their own decisions.

## Types of Child Care Programs

There are four main types of child care programs from which families may choose. These include *in-home child care, family child care, center-based child care,* and *school-age child care.* The best choice depends on the child's temperament, needs, and age. Some children do best in social environments where they can interact with other children. They are comfortable with activity around them. Others are not.

OtnaYdur/Shutterstock.com

**13-1** Parents, relatives, or nonfamily members may provide in-home child care.

### In-Home Child Care

Some parents prefer in-home child care in which one parent may choose to stay home, **13-1**. Parents may work different shifts so at least one parent is available to stay home with the children. Using an extended family member, such as a grandparent or an aunt, is another in-home child care option. Nannies and au pairs may also provide in-home child care.

**Nannies** are professionals hired to care for children in their own home. They may either live in the home or commute. Nannies typically have set work hours, even if they live in the home. They are often hired through agencies. Nanny services often require applicants to have child care training beyond high school or practical experience with good recommendations.

Nannies give one-on-one care to children and often develop close relationships with both the children and parents. They may work full- or part-time and often adjust their work schedule to fit the children's schedule. A nanny can oversee fieldtrips, such as going to the zoo or park, and provide transportation to other activities, such as swimming lessons. Nannies may also help with meal preparation for the children. For parents who travel for work and need flexibility in their child care, a nanny may be a good choice.

A drawback to having a nanny is that he or she is unsupervised in the home. Child care can be stressful. When the nanny is tired or sick, alternate care may be difficult to arrange. The nanny may leave for another job. The relationship between the child and nanny is intense. Therefore, losing a nanny may be traumatic for a child.

**Au pairs** are often from a different culture and are hired to live in the home and provide occasional child care as well as perform light household duties. This service often lasts for about six months to a year.

Part of the draw of using an au pair is for children to gain a cross-cultural experience while receiving care. Au pairs can expose children to another language and cultural traditions. Host families usually supervise au pairs and treat them as a member of the family. Au pairs also gain cultural experiences from the host families.

**Playgroups** are a good way for in-home care providers to give their children opportunities to play with other children as they socialize with other parents, **13-2**. Children involved in playgroups range in age, usually from birth to age 5. While children play and interact with each other, caregivers may discuss parenting challenges and receive support from others who may be experiencing similar issues. Playgroups may meet in an individual home, at a park, or another nearby location.

*paul prescott/Shutterstock.com*

**13-2**  Playgroups focus on socialization for both the children and parents.

# Family Child Care

**Family child care centers** are operated in the caregiver's private home for a small number of children. Often, there is just one caregiver to supervise the children. Using resources available in the home, caregivers provide nutritious meals and snacks, physical activity opportunities, developmentally appropriate activities, and guidance for infants, toddlers, and children.

Some family child care centers are licensed and operate with written expectations and policies. Licensed family child care centers have been approved by the state. This requires in-home centers to meet certain standards. Requirements vary by state, but often include regulations for the following:

- a safe environment
- maximum number of children receiving care (including the caregiver's own children)
- child-caregiver interactions
- provision of developmentally appropriate activities
- successful completion of background checks and safety inspections by accredited agencies

There are many advantages to licensed family child care centers. The center may be close to the child's home, which provides a familiar environment for the child. Family child care centers may also be less expensive and more flexible than center-based child care centers. Family child care centers may adjust rates based on attendance. Center-based child care centers may charge caregivers for full-time attendance, even when a child attends part-time. Another advantage of family child care centers is that caregivers can provide children with more one-on-one attention because there are fewer children in attendance, **13-3**.

*Diego Cervo/Shutterstock.com*

**13-3**  With fewer children in family child care, the risk for catching and spreading illnesses decreases.

Unfortunately, some family child care centers operate without licensing. A drawback to an unlicensed family child care center is that the care is unsupervised by outside agencies. In other words, if caregivers do not register their in-home centers with the state, they will not be subject to inspections. They may not meet safety and other child care standards. Overcrowding, unsafe environments, and unqualified caregivers may be some issues of concern with unregulated family child care centers.

## Center-Based Child Care

Center-based child care programs are provided in a center and not in a home. They may serve 20 children or 200 children. Center-based child care programs may be for-profit or nonprofit. *For-profit programs* are child care centers established to generate profit or money, as in other business operations. *Nonprofit programs* are not established for the purpose of making money. Places of worship and other community centers are examples of nonprofit programs. Parents, community members, or corporate donors may fund nonprofit organizations. Nonprofit centers are usually less costly than for-profit programs. Day care centers and preschool programs are two common options available for center-based child care.

### Day Care Centers

Most communities have day care centers. **Day care centers** offer care to large groups of infants, toddlers, and children with many caregivers, **13-4**. Day care companies, places of worship, community centers, hospitals, schools, or even corporations offering services to their employees may operate day care centers. Many day care centers are licensed as the result of meeting standards and passing periodic inspections. They also have clearly written policies for hours of operation, pick-up and drop-off times, disciplinary practices, and illness procedures.

*dotshock/Shutterstock.com*

**13-4**   Some day care centers operate in one building with children separated into rooms by age groups.

Day care centers may offer part- or full-time programs. In part-time programs, children attend day care for a few hours of the day. Full-time programs provide care for children for a significant portion of the day. Full-time programs often include meals, naptime, and other activities. Parents can choose part- or full-time programs depending on their scheduling needs. Some parents choose day care programs because of the socialization opportunities they provide for their children.

## Preschool Programs

Preschool programs focus on preparing children ages 3- to 5-years-old for the next level of schooling. Preschools focus on play and academics. While preschoolers learn new academic concepts, such as writing, reading, and math, they also learn communication and socialization skills. Programs can be full- or part-time. They often run for partial day hours or only on certain days of the week. Preschool programs are often scheduled around mealtimes, such as morning or afternoon care. These programs may offer snacks, but typically do not provide meals.

In addition to educational preparation, some preschool programs also provide meals and other services. For example, *Head Start*, a government-funded program, helps prepare low-income preschoolers for school. Educators, nutritionists, health

## Cultural Connections — Types of Preschool Programs

There are many types of preschool programs available for children ages 3 through 5. These programs may use pedagogy or andragogy teaching methods, differ in activities available, or differ in classroom organization. Three different types of preschool programs are Montessori, Waldorf, and HighScope programs.

### Montessori

Montessori preschools use the andragogy method of instruction, where students have more independence and learn through self-direction. Montessori teachers prepare developmentally appropriate activities, while setting any necessary safety limits or precautions. Preschoolers learn through hands-on experiences, using their senses of touch, sight, smell, hearing, and taste. For example, preschoolers will play with self-correcting games or use real food instead of play food.

### Waldorf

Similar to Montessori programs, Waldorf programs focus on using the senses to develop and learn. Originating in Germany, Waldorf programs are available globally. Caregivers create an environment resembling a home for children to explore and learn through their surroundings. Waldorf programs focus on creativity, nature, social skills, and other developmentally appropriate activities.

### HighScope

Preschoolers learn through self-direction. Ten areas of development are the focus of programs, including socio-emotional development, physical activity, language, mathematics, social studies, science, and creativity. Classrooms are divided by different play and learning activities.

### Research Activity

Research other types of preschool programs available. Which type of program do you think is best? Write a one- to two-page response outlining your argument.

professionals, social workers, and many other professionals work together to provide comprehensive services for economically disadvantaged children. Some Head Start programs are coordinated with other social programs to provide all-day child care. The result has better prepared children for their next level of schooling.

## School-Age Child Care

Traditionally, child care has been available for infants, toddlers, and preschool children. Child care needs do not stop, however, when children enter school. For caregivers who work full-time, school hours are usually shorter than their working hours. Sometimes schools start later than a working parent's starting time at work. The school day may end while a parent is still at work.

**Children in self-care** are unsupervised children who provide care for themselves for the few hours when a parent is away from the home before or after school. These children prepare themselves for school in the morning or return after school to an empty house. Also known as *latchkey children*, they are responsible for getting into their homes and directing their own care, such as preparing snacks or doing homework after school. States laws vary regarding the age children can begin to stay home alone.

One potential benefit to latchkey children is the opportunity for the child to learn about responsibility and independence. At times, children can become lonely, frightened, sad, and anxious. They may not know what to do in certain situations. In these situations, unsupervised children can be in danger. To prevent accidents or injuries, a child should never stay home alone, regardless of age, until the parent or caregiver determines that the child is capable of handling self-care responsibilities.

---

## *Safety* Connections          Safety When Home Alone

Finding adequate supervision and care for adolescents can be challenging for caregivers. After-school activities, sports, or clubs may not be an option. At times, young adolescents may need to stay home alone without supervision. The following guidelines can help increase safety when home alone.

- Have all emergency contact numbers readily available.
- Know how to carry through with an emergency escape plan, including fires, floods, etc.
- Know where to find first-aid equipment and the purpose of each item, and how to use first-aid techniques. In an emergency, call 9-1-1.
- Upon arriving home, if windows appear broken or doors are open, do not go inside. Walk to a neighbor's house and call caregivers. If necessary, call the police, who can perform an inspection and determine safety.

- Once at home, stay at home until caregivers arrive.
- Keep all doors and windows locked.
- Do not open the door for any unrecognized person. Do not feel obligated to respond to him or her. Never admit to being home alone.
- Make sure any remaining questions are answered that may be helpful to safety or well-being. This may include instructions about hazardous appliances, machines, or other items in the household.

### Speaking Activity

With a partner, discuss any pros and cons to staying home alone. Is there an appropriate minimal age for when individuals can stay home by themselves? What are your state's requirements for when children can stay home alone?

For children who are not ready for self-care, **school-age child care programs** provide care for them in safe, healthy, and stimulating environments. *Before- and after-school care programs* provide further care for children and adolescents before school begins or after school ends. These programs are often in the school the child regularly attends. School-age child care programs often provide help with homework, nutritional needs, or arrangements for other developmentally appropriate activities. After-school activities, including sports and interest-based clubs are among some of the care options that can also be beneficial to children and adolescents.

In addition to school-based care programs, other programs or *clubs* also provide care, mentoring, homework help, and appropriate activities. Clubs may meet in community centers, such as schools, places of worship, libraries, or other community locations. The purpose of these clubs is to help students meet educational needs, develop interests, or spend time with mentors, **13-5**. Language courses, art classes, and sports activities are just some of the options that are offered through these programs. Another main purpose of these clubs is for children and adolescents to feel a sense of belonging and a connection to their community. Clubs can provide a refuge from other unsafe locations, while helping students have their needs met.

## Checkpoint

1. What are the four main types of child care?
2. What is the difference between a nanny and an au pair?
3. List three possible advantages and disadvantages of a family child care center.
4. What is the difference between a day care center and a preschool program?
5. List two after-school child care options for school-aged children.

# Selecting Quality Child Care

With many child care options available, selecting quality child care can be challenging. There may be many differences when comparing child care centers and in-home caregivers, **13-6**. Hours of operation or employment, flexibility, cost, methods of instruction, activities, and types of discipline can vary. The amount of staffing available and the regulations may also differ.

When evaluating child care centers, one of the first factors to consider is the center's licensing and accreditation. Center-based child care must be licensed by the state in which they operate. Licensed centers have been approved by the state and have met all state child care regulations and minimal requirements. Not all child care centers, however, are accredited. **Accredited** child care centers are licensed and meet additional standards set forth by a professional child care organization.

In addition to a center's licensing and accreditation, parents research many other factors. Staffing, child care environment, parent participation, program activities, diversity, and facilities for children with special needs are all important factors. Needs fluctuate from family to family. Considerations vary in importance for different families. Determining these and other factors through research and observations of child care centers can determine the quality of overall child care. Parents can be well-informed concerning the suitability of a chosen child care center for an infant, toddler, or child.

| National Clubs and Organizations | | |
|---|---|---|
| **Name** | **Description** | **Website** |
| **4-H (Head, Heart, Hands, Health)** | Children in elementary school through high school work with mentors to address community concerns. Leadership and teamwork skills develop, while ideas for the future build. | www.4-h.org |
| **21st Century Community Learning Centers** | Government-funded community centers that focus on helping students meet educational standards. Help with homework and tutoring sessions are offered. | www.ed.gov |
| **Big Brothers Big Sisters** | Children are paired with big brothers or big sisters, who act as mentors to the children. Mentors may help with homework, sports activities, or subject-specific material. Mentors help children dream about their future and set goals. | www.bbbs.org |
| **Boys and Girls Clubs of America** | This program focuses on children's education, while providing a sense of belonging. Encourages children and adolescents to stay in school. Sports, creative arts, and other subject-specific activities are offered. | www.bgca.org |

*Goodheart-Willcox Publisher*

**13-5** These national clubs and organizations can offer an alternative to school-age care options, while providing a sense of community, developing interests, and building a future.

## Cultural Connections  Other Child Care Considerations

In addition to analyzing a center's licensing and accreditation, staff, environment, program activities, diversity, and special needs provisions, parents evaluate other factors in making care choices. Choosing a type of child care also depends on the parent's values and needs. Commute distance, hours of operation, and flexibility of schedules affect child care selections. Some parents prefer a certain setting, religion, culture, or method of instruction for their child. For most parents, cost is a significant part of the decision-making process. Finding high quality, affordable child care can be tricky.

Child care options are not all the same. Families must first decide what criteria will best meet their needs. Goal setting can help clarify personal values and important factors when selecting child care. Creating a list of short- and long-term goals, desired caregiver characteristics, and financial needs can help in the decision-making process. Families can also utilize community resources, such as a child care network to view information and recommendations about child care options.

### Speaking Activity

Interview a parent who has considered enrolling his or her child in a child care center. Ask about which factors were most important in determining child care needs. How did the research process start? What was a determining factor in the decision-making process? Write a two-page report summarizing your interview.

## Child Care Comparison

| Type of Child Care | Advantages | Disadvantages |
|---|---|---|
| In-home child care | • Children are in a familiar, comfortable setting.<br>• Nannies, au pairs, and family members can offer more individual attention.<br>• Risk factor for catching and spreading illness is reduced.<br>• Children can develop a closer relationship to in-home caregivers.<br>• Au pairs may offer cultural knowledge to a child. | • In-home caregivers may be unsupervised with children.<br>• Children may have less exposure socializing with children their own age.<br>• Substitute care may be difficult if the in-home caregiver is sick or away.<br>• If a nanny or au pair finds other employment, children can be negatively impacted. |
| Family child care | • Fewer children in care allows more individual attention and less chance of catching and spreading illnesses.<br>• Licensed centers are approved by the state and meet safety standards.<br>• Caregivers may be more flexible with a parent's schedule.<br>• May be more affordable. | • Some family child care centers may be unlicensed.<br>• Unlicensed centers may not meet safety and health regulations.<br>• Caregivers may be unqualified.<br>• Caregivers may be unsupervised. |
| Center-based child care | • Centers are licensed by the state.<br>• Staff members must meet certain qualifications to be hired.<br>• Preschools focus on educational and social skills.<br>• Center-based care may offer more socializing opportunities for children.<br>• Centers may have additional services or equipment for children. | • May be more expensive; centers may charge parents for full-time care, even if part-time care is used.<br>• Some programs may only provide part-time care.<br>• Centers may have a higher risk for spreading and catching illnesses.<br>• Children may not receive enough individual attention.<br>• Sick children may be advised not to attend the center. Parents may need to find alternative care. |
| School-age child care | • Programs may prevent some safety concerns for children in self-care.<br>• Programs may help children with homework and offer tutoring.<br>• Programs may help children develop interests and goals.<br>• Programs may provide children with a sense of belonging in their community. | • For before- and after-school programs, children may not want to remain in school after hours.<br>• Care may be limited to a certain age. |

*Goodheart-Willcox Publisher*

**13-6**  There are advantages and disadvantages to each type of child care.

## Staffing

The ages of infants, toddlers, and children at the center will determine the minimum number of caregivers needed. The appropriate number of caregivers available for each child is called the **child–caregiver ratio**. Certain age groups need constant attention and supervision, while other age groups require less consideration, **13-7**. Newborns, infants, and toddlers require more frequent care than children ages 5

## Child Care Guidelines for Caregiver to Child Ratios

| Age of Child | Ratio of Children to Caregivers* | Maximum Group Size* |
|---|---|---|
| Newborn to 2 years | 4 to 1 | 8 |
| 2 to 3 years | 6 to 1 | 12 |
| 4 to 5 years | 10 to 1 | 20 |

*Child–caregiver ratios and maximum group size vary by state. Ratios and group sizes reduce for children under care with special needs.

Goodheart-Willcox Publisher

**13-7**   Generally, the more caregivers available, the more individual attention infants, toddlers, and children can receive.

and above. They need more caregivers available to provide individual attention. The *group size* refers to the maximum number of children that can receive care in one room or center. Each state sets the maximum group size allowed in each type of child care center. Child care centers may have larger group sizes than family care centers because of more available spacing and staff.

### Appropriate Child–Caregiver Interaction

In addition to a child care center's child–caregiver ratio, the qualities of the caregivers and their interactions with the children are important. Caregivers often demonstrate characteristics reflecting quality child care, **13-8**. Caregivers who have a genuine interest in children and child development, who are patient, and who also enjoy the children they care for often tend to provide higher-quality care. They can help children optimize their physical, cognitive, and socio-emotional development.

Quality caregivers demonstrate positive, appropriate interactions with children. Appropriate interaction is indicated by positive physical contact, such as patting the child on the back, hugging the child, and holding her hand. Newborns thrive with focused attention. Infants need caregivers to hold them and nurture them. Infants need to be supported in their efforts to roll over, crawl, stand, and walk. Toddlers continue to need support in learning to talk, walk, and use fine-motor skills. Preschoolers need encouragement and support for mastering motor skills, language, and appropriate social interaction. Caregivers are important in supporting all types of growth and development.

## Characteristics of Quality Caregivers

| | | |
|---|---|---|
| adaptable | fond of children | loving |
| committed to ongoing education | honest | nondiscriminatory |
| compassionate | interest in child development | patient |
| empathetic | kind and caring | reliable |
| encouraging | knowledgeable | responsible |

Goodheart-Willcox Publisher

**13-8**   Quality caregivers share many common characteristics.

Besides physical interaction, quality caregiving can also be seen in emotional and social interactions with the children, **13-9**. Appropriate interaction includes listening to and talking with the children. Caregivers comfort children when they are distressed. They ask children questions and answer their questions. They offer encouragement and praise.

Guiding children's behaviors and choices and helping them make age-appropriate decisions is another part of appropriate child–caregiver interaction. Caregivers use the induction method of discipline over power assertion or love withdrawal. They do not shame children or react in anger. They do not ignore a child's behavior or give them the "silent treatment." Arranging an interview with the potential caregiver can help determine guidance techniques and other positive characteristics of the caregiver.

## Interviewing a Caregiver

Interviewing a caregiver, whether in-home or center-based, is important. Interviewing can help parents determine the qualities and qualifications of the potential caregiver. Compatibility between the parent and caregiver is also important, since they will both provide child care and work as a team. The parent can also determine compatibility between the caregiver and child. When interviewing a center-based caregiver, parents may need to arrange a meeting with the center's director. When interviewing a potential in-home caregiver, interviews may be in a community location or in the family home.

There are many questions to be asked prior to hiring an in-home caregiver, **13-10**. More than one interview may be necessary to gain a better sense of the caregiver's qualifications, attitude toward children, and personality. Any referrals, including those from a nanny referral service or personal recommendation, can be helpful when making caregiving decisions.

*Golden Pixels LLC/Shutterstock.com*

**13-9**   Positive caregivers smile, laugh, and play with the children while encouraging their development.

## Questions for an In-Home Caregiver Interview

- Why are you interested in working with young children? How are you prepared to do so?
- What are appropriate activities for children of this age? How will you meet the child's needs?
- Why did you leave your last job? Will your last employer provide a reference?
- How do you deal with stress?
- How will you communicate with the family about concerns, needs, and emergencies?
- Are you trained in first-aid procedures?

*Goodheart-Willcox Publisher*

**13-10** These are just a sample of questions to ask when interviewing an in-home caregiver.

### Parent Communication and Involvement

Parent to caregiver communication is important, since parents and caregivers are forming a care team. Although a parent remains the most important person to a child, quality caregivers can positively impact a child's development. Parents will need to provide additional instruction to caregivers. Caregivers will need to provide updates to parents on a child's progress and mention any concerns they may have.

Other than the child care's administration, parents will need to address many other topics when communicating with a caregiver. Parents discuss their expectations, special instructions, and other goals they may have for the child's care and development. Any special needs, such as medications, allergens, or special equipment needed for the child's care will need to be communicated. Discussing cultural background may also be helpful in understanding additional expectations of appropriate or inappropriate interaction.

Some centers may have frequent communication throughout the day. Other centers may report child progress every other day, weekly, or monthly. Methods of communication include in-person communication, e-mails, phone calls, and newsletters. Newsletters are a written or visual report of how children are progressing. Caregivers may report on individuals or the entire group.

The amount of parent involvement in child care centers may differ among locations. Parents are usually welcome to visit at any time caregivers are supervising their children. Some centers may ask parents to volunteer or help supervise with meal and snack preparation, arts and crafts, fieldtrips, or other activities.

## Program Activities

Program activities offered at a child care center will depend on the age and developmental milestones of each child. Quality care centers will base activities on developmentally appropriate practices. **Developmentally appropriate practices (DAPs)** are age-appropriate activities and teaching methods that consider each child's strengths, interests, and culture. Quality care centers also understand the previous stage of child development and upcoming milestones. Staff members should have an overall excellent understanding of child development to help create activities, **13-11**.

*Nolte Lourens/Shutterstock.com*

**13-11** Understanding the developmental abilities of an infant, toddler, or child is important in planning developmentally appropriate activities.

DAPs take into consideration the developmental milestones of an age group as well as individual preferences, learning styles, and interests. Caregivers and teachers incorporate individual learning styles and interests into activity plans to customize care to the individual. DAPs also consider an individual's culture for further insight into developing activities. Culture can affect many care aspects, such as language, foods, and play.

Some care centers will have activities that are developmentally inappropriate. **Developmentally inappropriate practices (DIPs)** are activities that focus on infants, toddlers, or children as a group without considering developmentally appropriate activities or individual preferences. DIPs may utilize only one type of teaching or caregiving strategy without variation or adjustment for individual needs. For example, a DIP may allow children free time to play in a reading room. A DAP may allow free time in a room with various playing areas, such as blocks and toys, arts and crafts, a water station, and a reading area. Unlike DIPs, DAPs strive to incorporate all major types of development into activities. DAP activities also make modifications for children with special needs.

## Providing for Special Needs

According to the Americans with Disabilities Act (ADA), child care centers cannot discriminate against children with special needs. Centers must be accessible for all children, including those with disabilities, **13-12**. For example, centers

## Case Study ???

### Selecting Child Care

Eva has a new job, but is now frantically looking for child care for her 3-year-old daughter, Marissa. Eva will work variable hours, but primarily eight hours per day. She has found four viable child care possibilities, all close to home. First, is a college student who would serve as a nanny. Although expensive, her fees are reasonable and within Eva's budget. The second choice is a local day care center that has many toys and an outside play area. The caregiver to child ratio is very good. Her next choice is right next door. A neighbor could provide childcare in her home. Marissa would be with two other children. Finally, Eva's cousin said that she could provide care. Marissa would be the only child. Because Eva knows that you have been studying lifespan development, she asks for your advice.

- Could all of these options provide good care for Marissa? If so, under what circumstances?
- Does one of these child care options seem better than the others? Why?
- Do you have any safety concerns about any of the options? Why or why not?

may need to install a ramp and have wider, clear aisles for children with wheelchairs. Caregivers must be knowledgeable about varying types of special needs. They can learn about individual special needs from parents, the child's doctor, or from outside training and education.

Many centers use inclusion as part of caregiving, and can modify activities as needed. For example, a child with a walking disability can still be included in arts and crafts activities, but may need assistance in playground activities. Similarly, caregivers offer or modify activities that are encouraging for gifted children and their interests and abilities.

## Environment

The environment of the child care center can reflect many aspects of quality care. Where the center is located, how it is maintained, and activities available are all relevant factors to a child's well-being. Values on safety, health, level of stimulation, and diversity in the center can all be reflected in the care center environment and equipment.

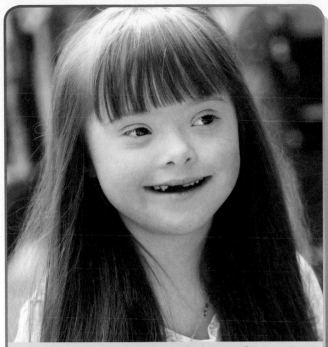

*Denis Kuvaev/Shutterstock.com*

**13-12**  According to ADA, child care centers, regardless of the type, must meet children's individual special needs.

### Safety and Health

The safety of the environment directly affects a child's health and well-being. Both indoor and outdoor areas need to meet state safety regulations. Licensed care centers go through periodic inspections to determine safety levels.

## Health Connections    Preventing Illnesses in Child Care Centers

One major concern parents have for child care centers is the increased risk of spreading illnesses. Since there are usually more children and staff members than in other child care options, illnesses can easily and quickly spread. Children and toddlers may unknowingly spread sicknesses through shared toys, foods, or other objects.

Parents can take some precautions in preparing their children for a child care center. Parents can make sure their children are up-to-date in receiving recommended inoculations. Inoculations can prevent some major sicknesses from developing and spreading. When children are feeling ill, allowing them to stay at home will help prevent spreading the illness. Staying home reduces the risk for other children and staff members to catch the sickness. Staying at home

also allows children to recover in a comfortable, familiar environment.

The child care center staff can also take daily precautions to prevent illnesses. Following through with proper handwashing procedures is a simple way to reduce the chances of spreading illnesses. Staff members should teach children proper handwashing techniques and ensure sanitizing occurs throughout the day. Toys, bathroom areas, food areas, and other play areas should be frequently sanitized.

### Speaking Activity

Interview a child care director about sick policies and sanitation procedures implemented at the child care center. Prepare a list of questions prior to the interview. Share your findings with the class.

Similar to a home, care centers should also be childproofed and have emergency precautions. For childproofing, any medicines and cleaning products should be out of reach. Toys should not have small or loose parts. Play areas should be tidy and free of hazardous items. Large, heavy items should not present a danger of falling or being pulled down by toddlers or children in the care center. Other unsafe objects, such as knives for mealtime and other pointed objects should be out of children's reach. Smoke and carbon dioxide detectors, fire extinguishers, and first-aid kits should all be properly functioning and present in the center. The center should also have emergency plans in place and staff members who are trained in the execution of these plans.

The surrounding area in the child care center should also be safe. Outdoor play areas should be in a safe location with no poisonous plants, bugs, or dangerous wildlife. If caregivers take children outdoors or leave the child center, the route taken and how children are transported to the location are safety concerns. The surrounding neighborhood and destination should also be safe.

The child care center should also maintain appropriate sanitation and health practices. Caregivers should appropriately implement hygienic practices, such as handwashing, food preparation, and toileting. Safety and sanitations dictate that caregivers wear disposable gloves when changing diapers to avoid passing germs. Toys should be clean, properly functioning, and safe. The overall center should be clean and well kept.

## Stimulation

If a child care center is visually stimulating, the center can be an interesting place for a child. In determining the level of stimulation in the environment, the surrounding artwork, colors, toys, and music can all be positive indicators. Calendars, the alphabet, and numbers displayed can be cognitively stimulating for a child. Displaying children's original artwork can indicate the value of the children's creative learning activities.

Rooms divided into different areas for varying kinds of play, reading, eating, and resting can also be stimulating to children. Areas should be welcoming and encourage exploration. Play areas can be engaging while teaching children new skills or concepts. With more activity options, children can feel excited about attending the care center.

## Cultural Connections    Diversity in Child Care Centers

Child care centers can include various cultures into child care programs. Developmentally appropriate activities inspired by other cultures can promote global awareness. Signs of diversity can be found in a variety of program activities offered as well as in the surrounding environment. Books, toys, artwork, and other objects from many cultures or about other cultures can indicate the level of cultural awareness in the center.

Diversity in the staff and children in care can also promote cultural knowledge. Children can learn from each other about cultures, customs, foods, and languages. Caregivers can also provide diverse music and games. Fieldtrips may be arranged to learn of another culture's dances, customs, and traditions. From an early age, children can learn not to form prejudices and stereotypes.

### Writing Activity

Arrange a visit and observe a local child care center. Determine the safety, health, stimulation, and cultural awareness in the center. Write a one-page record of your observations.

## Visiting a Child Care Center or Preschool

Visiting a child care center or preschool is one of the best ways to research child care options. Parents can learn a lot through observation. They can see how the facility runs, how caregivers interact with children, and how safe, healthy, and stimulating the environment is. Observing the level of comfort between children and caregivers is not something that can be determined by reading of the care center's policies and procedures. Rather, observing care centers can give parents an opportunity to view all aspects of the care center.

Observations can be objective or subjective. *Objective observations* are concrete observations that have a visible outcome. For example, watching caregivers prepare celery and peanut butter as a snack is an objective observation. The celery and peanut butter is the result of caregivers preparing the snack. *Subjective observations* are felt by the observer. Subjective observations may include listening for tone of voice or watching body language and other emotional responses. For example, a parent may notice a caregiver seems uncomfortable caring for a child or that the caregiver seems to favor girls instead of boys.

When visiting a child care center or preschool, creating a list of questions can help track concerns and record observations, **13-13**. If appropriate, ask the children questions about what they are doing, learning, or playing. Arrange a time to sit with the program director to ask specific questions.

After observing and asking questions, carefully consider how the program matches with the child's needs, the family's needs, and personal values. Although researching, visiting centers, and interviewing caregivers or directors may be time consuming, visiting more than one child care center or preschool is important for comparison and matching family values.

## Child Care Resources

There are several resources available for helping parents find the child care option that is right for their family, **13-14**. Some organizations offer accreditation to qualifying child care centers. They may also offer training, safety, and other advice to care centers. Some organizations also offer information to parents for tips on finding quality care programs. Other resources offer recommendations or find local care providers for parents.

---

### Child Care Program Observation Questions

- Is the program accredited? If so, by whom?
- How does the program care for children's physical, cognitive, social, and emotional needs? Are these developmentally appropriate? For example, ask the caregiver to give an example of a DAP for a 2-year-old.
- How are children assigned to groups or caregivers? What is the caregiver turnover at this center? How long does a child stay with one caregiver?
- What is the center's discipline policy?
- How does staff deal with separation anxiety issues? Toilet learning?
- What are the center's expectations for parents? Are parents welcome to visit and observe at any time?
- Is outdoor play incorporated into the routine?
- How are children monitored during playtime?
- What types of foods and beverages are offered during meal and snack times?

*Goodheart-Willcox Publisher*

**13-13**   These are possible questions to include when observing a child care center.

## Child Care Agencies and Resources

| Organization | Description | Website |
|---|---|---|
| **National Association of Child Care Resource and Referral Agencies (NACCRRA)** | Nonprofit organization that ensures quality child care in most communities around the country. NACCRRA train child care workers and provide resources for parents seeking information. | www.naccrra.org |
| **National Association for Family Child Care (NAFCC)** | Nonprofit accrediting agency for family child care providers. Offers family child care centers ongoing child development training and education. | www.nafcc.org |
| **International Nanny Association (INA)** | Nonprofit organization that creates a network of in-home care providers. Offers training and referrals. | www.nanny.org |
| **National Association for Education of Young Children (NAEYC)** | Accrediting organization that focuses on the education of early childhood. Offers training and resources. | www.naeyc.org |
| **U.S. Department of Justice** | Outlines regulations child care providers must follow under the Americans with Disabilities Act. | www.ada.gov |

*Goodheart-Willcox Publisher*

**13-14**  An array of resources are available to help parents who are considering child care options.

Many local communities offer child care referral services. These referral sources may be printed or online information about child care centers and preschools in the community. If hiring an au pair or other in-home care provider, personal background checks and referrals should be used to gain additional information. Referrals may also describe caregiver or teacher qualifications, facilities, extra services, or operating procedures.

### Evaluating Child Care After the Selection

Parents should continue to monitor child care choices after they have made their selection, too. Parents can evaluate how the child is adjusting to the new setting or situation and how caregivers meet child care needs. Commuting, activities, scheduling flexibility, and any other factors continue to be assessed to determine the family's needs, goals, and plans.

A good relationship between parents and caregivers should be maintained. Positive, respectful, open communication is critical. Caregivers will need to know if parents are dissatisfied. Communication can help clear any possible misunderstandings.

### Checkpoint

1. List five major concerns of parents when selecting child care.
2. Define the term *child–caregiver ratio*.
3. List five characteristics of quality caregivers.
4. What is the difference between a DAP and DIP? Give an example of each.
5. List four factors in a child care environment that can reflect the center's values.

# Older Adult Care and Services

Older adults have the same needs as people in any stage of life. They need good nutritious food and regular physical activity. They need intellectual stimulation. They need interaction with others, to be shown love and care, and to feel valued.

At times, families may need to provide alternate care when older adult family members are unable to care for themselves. Several housing alternatives were discussed earlier in the text, and include independent living communities, assisted living communities, retirement homes, and hospice care. Depending on specific needs, these can be good choices, especially when there is a desire to maintain as much independence as possible. Alternative living arrangements, however, do require relocation.

For older adults living with their family members, other part-time care options in addition to family care may be necessary. Because of the daily physical and emotional demands of caring for another, families may often need to seek additional quality care for older adult family members. Employed family members are often reluctant to leave their vulnerable older adult family members alone. For them, adult day care may be a good alternative. **Adult day care** centers offer safe environments staffed by health and other care specialists. Centers provide services during mornings and afternoons and offer age-appropriate activities, physical activities, meals, hobbies, and social activities, **13-15**.

Social and intellectual stimulation occurs through interactions with staff and other participants at adult day care centers. Centers may offer *intergenerational activities*, which provide opportunities for people of different generations to spend quality time together. For example, children or adolescents and older adults can exchange stories, share a meal, play games, or arrange other activities. Adult day care centers can be physically, cognitively, and socio-emotionally beneficial for the older adult.

*Monkey Business Images/Shutterstock.com*

**13-15**   Adult day care centers provide good socialization opportunities for older adults.

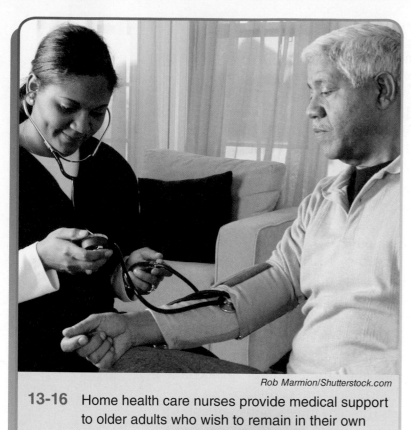

*Rob Marmion/Shutterstock.com*

**13-16**  Home health care nurses provide medical support to older adults who wish to remain in their own home.

For some older adults, leaving the home to attend adult day care is not an option. This may be due to cost, unavailability of local programs, mobility concerns, or health issues. Language or cultural practices may also be a communication barrier. For others, they may be uncomfortable interacting with others in a large group.

Many older adults do not want to leave their homes. With decreasing physical abilities, however, daily tasks such as personal grooming, meal preparation, safety and security, and home upkeep become difficult. Older adults living independently may have a home health care worker who lives with the older adult or checks on them periodically, **13-16**. Sometimes this is a trained home health care nurse who can provide medical care. In other situations, untrained workers or volunteers can offer companionship and help with daily living, but cannot offer medical support.

Although often overlooked, a large proportion of in-home caregivers are unpaid family members. Typically, they are the spouses, adult children, and extended family members of the aging adult. Not only are family caregivers unpaid, they are often employed outside the home as well. Caregiving creates costs and benefits, which can provide both satisfaction and stress. To help determine additional caregiving needs for older adults, many resources are available to offer caregiving information and support.

## Resources for Finding Quality Older Adult Care

Like child care, older adult care must meet the needs of the person receiving care as well as the family members who interact with the caregivers. Assessing the older adult's physical, cognitive, and socio-emotional needs can help determine proper care. A survey of what is available and evaluating the attributes of each possibility is necessary to make an informed decision. Visiting centers and making observations is important. If an in-home caretaker is desired, rigorous interviews as well as background checks should be conducted.

Several resources can make the process of finding older adult care easier for families. Some resources can also provide support for caregivers. Community programs may offer day care, caregiving centers, or feeding and activity programs for children or older adults. Grocery or meal delivery services are common. Places of worship often provide social networks or special events. Community centers that offer classes and activities tailored toward older adults can provide intellectual and social stimulation. They can also provide relief for caregivers.

## Cultural Connections — Services for Older Adults Living Independently

For older adults living independently, some services are available to help with physical, cognitive, and socio-emotional needs. These services can help older adults with a variety of tasks in the home, which may allow them to live independently for a longer time. Programs may be organized through associations, places of worship, or volunteers from community centers.

Some programs offer meal options, companionship, or cleaning services. Meal services provide nutritional meals in the homes. These services can help ensure adults are receiving proper nutrition. In other services, volunteers may visit older adults to help with housekeeping, self-care, transportation, or other needs. They may also offer companionship. Games, story exchanges, and other activities may be part of the schedule.

### Speaking Activity

With a partner, discuss the possible responses an older adult might have to these in-home services. How might these services beneficially impact an older adult? Are there disadvantages?

Cities, counties, and individual states often offer government resources. These services can usually be found quite easily through an online search. Community programs may be supported financially by local and state government funding. Government resources can provide information about health care programs, housing options, transportation options, and older adult care.

Local support groups can be found in many communities. Sometimes these are associated with hospitals or with religious organizations. Support groups are important as an outlet for caregivers. They provide an opportunity for caregivers to still feel connected rather than isolated. Ideas can be shared with other caregivers and encouragement given.

Once adult care is selected, the family and the older adult continue to assess the quality of care. Adults and caregiver staff can determine if the care provided meets older adult needs. Family members often visit the older adult family member in order to ensure caregivers are providing quality care by meeting physical, cognitive and emotional needs.

## Checkpoint

1. List three housing arrangements for older adult care.
2. Define adult day care.
3. Why is it important for family members to continue to evaluate the quality of care after an adult care option is selected?

## Summary

Children and older adults are two of the most vulnerable groups in society. When searching for child care, children need quality care in a safe, stable environment. They need a quality caregiver who can help infants, toddlers, and children optimize their physical, cognitive, and socio-emotional growth.

In-home child care may be provided by a nanny or au pair. When families seek child care outside the family, there are several options, which may include day care, family center child care, part-time day care, and preschool. Playgroups also provide social interaction for both the child and parent. Parents must evaluate individual programs, staffing, program activities, environment safety, and special needs provisions.

School-aged children continue to need care outside of school hours. Many communities offer before- and after-school programs that focus on homework activities, mentoring, sports, or other special interests.

Older adults may also need additional care from specialized caregivers. Adult day care programs provide physical, intellectual, social, and emotional stimulation for older adults. If the older adult is not mobile and leaving the home is not possible, a home health care worker or nurse may provide needed care.

## Vocabulary Activity

In teams, create categories for the key terms and classify as many of the terms as possible. Then, share your ideas with the remainder of the class.

## Critical Thinking

1. **Compare and contrast.** Reflect on the caregivers you had as a child. Did you have favorite babysitters or child care providers? What has contributed toward your positive memories? Did you have less favorite experiences? What insight does this comparison offer?

2. **Predict.** Predict the employment trend for in-home nannies and au pairs. Verify your prediction by consulting a government job outlook resource.

3. **Analyze.** When might parents select an in-home caregiver instead of a child care center? What factors may contribute to the parents' decision?

4. **Determine.** How should preschools ensure the safety and protection of children? What about child care in other community centers?

5. **Evaluate.** Why are child care centers required by the state to meet regulations to earn a license?

6. **Draw conclusions.** Make a list of questions to ask someone who you were considering hiring to babysit a child for you. What would you hope to learn from the answers given by the potential caregiver?

7. **Cause and effect.** How might a parent's loss of job benefit a child's care in the short run? How might it hurt child care if the unemployment continued?

8. **Assess.** Find the two closest child care providers in your neighborhood. Visit each one and gather information about the program or service. Which do you think is the better program? Why?

9. **Identify.** How does your family interact with and/or care for older adult family members? How do resources such as time or money play a role? How do cultural expectations and traditions play a role?

10. **Make inferences.** What are some of the older adult care housing options available in your neighborhood? How does the number of adult living facilities in your neighborhood reflect the surrounding population and their needs?

## Core Skills

11. **Writing.** Write a two-page paper about how you would design a child care facility. What would be the essential components of the space? How would the place look (colors, textures, furniture style, etc.)? What toys would you include? Include drawings if desired.

12. **Listening.** Interview a working parent about how he or she selected child care.

13. **Reading.** Read a book about brain development and the type of environments that best promote a young child's learning.

14. **Math.** Find a source that reports the average family income in your local area. What child care resources might be financially reasonable for an average family?

15. **Speaking.** Interview an older family member about his or her interests and activities. Share one of your family traditions with your classmates. Traditions may relate to clothing, food preferences or preparation, or other lifestyle choices.

16. **CTE Career Readiness Practice.** Visit a house or housing complex that is for sale or conduct an online virtual tour of a house for sale. Assess the features that require adaptation for an older adult who intends to remain in his or her own home rather than move to an assisted living facility. What problems exist with certain features of the dwelling? Provide evidence for adaptations that offer solutions to the problem.

## Research

17. Search for local clubs or organizations that are available to provide care, mentoring, homework help, and other activities to school-age children. What services do the organizations provide? Create a pamphlet of your findings.

18. Research child care services in other countries. Are they similar to care centers in the United States? How are they different? Write a one-page report of your findings to present to the class.

## Event Prep

19. Arrange to interview an older adult about how child and adult care has changed since he or she was young. Develop a list of interview questions prior to the interview. After the interview, create an electronic presentation of your questions and answers to share with the class. You may wish to expand your project by developing an FCCLA *Families Today* or *Parent Practice project* for *Families First*. Use the FCCLA *Planning Process* to guide your project planning. See your FCCLA adviser for further information.

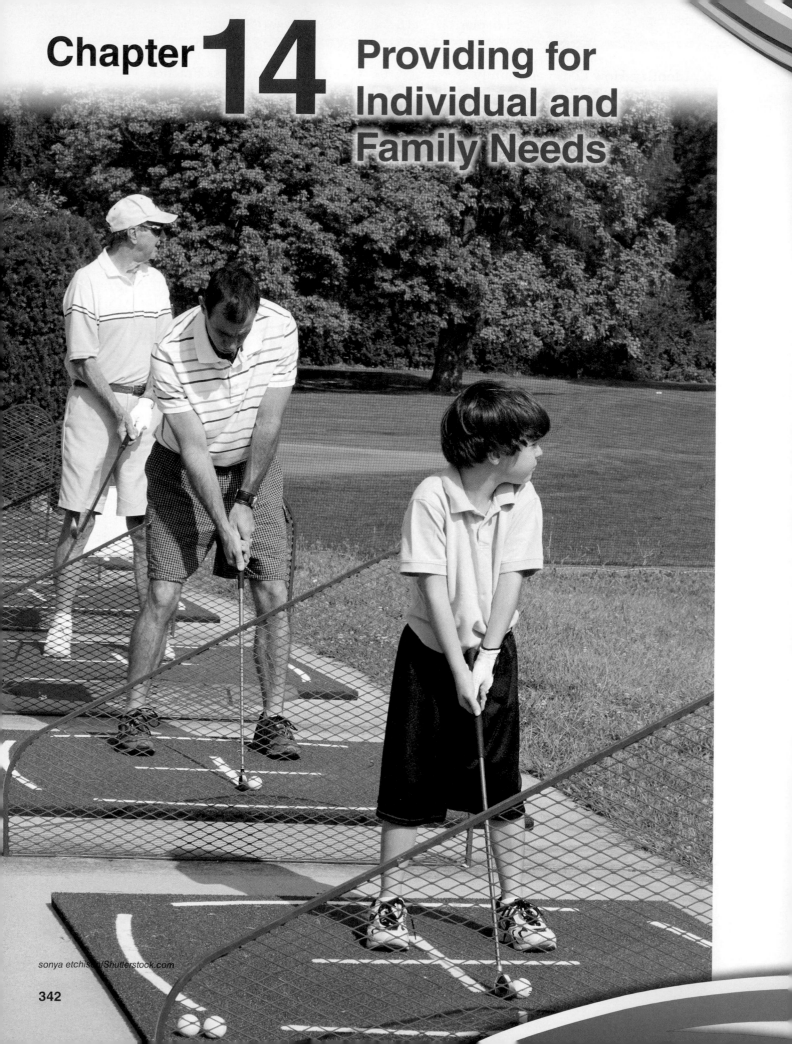

sonya etchison/Shutterstock.com

# Objectives

After studying this chapter, you will be able to

- summarize the basic needs of every human.
- determine ways to best manage resources to meet individual and family needs.
- analyze types of child neglect and abuse.
- analyze causes and effects of child neglect and abuse.
- analyze prevention and treatment of child neglect and abuse.
- analyze types of elder abuse and recognize possible signs and symptoms.
- give examples of programs and services for victims of elder abuse.

## Reading Prep

Before reading this chapter, look at the chapter title. What does this title tell you about what you will be learning? Compare and contrast the information to be presented with information you already know about the subject matter from sources such as videos and online media.

## Key Terms

| | | |
|---|---|---|
| budget | physical neglect | sexual abuse |
| fixed expenses | medical neglect | elder abuse |
| flexible expenses | educational neglect | self-neglect |
| impulse buying | emotional neglect | abandonment |
| lease | child abuse | material exploitation |
| mortgage | physical abuse | Adult Protective Services (APS) |
| child neglect | emotional abuse | |

**Visit the G-W Learning Companion Website to:**

- **build** vocabulary with e-flash cards and interactive games;
- **assess** what you learn by completing self-assessment quizzes; and
- **expand** knowledge with activities that extend learning.

G-WLEARNING.com  www.g-wlearning.com/development/

Basic human needs remain the same throughout the lifespan. People need air to breathe. They need to feel love and acceptance from others. Infants and young children are unable to meet their own needs and must rely on adults to help them. As children grow and develop into adults, they assume responsibility for themselves and often become caregivers who must ensure that their own children's needs are being met.

Everyone needs resources to be able to meet their needs. People need to be able to purchase food, clothing, and shelter. The ways in which people manage their resources varies, however. Because young children and older adults are some of the most vulnerable members of society, they need additional help and protection.

# What Every Human Needs

All people need the same basic things to survive. How people meet these needs varies greatly. Abraham Maslow's *Theory of Human Needs* identifies people's needs in order of priority. (See Figure 1-7 on page 12 of this text.) For example, physical needs are the first priority. People then need to feel safe and secure in their surroundings. They need to feel love, acceptance, and respect from others. Only after meeting these needs to some extent can people realize their full potential.

## Physical Needs

Everyone has the same basic needs in order to survive. They need food and water to grow and thrive. They need clothing and shelter to protect them from the elements. People need to get plenty of sleep each night in order to function properly the next day. Physical needs also include adequate medical and dental care. Meeting these basic physical needs is critical to health and well-being. Adults are responsible for helping children meet their basic needs, 14-1. Adults need to effectively meet their own basic needs as well. Once people meet these basic needs, they can focus more on meeting other needs.

## Safety and Security

All people have a need to feel safe and secure. Children need to feel safe to learn and grow. Adults need to feel safe to promote positive well-being. People need to feel safe in their homes, schools, and communities. Adults need to be able to protect children from harmful people, objects, and situations. For example, installing a home alarm can offer protection from intruders entering the home. Childproofing can help ensure the environment is safe for children's explorations.

Security comes from stability. Stability gives a sense of comfort. People need to experience a sense of stability in their daily schedules and activities. Structured routines, such as establishing times for specific activities and rest, help people know what to expect from life. Too many people coming in and out of daily life, and relationships changing frequently and rapidly, can disrupt a sense of stability for a child or an adult. If too much energy goes into creating a sense of stability, there is less time to focus on growth and development.

Monkey Business Images/Shutterstock.com

**14-1**  Adults need to provide children with nutritious meals to promote healthy growth and development.

## Love and Acceptance

From babies to older adults, everyone needs to feel the love and acceptance of others. Parents and caregivers need to show babies physical affection. When caregivers cuddle infants and comfort them, children learn about positive interactions, **14-2**. Young children learn how to develop relationships with others by modeling their caregivers' behaviors. Older children, teens, and adults all need physical affection, which promotes emotional and social health. Developing encouraging and supportive relationships with family and friends can help fulfill a person's need for love and acceptance throughout the lifespan.

Sergey Mironov/Shutterstock.com

**14-2**  Physical affection is critical for babies as learning increases.

*Stephen Coburn/Shutterstock.com*

**14-3** People can gain a sense of value or worth through their achievements.

## Esteem

The need for esteem involves a person's need to feel respected and valued. People need to feel they are worthy and important. They need to establish self-esteem and self-respect. Interaction with caregivers is especially critical to the development of children's self-esteem. Being positive and praising children as they learn new skills can help them feel good about themselves and their accomplishments, thereby developing self-esteem. Positive interactions with teens and adults let them know they are cared for and valued. When people engage in activities that interest them, they can build confidence and self-esteem through their accomplishments, **14-3**.

## Self-Actualization

The need for self-actualization, to fully realize one's own potential, is a lifelong process. According to Maslow, people cannot begin to reach this higher-level need until at least partially fulfilling other needs. At this level, people have self-awareness and are confident in themselves and their abilities. They are not as concerned about the opinions of others. Instead, people are more concerned about personal growth. They want to know what they can do to reach their full potential and be the best they can be.

## Checkpoint

1. List people's needs in order of priority as described in Abraham Maslow's *Theory of Human Needs*.
2. Identify three physical needs of every human.
3. Describe how security comes from stability.
4. How can people fulfill their need for love and acceptance throughout the lifespan?
5. Give an example of how caregivers can help children develop self-esteem.
6. What is self-actualization? Why is self-actualization a lifelong process?

# Managing Individual and Family Resources

Resource management is important for meeting the needs of individuals and families. Money is an important resource people use to help meet their needs. Personal knowledge and time are important resources people use to meet needs. Other people can also be a useful resource. Many times, individuals combine resources to meet their needs. For example, people may use their knowledge of nutrition to spend their money wisely when making food choices.

Setting goals and using the decision-making process can help people form a plan for how to meet their needs. Knowing how to manage finances is one of the first steps in providing for such basic physical needs as food, clothing, and shelter. Because traveling to work and other places to obtain resources is often necessary, transportation becomes a basic need of many individuals and families.

## Finances

Finances are money-related issues, including income, expenses, and savings. Money earned through work is called *income*. Income is a source of money that individuals and families use to help meet their needs. Individuals and families spend money on *expenses* or goods and services that require payment. Food, clothing, housing, and transportation are examples of expenses. The remaining amount of money after income is received and expenses are paid is called *savings*. How people manage their finances is important, since financial choices impact each member of a family. Many families develop a budget to help them manage their money. A **budget** is a written financial plan to manage income, expenses, and savings.

## Case Study ???

### Financial Planning

Jerome is a senior in high school. Next year, he will be attending a state university. He currently has a part-time job at a supermarket, which he has had for one year. Jerome knows he will encounter many expenses when he attends college. Other than tuition, he and his parents will have to pay for housing, transportation, books, food, and clothing. His parents have agreed to pay for half of his college expenses, but Jerome will have to pay the other half.

In the last year of high school, Jerome and his friends are enjoying spending as much time together before everyone attends a different college. Together, they dine out, go to a movie theater, or gym at least once a week. The group also goes shopping some weekends, which leads Jerome to occasionally make unplanned purchases. Jerome, however, is usually able to maintain the same amount of money in his bank account each month.

Although Jerome will have financial assistance from his parents, he is still concerned about paying his half of the college expenses. In the meantime, he is enjoying spending time with his group of friends.

- How can creating a budget help Jerome manage his finances?
- What expenses does Jerome encounter while spending time with friends? How can he minimize these expenses?
- Is Jerome currently saving money? losing money?
- What is another option available for Jerome to gain financial aid?

## Budgeting

There are many benefits to creating a budget. By viewing a written list of expenses, people can see how they are spending their money, 14-4. Budgeting can help individuals and families determine when they can afford to purchase items. Using a budget can also help people plan and save for future expenses, such as emergencies, vacations, homes, and cars. There are five basic steps to creating a budget.

1. **Define goals.** Determine current and future needs and wants. Short- and long-term goals should be included. Short-term goals may include paying a medical bill, attending a concert, or purchasing an appliance. Long-term goals may include paying college tuition, going on vacation, or buying a home.

2. **Determine income.** Determine the total amount of income available for a specified period. For example, consider how much money is available each week or month.

3. **Identify spending needs.** Determine expenses. Fixed expenses are costs that do not vary from time period to time period. Rent, car payments, and insurance premiums are examples of fixed expenses. Flexible expenses are costs that fluctuate or vary in price and frequency. Entertainment and clothing purchases are examples of flexible expenses. Many budgets also include a miscellaneous category for unplanned expenses not mentioned in the fixed or flexible categories. List the approximate monthly cost of each service or item next to each type of expense. Add the amount of fixed and flexible expenses together to view the total expenses per month.

4. **Evaluate.** After all expenses are listed, review the monthly budget. How does the number of expenses compare to the total amount of income? Are expenses greater than income? If so, overspending will result. If income is

| My Monthly Budget | | |
|---|---|---|
| **Income** | | |
| Allowance | $40 | |
| Babysitting | $50 | |
| Gifts | $5 | |
| Total income | | $95 |
| **Expenses** | | |
| Fixed expenses | | |
| Lunch | $30 | |
| Savings | $10 | |
| Flexible expenses | | |
| Magazines | $5 | |
| Snacks and Eating out | $10 | |
| Clothing and accessories | $20 | |
| Transportation | $10 | |
| Other flexible expenses | $10 | |
| **Total expenses** | | $95 |

*Goodheart-Willcox Publisher*

14-4  Budgets can help prevent overspending.

equal to expenses, then overspending will not occur, but saving money will not be possible either. Saving money can only occur when income is greater than expenses.

5. **Revise as needed.** After evaluating a budget, make adjustments as necessary. Financial adjustments may include eliminating or reducing expenses. Prioritizing can help identify which expenses are needs, and which expenses are only wants.

Following a budget is an organized way for individuals and families to manage finances. Common categories included in many budgets are food, clothing, housing, and transportation costs.

## Food

Food is a basic need that everyone must have in order to survive. Therefore, finding affordable sources of good, nutritious food is important. There are many factors to consider when making food purchases. Establishing a budget for food purchases can help individuals and families make wise spending choices. Knowing where to shop is also important. Understanding what types of foods to buy is necessary for people to meet their nutritional needs.

After determining how much money is available for food purchases, the next step is to create a shopping list. Shopping lists can help people stay within budget. Creating a shopping list involves planning meals to determine which foods are needed throughout the week. Using weekly food ads can help people plan more cost-effective meals.

Shopping lists are an organized, visual way to ensure people are receiving nutrients from all the food groups. Once at the store, shopping lists help food purchasers shop quickly and efficiently. Lists can also prevent shoppers from **impulse buying** (making unplanned purchases) while at the store.

---

## *Safety* Connections    *Maintaining Financial Records*

In addition to budgeting, keeping track of financial records is another important aspect of financial management. This means keeping, maintaining, and updating financial records. Financial records include paystubs, bank statements, receipts, bills, and any other financial documents. Paystubs should be kept for tax purposes. Keeping receipts and bank statements serve as proof of purchase for goods and services. Receipts can be kept in case a refund becomes necessary.

Many people use online services to help with personal financial management. Most banks offer online banking, which allows access to personal bank accounts and statements from a private or public computer. Take safety precautions when establishing online banking. When creating a password for the online bank account, use a secure password that no one else can guess. Do not share the password with others. Periodically changing the password can also add to the security of personal financial information.

Keeping accurate financial records can prevent some potential problems in the future. Financial records can protect a person against claims of nonpayment or underpayment. Sometimes, an establishment may not be up-to-date with their financial records. If a company does not keep a financial record of a business transaction, an individual may be asked to produce proof of payment. Keeping evidence of payment may possibly prevent some legal problems and quickly resolve any miscommunications or issues.

### Writing Activity

Keep a log of any purchases you make throughout one week. At the end of the week, calculate the total expenses you encountered. Create a pie chart dividing the expenses according to categories, such as *food*, *clothing*, or *transportation*. Keep all receipts. Which receipts may you need to keep the longest? Why?

*Consumers*, or people who purchase goods and services, have many options available to them when shopping for foods. Knowing where to shop can help families maintain their food budget. Following are five types of food stores:

- *Supermarkets* offer a variety of prices and sell many types of foods, including fruits, vegetables, whole grains, dairy, and protein foods, **14-5**. Items are available in many forms and stages of preparedness.
- *Discount or warehouse supermarkets* offer a similar variety of goods as supermarkets. Products often come in bulk, which means purchasing a larger quantity of an item, often at a lower price per unit. Bulk purchasing can be cost-effective when purchasing for families.
- *Convenience shops* have fewer options for food items. Foods sold usually have a longer shelf life and are often precooked or partially prepared. Stores may have longer hours than supermarkets, and usually charge a higher price for convenience.
- *Specialty stores* feature one type of food item. Bakeries and cheese shops are examples of specialty shops.
- *Farmer's markets and roadside stands* offer fresh foods sold directly from the farmer to the consumer. They are usually available at certain times, such as when produce is in-season.

When food shopping, reading the nutritional value of each food item can help consumers make wise, healthful food choices. The *Nutrition Facts* panel is federally required information on food packaging that includes the food's serving size, servings per container, calories, nutrition content, and Percent Daily

*I. Pilon/Shutterstock.com*

**14-5** Supermarkets often have specialty items, including ethnic foods, delis, and bakeries.

Values, **14-6**. The nutrition content informs consumers about the vitamins, minerals, and other nutrients the food product contains. The Percent Daily Values are the percentages of each type of nutrient or ingredient the food contains in comparison to the average daily diet. High percentages indicate a large amount of a nutrient or other substance.

For some people, limited financial resources negatively affect food purchasing. To help low-income families, the U.S. Department of Agriculture, the Food Research and Action Center (FRAC), and many other organizations have worked together to create several federal anti-hunger programs, **14-7**. There are also many food assistance programs available for school programs, child and adult care centers, and emergency disaster relief. Many nonprofit organizations, such as food banks, community and club organizations, and religious organizations also provide local support.

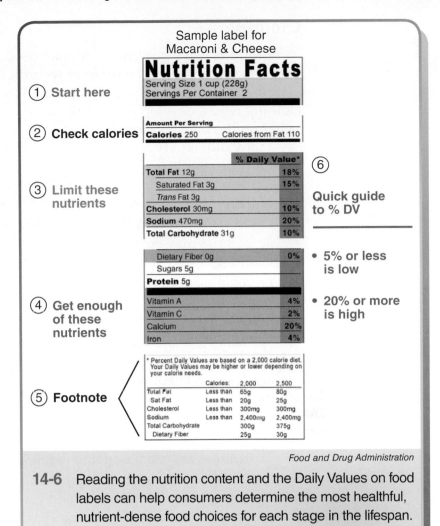

*Food and Drug Administration*

**14-6**  Reading the nutrition content and the Daily Values on food labels can help consumers determine the most healthful, nutrient-dense food choices for each stage in the lifespan.

## National Programs for Food Purchasing Assistance

| Program | Description |
|---|---|
| **Supplemental Nutritional Assistance Program (SNAP)** | Formerly known as *Food Stamps*, this program offers families financial assistance for purchasing foods. Supervised by U.S. Social Security. |
| **Special Supplemental Program for Women, Infants, and Children (WIC)** | Program that provides food assistance to infants, children through age 4, and pregnant and lactating women. |
| **Commodity Supplemental Food Program (CSFP)** | This program provides nutritional foods to community locations as dietary supplements for women during pregnancy and postpartum stage, infants and children through age 6, and adults age 60 and older. Program is operated by the U.S. Food and Nutrition Service. |
| **WIC and Senior Farmers' Market Nutrition Program (FMNP)** | Two separate programs that offer supplemental food from farmer's markets and roadside stands. WIC FMNP is for infants, children through age 4, and pregnant and lactating women. The senior program (SFMNP) is for adults age 60 and older. |

*Goodheart-Willcox Publisher*

**14-7**  Many food assistance programs are available to help people with limited resources fulfill their basic need for food.

# Clothing

Clothing helps meet many human needs. Physically, clothing provides warmth, protection, and a sense of security. Clothing also expresses individual style and communicates a message about the wearer. Determining individual clothing needs, developing a family budget, and knowing where to shop can help families manage clothing needs.

Many different types of vendors or stores sell clothing, which allow consumers many purchasing options. Following are some basic vendors for apparel:

- *Department stores* are larger stores that offer many clothing and accessory options. Different sizes, brands, and styles are available in a variety of prices.

- *Outlet stores* offer similar items as department stores. Clothing and accessories may be out of season, discontinued, or slightly damaged. Clothing is sold at a discounted rate from the main department store.

- *Discount stores* stock various types of clothing items and brands for lower prices. Items may be of different quality than other stores, but many quality items can be found for bargain prices.

- *Specialty shops and boutiques* sell clothing for one particular market. For example, a sports apparel store only features clothing and other items that are sports-related. A boutique may offer clothing only for infants.

- *Thrift shops* sell a variety of clothing for highly discounted rates. Clothing options may range from vintage to modern in brand names or generic names. Clothing may be in damaged or good condition. Clothing found in thrift stores are often donated items.

- *Yard and garage sales* are similar to thrift shops, but personal vendors sell items from their home or yard. Yard and garage sales usually offer clothing, among other items, for discounted rates. Quality, style, condition, and prices vary.

## Selecting Clothing for Family Members

As individuals grow and develop throughout the lifespan, so will their clothing needs. As growth occurs, people need different sizes of clothing. As people

## Cultural Connections    Global Economy

Before the Internet, shopping was mostly limited to local shops and stores. Consumers would rely on the business to *import* items or purchase special items from other places and have them shipped to a local location. Today, consumers can purchase almost any item from almost any country without relying on local options.

There are a variety of options for purchasing goods and services. Consumers can continue to make in-person purchases at local stores and service shops. Most stores also have online stores. Using an online service to purchase or sell any type of good or service is called *e-commerce*. Selling and purchasing specifically retail goods (merchandise) online is called *e-tailing*. Consumers may also purchase items through smartphones or other mobile devices, called *m-commerce*. Sometimes, more options are available online than in the physical store. E-commerce can also offer consumers access to stores that are not locally available.

### Speaking Activity

With a partner, discuss the pros and cons of online shopping. Which method of shopping does each person prefer? Are there other shopping methods available?

age, physical needs and individual styles change and develop. Understanding clothing needs at different ages can help families make wise purchasing decisions.

### Infants

Infants need soft, warm, comfortable clothes. Infant clothing often features snaps that allow caregivers to easily change diapers. Selecting clothes by the infant's length and weight can give a more accurate size than suggested sizes by age. Since infants grow and develop rapidly throughout the first year, caregivers often shop for clothing in the next size to prepare for the infant's next stage of growth. By law, all clothing made for infants, toddlers, and children must be flame resistant.

### Toddlers

As toddlers are learning to self-feed, toilet learn, and master motor skills, clothing often becomes stained or dirty, **14-8**. Caregivers search for soft, durable clothing that is also colorful. Since toddlers are learning to self-dress, many clothing options include self-help features, such as snaps and elastic waistbands. Selecting clothing by toddler height and weight can also help caregivers select the most accurate clothing size.

### Preschoolers and School-Age Children

Preschoolers and school-age children continue to grow and have much more mobility. They may enjoy selecting their own clothing and demonstrating self-help abilities. Clothing with zippers, Velcro, and buttons allow preschoolers to dress themselves. School-age children develop their own clothing preferences. They are also involved in many activities, such as outdoor play, special occasions, and school. Caregivers select clothing appropriate for the type of activity that is not too tightly fitting.

Olesia Bilkei/Shutterstock.com

**14-8** Toddlers are more mobile and need clothing that allows for much movement and exploration.

### Adolescents

During adolescence, individuals develop their own sense of style. They decide which type of clothing best fits their personality, and select clothing accordingly. The type of clothing sends a message about the person wearing the clothing. Adolescents also have clothing for special events, such as swimming, school dances, sports, and work options.

### Young Adults

Young adult clothing needs also change. As young adults work and develop their careers, many integrate business attire into their wardrobes. Young adults working in a trade profession require sturdy, comfortable clothing to perform job duties. Clothing needs may also develop for maternity needs, travel, or relocation to a new climate. Planning a *wardrobe inventory*, or evaluating the clothing already owned and items still needed, can help people determine shopping strategies, **14-9**.

### Middle-Aged Adults

Middle-aged adults continue to select clothing that reflects lifestyle choices. Work attire, comfort, and personal style remain important factors. Middle-aged

| Wardrobe Inventory | | | | |
|---|---|---|---|---|
| **Clothes** | **Description** | **Keep** | **Repair** | **Discard** |
| Shirts/tops | | | | |
| Sweaters | | | | |
| Sweatshirts | | | | |
| Sweatpants | | | | |
| Jeans | | | | |
| Pants | | | | |
| Suits | | | | |
| Sport coats | | | | |
| Dresses | | | | |
| Skirts | | | | |
| Undergarments | | | | |
| Socks | | | | |
| Shoes/boots | | | | |
| Jackets | | | | |
| Coats | | | | |
| Accessories (belts scarves, etc) | | | | |

*Goodheart-Willcox Publisher*

**14-9** Preparing a wardrobe inventory such as this one can help people identify clothing needs.

adults often have focused interests, such as tennis, hiking, or culinary arts that require specific clothing. Although adults are no longer growing, weight may fluctuate, and trying on garments before completing a purchase can ensure clothing is properly fitting.

### Older Adults

Clothing needs for older adults depend on the needs of each individual. Some older adults may continue to wear clothing items from middle adulthood. Other older adults may need new clothes to help ease changes related to aging. For example, clothing with snaps and buttons can become painful and frustrating for adults with arthritis. Clothing with elastic waist bands may be easier and more comfortable to wear. Nonrestrictive clothing that allows for movement and comfort are important considerations.

## Shelter

Shelter provides people with physical protection from weather. Shelter also provides warmth, safety, and security. Families select housing based on family size, finances, and location. Other factors, such as special needs and available resources near the home, are also considerations when selecting housing.

The two main types of housing are single-family housing and multiple-family housing. *Single-family housing* shelters one family. The house is an individual building or structure that does not share a wall or other outdoor resources with another family. *Multiple-family housing* may shelter two or more families. Apartments, townhomes, and duplexes are examples of multiple-family housing, **14-10**. People can rent or buy housing.

*Philip Lange/Shutterstock.com*

**14-10** In multiple-family housing, people often share at least one common wall, and they may share outdoor resources, such as a swimming pool.

When people rent housing, they pay the owner of the housing a monthly fee. People sign a **lease**, a legally binding rental agreement. Leases usually include the length of time the person will rent, the amount of rent, and any other rental conditions. For example, some leases may specify who is responsible to pay for utilities, how many people can live in the home, or if pets are allowed.

There are many advantages and disadvantages to renting housing. Renting can be more flexible, since occupants are not permanently in one place. This may be optimal for single people or families in the beginning stage of the family life cycle. Renters are also not responsible for home maintenance repairs, such as painting, plumbing, heating, or other home fixtures. A disadvantage to renting is paying rent, which can be expensive. Renters are paying money for property they will not eventually own. Renters may also experience the stress involved with relocating when their lease expires.

When families choose to buy, they own the home. Although homeowners do not pay rent, they may need a mortgage. A **mortgage** is a legally binding contract in which property is security for borrowed money. Many homeowners obtain a loan through a financial institution and then repay the loan in installments. Mortgages do not include other home-related expenses, such as bills for electricity, water, or repairs.

Home ownership also has advantages and disadvantages. When families buy a home, they have security and stability. There is no lease and families can stay in one place without paying rent. They can make any adjustments to the home, such as new paint, additions, or any other structural changes. If a family decides to relocate, they may rent their house for added income. One disadvantage to owning a home is the responsibility for maintenance. When the house is in need of repairs, owners are responsible for fixing any damages.

For some, making housing payments is a significant struggle. Financial assistance may be needed in order to meet monthly payments. For economically disadvantaged people, the U.S. Department of Housing and Urban Development offers housing assistance, **14-11**. Housing assistance for emergency relief is also available. Some private and nonprofit organizations may also offer housing assistance.

## Transportation

Transportation is a need for many people. Without transportation, individuals may not be able to get to work to earn the money they need to buy food, clothing, and shelter. The two main types of transportation are private and public transportation. Private transportation includes personal vehicles, bicycles, or scooters. Public transportation includes buses, trains, boats, airplanes, or subways.

Transportation options differ for urban, suburban, and rural areas. In urban areas, there are usually many more options for public transportation. Public transportation may be frequent, affordable, and easy to use. In suburban areas, stations for trains and buses may be farther apart than in urban areas. Public transportation may also run on less frequent schedules. Rural areas usually have less public transportation options.

Deciding which transportation option to use depends on many factors. Where people live, distance to destination, and finances are just some of the factors affecting transportation needs. Driving a car is the most common type of transportation method. People may decide to either lease or buy a car. At the end of the lease period, an individual must return the car and make other transportation arrangements. Buying a car means the individual owns and maintains the car. The process for buying a car is similar to the process for buying a home. Individuals can pay the full amount or obtain a loan and make monthly payments.

| Federal Housing Assistance Programs | |
|---|---|
| **Program** | **Description** |
| **Public Housing Program** | Offers affordable housing to low-income families, older adults, and individuals with disabilities. Housing agencies manage housing units and charge rent on a sliding scale based on income. |
| **Housing Choice Voucher Program** | Vouchers are given to eligible low-income families, older adults, and individuals with disabilities. Families can select eligible housing and use vouchers to help pay rent. |
| **Supportive Housing for the Elderly Program** | Helps low-income adults age 62 and older with rent assistance for housing that offers support and caregiving services. |
| **Supportive Housing for Persons with Disabilities** | Offers low-income individuals with disabilities rental assistance for housing that offers specialized support and caregiving services. |
| **Rural Renting Housing Loans** | Government administers property loans to individuals or organizations to provide affordable rent to low-income families, older adults, and those with disabilities in rural areas. |

*Goodheart-Willcox Publisher*

**14-11** These housing assistance programs allow people who are economically disadvantaged to more comfortably afford housing.

## Cultural Connections   Improve Fuel Economy

World events, such as high fuel costs can affect a family budget. To avoid high fuel costs, consider walking or biking to nearby destinations as a family. The physical activity is good for family members and allows you to spend quality time together. Taking advantage of carpooling and rideshare programs can significantly reduce weekly fuel costs and possibly reduce repair bills. Using public transportation, if available, is another good way to reduce fuel costs. Combining trips to run errands can save families time and money.

The most important fuel economy decision a person makes occurs when choosing which vehicle to purchase. A vehicle that gets 40 MPG is much more cost-effective than a vehicle that gets 30 MPG. The difference could amount to a savings of several thousand dollars in just five years. One type of fuel-efficient vehicle is a hybrid. A *hybrid* car has an engine that combines the benefits of a traditional gasoline engine with an electric motor. The greatest benefits of hybrid cars include better fuel economy and lower pollutant emissions into the atmosphere.

### Research Activity

Conduct a search to learn about ways to improve fuel economy by driving more efficiently. Create a list of tips to share with the class.

## Checkpoint

1. What is a budget? List the five steps used to create a budget.
2. Differentiate between fixed and flexible expenses. Give an example of each.
3. What type of information is included on the *Nutrition Facts* panel? Give an example of how this information might impact food purchasing decisions.
4. What are self-help features on clothing and why are they helpful for toddlers?
5. Differentiate between a lease and a mortgage.
6. Compare and contrast the two main types of transportation options.

# Protecting Children and Adolescents

In the late 1800s and early 1900s in the United States, people viewed children differently. Children were seen as economic property. At an early age, typically around puberty, children were perceived as "little adults" and were expected to work to help support the family. Many children did not complete high school, but rather worked on farms or in factories.

Today, children and adolescents are treated much differently. They are protected by laws. These laws are often combined and referred to as *children's rights*. These laws state that children have the right to be treated as humans with dignity and respect. At the same time, children and adolescents are not adults. They lack the moral maturity to share adult rights such as working full-time, voting, enlisting in the military, or choosing to marry. Parents and caregivers are responsible for protecting children's health and well-being.

 **Cultural Connections** — **Convention on the Rights of a Child**

The *Convention on the Rights of a Child* is a document accepted internationally that defines the rights of all children. These rights are written as 54 articles. The articles include safety, health, education, economic, and social rights. These rights take into account the overall well-being of children for optimal physical, cognitive, and socio-emotional development.

According to the Convention, the articles fall in the following four main categories:

- *Nondiscrimination.* These articles acknowledge the right for children to participate in activities that are beneficial to them, including education, health, and culture.

- *Devotion to the best interests of the child.* This category describes the government, state, or adult obligation to ensure children are provided for, which includes economic means.

- *The right to life, survival, and development.* Articles in this category aim to protect the right of children to exist and continue living.

- *Respect for the views of the child.* These articles recognize that children may have independent views and have the right to express them.

**Reading Activity**

Visit www.unicef.org to read the 54 articles in the *Convention on the Rights of a Child.* How do these rights differ from the rights of children in earlier centuries?

Internationally, children and adolescents have only been declared to have rights in the last half of the twentieth century. What started as a movement to protect children and adolescents from long labor hours working on farms or in factories, has transformed into today's protections, which cover many things. These include laws, policies, agencies, and services that affect children's and adolescents' health and social welfare along with their educational needs, **14-12**.

| Resources for Protecting Children's Rights | | |
|---|---|---|
| **Agency or Service** | **Type of Right Protected** | **Description** |
| **Child Protective Services** | Safety, health | Investigates reports of abuse, mistreatment, or otherwise unsafe environments for children. Run by each state. |
| **Children's Defense Fund** | Health, education, safety, financial standard of living | Nonprofit organization focusing on low income, minority, and special needs families. |
| **Early Intervention** | Health | State program for children under age 3 who have a disability or developmental delay of any type. Helps children progress in development. |
| **Medicaid and Children's Health Insurance Program (CHIP)** | Health | Government agency that provides health coverage to children from low-income families. |
| **Save the Children** | Health, education, safety | Global organization that provides aid when disasters occur. Provides food, medical care, and education, and helps communities rebuild after disaster. |
| **United Nations Children Fund (UNICEF)** | Education, health, safety | Global organization that provides education, immunizations and vaccinations, clean water and sanitation, nutrition, and emergency relief. |
| **United States Department of Education** | Education, special needs | Provides grants for the education rights of homeless youth in every state, as well as the District of Columbia and Puerto Rico. Also enforces Individuals with Disabilities Education Act (IDEA). |
| **United States Department of Labor** | Child labor prevention | Establishes and enforces child labor protection laws, including age restrictions, types of jobs, and number of hours minors can work per week. |

*Goodheart-Willcox Publisher*

**14-12** Many agencies, organizations, and services exist to help protect the rights of children and adolescents.

# Child Neglect and Abuse

Children and teens need care. They need food, clothing, and a place to call home. They need to be educated and nurtured. They also need protection from danger. Sadly, some children and teens suffer from neglect or abuse by adults. Both neglect and abuse of children are illegal. **Child neglect** involves endangerment of or harm to a child caused by an adult's failure to provide for the child's basic needs. Types of child neglect include physical, medical, educational, and emotional neglect.

- **Physical neglect** refers to a failure to provide such basic needs as food, clothing, shelter, or appropriate supervision.
- **Medical neglect** involves a failure to provide necessary treatment for injuries, illnesses, or other health conditions.
- **Educational neglect** is a failure to conform to a state's legal requirements to provide for a child's education or special education needs.
- **Emotional neglect** involves a failure to meet a child's emotional needs or to provide psychological care, or to allow a child to use alcohol or drugs.

**Child abuse** involves threatening to or inflicting harm on a child. Types of child abuse include physical, emotional, and sexual abuse.

- **Physical abuse** involves inflicting injury through beating, hitting, shaking, biting, punching, kicking, or by other means. Physical abuse often results in bruises and repeated injuries such as broken bones, cuts, or scrapes.
- **Emotional abuse** includes constant criticism, threats, or rejection that harms a child's sense of self-worth and emotional development. Withholding love, support, or guidance is also a part of emotional abuse.
- **Sexual abuse** includes inappropriate behavior toward or with a child including touching, sexual acts, and exposure to pornography.

## Causes

You may often wonder why some adults neglect and abuse children. There is no one single cause of child neglect and abuse. The causes for neglect and abuse may vary, but they still produce the same hurtful results. Sometimes causes may pass from generation to generation as parenting is learned. When a child is a victim of abuse, he or she might think this is normal behavior. When the child grows up and has children, he or she may repeat the abusive behavior for lack of another known way.

Some people believe that abuse is prevalent because of the amount of violence viewed in society. Children who live in dangerous neighborhoods may be more likely to experience abuse. Adults who grew up in violent communities as a child are also more likely to abuse their own children.

Neglect and abuse can occur across all socio-economic, cultural, and ethnic groups. There are certain risk factors that researchers commonly associate with neglect and abuse. These risk factors can be grouped into four types, which include parent or caregiver, family, child, and environmental factors, **14-13**.

| **Risk Factors for Child Neglect and Abuse** | |
| --- | --- |
| **Type of Risk Factor** | **Contributing Factors** |
| **Parent or caregiver** | • Low self-esteem<br>• Impulsive<br>• Depressed<br>• Stressed<br>• Antisocial behavior<br>• Family history of abuse<br>• Substance abuse<br>• Mental illness<br>• Lacks knowledge about child development<br>• Has unrealistic expectations that a child is unable to meet<br>• Focuses on a child's negative actions without acknowledging positive actions |
| **Family** | • Domestic abuse<br>• Unemployment<br>• Low-income/poverty—less care and other opportunities available for child<br>• Large family with many children<br>• Single-parent household |
| **Child*** | • Between birth and age 3, children are most vulnerable, dependent, and defenseless<br>• Has physical, cognitive, or socio-emotional disabilities or special needs |
| **Environmental** | • Low-income neighborhoods<br>• Violent neighborhoods<br>• Lack of social support |

*Children are not responsible for being victims of abuse or neglect. Research suggests children who have been abused or neglected may possess similar characteristics.

Goodheart-Willcox Publisher

**14-13** Although there are no universal causes of child mistreatment and abuse, these are common contributing factors among situations involving child mistreatment and abuse.

Although children are never responsible for the neglect or abuse they may experience, researchers have found some common factors shared among neglected and abused children.

Many of these risk factors relate to stressors. As some of the most vulnerable members of society, children become easy targets. They are the targets of anger and wrath from adults who are frustrated and stressed. Economic distress brought on by unemployment, inadequate pay, or illness in the family are often associated with abuse. Lacking parental skills plays a part. Parental personality issues such as a need to control, low self-esteem, anger issues, social isolation, or difficulty coping with stress are often factors. Depression and other mental health problems may be factors. Alcohol and substance abuse frequently play a part, too.

The presence of risk factors does not necessarily mean that neglect or abuse is taking place. Some adults may present certain risk factors, but never neglect or abuse their children. Identifying risk factors, however, can help determine the type of support services or interventions that may benefit families.

## Effects

The effects of both neglect and abuse are devastating to children and teens. Physical neglect of children may cause them to fail to thrive. Growth and development may be severely impacted. Immediate health effects of physical abuse such as bruises, burns, or broken bones may heal, but emotional scars remain. Some victims of physical abuse suffer long-term effects such as permanent brain damage or other disabilities. Some do not survive at all. Victims of sexual abuse may suffer internal and external injuries, contract STIs, or become pregnant. They also experience emotional trauma, which often results in depression that can continue long after the abuse stops.

Many times physical and emotional abuse exist together. When physical and emotional abuse occurs together, the result often confirms questionable signs of physical injuries. Children and teens who suffer from physical and emotional abuse are often withdrawn. They may have trouble making friends or they may be uncomfortable around adults. They may be hesitant to state their thoughts or needs. They often have low self-esteem and may suffer from depression. On the other hand, some children who experience physical and emotional abuse demonstrate aggressiveness and uncontrolled anger toward others, especially younger children and animals.

Even after proper care is given and abuse stops, the effects can impact children and teens well into their adult years. Most typically, long-term emotional problems follow. Without intervention, the cycle will likely continue to the next generation. Many parents who abuse children were often victims of abuse as well.

## Prevention

The cycle of child neglect and abuse does not have to repeat in the next generation. Individuals, families, communities, and society can all play a part in preventing child neglect and abuse. Raising public awareness of child neglect and abuse through public service announcements can promote healthy parent-child relationships and child safety. Many organizations provide educational materials that can help inform individuals about child neglect and abuse, **14-14**.

Parent education is critical in stopping the neglect and abuse of children. Parent education should increase the parents' knowledge of children. Learning about developmental stages can give parents a better understanding of reasonable expectations for their children's behavior. Education should also include showing parents how to appropriately and effectively discipline their children. In addition to parent education, children need to learn safety and protection skills.

Recognizing risk factors often associated with child neglect and abuse is also important. When risk factors are present, families can be connected to appropriate social programs. Local government sources, doctors, religious organizations, schools, hospitals, health centers, and law enforcement agencies can provide referrals to support systems within the community.

*Home visitation* is one example of a support service that can help new parents learn more about child development and healthy parenting. Professionals monitor families in their homes and provide one-on-one parent education.

*Respite and crisis care programs* are another example. These programs offer temporary relief to caregivers by providing care for children for a specified time. Because abusive behaviors are often linked to stress, community resources that can lower family stress including financial resources, child care, housing, and supplemental nutritional assistance are also available.

Parents who are stressed, frustrated, and struggling need to have opportunities to discuss and find support from others who also struggle. Counselors and support groups can alleviate stress and the feeling of isolation for parents. Child abuse hotlines, provided through crisis intervention centers, can provide immediate relief for parents who need someone to talk to during times of crisis.

| Child Mistreatment and Abuse Resources | |
|---|---|
| **Organization** | **Website** |
| **Administration for Children and Families** | www.childwelfare.gov |
| **AVANCE** | www.avance.org |
| **Child Help** | www.childhelp.org |
| **National Exchange Club Foundation** | www.preventchildabuse.com |
| **Prevent Child Abuse America** | www.preventchildabuse.org |
| **The Child Abuse Prevention Center** | www.thecapcenter.org |

*Goodheart-Willcox Publisher*

**14-14** There are many sources offering information about child abuse prevention and intervention, parenting tips, help for abuse victims, and other related information.

## Cultural Connections

### What You Can Do to Prevent Child Neglect and Abuse

Child neglect and abuse affects families and society as a whole. Preventing child neglect and abuse will go a long way toward supporting strong families and producing productive citizens. Reducing stress is a key to helping parents cope. Family support services can help. Providing education opportunities can help parents learn better parenting skills. Providing employment opportunities alleviates financial stress. Building a sense of community eases the stress of isolation.

How can you affect change? As an individual citizen, there are many ways to be actively involved in the fight to prevent child abuse. You can get to know the people around you and offer help to a family to reduce their stress. You may offer your time to babysit, run errands, or provide a meal. Volunteering at local community agencies is another way to help children and families in need. Recognizing signs of abuse and then reporting the situation can help protect a child. By becoming aware of the support services in your area, you will be able to share this information with others.

### Writing Activity

Examine issues of child abuse and neglect within your community. Determine areas of need and write a plan to affect change.

### Reporting

If you are in a situation where you suspect neglect or abuse of a child or teen, you have a responsibility to report the situation. If you are a minor yourself, you need to contact a responsible adult and share your concerns. A parent, teacher, or school guidance counselor are some possible options. Be clear in your descriptions of what you have seen and heard. If you are employed as a child care worker at a day care center or school, you should report the situation immediately. If you are unaware of reporting procedures, speak to your employer about your concerns. He or she will know how to properly report the concern to legal authorities. If the adult you confide in does not take your concerns seriously, voice your concerns to another adult. Do not confront the suspected abuser because you may risk putting the child in more danger.

### Treatment

When cases of child neglect or abuse are confirmed, treatment for the children can begin. In cases of physical abuse or neglect, immediate medical treatment is needed. Doctors will exam the child, provide necessary care, and document their findings. Caseworkers from child protective services agencies often become involved to make decisions about the children's welfare. Caseworkers act as advocates for the children and can help identify support systems that could benefit children and their families. Referrals for necessary services are determined on a case-by-case basis. Some commonly used services include foster care, counseling, and individual and group therapy.

Treatment for sexual and emotional abuse often involves individual therapy. In some cases, group therapy is also encouraged. Qualified mental health professionals can assess the children to determine exactly what type of treatment would benefit them the most. Treatment programs can then be developed to

---

## *Safety* Connections    *Signs of Child Neglect and Abuse*

Just as there are many types of child neglect and abuse, there are also many signs that may indicate neglect or abuse. The following are a few signs of child neglect or abuse that a child may show:

- is malnourished
- lacks basic physical items, such as clothing or shelter
- has clothing that is ill-fitting, inappropriate for the weather, or that is used to cover physical marks
- does not receive proper hygiene practices, such as bathing or dental care
- is abandoned for long hours
- has multiple, recurring bruises
- does not feel cared for, secure, or loved
- fears parents and other adults
- does not want to go home
- shows a significant decrease in grades or extracurricular performance
- has advanced or detailed sexual knowledge

Child neglect and abuse can also be detected through parents. Refusing the child medical treatment for any reason can be detrimental to the child's well-being. Failing to give the child proper schooling or education is another sign. A parent may also admit to disliking a child or to being indifferent toward the child.

Although anyone can report child neglect or abuse, *mandated reporters* are people who are legally required to report suspected instances of child abuse and neglect. Laws vary by each state, but many include professions who work with children, such as teachers, caregivers, health care providers, and lawyers.

### Research Activity

What are other signs of child neglect and abuse? Research signs of each type of neglect and abuse. Create a public service announcement and share your announcement with the class.

address children's individual needs. Integrating family members into children's treatment often occurs with goals to promote child safety and family education, and to reduce the risk of abuse recurring.

Treatment for the abusers is also determined on a case-by-case basis. Depending on the severity of the abuse or neglect, some adults may not be allowed to see their children or may have their parenting rights terminated. Because child neglect and abuse is illegal, adults may be convicted of a crime and ordered to receive therapy.

## Checkpoint

1. How were children in the U.S. perceived in the early 1900s? How does their treatment differ today?
2. How does child neglect differ from child abuse? Give an example of a form of child neglect and a form of child abuse.
3. What are the four types of risk factors associated with child neglect and abuse? Give an example of a risk factor for each type.
4. Give an example of how neglect or abuse affects children.
5. List three ways to prevent child neglect and abuse.
6. What should you do if you suspect neglect or abuse of a child?
7. Describe possible treatment options for victims of child abuse.

## Protecting Older Adults

As older adults develop physical or mental problems, they often become quite frail and vulnerable. Older adults need assistance to perform many daily tasks that they are no longer capable of performing themselves. They must rely on others to help them meet their needs.

Unfortunately, as older adults become more frail and vulnerable, they may become victims of elder abuse. **Elder abuse** involves any act that threatens or harms the health or well-being of an older adult. Elder abuse may occur in different places, such as the older adult's home, a family member's home, or a community living facility or other care facility. Family members, friends, employees of care facilities, and others may abuse older adults in many different ways.

The causes of elder abuse are complex and varied, just as in cases of child abuse. Oftentimes, a combination of factors will contribute to the abuse. These may include psychological, economic, and social factors. When there is a history of abuse in the family, the cycle of violence is more likely to repeat. Substance abuse, depression, and isolation are other possible risk factors for abuse.

Researchers generally believe that far more family members abuse their elders than outside caregivers. Elder abuse at the hands of caregivers who are family members may be intentional or unintentional. This speaks to the tremendous amount of strain, stress, guilt, and isolation some adults experience as caregivers. Regardless of the causes of the abuse, the results can be devastating, and possibly even deadly.

Sadly, many incidents of elder abuse go unreported. Learning to identify various types and possible signs of abuse, and then reporting the abuse, can help older adults get the quality level of care they deserve.

## Safety Connections        Caregiver Stress

Providing care for an older adult family member can be physically and emotionally overwhelming. Caregivers can become physically distressed when older adults need help with everyday tasks, such as mobility, eating, and toileting needs. While providing care, caregivers may experience many emotions, including anger, frustration, sadness, depression, and withdrawal. Witnessing a family member become dependent is difficult for both the caregiver and the older adult. As a result, some caregivers may become overwhelmed. When stressed, caregivers may forget to take care of themselves or cause unintentional harm to the older adult.

There are many coping strategies available for managing caregiver stress. Following are a few tips to help caregivers cope:

- *Meet personal needs.* The caregiver's personal needs remain important. Maintain healthful eating habits, level of physical activity, and regular sleeping hours. Continue personal interests and spend time with family and friends. When a caregiver is healthy, he or she is better able to

provide care and cope with stress.

- *Become knowledgeable about the illness or disease.* When the caregiver is knowledgeable, he or she can provide optimal care.
- *Use time management.* Create a schedule to help achieve daily goals.
- *Know limits.* Recognize personal limits and know when to take a break.
- *Communicate.* Ask for help when needed. One caregiver cannot provide care 24 hours a day. Another caregiver or other arrangements may be necessary. The older adult may be able to provide some help.
- *Find a support group.* Caregivers are not alone in their struggles. Specialized support groups are available to provide support and share coping strategies.

### Speaking Activity

With a partner, discuss how coping strategies beneficially impact the caregiver and the older adult. Add two additional strategies or examples of coping methods. Share your results with the class.

## Types of Elder Abuse

The types of elder abuse are similar to the types of child abuse. Elder abuse may include physical abuse, sexual abuse, and emotional or psychological abuse. Older adults may be mistreated in other ways, too. Older adults may become victims of neglect, abandonment, and material exploitation. Through neglect, older adults may be left bedridden. They may not receive their needed medications. Caregivers may fail to provide a safe environment for the older adult.

At times, older adults may become victims of self-neglect. **Self-neglect** involves behaviors committed by the older adult that endanger his or her health, safety, and overall well-being. Self-neglect can be intentional or unintentional. For example, some older adults may become depressed and refuse to take prescribed medications or follow safety precautions. Other older adults may not be able to remember whether they took their medications or ate a meal.

Older adults become victims of **abandonment** when a person who has assumed responsibility for the care of an older adult deserts, or leaves, the older adult. Many times, the caregiver is a family member who cannot handle the constant strain and stress of providing a high level of care for another individual.

Another common form of mistreatment older adults fall victim to is material exploitation. **Material exploitation** is the misuse of an older adult's financial

## *Safety* Connections    *Victims of Material Exploitation*

Older adults are the most likely age group to become victims of material exploitation. The most common types of scams are related to purchasing jewelry and coins, investing, collecting cash prizes for a small fee, and donating. Scams can occur through the phone, e-mail, Internet, or in person.

According to a recent study conducted by the University of California, Los Angeles, the ability to assess trustworthiness in people significantly decreases in older adulthood. When compared to younger adults, older adults do not easily identify facial expressions that indicate dishonesty. This same area of the brain involved with assessing dishonesty also plays a part in making financial decisions. Combining financial matters with an older adult's decreased ability for distinguishing honesty creates a result of older adults as victims.

Older adults may also be victims of identity theft. *Identity theft* is when a person's identity, including name, Social Security number, and financial information is stolen. The information is then used to fraudulently acquire new credit cards and loans, or to make other purchases. Consequences of identity theft include debt and ruined credit.

Older adults and caregivers can protect against scams and identity theft. Do not give out personal information, such as Social Security numbers, credit card numbers, and bank information. Do not feel obligated to listen to a salesperson and hold a conversation. Be cautious. Offers, investments, or deals that sound too good to be true, probably are.

### Reading Activity

Find a newspaper article about a financial scam. What type of scam was involved? Who were the victims? What were the consequences? Summarize your article for the class.

resources, property, or possessions. Stealing money or possessions from an older adult, forging an older adult's signature, or targeting an older adult as part of a financial scam are all examples of material exploitation. Caregivers or nonfamily members may be responsible for the material exploitation of older adults. Sometimes, caregivers might feel they are "owed" these items because of the care they are providing for the older adult.

## Signs and Symptoms of Elder Abuse

Being able to recognize signs and symptoms of elder abuse can be difficult. Sometimes, possible signs and symptoms may appear to be a result of disease conditions or frailty. This may be true, but a caregiver who is the abuser may also use disease symptoms as a way to hide the abuse. Possible warning signs of abuse may include frequent arguments between the older adult and caregiver, and changes in the older adult's behavior. If you suspect abuse, but are still not sure, the presence of other possible signs and symptoms may help you determine if abuse is actually occurring, **14-15**.

## Elder Abuse Programs and Services

Many older adults who are victims of abuse do not report the incidences, even if they are capable of doing so. Because the abuser is often a family member, the older adult may be afraid to report the abuse for fear of what the abuser might do. If the abuser is an adult child, the older adult may be ashamed of the abuser's behavior. Perhaps the older adult does not want the person to get in trouble. The older adult may also be afraid that no one will be left to take care of him or her. Older adults should be encouraged to report cases of abuse to a doctor, family friend, or other trusted person.

## Possible Signs and Symptoms of Elder Abuse

| | |
|---|---|
| **Physical abuse** | • Bruises and lacerations<br>• Broken bones<br>• Open wounds or cuts<br>• Untreated injuries<br>• Sprains and dislocations<br>• Broken eyeglasses<br>• Marks from physical restraints<br>• Lab results of medication overdose or under utilization<br>• Sudden changes in older adult's behavior<br>• Caregiver refusal to let visitors see the older adult alone |
| **Sexual abuse** | • Bruises around the breasts or genital area<br>• Unexplained vaginal or anal bleeding<br>• Unexplained STIs<br>• Torn, stained, or bloody underclothing |
| **Emotional or psychological abuse** | • Emotional upset and agitation<br>• Withdrawn<br>• Noncommunicative or nonresponsive<br>• Unusual behavior that mimics dementia, such as rocking, sucking, biting, or mumbling to self |
| **Neglect (includes self-neglect)** | • Dehydration and malnutrition<br>• Untreated bed sores or wounds<br>• Untreated health problems<br>• Poor personal hygiene<br>• Unsanitary living conditions, such as soiled bedding or clothing, presence of bugs, or lice on person<br>• Unsafe or hazardous living conditions, such as no heat or running water, faulty wiring, and other fire or safety hazards |
| **Abandonment** | • Desertion of the older adult at a hospital, nursing facility, or other public place |
| **Material exploitation** | • Sudden changes in financial condition<br>• Unexplained large withdrawals of money from a bank account<br>• The addition of names on the older adult's signature card<br>• Unauthorized ATM withdrawals<br>• Unauthorized debit or credit card purchases<br>• Sudden changes in a will or other financial document<br>• Disappearance of possessions or money<br>• Unpaid bills or substandard care despite available resources<br>• Sudden appearance of uninvolved relatives or other people claiming rights to finances or possessions<br>• Provision of unnecessary services |

*Goodheart-Willcox Publisher*

**14-15** Symptoms such as these should be investigated to determine cause and identify possible treatment options.

If you have determined that elder abuse is occurring, you have a responsibility to report the abuse. **Adult Protective Services (APS)** is the primary agency that investigates claims of elder abuse and neglect. In fact, approximately 70 percent of APS caseloads involve elder abuse. When APS confirms cases of abuse, the agency helps the victims of abuse receive necessary help and protection.

## Safety Connections          Preventing Elder Abuse and Neglect

Elder abuse and neglect can occur intentionally or unintentionally, especially when caregivers are family members or friends. They are often not professionally trained. They may not know the best care practices or realize the full extent of caregiving that is needed. One of the most common risk factors in perpetrators of elder abuse or neglect is a stressed caregiver. Stress can affect decision-making skills, which can result in harm to the older adult.

Caregivers may knowingly or unknowingly neglect certain needs. Caregivers may knowingly neglect elders when certain tasks seem unpleasant. They may delay the task or choose not to do it at all. Caregivers can also unintentionally cause harm. A lack of knowledge and communication can contribute to likeliness of causing neglect. For example, an older adult may wish to be less of a burden and desire to perform a task independently. He or she

may try to reduce caregiver responsibilities, even if the task is too difficult or demanding to complete. This may result in missed needs, accidents, and injuries.

Elder neglect and abuse can be prevented when caregivers are able to manage stress, become more knowledgeable about the illness, understand and accept caregiving responsibilities, have support from other caregivers, and avoid substance abuse. If elder neglect or abuse is suspected, report it immediately.

### Reading Activity

Find a nonfictional article or book about a case of elder neglect or abuse. Determine which type of neglect or abuse the older adult experienced. What was the effect on the older adult? What were the signs of neglect or abuse? How could this situation have been prevented?

Other agencies that may provide assistance and investigate claims of elder abuse include the following:

- Area Agency on Aging
- County Department of Social Services
- Administration on Aging (AoA)
- U.S. Department of Health and Human Services
- National Center on Elder Abuse
- Area Association of Retired Persons (AARP)
- Eldercare Locator
- Long-Term Care (LTC) Ombudsman Services (for claims of abuse in nursing homes)

In addition to agencies that provide assistance, each state has an elder abuse hotline or reporting number. If the older adult lives in another state, you can call the APS agency located in the state in which the older adult lives.

Victims of elder abuse need support and help to recover. By spending time with them and just listening, you can show that you care. Sharing information about available services can also help. Many times, counseling may be necessary to help older adults recover.

## Checkpoint

1. What is material exploitation?
2. Give an example of a possible sign and symptom of each type of elder abuse.
3. What is Adult Protective Services?
4. List five agencies that may provide assistance and investigate claims of elder abuse.
5. Why do many incidents of elder abuse go unreported?

## Summary

According to Abraham Maslow's *Theory of Human Needs*, all people have the same basic needs for survival. Physical needs must first be met, followed by safety and security, love and acceptance, esteem, and self-actualization. To meet these needs, resource management, including financial management, is necessary. Creating a budget allows for short- and long-term financial management.

Children and older adults are the most vulnerable age groups. Many agencies and resources protect children and older adults. Caregivers are responsible for providing for and maintaining safety and well-being. Child and elder neglect occur when a caregiver fails to provide for basic needs. Types of neglect include physical, medical, educational, and emotional neglect. Child and elder abuse occur when an adult threatens to or inflicts harm. Types of abuse include physical, emotional, and sexual abuse. There are legal consequences to neglect and abuse.

Causes of neglect and abuse vary. Common factors include personal background of abuse, substance abuse, and lack of caregiving resources. Neglect and abuse can be prevented through public awareness and education. Any suspected cases of neglect or abuse should be reported. Many treatment options are available for victims.

## Vocabulary Activity

Classify the terms into categories. Then pair up with a classmate and compare how you classified the terms. How were your lists similar or different? Discuss your lists with the class.

## Critical Thinking

1. **Draw conclusions.** What resources do you use to meet your basic needs?
2. **Make inferences.** Think of someone you know who seems close to the level of self-actualizing. What characteristics and traits do they possess that make you think they are reaching self-actualization?
3. **Determine.** What are your monthly fixed and flexible expenses?
4. **Analyze.** Look at the *Nutrition Facts* panel for three similar food products. Which product would you choose? Why?
5. **Identify.** Look at several clothing options for toddlers. Which self-help features are included on each clothing item?
6. **Assess.** Create a wardrobe inventory that shows the clothing you already own and the items you still need.
7. **Compare and contrast.** Use online or print sources to find available apartments for rent in your community. Compare the features of each apartment. Which apartments offer similar features? How do the prices differ for the apartments?
8. **Cause and effect.** If a young child is emotionally abused, how might this abuse affect his or her growth and development?
9. **Evaluate.** Why does abuse of children continue throughout the world? How does power play a role?
10. **Predict.** Do you predict that elder abuse and neglect will increase or decrease in the coming years? Why? What could be done to decrease elder neglect and break the cycle of abuse?

## Core Skills

11. **Writing.** Develop a meal plan for your family for one week. Check to see which items you already have on hand, and then write a shopping list of all the items you would need to purchase.

12. **Math.** Imagine you are going to visit a friend who lives 200 miles away. Your car's gas mileage is 32 MPG. Using the current gas price in your area, determine how much you will spend on gas during your trip. (Divide total trip miles by MPG, and then multiply the total by the current gas price.)

13. **Listening.** Interview an employee from a local social service agency about the various types of resources they offer to help individuals and families meet their basic needs.

14. **Reading.** Read a book about an adult who was a victim of abuse as a child. How did the abuse influence lifestyle decisions this person has made?

15. **Speaking.** In small groups, discuss ways to prevent child and elder abuse.

16. **Writing.** Write a paper on the responsibility of citizens and society in the care and protection of children and adolescents. How do legislation and public policies affect children and adolescents?

17. **Writing.** Write a summary of various resources focusing on children and adolescents. Include services provided by agencies that protect the rights of children and adolescents.

18. **CTE Career Readiness Practice.** Water is a basic need for everyone. Clean, pure drinking water, however, is not available to many people in various parts of the world. Identify key areas where this is a problem. What are some cost-effective ways to provide clean, pure drinking water? What are the social and economic impacts of countries failing to provide basic water purification for their citizens? Write a report of your findings to share with the class.

## Research

19. Conduct research to learn more about the forms, causes, effects, prevention, and treatment of child neglect and abuse. Write a two-page paper of your analysis to share with the class.

20. Search online to find out about your state's laws regarding elder abuse. How does your state define elder abuse? Who is mandated to report cases of abuse and neglect? What is the reporting procedure? Create a presentation of your findings to present to the class.

## Event Prep

21. Create a personal spending plan to follow for one month. Adjust your plan as necessary and take notes about how well the plan works or about any challenges you may face. Why is following a budget a helpful habit to practice? You may wish to expand your project by developing an FCCLA *Financial Fitness* project. Use the FCCLA *Planning Process* to guide your project planning. See your FCCLA adviser for further information.

# Part 4

# Career Preparation and Opportunities

Stephen Coburn/Shutterstock.com

**Chapter**

# 15

Preparing for Careers

**Chapter**

# 16

Career Paths in Education and Training

**Chapter**

# 17

Career Paths in Human Services

## FOCUS ON

# Truthful Applications

When applying for a job or a volunteer position, or submitting a college application, being truthful is important. Inventing accomplishments to gain a position is unethical and could cost you a future opportunity to be a part of that organization. This means always telling the truth about your skills, experience, and education—do not embellish. Play up your strengths without attempting to create the illusion of being someone you are not. Present your information in a positive light, but be honest. What could happen if someone applying for a helping or teaching position did not follow these practices?

# Chapter 15 Preparing for Careers

Andrew Taylor/Shutterstock.com

# Objectives

After studying this chapter, you will be able to

- identify personal interests, aptitudes, and abilities and assess how they can help in choosing a career.
- demonstrate how to research careers.
- recognize the importance of establishing short- and long-term goals when developing a career plan.
- compare and contrast various ways to find a job.
- demonstrate how to prepare a letter of application, résumé, and portfolio.
- demonstrate how to interview for a job.
- describe skills that are necessary to maintain and succeed on a job.

## Reading Prep

Scan this chapter and look for information presented as fact. As you read this chapter, try to determine which topics are fact and which are the author's opinion. After reading the chapter, research the topics and verify which are facts and which are opinions.

## Key Terms

occupation
career
interests
aptitudes
abilities
career assessments
major
internships
job shadowing

career plan
networking
career fairs
job application
résumé
references
letter of recommendation
letter of application
portfolio

interview
employability skills
body language
critical thinking
team member
leadership
work ethic
entrepreneurship

### Visit the G-W Learning Companion Website to:

- **build** vocabulary with e-flash cards and interactive games;
- **assess** what you learn by completing self-assessment quizzes; and
- **expand** knowledge with activities that extend learning.

**G-WLEARNING**.com    www.g-wlearning.com/development/

Daily decisions, such as deciding what to eat for lunch or what clothes to wear to school, generally take little time and energy. There is not much perceived risk. Major decisions, such as deciding whether to attend college or to get a job after graduating high school, require much more time and effort. To some people, decisions about work may seem overwhelming. By learning about work and workplace expectations, people can make informed decisions.

# Exploring the World of Work

Work is the effort a person puts into completing a task. The work a person does may be paid or unpaid. For instance, babysitting is an example of paid work. Schoolwork is an example of unpaid work. For the purposes of this text, *work* refers to paid jobs.

One of the most important reasons people work is for financial gain. People need money to help provide for their needs. They need to be able to pay for food, clothing, and shelter. Many times, people need money to support themselves and other family members. Money is not the only reason people work, however. Another reason people work is to do a job they enjoy. People also work for the sense of accomplishment they gain when they perform their job well.

Exploring the world of work requires an understanding of such terms as *occupation* and *career*. An **occupation** is the job a person does for a living. Examples of occupations may include child care worker, police officer, construction worker, or sales representative. A career is a broader concept. A **career** is a progression of related jobs a person has over an extended period of time. A person's occupation may change numerous times throughout his or her career. Most jobs fall within the general occupational or industry categories shown in Figure **15-1**.

| Common Occupational or Industry Categories | |
|---|---|
| **Category** | **Type of Job Emphasis** |
| **Agriculture, food, and natural resources** | Agricultural products such as food, natural fibers, wood, plants, and animal products; the production, distribution, marketing, and financing of these products |
| **Architecture and construction** | Design, plan, or construct building structures; building management and maintenance |
| **Arts, A/V technology, and communications** | Visual and performing arts, journalism, and entertainment; designing, directing, exhibiting, writing, performing, and producing multimedia |
| **Business management and administration** | Plan, organize, and evaluate business operations; sales, support services, and administration |
| **Education and training** | Teach in various learning environments; educational support services and administration |
| **Finance** | Investments, banking, insurance, financial planning, and financial management |
| **Government and public administration** | Local, state, and national government jobs |

Goodheart-Willcox Publisher

**15-1**   Which occupational areas are of interest to you?

(Continued on next page)

| Common Occupational or Industry Categories | |
|---|---|
| **Category** | **Type of Job Emphasis** |
| **Health science** | Health and medical services |
| **Hospitality and tourism** | Foodservice, lodging, travel, and tourism |
| **Human services** | Child and adult care services, counselors, therapists, home care assistants, and consumer services |
| **Information technology** | Relate information through communication systems, computers (including hardware, software, Internet), and other media |
| **Law, public safety, corrections, and security** | Public safety and security |
| **Manufacturing** | Production of goods; sourcing and distribution |
| **Marketing** | Sale of goods; advertising, marketing, forecasting, and planning |
| **Science, technology, engineering, and mathematics** | Scientific research, scientific services, and product development |
| **Transportation, distribution, and logistics** | Movement of people or goods through flight, rail, car, biking, trucking, walking, or by other means |

*Goodheart-Willcox Publisher*

**15-1**  (Continued.)

## Identifying Interests, Aptitudes, and Abilities

Thinking about which career to pursue involves learning about individual interests, aptitudes, and abilities. **Interests** are things a person enjoys learning about or doing. Learning about personal interests can help identify possible careers to pursue. For example, people who enjoy working with others may be interested in pursuing a career in human services. A career in finance may be of interest to people who enjoy working with numbers and money.

**Aptitudes** are natural talents people possess. They denote a potential for doing a certain activity. For example, some people may have an aptitude for music and can play an instrument or sing well. Some people may have an aptitude for something they have not yet discovered. Careers require certain aptitudes. For example, a person who has an aptitude for words may be successful in a writing or public speaking career.

**Abilities** are acquired skills. Having an aptitude in a certain area makes learning a skill easier, **15-2**. For example, a person who has an aptitude for math may learn how to perform complex calculations much more quickly than a person who has a low aptitude for math.

*George Dolgikh/Shutterstock.com*

**15-2**  Having an artistic aptitude makes learning how to paint much easier and fun.

### Career Assessments

**Career assessments** are useful tools that help people to better understand their strengths by identifying their interests, aptitudes, and abilities. Career assessments can help people determine the type of career that best matches their skills. Assessments, if viewed critically, can be very useful in guiding career decisions. Typical types of career assessments include

- interest inventories
- aptitude and ability tests
- value assessments
- career development assessments (types of careers that match interests, values, and aptitudes)
- personality or management style inventories

The best place for students to find a good career assessment tool is in the school counseling center. School guidance counselors are trained to help students select the most appropriate assessment test and interpret the results. High school is a great time to take advantage of these readily available services. Adults considering career transitions may find out about testing options through career counseling services.

## Determining Education and Training

When thinking about careers, it is important to consider the amount of education and training necessary to obtain a job. Some jobs only require on-the-job training, while others require many years of education beyond high school, **15-3**.

*Minerva Studio/Shutterstock.com*

**15-3** Becoming a doctor requires many years of education beyond high school.

Because many jobs require college degrees, people often decide to attend college to become a professional in a field of choice. Colleges prepare students with specialized education relevant to a particular career option. When students enter college, they select a **major**, or area of study that outlines classes needed to complete a program and achieve a particular degree.

An *associate's degree* is a two-year degree earned through community colleges. A *bachelor's degree* is a four-year degree earned through colleges and universities. Bachelor's degrees are commonly required as a minimum for many jobs today.

Higher-level degrees include a master's degree and a doctorate degree. A *master's degree* is earned after a bachelor's degree and requires additional years of schooling. A *doctorate degree*, or Ph.D., is the highest degree a person can earn.

## Work-Based Learning

Work-based learning provides opportunities for students in high school and college to learn about occupations in a classroom and workplace setting. *Co-op programs* are high school work-based learning experiences. Students usually go to classes for several hours each day and then to work for several hours. Work-based learning programs at the postsecondary level are **internships**.

When an internship is established, a company or organization agrees to provide a college student with an opportunity to gain exposure to an occupational area. An internship is a mutually beneficial arrangement for both the organization and the student. Internships may be paid or unpaid, and often last for several quarters or a semester. An internship often counts as course credits toward a major. Many areas of study require the successful completion of an internship in order to earn a degree.

## Certification and Licensing

Some people may earn a certificate or license for a particular occupation by meeting certain educational and work requirements. A *certificate* is validation that a person has specialized knowledge and is qualified for a particular aspect of work in a given field. Teachers, nurses, and project managers are all examples of occupations that require professional certification.

---

### Cultural Connections   College Study Abroad Programs

While earning a college degree, some people take advantage of study abroad programs. These programs allow students to attend classes at a university in another country while earning credits toward their degree. Many colleges and universities offer study abroad programs. Additional expenses for these programs typically involve travel costs and living expenses. Study abroad opportunities are often available in such places as England, France, Germany, Italy, Argentina, China, and Japan. Opportunities will vary from school to school.

Studying abroad gives students a chance to gain global experience in their field of study. Students may also have an option to learn even more in-depth knowledge about another culture by living with a host family. Learning a foreign language is yet another benefit of studying abroad.

#### Research Activity

Research college study abroad programs available at colleges and universities that might interest you. What study abroad destinations are available? What are the program requirements? Share your findings with the class.

To earn a *license*, people must successfully meet regulations determined by a specified government agency. A license may be required for occupations such as counselors, dentists, bus drivers, firefighters, or real estate agents. Both certificates and licenses expire and must be renewed.

## Checking the Job Market

Labor market changes are an important consideration when choosing a career or industry to pursue. If a particular field is expecting low or no growth in the job market, then obtaining a job may prove to be difficult. On the other hand, demand changes over time for workers skilled to handle certain jobs. What might be a hot job market for a specific job category one year may be a very slow market five years later. Checking into the projected job growth in fields of interest can help people make informed career decisions.

The *Occupational Outlook Handbook* (OOH) identifies the fastest growing occupations, as well as those with the most projected job openings. The OOH also includes information on education and training requirements, salary forecasts, and job duties. The U.S. Department of Labor updates the OOH every two years.

## Investigating Careers

There are a number of ways to explore and investigate potential career areas. Some good sources of career information include the school career center, the local library, news sources, and electronic databases. The Internet offers innumerable resources to students and job seekers, **15-4**. People can learn about occupations, educational requirements, job outlook, job duties, and potential earnings. Remember though, all information available on the Internet is not necessarily valid or reliable.

| Career Internet Resources | |
|---|---|
| **Source** | **Internet Address** |
| **USAJOBS**, the U.S. Federal government's official job site | www.usajobs.gov |
| **Occupational Outlook Handbook**, U.S. Department of Labor (Bureau of Labor Statistics) | www.bls.gov/ooh/ |
| **Occupational Outlook Quarterly**, U.S. Department of Labor (Bureau of Labor Statistics) | www.bls.gov/opub/ooq |
| **U.S. Department of Labor, Employment and Training Administration** | www.doleta.gov |
| **O*NET Online** | www.onetonline.org |
| **CareerOneStop** | www.careeronestop.org |
| **Mapping Your Future** | www.mappingyourfuture.org |

*Goodheart-Willcox Publisher*

**15-4**  Use reliable sources such as these when searching for career information online.

One of the best ways to learn about a certain career is to get firsthand knowledge. **Job shadowing** involves observing someone in his or her job for a few hours or a day. Through job shadowing, a person can get a close-up look into the daily tasks and activities of a job. Job shadowing can also help people assess whether the job or career is something that might be of interest to them.

Job shadowing is a very short-term investment of time and energy. Teachers or counselors may be able to help students set up a job shadowing opportunity. Students can also arrange their own job shadowing experiences. As long as safety, confidentiality, or job schedules are not an issue, many people are open to the idea of having a student shadow them for a few hours or a day.

*Volunteering* for an organization is another way to learn about careers. Volunteering opportunities may be local, national, or international. Those who volunteer gain new experiences, while also providing an important free service for the organization. By volunteering, people can learn inside information about a career area and make key contacts with professionals in the field.

*Informational interviews* are another great way to learn more about a career field, **15-5**. By setting up an informational interview, students have the opportunity to talk with some of the key professionals in their field of interest. By asking strategic questions, students can gain tremendous knowledge about the industry, career options, training, and education needed to enter the field. Examples of questions to ask during an informational interview might include the following:

- How would you describe your typical day?
- What do you like and dislike about your job?
- How would you describe the work environment?
- How did you get into this field?
- What advice do you have for me as a student?

When participating in informational interviews, be sure to always leave a good impression. Send a thank-you note or e-mail after the interview to indicate how the experience was particularly beneficial.

*william casey/Shutterstock.com*

**15-5** Informational interviewing allows people to meet professionals and explore career options.

## Developing a Career Plan

After deciding on a career to pursue, the next step is to form a career plan. A **career plan** is a detailed plan outlining all the steps needed to reach a career objective. Career plans involve setting and accomplishing many short- and long-term goals before achieving the objective. Developing a career plan helps create a manageable map for the future by breaking down the objective into smaller steps.

Many high schools require students to adopt a program of study, which maps the courses and learning experiences that a student will achieve in preparation for a specific career area. After customizing the program into a *personal plan of study*, students have a clear idea of how their secondary studies and experiences will prepare them for a desired career.

The career chosen will require some type of specialized education and training, ranging from on-the-job training or postsecondary courses to a Ph.D., **15-6**. For example, if a bachelor's degree is required, one short-term goal may be to list colleges and universities that offer a degree in the selected field. Long-term goals may be to meet the school's entry requirements to be accepted, and then to successfully graduate.

Many careers require additional experience and training, which may include internships, volunteer opportunities, or work experience. Consider these carefully. Students who develop a personal plan of study know which high school activities and experiences are valuable for their respective career choice. A position may also require specialized experience, such as earning a certificate or license.

When developing a career plan, many resources are available to help set and reach goals. Personal resources, such as career guidance counselors, family members, or professionals in the field, can offer strategies and support to help reach goals. Other resources may include the library, Internet, career and technical student organizations, or programs that can help an individual develop skills and experience. Setting realistic, achievable goals can help strengthen the career plan. Evaluating career plans and then revising as necessary is also very important.

*Andresr/Shutterstock.com*

**15-6** Earning a degree is often a requirement for entry into many careers.

## Checkpoint

1. Differentiate between an occupation and a career.
2. What are your interests, aptitudes, and abilities? Give two examples of each.
3. What are career assessments? List three typical types of career assessments.
4. Describe four types of college degrees.
5. Differentiate between a certificate and a license.
6. Why is it important to consider labor market changes when choosing a career or industry to pursue?
7. Describe three ways to investigate potential career areas.
8. Give an example of three short- and long-term goals for a career plan.

# Finding Job Openings

After investigating careers and developing a plan, the job search can begin. Job leads come from any number of sources including people, the Internet, and career fairs. Help-wanted ads in the newspaper can be a resource when conducting a job search. Many of these ads are also available online. Some businesses post help wanted signs where people passing by can see them. People often use a combination of methods to find job openings.

## Safety Connections

### Labor Laws Protecting Minors

Employment and hiring laws protect Americans. For youth, special laws apply. These laws regulate the number of hours a minor can work, the type of work, and the hours of the day a minor can work. The U.S. Department of Labor regulates labor laws.

Minors who are 14 or 15 years of age can work no more than 3 hours on a school day and no more than 18 hours during a school week. During school breaks, they can work 8 hours a day, 40 hours a week. They can work between 7 a.m. and until 7 p.m., but hours are extended to 9 p.m. during the summer. For those who are age 16 and older, there are no restrictions on number of hours or time of day. Individual states may have stricter laws about working hours, however.

The type of work a minor can do is regulated, too. For those ages 13 and younger, they can deliver newspapers, babysit, be an actor, or work for their parent's business if it does not include manufacturing or other jobs considered hazardous. Between the ages of 14 and 16, minors can perform a variety of jobs including working in a grocery or retail store, restaurant, park, theater, or gas station. They are prohibited from working in hazardous jobs, driving jobs, operating power-driven machines or office equipment, sign waving, or door-to-door sales. After age 16, minors can work in most occupations except those considered hazardous, such as operating machinery. Different rules apply to farming. Again, individual states may have more strict rules.

### Writing Activity

Research your state's current labor laws for minors. Write a one-page report of your findings.

## Networking

**Networking** is the act of meeting and making contact with people who may be of help in finding a job. The key to networking is making connections between people. Networking opportunities can happen with teachers, coaches, family members, friends, neighbors, and other community members. Networking can take place in quiet conversations or in large group settings.

Other networking resources may include contacts met through volunteer organizations, clubs, and hobby groups. Participation in career and technical student organizations (CTSOs) such as FCCLA or Educators Rising can provide good networking opportunities. Joining a *professional organization* is a way for people to meet other professionals already in a chosen career field. For example, the *National Organization for Human Services (NOHS)* is a professional organization for people working in the field of human services. The *National Association for the Education of Young Children (NAEYC)* is a professional organization for people working with young children.

Professional organizations keep members informed about what is currently happening in the industry. They provide professional development opportunities for members to update their skills. They may advocate and implement social policy. Some professional organizations also issue certifications to members who have met specific qualifications.

## The Internet

Internet job boards are a quick and efficient way for employers to get the word out about a job opening, **15-7**. People can search for many different types of

Yuri Arcurs/Shutterstock.com

**15-7**  The Internet is a popular tool people use when trying to find a job .

jobs or narrow the job search by identifying specific search criteria. For example, people may search for jobs within a specific region, industry, salary range, or by the amount of experience needed.

Using certain *keywords*, such as a company name, an occupation, or a specific city, can help people refine their job search even further. By searching with keywords, people can indicate whether they want full-time, part-time, or temporary work. When people know of certain companies in which they would like to work, they can go directly to the company's website to check for current job openings.

### Career Fairs

Imagine dozens of potential employers in one place and at one time. **Career fairs** are events where employers network with potential employees. Career fairs may also be referred to as *career expos* or *job fairs*. Communities and schools often host career fairs. Career fairs offer job seekers the convenience of interacting with many employers at once. This can save people both time and energy in making an initial contact. Career fairs also benefit job seekers by giving them an opportunity to practice interaction skills.

Spending time preparing for career fairs can give people the best chance to make positive contacts with potential employers. To successfully navigate a career fair, people might first find out which organizations will be present. They can then research as many of these companies as possible before attending the job fair. Thinking of possible questions to ask recruiters will demonstrate a person's interest and preparedness. Job seekers should be prepared to discuss their career objectives and any relevant experience, skills, and strengths with recruiters. Practicing what to say before attending the career fair can be very helpful.

## Checkpoint

1. List three ways to find job openings.
2. What is networking? List two good networking resources.
3. Describe how using keywords can help people refine their online job search.
4. What is a career fair? Give an example of how a person can spend time preparing for a career fair.

## Securing Employment

After finding a job lead to pursue, the next step is to apply for the position. This often requires the completion of an application. Many potential employers also require applicants to provide an organized summary of their qualifications and achievements. Before employers make a decision to hire someone, they conduct interviews. If offered a position, a person must decide whether to accept or reject the offer.

## Completing a Job Application

A **job application** contains information about the qualifications and skills of a person seeking employment with a company. Many job applications require similar types of information, such as contact information, education, and work history, **15-8**. Some companies prefer job seekers to fill out an application in person, while others accept applications online through their website.

Many times, the job application is the first piece of information an employer receives about the potential employee. Therefore, it is important to make a good impression. Before completing an application, read the document and then carefully follow the directions. Applications should be neat and legible with no spelling or grammatical errors. Everything stated on the application must be true. Answer all questions completely. Do not leave any blank spaces unless instructed to do so. If something does not apply, simply state *not applicable* or *n/a*.

## Preparing a Résumé

Many employers request that job seekers submit their résumé when they fill out an application. A **résumé** is an organized summary of a person's education, qualifications, and work experience. A résumé is a written publicity piece about a person because it "sells" the individual to an employer. It shows how a person could be a good match for a position. Putting together a good résumé is essential in order to get the attention of an employer and gain an interview.

In order to write a good résumé, a target audience needs to be identified. This enables a person to summarize relevant experiences that might mean the most to a prospective employer. Many career specialists agree that a résumé should only be one page in length. A good résumé includes contact information, a career objective statement, education and work history, volunteer experiences, and any special skills or qualifications, **15-9**. When listing specific accomplishments, using active rather than passive verbs will communicate energy. To ensure accuracy, a person may want to have at least two people carefully check the résumé to make sure there are no spelling or grammar errors.

---

### Commonly Requested Information for Job Applications

- **Contact information.** This includes your full name, mailing and e-mail addresses, and phone number. Use an e-mail address that is professional and not offensive.

- **Education history.** This includes schools attended and degrees received. Know the dates of attendance and graduation. Be prepared to also list any certifications, as well as any special skills or qualifications.

- **Work history.** This includes current and previous positions. Be sure to know job titles and responsibilities, employer's contact information, supervisor's name and job title, salary, start and end dates of employment, and reason for leaving. Volunteer experiences may also be included.

- **Availability.** This includes days and hours you are available to work and whether you are looking for a full- or part-time position.

*Goodheart-Willcox Publisher*

**15-8**  Having the correct information readily available can make filling out job applications easier.

**Claire Johnson**
1234 Stone Lane
Portland, OR 97212
333.555.4475
cjohnson@provider.com

| | |
|---|---|
| **Objective** | To gain experience working with young children by assisting summer camp counselors. |
| **Education** | Portland High School, Portland, Oregon, 20XX to present. |
| | Focus on human services with an emphasis in child development courses. Proficient in Microsoft Word, Excel, and PowerPoint, and in Photoshop. |
| | Graduating in June 20XX. |
| **Experience** | Volunteer, Portland Grade School After-School Child Care Program, 20XX to present. |
| | Supervise craft activities, playtime, and games, and help with homework. |
| | Babysitter, 20XX to present. |
| | Provide child care for neighborhood children between the ages of 6 months and 12 years. |
| **Honors and Activities** | Portland High School honor roll, 20XX. |
| | Secretary, Family, Career and Community Leaders of America (FCCLA), Portland High School chapter, 20XX to present. |
| | Recreation Leader, Boys and Girls Club, Summer 20XX. |
| | Member, Portland High School yearbook committee, 20XX to present. |

*Goodheart-Willcox Publisher*

**15-9** A good résumé is carefully constructed, well-organized, and tailored for a particular audience.

There are many resources to help in writing a good résumé. If people have little or no work experience, they may wish to focus on skills and abilities they possess from volunteer and extra-curricular activities. If people have relevant job experience, they can highlight this experience in their résumé. High school guidance counselors and teachers are great resources for helping students write résumés that enhance the skills, knowledge, and abilities they possess. Résumé writing advice also abounds on the Internet.

### References

Employers may request the contact information of about three or four personal references be included with a résumé. **References** are people other than relatives who know a person and can attest to his or her work habits, skills, and abilities. Teachers, coaches, and former employers or coworkers can make good references. Because of the limited space available in a résumé, people may choose to prepare a separate list of references.

Before listing people as references, always check with them first and ask their permission. Employers will often call an applicant's references and ask specific questions about the person's qualifications. Therefore, job seekers will want to make sure their references are willing to positively recommend them. People may ask their references to write letters of recommendation. A **letter of recommendation** is a formal written letter outlining a person's qualifications to perform a job.

### Writing Letters of Application

A **letter of application** accompanies a résumé and provides additional details about why a person is qualified for a job, **15-10**. If a job seeker has an opportunity for an in-person introduction, a letter of application may not be necessary. For the vast majority of job seekers, however, letters of application are important.

If a person does not have an abundance of work experience, a letter of application can focus on career goals and expected job outcomes. Generally, three or four paragraphs will do the job. If a letter of application is too long, it will often go unread. If the letter is too short, it may come across as hurried or careless.

## Creating a Portfolio

A **portfolio** is a dynamic, ever-growing, and changing collection of work that illustrates a person's abilities and achievements. A portfolio shows what a person has learned over time and can be a great tool to use when interviewing for a job.

Think of a portfolio as an opportunity to display skills and abilities visually. Portfolios can be represented in a variety of forms such as binders or personal websites. Remember, a portfolio is a work in progress. Keep a portfolio organized and up-to-date by adding or removing items as necessary. Following are some suggested items to include when developing a portfolio:

- a current résumé
- letters of recommendation
- a list of references
- work samples that showcase specific skills
- documentation of awards and honors
- summaries of volunteer experiences
- certifications, if any

## Interviewing for Jobs

Employers carefully review applications and résumés to decide which candidates they think might be a good match for a job opening. These people are then asked to schedule an interview. An **interview** is a meeting between an employer and a potential employee.

1234 Stone Lane
Portland, Oregon 97212
March 3, 20XX

Ms. Sandy Smith
Camp Director
Portland Summer Camp
Portland, OR 97212

Dear Ms. Smith:

I am interested in working as an assistant at Portland Summer Camp this summer. My Portland High School guidance counselor, Mr. Wilder, suggested I contact you about any entry-level positions you might have available.

This job would be an excellent learning experience for me. I also have much to offer as an employee. I have taken child and lifespan development courses in high school. As a volunteer at the Portland Grade School After-School Child Care Program, I work with over 30 children ages 5 through 12 each week. My duties are to supervise craft activities, playtime, games, and homework completion. As a babysitter for the past three years, I have provided care for children ages 6 months through 12 years. Last summer, I was the Recreation Leader at the Boys and Girls Club where I planned and supervised activities and crafts for 20 children of various ages. These experiences have confirmed my love for working with children. My long-term career goal is to eventually be a child care director after I graduate from college and gain enough experience.

Enclosed is my résumé. I would appreciate the opportunity to discuss how I could be of service to Portland Summer Camp. Please contact me at 333.555.4475 or at cjohnson@provider.com. Thank you for your time and consideration.

Sincerely,

*Claire Johnson*

Claire Johnson

*Goodheart-Willcox Publisher*

**15-10**   A letter of application is an introduction for a résumé that highlights how relevant personal experiences can benefit a prospective employer.

Preparing for an interview is the key to being successful. It involves researching the company and studying the job description. Company websites provide much useful information that can help interviewees show they are knowledgeable about the company. Employers are more likely to respond positively to people who are able to ask insightful questions about a potential place of employment.

# Cultural Connections Job Discrimination

Federal law prohibits job discrimination in all hiring processes including applications and interviews. Specifically, Title VII of the Civil Rights Act of 1964 prohibits employment discrimination based on race, color, religion, sex, or national origin. For both applications and interviews, questions that discriminate against you are illegal in the United States.

There are several federal laws that protect specific groups of workers. For example, the Equal Pay Act of 1963 (EPA) protects men and women who perform substantially equal work in the same establishment from sex-based wage discrimination. Age discrimination is also prohibited under the Age Discrimination in Employment Act of 1967 (ADEA), which protects individuals who are 40 years of age or older.

Americans with disabilities are also a protected group. In 1990, Title I and Title V of the Americans with Disabilities Act (ADA) were enacted to prohibit employment discrimination against qualified individuals with disabilities. The ADA does not prohibit an employer from establishing job-related qualification standards. These standards are within the employer's authority and employers may seek to hire the most qualified candidate. If candidates with disabilities meet the employment standards, reasonable accommodations must be made to enable employees to perform the job.

## Writing Activity

Learn more about the types of interview questions that request illegal information or are discriminatory. Write a list of 10 illegal interview questions to share with the class. Which questions were also identified by classmates?

Interview preparation also includes answering typical interview questions, **15-11**. Answering questions with a personal story about an achievement is a good way to make a lasting impression with interviewers. To prepare, identify sample questions, write responses, and then practice answer delivery. Conducting several mock interviews with family and friends before an interview is a good way to get honest feedback and identify questions that are more difficult to answer.

---

### Sample Interview Questions

1. Tell me about yourself.
2. What are your strengths and weaknesses?
3. What are your long-term career goals?
4. What is your proudest achievement?
5. What is the most important thing you learned in school?
6. What were the responsibilities of your last position?
7. How would you describe your work style?
8. What was the most difficult assignment you have ever had? How did you handle it?
9. How would you handle a situation that requires you to finish multiple tasks by the end of the day, and there is no way you can complete them?
10. What can you do for this company that other applicants cannot?

*Goodheart-Willcox Publisher*

**15-11** Sample questions to answer during an interview, as well as other helpful interviewing tips, abound on the Internet.

To make a good impression at the interview, plan to arrive about 10 minutes before the scheduled time. Bring necessary paperwork such as a résumé, list of references, letters of recommendation, and a portfolio. Turn cell phones off to avoid interruptions. Be well-groomed and dress appropriately to appear professional and respectful. Clean and well-pressed suits, blazers, dress shirts, dress pants, or dresses are typically good choices. Dirty or ripped clothing, extreme hairstyles, and obvious piercings or tattoos can prevent a person from getting a job. Greet the interviewers with a firm handshake and use formal language rather than informal greetings that may be used with friends.

Group interviews are a common way of interviewing potential employees. Group interviews allow employers to observe several things including how well a person works with others and can handle stress. Interviewers understand that an interviewee is "on the spot" and probably a little nervous. If interviewers are new or untrained at interviewing, they may be nervous, too. Even so, try to avoid appearing apprehensive. Steer clear of nervous habits such as fidgeting, quick or jerky movements, and either staring or avoiding eye contact. Try to appear confident, but not arrogant.

After interviewing, immediately send a thank-you note or e-mail to every interviewer. Thank them for their time and restate an interest in working for the company. Do not delay or procrastinate. Sometimes this is a deciding factor in the selection process.

## Case Study ???

### Honesty in Claiming Work Experience

Last summer, Amy thought she had found the perfect summer job. The community park district was hiring assistants to work at a summer sports camp for preschoolers. Amy wanted a job working with young children, which would help her gain experience to eventually achieve her career goal of becoming a kindergarten teacher. Amy applied for the position and was thrilled when she was hired.

Before she started working with the children, Amy attended an orientation to learn about the camp, its members, and her specific job duties. On her first day working with the children, she thought the new job would go well. She loved the preschoolers, the work responsibilities, and her coworkers. Unfortunately, at the end of Amy's second day of work, her supervisor informed her that the city had cut funding and her job had been eliminated.

This summer she found another job that seemed perfect. She would be working with a local organization to help plan sports events, arts and crafts, and dance classes for children. This new job requires experience working with children. Technically, she was employed last summer and worked with preschoolers, even if the job only lasted two days.

- Is it honest for Amy to claim her two days working for the community park district as experience working with children?
- What might be the benefits of doing so?
- What might be the disadvantages of claiming experience working with young children through the park district?
- Could claiming experience working with children negatively impact the children? If so how?

## Weighing Job Offers

There are many considerations to debate when deciding whether to accept or reject a job offer. It may be helpful to break the evaluation process into several categories to review. These include work schedules, job duties, wages and benefits, transportation, potential for advancement, and personal needs. Thoughtfully evaluating the selection criteria can help in making an informed and rational decision. Asking family members and friends for their input can also help in the decision-making process.

Once a decision is made, let the employer know as soon as possible. When accepting a job offer, a start date can then be determined. If rejecting an offer, call the employer and convey the message in a courteous and professional manner. Remember, people must often apply for several jobs before receiving an offer. Do not be discouraged, just keep trying.

## Checkpoint

1. List four types of information commonly requested when filling out job applications.
2. What is the main function of a résumé? a letter of application?
3. How does a portfolio differ from a résumé in function?
4. Describe how to best prepare for an interview.
5. Name five ways to make a good impression at an interview.
6. List six categories to review when evaluating job offers.

# Succeeding at Work

Employers expect their employees to have certain **employability skills**, which are basic skills needed to obtain and succeed on a job. Employability skills are transferrable to any part- or full-time job. These involve basic academic, technology, communication, and decision-making skills. To succeed on the job, employees also need to be effective leaders and team members, and demonstrate positive behaviors and attitudes.

## Academic Skills

Being able to read and write are basic literacy skills important to any job. Employees need to be able to read and understand instructions and project materials. They need to be able to demonstrate effective writing skills in communications with supervisors and coworkers. Reports, presentations, correspondence, and articles must all be clear, concise, and error-free.

Other academic skills that employers expect employees to have are basic math and science skills. People need to be able to add, subtract, multiply, and divide to perform simple tasks, **15-12**. For example, math skills are required to balance a checkbook, make change, develop a budget, or calculate gas mileage. Science involves general knowledge about the world and how things work. Employees use scientific principles when they learn new processes, examine problems, and propose possible solutions.

## Technology Skills

Having basic technology skills is a necessity in today's job market. Employers expect their employees to be able to conduct Internet research, prepare electronic presentations, write reports, input data into spreadsheets, or use company-specific software. Technology allows employees to complete tasks more quickly, thereby increasing productivity. Successful employees are able to use technology tools efficiently and learn new skills quickly as advancements are constantly being made.

## Communication Skills

Communication in the workplace occurs with supervisors, coworkers, customers, and vendors. Therefore, good verbal and nonverbal communication skills are essential. Employees must be able to demonstrate effective speaking and listening skills. They must be able to write messages that are easily understood by others. Using text messaging abbreviations and slang are not preferred methods of communication in most workplaces. Instead, employees need to possess business communication skills. This means using proper grammar, spelling, and word choice.

*bikeriderlondon/Shutterstock.com*

**15-12**  Basic knowledge of fractions is often used for measurement.

## Cultural Connections    Writing Styles

Writing messages to friends or family is often very different from writing messages in the workplace. This is because the messages are written using different styles. An *informal* writing style is similar to the way a person speaks. Informal writings often include slang, contractions, and short, incomplete sentences. Writing informal messages allows the writer to easily express emotions and feelings. Exclamations and emoticons are commonly used. Examples of informal writings can often be seen in text messages and e-mails to friends.

Academic reports and business communications require a *formal* writing style. Formal writings do not use slang, abbreviations, or contractions. The sentences are typically longer, complete, and more complex. Formal writing is not personal and does not use first or second person words such as *I*, *we*, or *you*. Messages are carefully composed and reviewed to make sure there are no spelling, grammar, or punctuation errors. Being able to effectively use a formal writing style is a skill that is necessary to succeed in the workplace.

### Writing Activity

Choose a topic that concerns you and write a two-page report about it to practice using a formal style of writing.

Body language, or nonverbal signals such as facial expressions, gestures, posture, and eye contact, can speak volumes in the workplace. Body language can communicate both positive and negative messages. For example, a smile when offering praise communicates a positive message. Maintaining good eye contact indicates a person is listening to what the speaker is saying. Frowning and sitting with arms crossed may reflect a lack of interest. Because communication is so important in the workplace, many employers evaluate their employees' communication skills.

## Decision-Making and Problem-Solving Skills

Employers expect their employees to be able to investigate and resolve problems in the workplace. Critical thinking involves looking closely at a situation and weighing possible outcomes before determining a solution. Employers want employees who are able to deal with issues and make good decisions. Decision-making skills are necessary at any level in the workplace, from entry-level to management positions. By using decision-making and problem-solving skills in the workplace, employees are able to value each other's opinions and work together to achieve a common goal.

## Effective Team Members and Leaders

Another important skill for any career is the ability to work as a team member. A team member is a person who works with other members of the group to help achieve a common goal. When people work together, projects and goals can be accomplished efficiently. Team members use *teamwork*—they work together to examine a problem, form a plan, and achieve the goal as a unit.

Team members use many skills to work as part of a team, 15-13. They use communication and cooperation skills to work with other team members. They do not cause conflict, spread gossip, or form cliques. Instead, team members are friendly toward fellow teammates. They recognize that team members are diverse and are able to understand and accept their opinions. Team members have good interpersonal skills and can communicate effectively with others. They listen to others and speak clearly. They participate in the team by asking or answering questions. They may offer helpful information and accept help as needed. Team members accept responsibility for the progress of the team and actively work toward accomplishing the goal.

| Skills and Qualities of an Effective Team Member | | |
|---|---|---|
| • Good communicator | • Honest | • Supportive |
| • Good listener | • Fair | • Committed |
| • Positive attitude | • Reliable | • Competent |
| • Creative | • Respectful | • Dependable |
| • Enthusiastic | • Adaptable | • Disciplined |

*Goodheart-Willcox Publisher*

**15-13** Effective team members possess skills and qualities such as these.

Teams often have a leader. **Leadership** is a quality that involves organizing, guiding, and taking responsibility for a team. People may volunteer for, be voted into, or assigned leadership roles. Different leaders have different styles of leadership. Effective leaders demonstrate similar qualities and skills when leading a team, **15-14**. They encourage members to use their skills and talents. They are supportive, accommodating, and responsible. Responsible team leaders acknowledge when there is a problem and work to solve the issue. They accept issues and accomplishments. They acknowledge team member contributions and give credit to the team as a whole.

There are many opportunities to develop leadership skills. School clubs and CTSOs have natural opportunities to demonstrate leadership. These groups often offer students the opportunity to serve on the club's board. Other groups, such as in music and performing arts, sports, or other special interest groups also need student leaders to help maintain the group. In larger groups, leaders within subsets can help unify and organize the group. Leadership opportunities may also be informal, such as when organizing activities with friends or family.

## Essential Behaviors

*Professionalism* is behavior that is expected in the workplace from employees. Dressing appropriately, avoiding use of slang, and being courteous are some examples of behaving professionally. Professionalism also includes having a good work ethic, having a positive attitude, being responsible, and being cooperative.

To achieve workplace success, employees need to have a good work ethic. A **work ethic** is a personal belief in the value of work and its ability to strengthen character. People do not have the same work ethic. Some employees think that just showing up to work is enough. Others are extremely hard working and want to do the best job they possibly can. They demonstrate positive behaviors such as being dependable, reliable, trustworthy, and respectful. They also have a positive attitude.

Demonstrating positive behaviors and attitudes go a long way toward job success. Employers need workers who are dependable and can be trusted to do

---

### Effective Leadership Qualities and Skills

- Values each team member
- Encourages team member participation
- Offers support to individuals
- Does not always dominate conversations
- Listens to team member suggestions, ideas, and plans
- Motivates team members
- Uses problem-solving skills
- Accepts responsibility for the team and progress on projects
- Acts as a mediator to resolve conflicts
- Communicates openly and effectively with team members
- Accepts help and criticism

*Goodheart-Willcox Publisher*

**15-14** Effective team leaders demonstrate many qualities and abilities.

what they say they will do, **15-15**. They show up for work on time. They are consistent in temperament and reactions to situations. Dependable employees are willing to help where needed. They are reliable and steadfast. They are also trustworthy, loyal, and faithful to their employer.

Good employees are responsible. Being responsible means being committed in all activities, relationships, and actions. Responsibility means carrying a project through to the end whether or not the process is easy. When working on a team, responsibility means giving a best effort even if one team member does not do the same. Accepting responsibility means not blaming someone else when things do not go exactly as planned. The more responsibility employees are able to demonstrate to their employer, the more responsibility they are often given.

In addition to being dependable and responsible, employers need employees who are trustworthy, or honest. Honesty is an essential behavior for all employees. Employers need to know that their employees will not lie to them or steal from them. One way employees may steal from their employers is to spend work time using the computer or phone for personal matters. Good employees are productive and remain focused on their projects.

Employees are more likely to succeed when they are able to cooperate with their supervisors and coworkers. Successful workers value the opinions of others and are flexible and willing to try new processes. They respect others, even if they do not agree with them. They are able to work together and compromise to achieve goals. Successful employees are also able to give and accept constructive criticism in order to improve work performance.

Disagreements will happen in every job, but some disagreements can become conflict. When this happens, *conflict management skills* can help the parties involved work through the conflict peacefully. Speaking and listening are both important skills in resolving conflicts. They can help in reaching a *compromise*, an agreement in which each side makes concessions with the goal of ending the conflict.

Yuri Arcurs/Shutterstock.com

**15-15** Employers greatly value employees who are dependable.

Having a positive attitude means being optimistic and taking satisfaction in a job well done, 15-16. Instead of continually complaining to fellow workers, a person with a positive attitude can see the good in situations. These people are generally more pleasant to be around and their positive attitude often rubs off on coworkers. A positive attitude is very important and highly valued by employers.

## Leaving a Job

There are many reasons for leaving a job. Perhaps the job was not such a good fit after all. Maybe a more advanced position is available at a different company. Whatever the reason, it is considered good practice to give an employer at least two weeks' notice. This gives the employer time to hire and train another employee. Of course, if the position poses a safety risk, it may be necessary to leave immediately.

When giving notice, employees often write a letter of resignation to their supervisor. There is no need to go into a long written explanation. Simply state the last day of employment and thank the employer for the opportunity to work for the company. The most important thing is to remain positive and be professional, even if the work was not enjoyable. A former employer can be a good reference on a résumé.

*Golden Pixels LLC/Shutterstock.com*

**15-16** Coworkers appreciate working with others who have a positive attitude.

## Checkpoint

1. What are employability skills? What specific skills do they involve?
2. Give one example each of how body language can communicate a positive message and a negative message in the workplace.
3. Identify five skills or qualities each of an effective team member and leader.
4. What are two ways you can develop leadership skills?
5. After landing a job, what are five attitudes or behaviors that can make you more successful as an employee?
6. If resigning from a job, to whom and how should you give notification?

## Entrepreneurship

**Entrepreneurship**, the process of creating and managing one's own business, is another form of employment. *Entrepreneurs* are people who establish and run their own business. They decide which service or good to provide, how to provide it, when, and at what cost. Establishing a new business requires a lot of work, **15-17**. To help prepare for business management, entrepreneurs create

*mangostock/Shutterstock.com*

**15-17**  Entrepreneurs assume all the responsibilities and risks for managing their own business.

a *business plan*, a detailed plan for running the business. Business plans include details about the product or service, how to provide the product, how to market and sell the product, and related finances. Entrepreneurs evaluate their plan and decide if adjustments need to be made in any part of the business. They gain profits, realize losses, and decide if additional workers need to be hired.

Successful entrepreneurs often possess common characteristics. In addition to having a specialized skill, they are also ambitious, confident, patient, and hard workers. They have excellent communication and leadership skills. They acknowledge when there are problems, and act to resolve any issues. Successful entrepreneurs have a clear understanding of the financial challenges of how to develop a budding business into a profit-making venture.

Opportunities for entrepreneurship are endless. The decision to become an entrepreneur depends on many factors. Entrepreneurs examine the market and determine if they can fulfill a need. They have a specialized skill they can use to create a profit. Combining a skill with a new type of business or creating a new approach to a preexisting business can create business opportunities. For example, in an area with many school-aged children, an adolescent may decide to open a babysitting program during the summer. Deciding which business to operate depends on the entrepreneur, the quality of the product or service, the market, and the business plan.

## Cultural Connections — Entrepreneurial Opportunities

How do entrepreneurs establish a business? Becoming an entrepreneur starts with an idea. From there, the entrepreneur researches and analyzes the market and many details related to starting a business. Then, the entrepreneur develops the idea into a feasible business plan.

Entrepreneurial opportunities come in various forms. Perhaps an idea relates to a unique concept for a product or service relating to clothes, food, music, science, art, or convenience. Technology provides many business opportunities. For example, many businesses incorporate technology into their organizations, regardless of the type of industry. The technology may be a part of the service or product itself, or it may help run the business. Either way, technology can help a local business become global, which considerably expands the market. Technology can also help modernize a business, which is important in a digital age where many consumers expect the latest forms of technology.

### Research Activity

Create and develop your own entrepreneurial idea. Ideas may be to improve a preexisting business or introduce a new product or service. Then research the market and analyze the types of information that need to be included in a business plan.

## Checkpoint

1. What is entrepreneurship?
2. How does a business plan help entrepreneurs establish a business?
3. What are common qualities of entrepreneurs?
4. List at least two examples of entrepreneurship opportunities.

## Summary

Preparing for a career takes time and thought. Exploring careers can be done online or through interactions with others. Career assessments can provide insights into personal interests, skills, and aptitudes. Informational interviews can provide insight into a career field. Job shadowing can, too. Volunteering, internships, or on-the-job training can add to a person's list of experiences.

When seeking employment, job seekers need to first fill out an application. Résumés, letters of application, and portfolios are also used when seeking employment. Employers use these to decide who might best fit their needs as a potential employee.

Interviews are formal conversations between employers and potential employees. Interviews serve as an opportunity for both the employer and the job seeker to evaluate whether or not they are a good match. Preparation and practice will lower anxiety and present applicants in the best possible light.

To succeed on the job, employees need to have basic employability skills. Essential behaviors such as dependability, responsibility, and respect are highly valued in the workplace. A positive attitude is also important. Entrepreneurship, or the process of creating and managing one's own business, is another form of employment.

## Vocabulary Activity

Divide into two teams. Play charades to act out the meaning of each of the terms. Each team member will draw a slip of paper with a term prepared by your instructor. As team members identify the terms, the team gets a point. The team that acts out and identifies the most terms wins the game.

## Critical Thinking

1. **Compare and contrast.** Pick two career fields that you might be interested in and make a chart that compares their differences and similarities.
2. **Identify.** Consult with your high school guidance counselor and arrange to take a career assessment to identify your interests, aptitudes, and abilities.
3. **Make inferences.** How might your interests, aptitudes, and abilities change throughout adulthood?
4. **Determine.** Summarize your current work ethic practices. How will you continue to develop your work ethic as you proceed in your career?
5. **Predict.** Make a list of problem-solving techniques. If you were in a leadership position, how would you implement these techniques to solve problems efficiently?
6. **Identify.** What are some ways you demonstrate professionalism at school or your job? How will you demonstrate professionalism in your future career?
7. **Predict.** What might be the hottest job trends in 10 years? 20 years?
8. **Evaluate.** Look at an advertisement for a job opening. What do you assume about this job as far as responsibilities are concerned? What unanswered questions do you have? Would this be a job that would interest you? Why or why not?
9. **Determine.** Choose at least three people you know, other than family members, who would say positive things about you and your work habits. Ask their permission to use them as references.
10. **Analyze.** Think about your employability skills. Why are these skills necessary for career success? What actions could you take to improve these skills?
11. **Assess.** What leadership and teamwork qualities do you already possess? What qualities do you need to develop to

become an effective leader and team member?

12. **Cause and effect.** If a person writes negatively about his or her boss on a social networking site, how could this affect future employment?

# Core Skills

13. **Listening.** Schedule an informational interview with an employer in a field that interests you. Prepare a list of strategic questions to ask to help you gain knowledge about the industry, career options, training, and education needed to enter the field.

14. **Speaking.** With a partner, role-play using effective verbal and nonverbal communication in the workplace.

15. **Math.** Most jobs rely on math knowledge and skills. Choose a particular job or profession. Brainstorm with a classmate to come up with a list of ways that the job relies on or requires math knowledge and skills.

16. **Reading.** Read a book about how to maintain and succeed on a job. What advice did you find particularly helpful?

17. **Writing.** Determine a perfect entrepreneurial opportunity for you in the educational field. Write a paper showing how you used decision-making skills to come to this conclusion. Include an evaluation of the education requirements necessary for this job. What short-term jobs will help you meet your long-term career goal?

18. **Speaking.** In teams, create a video of team members practicing effective conflict management skills. Share your videos in class and discuss the effectiveness of the conflict resolution. Also discuss the teamwork skills you used to complete the assignment.

19. **Writing.** Write a letter of resignation. With a partner, role-play appropriate ways to resign a position.

20. **CTE Career Readiness Practice.** Imagine you are a certified fitness trainer at a facility that specializes in rehab for workplace injuries. You work closely with several physical therapists. A number of clients have expressed interest in a class you lead on learning how to balance their energy requirements for a healthy lifestyle. What topics would you use in the class? How would you help people develop a fitness routine? How would you use your leadership skills to motivate, inspire, and persuade your clients to make fitness and energy management a goal for life?

# Research

21. Research the educational requirements for careers that interest you. Based on your findings, how much education will you need to obtain employment in the field that interests you the most? Create short- and long-term education goals to include in your career plan.

22. Explore five career resource websites to learn more about the information available. Create a table of your findings.

# Event Prep

23. Develop a letter of application and résumé for a job that interests you. Be sure to include your relevant educational, job, and volunteer experience. Also include any applicable leadership roles. Update your portfolio, including samples of work, assessment results, and scholarship applications. Work with a partner to practice conducting mock job interviews for the position and presenting your portfilio. You may wish to expand your project by participating in an Educators Rising *Job Interview Competition*. See your adviser for further information.

# Chapter 16

# Career Paths in Education and Training

oliveromg/Shutterstock.com

## Objectives

After studying this chapter, you will be able to

- compare and contrast career opportunities for teachers at various levels *within* schools.
- summarize career opportunities for teachers and trainers *outside* of schools.
- identify career opportunities in the professional support services pathway.
- give examples of career opportunities in the administration and administrative support pathway.
- evaluate employment opportunities and trends in the field of education and training.

## Reading Prep

As you read this chapter, think about what you are learning. How does this compare and contrast with similar information you have learned in other classes?

## Key Terms

nonsectarian
prekindergarten programs
self-contained classrooms
middle schools
junior high
collaborative learning

high school
special education teachers
corporate trainers
cooperative extension educators
parent educators
school guidance counselors

career counselors
speech-language specialists
children's librarians
curriculum
curriculum developer
program director

**G-WLEARNING.com**

### Visit the G-W Learning Companion Website to:

- **build** vocabulary with e-flash cards and interactive games;
- **assess** what you learn by completing self-assessment quizzes; and
- **expand** knowledge with activities that extend learning.

www.g-wlearning.com/development/

The education and training occupational category offers exciting professions in three career pathways: *Teaching and Training, Professional Support Services*, and *Administration and Administrative Support*. Each pathway addresses related occupations that require similar knowledge and skills. This chapter explores some of the occupations in each pathway, as well as the knowledge and skills necessary to succeed. By learning about the various types of career opportunities within this field, you can decide if a career in education and training is right for you.

## Teaching and Training

Some of the job titles within the teaching and training pathway include teacher, child care worker and director, coach, fitness trainer, and nanny. Careers in teaching and training can be both frustrating and rewarding at the same time. They require patience, persistence, and an appreciation for diversity and individuality. What makes teaching truly different from many other professions is the potential long-term effect a teacher can have on the lives of others.

Think about the teachers you have known. Which were your favorites? What was it about these teachers that made them successful? Most likely, your favorite teachers were not all alike. Good teachers come in many forms. They may be outgoing and dramatic or soft-spoken and reflective. Their approaches to life can be very different from one another, too.

Although teachers may vary, good teaching requires a common set of skills. Effective teachers motivate, inspire, and influence their students, **16-1**. They communicate well with both students and adults. In addition, effective teachers are well organized as they deal with the planning, record keeping, and many administrative tasks that go along with the job. While there are many other skills, these are some of the most basic.

In the following sections, you will learn much more about aspects of teaching that you may not have considered. You may want to make opportunities to try out some of the tasks associated with teaching. You may choose to observe teachers and students. You may also take part in activities with children of various ages. With more knowledge, experience, and insight into your own goals and aptitudes, you will be better able to make a career decision.

*Blend Images/Shutterstock.com*

**16-1** Effective teachers convey their own enthusiasm for learning.

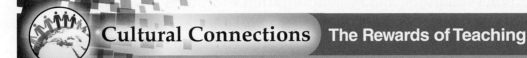

## Cultural Connections    The Rewards of Teaching

Many experienced teachers will tell you that teaching is inspiring and challenging, and each teaching experience is unique. Because every student has his or her own learning style and personality, teachers are challenged to find how to best help each individual learn.

Teaching is a career that makes a long-term difference in the world. Because learning takes time, seeing the effects of a teacher's efforts requires patience. Still, there are everyday victories. A young child successfully deals with conflict on the playground. A struggling student passes a difficult test. A reluctant reader chooses a challenging book from the library.

To be a successful teacher, understanding human lifespan development is critical. Teachers see their students develop physically, cognitively, and socio-emotionally. Teachers see their students learn, day by day.

Most teachers agree that seeing students develop new knowledge and skills and gain confidence can be the most rewarding part of teaching. Teachers have the satisfaction of knowing they played a significant role in that process.

### Listening Activity

Interview a teacher whom you admire to find out what this person feels are the most rewarding parts of teaching. Why did this person decide to become a teacher?

## Teaching in Schools

Most teachers work in schools. For teachers who work in a school system, there is a great variety of students and school settings. Schools range from small to large, rural to urban, and preschools to universities. Schools are public and funded by tax dollars or private and funded by other sources. Most private schools are sponsored by religious organizations, while the vast majority of schools are public, or **nonsectarian** (not based on any religious affiliation). Schools are normally divided by grade levels, **16-2**. The purpose of all schools, however, is the same—to promote learning.

| Common School Designations | | |
|---|---|---|
| **Level** | **Grades** | **Typical Ages** |
| **Preschool** | | 2 through 4 |
| **Prekindergarten** | | 4 through 5 |
| **Elementary** | Kindergarten through grades 4, 5, or 6 | 5 through 11 |
| **Middle school** | Grades 5 or 6 through 8 | 10 through 13 |
| **Junior high** | Grades 7 through 8 or 9 | 12 through 14 |
| **High school** | Grade 9 or 10 through 12 | 14 through 18 |

*Goodheart-Willcox Publisher*

**16-2**   Although these are typical school designations, variations are fairly common.

## Child Care, Preschool, and Prekindergarten Programs

More and more children are enrolled in educational programs prior to kindergarten. *Child care programs* focus primarily on providing a safe, caring, and challenging learning environment. Preschool and prekindergarten programs have a stronger educational focus. *Preschool programs* are generally for children ages 2 through 4. **Prekindergarten programs**, where available, are for children who will be in kindergarten the following year. Prekindergarten programs are often referred to as *Pre-K*.

Preschool and Pre-K teachers plan activities that build on children's curiosity and interest in play. These activities are based on experience with children and a thorough understanding of child development and learning. The activities help children develop the many skills they will need for kindergarten and beyond.

## Elementary Schools

Significant developmental changes occur between kindergarten and fifth grade. The physical, intellectual, social, and emotional differences between a kindergartener and an 11-year-old are enormous. In this time span, small children grow into preteens. They learn to read, compute, and tackle more complex information. They make friends and figure out how to handle disagreements. They deal with feelings and develop a sense of who they are. In these early years, students often have classroom experiences that affect their success or failure in school, work, and even their personal lives.

Many elementary school teachers teach in **self-contained classrooms**. This means the same teacher and group of students remain in one classroom most of the day, with most or all subjects taught by one teacher. Elementary school classrooms are typically active and visually stimulating. Lessons may incorporate games, music, art activities, computer programs, and visuals, as well as textbooks and teacher presentations, **16-3**. Most traditional elementary schools employ teachers who specialize in one grade level, although some school systems are structured so teachers instruct across several grades.

## Middle Schools and Junior Highs

Many schools place older preteens and young teens in their own school. They recognize that students these ages have different needs. **Middle schools** usually include grades 5 or 6 through 8. Schools with a **junior high** system include students in grades 7 through 8 or 9. Even if these students remain physically within the same building with younger grades, methods of teaching and learning change.

There are good reasons for these divisions. Brain development at this stage moves thinking to a higher level. Students think faster and more creatively. They can identify multiple solutions to problems. They also become able to think abstractly. Students who think abstractly are interested in why things are as they are. Abstract thinkers can also connect how they feel to what they are thinking.

These changes in thinking and learning make the role of middle school and junior high teachers different from that of elementary school teachers. Because students study topics in more depth, most teachers specialize in teaching one or two areas, such as social studies, science, or

Zurijeta/Shutterstock.com

**16-3** Elementary school teachers use a variety of teaching methods.

math. This means that students have several teachers during the day—preparing them for the system they will have in high school. Learning is often less structured, incorporating more projects and activities. Students can be lively and creative. Because learning social skills is so important in this stage of life, students often work in groups and solve problems together, **16-4**. This is known as **collaborative learning**.

Middle school and junior high students are expected to become more responsible for their own learning and behavior. Information and tasks are more complex. Students learn to structure their time and to make, organize, and carry out plans. Teachers help them systematically build these and other skills and habits needed for high school.

Monkey Business Images/Shutterstock.com

**16-4** Through collaborative learning activities, students are able to learn about subjects as they learn how to work with others.

## High Schools

**High school**, grades 9 or 10 through 12, brings new subjects. General math gives way to algebra, geometry, and trigonometry. Topics are studied in much more depth. Students are also expected to take primary responsibility for their learning. In addition to often having homework in each subject every night, long-term projects are also common. Students are expected to ask for help if they do not understand topics. More assignments require complex thinking skills, and students routinely practice solving problems by gathering and evaluating information.

High school teachers typically specialize in one subject or a group of related subjects. In small schools, however, teachers may have a more diverse teaching load. More content knowledge is needed to teach high school courses. Teachers must have at least a bachelor's degree from a four-year college or university and be certified to teach in their state. Training for high school teachers is more focused on the subject areas they have chosen.

Even with curriculum guidelines, teachers still have some flexibility in what and how they teach. They determine how much to emphasize various topics and how to best present them. Which topics will they assign for papers? Can a concept be learned most effectively through a teacher presentation, group discussion, lab experience, or some combination of these and other techniques? What methods used to promote learning is among the aspects controlled by individual teachers.

High school teachers usually have additional responsibilities besides teaching. They may monitor study halls, serve as advisors for school clubs, coach sports, and chaperone events. Some of these responsibilities are considered part of their regular teaching duties, while they may receive extra pay for others. Many teachers are willing to help students outside of class to make sure they understand assignments.

## Teaching Specialists

In addition to regular classroom teachers, most schools also rely on teachers who play special roles. In elementary school, students may have teachers who only teach music, physical education, or a foreign language, **16-5**. Reading specialists typically work with students who have difficulty with that key skill. They are trained to identify specific reading problems and help students move ahead.

**Special education teachers**, those who work with students who have special learning needs, also fall in this category. Special education teachers use various techniques to help students learn. The needs, strengths, and weaknesses of each individual student are carefully considered, and an Individualized Education Plan (IEP) is developed. This is done by a team of teachers and specialists (often a therapist and psychologist), in addition to the child's parents.

Many special education teachers work with students with mild to moderate learning difficulties. These students typically spend most of their day in regular classrooms. Some special education teachers assist students with specific impairments in speech, hearing, sight, or language. They often help regular classroom teachers adapt their teaching for these students. Others help children deal with emotional problems that impact learning. A few special education teachers work with students with more severe cognitive disability or autism. With these students, they work on both basic literacy skills and life skills. Life skills can include social, self-care, and job-related skills for high school students.

oliveromg/Shutterstock.com

**16-5** Many schools hire teaching specialists, such as music teachers.

## College and University Faculty

Many postsecondary teaching positions are available in trade and technical schools, community colleges, four-year colleges, and universities, **16-6**. Examples of jobs at this level include professor, assistant professor, associate professor, instructor, faculty member, or lecturer. In addition to teaching courses pertaining to a particular subject, educators must also conduct research in their field and publish their findings. Most postsecondary educators must have a Ph.D., but some community colleges may accept a master's degree. When working in trade and technical schools, professional work experience in a particular field is necessary to obtain employment.

Diego Cervo/Shutterstock.com

**16-6** Postsecondary teachers instruct students beyond the high school level.

## Safety Connections    *Coaching Safety*

Besides training athletes about rules and strategies for a particular sport, coaches are also responsible for the safety of each team member. Coaches must ensure that athletes follow safety guidelines and use proper safety equipment. Coaches need to recognize signs of injury or any other factors that may affect team members' well-being. Coaches must also ensure that athletes are not threatening the safety of another student, either intentionally or unintentionally.

Sports safety programs teach coaches about the prevention and care of common illnesses and injuries. They review guidelines that can help ensure player safety. First-aid training is also necessary to safely treat injuries when they do occur. Courses in lifespan development, sports nutrition, and sports medicine are also helpful.

### Speaking Activity

How can knowledge of lifespan development further promote the safety of athletes? With a partner, discuss how sports safety relates to physical, cognitive, and socio-emotional well-being.

## Coaches

Many schools and universities also have coaches for specific sports and physical activities. Coaches are responsible for training students in the rules, practices, and strategies of a particular sport. They provide athletic training and nutritional advice. They ensure safety practices are being followed and maintained. Coaches also support athletes and help students develop their strategies and skills. Specialized coaches manage a particular team, such as basketball, football, or volleyball.

## Teaching in Other Settings

Trained and skilled teachers do not always teach in the school system. Because education is key to so many aspects of society, teachers find their skills in demand in other places as well. Opportunities are quite varied. A few examples are described here.

### Business and Industry

Many businesses and industries provide education to their employees. The teachers who provide this education are often called **corporate trainers**. The types of education they offer depend on the situation. Some programs focus on technical work skills, while others teach team building and leadership skills. International companies may hire people to teach employees moving to other countries the languages, customs, and work practices they will need to know.

Large companies often employ corporate trainers as full-time employees. Others work for a specialty company that provides corporate trainers on an as-needed basis. Entrepreneurial opportunities also exist for corporate trainers who desire to be self-employed.

Businesses employ teachers for many other purposes, too. For example, a teacher may be hired by a cruise ship company to teach the history of cruise destinations. Teachers provide classes or one-on-one instruction to children undergoing long-term hospital treatment. Whatever the challenge, basic teaching skills are simply adapted to fit the situation.

## Cultural Connections — Overseas Teaching Professions

English is taught as a foreign language in many schools and communities around the world. This provides teaching opportunities for English teachers who want to work abroad. Teaching experiences abroad may be short-term, often called *exchanges*, or long-term. Many teaching abroad programs partner with local schools, colleges, or universities.

Many private businesses or organizations also offer teaching opportunities abroad. These opportunities may be through a religious or nonsectarian organization. Teachers working in nonsectarian organizations help employees of local companies or organizations learn English skills, business terminology, conversational skills, and terms relating to the profession or organization.

Some programs offer housing with a host family to submerge the participant in another culture, while the host family learns about the English language. This creates a cultural exchange in which people learn directly from each other. Exchange programs offer orientation classes and support for the teacher throughout the teaching abroad experience.

### Writing Activity

Imagine yourself teaching English or another subject abroad. Write a one-page reflection paper about the pros and cons of teaching overseas.

## Adult Education

In a society where jobs require up-to-date knowledge and skills, adult education is an ongoing need. Literacy programs, for example, may focus on teaching adults to improve reading skills or learn the English language. For adults without a high school diploma, alternative programs can provide the equivalent of a diploma. Other programs provide specific job or technical skills in areas such as computer training.

Adult education teachers plan, deliver, and evaluate educational programs. Their roles are similar to elementary, middle school, high school, and college educators, but their audience is different. Like other teachers, they use lecture, hands-on learning, computer programs, group work, and projects to teach course content. Their teaching must reflect the latest in their field's knowledge and practices. As in all teaching, personal interaction between students and the teacher is important.

Adult education programs are often government funded. Sometimes they are supported through private funds and/or corporate contributions. Community colleges and universities may also provide adult education programs, although these do not normally lead to a degree. Adult education teachers can also be found in job training centers, community centers, or any environment where training and education programs are needed, **16-7**.

## Cooperative Extension Service

**Cooperative extension educators**, or agents, are community teachers. They provide educational programs in family and consumer sciences, 4-H youth development, agriculture, and community and rural development. They provide information and technical assistance for community residents on topics such as parenting, financial planning, and gardening.

Monkey Business Images/Shutterstock.com

**16-7** Adult education career opportunities range from teaching one course to full-time positions.

Cooperative extension educators commonly coordinate youth 4-H activities and recruit, train, and develop community leaders. They are professional employees of state universities who are supported by the federal government. Their varied duties include offering formal and informal educational programs to communities in their region.

## Sports and Fitness Programs

Most communities have opportunities for people of all ages to learn and play sports and improve their physical fitness. These depend on coaches, athletic trainers, athletic directors, aerobics instructors, camp directors, and recreation specialists. These teachers must have sports and fitness knowledge and experience, although a college degree is not always required. They must be able to motivate others to learn and to accomplish goals. They may work for private gyms, community organizations such as the Boys and Girls Clubs of America, summer camps, or parks departments, **16-8**. Entrepreneurial opportunities are also available for people who want to be self-employed as coaches and trainers.

holbox/Shutterstock.com

**16-8** Fitness clubs often hire instructors to lead exercise classes.

## Knowledge and Skills

Teaching is a career field that offers variety, challenges, and rewards. For public schools, teacher preparation standards vary by state. Teacher preparation can be described in four steps: high school education and training, college education and training, student teaching and experience, and certification, **16-9**. Trainer standards, on the other hand, vary by organization and the needs of the learners and may not require a degree or certification.

Teachers and trainers both must know how to teach. In other words, they must know how to effectively communicate and instruct. They must understand how children, youth, and adults change at different stages of life. They must know how to manage a classroom. They must know how to work with parents and administrators and how school systems work. If they work with adults, teachers need to understand the needs of their learners.

Teachers and trainers must have content knowledge and expertise in a subject. They must keep up to date. They need to know the English language, including writing and reading skills. They must teach what is required by the organization or their school, district, and state. Overall, they must meet the intellectual, physical, emotional, and social needs of students.

High school is a perfect time to begin exploring the teaching field. It is also a good time to gain experience working with children and youth. You can set goals, gain experience, and learn more about children and youth. You can do well in school and observe the educational environment first-hand. You can explore college teacher preparation programs. You can apply to college programs that begin your career path toward teaching.

| Education Requirements for Teaching and Training Occupations | |
|---|---|
| **Occupation** | **Education Requirements** |
| **Child care worker** | High school diploma, Child Development Associate (CDA) credential |
| **Nanny** | High school diploma, Child Development Associate (CDA) credential |
| **Child care director** | Bachelor's degree, 1 to 5 years work experience in related field |
| **Teacher assistant** | High school diploma or associate's degree |
| **Preschool teacher** | Associate's degree |
| **Elementary school teacher** | Bachelor's degree, state-issued license |
| **Middle school teacher** | Bachelor's degree, state-issued license |
| **High school teacher** | Bachelor's degree, state-issued license |
| **Special education teacher** | Bachelor's degree, state-issued license |
| **Postsecondary teacher** | Doctoral or professional degree |
| **Coach** | High school diploma, experience with the sport |
| **Fitness trainer** | High school diploma, certification |

*Goodheart-Willcox Publisher*

**16-9**   Requirements for teaching and training occupations vary.

# Case Study

## Teaching Challenges

Samira always wanted to be a high school teacher. She enjoys helping others and has a variety of experience tutoring younger students, peers, and older adults. Samira earned a bachelor's degree and a teaching certificate. She is aware of the rewards of teaching, but is concerned about the many challenges. Although Samira has experience working closely with individuals, she lacks experience leading an entire classroom.

Samira is aware that the conditions under which teachers work are not always ideal. Classes can be large and workloads heavy. School districts vary in their ability to provide teachers with up-to-date textbooks, educational technology, and other learning aids. Schools also reflect the problems of society. Poverty, drug and alcohol abuse, and similar societal problems affect students. Teaching can also be emotionally draining. Teachers must sometimes cope with disrespect, unruly behavior, and even violence in schools.

Samira has a friend, Mark, who after teaching high school math for a year, decided that teaching was not the profession for him. Mark cautions Samira about potential scenarios and conflicts that can arise at any time while teaching. Samira is concerned that she may have a similar experience as Mark.
- What advice would you offer to Samira about her teaching concerns?
- How can Samira learn from Mark's experiences?
- What other opportunities relating to teaching and education could Samira investigate?

## Checkpoint

1. Why are the personal rewards of teaching often considered long-term?
2. How do child care programs differ from preschool and prekindergarten programs? How are they the same?
3. What are self-contained classrooms? At what level are they most commonly used?
4. What is collaborative learning? At what level is it first used extensively?
5. What are the minimum educational requirements to be a teacher?
6. Why would having a bachelor's degree with teaching certification be an asset in training or teaching situations outside of school, even if it is not required?

# Professional Support Services

There are many professional supporting roles within the field of education. These jobs are often creative and flexible, providing invaluable support to education and training systems. Similar to administration and administrative support, many of these jobs are highly specialized, **16-10.**

## Sample Occupations

Job titles in the professional support services pathway include parent educator, school and career counselor, speech-language specialist, and children's librarian. All of these occupations require a degree. To become a parent educator, a bachelor's degree is required. Other occupations within this pathway typically require more than a bachelor's degree.

| Education Requirements for Professional Support Services | |
|---|---|
| **Occupation** | **Education Requirements** |
| **Parent educator** | Bachelor's degree |
| **School guidance counselor** | Master's degree |
| **Career counselor** | Master's degree |
| **Speech-language specialist** | Master's degree |
| **Librarian** | Master's degree |
| **School psychologist** | Doctoral degree, state-issued license |

*Goodheart-Willcox Publisher*

**16-10**   Most careers in the professional support services pathway require at least a master's degree.

### Parent Educators

Some school districts, hospitals, places of worship, and other community organizations provide parent educators. **Parent educators** come from a variety of backgrounds and offer training and encouragement to parents. They may facilitate discussion among parents of newborns. They may organize playgroups that focus on good parenting skills. They may offer classes on how to communicate with teens. Parenting coaches can share knowledge and skills while offering encouragement and a community for parents to interact and ask questions.

### School and Career Counselors

Counselors are an important type of support professional. **School guidance counselors** help students learn social skills, solve issues, cope with personal crises, and make education and career decisions. They can help students determine their interests, aptitudes, and abilities, and decide which courses they need to take to follow a specific career path.

**Career counselors** help people make career decisions by leading them through the process of choosing and preparing for a career. They often offer assistance in completing résumés and preparing for interviews. Career counselors may work in colleges or government career centers, **16-11**. Entrepreneurial opportunities are available for those who wish to work in private practice.

### Speech-Language Specialists

Communication is critical to learning. Some children struggle with speech. They may stutter, struggle to form sounds and words, or have trouble hearing or understanding language. When a child struggles with speech or language disorders, it affects their learning. **Speech-language specialists** are trained to diagnose and provide treatment that helps each individual student. They work closely with the student's doctor, family, and teachers to address the speech or language challenge at all levels.

### Children's Librarians

Libraries and other learning resources are an important part of every school. Librarians specialize in books and other online materials that can enhance learning. They order books, maps, computer software, and other visual materials that boost learning. Some librarians specialize in resources for young children, **16-12**. They are called **children's librarians**. Other

Dennis Owusu-Ansah/Shutterstock.com

**16-11**  Many employers request that career counselors have a master's degree.

K. Miri Photography/Shutterstock.com

**16-12** Children's librarians may work in schools, public or private libraries, museums, or bookstores.

librarians specialize in older children, teens, or adults needs. Besides remaining current in what is available and desired, they offer reading sessions or story times, teach reading or research skills, and help students navigate computer software or Internet resources.

## Knowledge and Skills

Occupations in the professional support services pathway require highly specialized knowledge and skills plus these personal qualities—creativity, patience, and caring. These professionals must be able to work well with students, teachers, family members, and other professionals in the community one-on-one or in a group setting. They must have the desire to contribute to a student's success. Providing support services and then evaluating outcomes is critical in order to enhance the student's learning and environment.

## Checkpoint

1. List five examples of professional support services occupations.
2. What is the difference between a school guidance counselor and a career counselor?
3. List some of the qualities needed to work in the professional support services pathway.

# Administration and Administrative Support

There are many people involved in successfully running an educational organization, such as a school, day care center, or museum. In addition to instructors, schools and educational organizations need staff to help the organization run smoothly. Supporting staff in educational organizations is called *administration and administrative support*. People working in these careers mainly work behind the scenes. Essentially, they help lead, manage, and support the instructors. These professionals must also be comfortable working with many people, as a learner, leader, and team member.

## Sample Occupations

Schools and universities could not efficiently function if only instructors were present. Administrative support help manage daily job duties involved in an educational organization. Administrative support comes in many forms, **16-13**. Examples of administration duties include deciding what will be taught, training and supporting teachers or instructors, and measuring the effectiveness of teaching and student learning. These professionals also lead and manage other educational activities within the organization. Professionals in administration and administrative support roles have at least an associate's degree. Many positions require a higher degree, such as a bachelor's or master's degree. Examples of job titles in administration and administrative support include curriculum developer and program director.

## Curriculum Developer

Before a school year or course begins, the information that will be taught must be decided, developed, and planned. **Curriculum** describes the material and content taught in a school or program. Curriculum includes all the courses taught in a program of study and the material taught in each course.

A **curriculum developer**, also called an *instructional coordinator*, helps develop course content in a program of study or specific course. Curriculum developers

| Education Requirements for Administration and Administrative Occupations | |
|---|---|
| **Occupation** | **Education Requirements** |
| **Curriculum developer** | Master's degree |
| **Program director** | Bachelor's degree |
| **Elementary, middle, or high school principal** | Master's degree |
| **Postsecondary college administrator** | Master's degree |
| **Interpreter** | Bachelor's degree |
| **Translator** | Bachelor's degree |

*Goodheart-Willcox Publisher*

**16-13** Minimum education requirements vary for entry-level positions in the administration and administrative support pathway.

stay informed of educational standards set at national, state, and district levels. They ensure the curriculum meets educational standards and will prepare students for the next course or level of education, **16-14**. Curriculum developers may recommend the purchase of instructional materials, such as textbooks, teaching aids, learning equipment, and technology.

Curriculum developers are also responsible for training instructors. This may include training them on how to use materials effectively in the classroom. Curriculum developers may also attend and lead sessions relating to new research, teaching strategies, or other new developments within the field. They may also observe a classroom and provide feedback to the instructor for improving teaching methods.

## Program Director

A **program director** oversees the mission, goals, and programs of an organization, such as a child care center. Program directors develop programs, organize how they are run, and evaluate the program's progress and success. They hire caregivers, instructors, and supporting staff, and provide orientation and training. This is a supervisory position that requires a combination of educational expertise and experience. Most program directors also work with state and federal agencies to secure grants, maintain health and safety regulations, and stay up-to-date with current developments relating to their program.

Rob Marmion/Shutterstock.com

**16-14** Curriculum developers establish the curriculum that helps teachers determine what to teach.

## Knowledge and Skills

To work in any career within the administration and administrative support pathway, professionals use a variety of knowledge and skills. They have foundational skills in addition to the skills needed to work in the education and training industry. They are also comfortable working closely with others, managing staff, and recognizing legal and political factors relating to job duties and the organization.

Pavel L Photo and Video/Shutterstock.com

**16-15** Administration and administrative support professionals are comfortable attending and leading training sessions.

Many careers in the administration and administrative support pathway involve management and leadership. Administration professionals supervise and/or train instructors or caregivers within an educational institution. This requires knowledge of the most up-to-date research, teaching strategies, educational standards, technology, and health and safety practices, **16-15**. They must not only be aware of recent trends and development, but also know how to incorporate new knowledge into their organization. They enjoy lifelong learning. Administration professionals enhance the learning environment and motivate learners. They also support and motivate the instructors.

Administration and administrative support professionals are also aware of legal, cultural, and political factors that are relevant to the organization. Many laws and regulations are involved in educational settings. Administration professionals are informed of these laws. They are also culturally knowledgeable and comfortable with diversity. They address political concerns and may create new rules and regulations to better ensure the organization continues to run smoothly.

## Checkpoint

1. What are the essential tasks of administration and administrative support professionals?
2. List two examples of administration and administrative support occupations.
3. What are some of the qualities of professionals who work in the administration and administrative support pathway?

# Employment Opportunities and Trends

Fortunately, there will always be a need for talented professionals in the field of education and training. Education is the key to a successful society. Children need to be educated to be contributing members of society. Adults need to learn new skills and knowledge. In fact, job out-look predictions show that over the next ten years, the United States will need over two million new teachers in schools alone. This is because many current teachers will be retiring soon and there is a national movement for educational reform. Many people believe that having more well-trained teachers will help students get a better education, **16-16**.

Teachers of core subjects, such as math and science, and teachers who speak more than one language will be in demand. *Bilingual education* (teaching in two languages) is growing in many parts of the country. Teachers who have the skills to teach in two or more languages will be in great demand.

Teacher shortages already exist in some geographic areas, including inner-city and rural schools. In addition, popu-lation growth is expected to be greater in some states than others. Consequently, the demand for teaching jobs is expected to increase. Taking advantage of oppor-tunities currently available can help you develop the knowledge, skills, and qual-ities that make an excellent teacher.

*AVAVA/Shutterstock.com*

**16-16** If you want to teach, develop the knowledge, skills, and qualities that will make you a great teacher.

## Checkpoint

1. What is the key to a successful society?
2. List two reasons the demand for teachers is projected to increase.
3. Identify two areas that are projected to have a higher demand for teaching opportunities.

## Summary

The three pathways within the education and training industry are *teaching and training, administration and administrative support*, and *professional support services*. There are many career opportunities within each pathway. Traditional classroom teaching and training opportunities exist at the preschool through adult level of education. Professionals in the field may work in schools or businesses. Entrepreneurial opportunities are also available.

Professionals working in educational settings have specific knowledge and skills. Teachers have a desire to share their love of learning. They spend most of their time planning, presenting lessons, and evaluating learning. They often have additional responsibilities, such as supervising extracurricular activities. Teachers provide opportunities to help their students learn and succeed. Teaching can be a rewarding and fulfilling career, as well as challenging.

Professional and administration support service careers help run the educational organization. Professionals may work in highly specialized subject areas with other faculty members, students, or community members. Keeping up-to-date on the latest knowledge within the field is critical.

## Vocabulary Activity

With a partner, use the Internet to locate photos or graphics that depict the terms. Print the graphics or use presentation software to show your graphics to the class, describing how they depict the meaning of the terms.

## Critical Thinking

1. **Make inferences.** Which personal characteristics are the most important for teachers to have? Why?

2. **Determine.** Should teachers be held to a higher moral and ethical standard than other professionals? Why or why not?

3. **Analyze.** Who was your favorite elementary school teacher? What did you like the most about this teacher? Why?

4. **Evaluate.** Ask a group of family and friends to list their top three characteristics of a good teacher. Compile their suggestions into a master list, noting which characteristics were mentioned the most frequently. Is there any similarity between the responses?

5. **Assess.** Ask permission to observe the activities of one of your teachers for a day. What are the most effective activities you observed?

6. **Cause and effect.** Watch a movie or feature film about a teacher. Describe the film's script or story. What challenges did the students and teacher face in this story? What were the critical events that lead to the story's ending? Was it a positive ending? Was there a moral to this story? If so, what was it?

7. **Compare and contrast.** Think of a time when you used collaborative learning in a class project. How did this experience compare and contrast to a time when you had to complete a project alone? What were the benefits? What were the challenges?

8. **Predict.** As a college student, in what type of environment could you best learn?

9. **Draw conclusions.** Visit the children's section of a library and browse through the book collection. How are the books organized? Who is primarily using this library section? How are they using it? Can you draw conclusions about the library patrons?

10. **Identify.** Identify all the professional and administration support service occupations associated with your school.

## Core Skills

11. **Writing.** Interview a teacher or other professional in your school about the rewards and challenges of a career in education. Write a reflection paper summarizing the interview.

12. **Speaking.** Find a newspaper article or online report about a public policy issue affecting K-12 schools in your area. Report on the issue to your class.

13. **Listening.** Interview a person established in his or her career. Ask the person how new ideas, methods, and standard procedures or expectations are learned on the job. Do they employ corporate trainers?

14. **Reading.** Go to a library and find a magazine for teachers or trainers. Read at least five of the articles.

15. **Math.** Prepare a practical math lesson and teach it to someone else. You could teach someone how to figure gas mileage, measure a room, or convert tablespoons to cups when measuring in cooking.

16. **CTE Career Readiness Practice.** Obtain a copy of a career-search book (such as the latest edition of *What Color Is Your Parachute?*). Read the book. Then write a book report analyzing and identifying the important guidelines the author suggests for finding meaningful employment, including identifying your personal career and educational goals. Select two topics you found most valuable to share with the class. Give evidence from your reading to support your reasoning.

## Research

17. Find out who decides the curriculum that will be taught in your school, district, and state. How are curricula decisions made?

18. Research a career in the occupational category of education and training. What required courses and other electives would you need to pursue this career? Create a plan of study to record your findings.

## Event Prep

19. Learn more about an education professional support services career through job shadowing and interviewing a professional within the field. Develop an interview form prior to the experience to record information about education requirements, work experience, and job duties. You may wish to expand your project by participating in an Educators Rising *Exploring Support Services Careers Competition*. See your adviser for further information.

# Chapter 17

## Career Paths in Human Services

Rob Marmion/Shutterstock.com

# Objectives

After studying this chapter, you will be able to

- compare and contrast career opportunities for counseling and mental health services professionals.
- identify career opportunities in the family and community services pathway.
- summarize career opportunities for consumer services workers.
- recognize job duties of various human services workers.

## Reading Prep

Before you begin reading the last chapter of this text, consider how the author developed and presented information. How does the information in one chapter provide the foundation for the next? Why do you think the author decided to make this chapter the last chapter?

## Key Terms

counselor
marriage and family therapist
mental health counselor
rehabilitation counselor
psychologist
social worker

community service director
development director
executive director
social and human services assistant
case manager

emergency and relief worker
consumer advocate
financial advisor
hospital patient account representative
home care aide

## Visit the G-W Learning Companion Website to:

- **build** vocabulary with e-flash cards and interactive games;
- **assess** what you learn by completing self-assessment quizzes; and
- **expand** knowledge with activities that extend learning.

G-W LEARNING.com   www.g-wlearning.com/development/

If you enjoy helping others, then a career in human services may appeal to you. *Human services* is a broad career field that involves helping others to improve their quality of life throughout all stages of the lifespan. Human services professionals help individuals, families, and communities learn to function effectively and meet basic needs. Because families exist in every culture and in every region, the skills held by human services professionals are greatly needed.

Human services professionals work in five different career pathways: *Counseling and Mental Health Services*, *Family and Community Services*, *Consumer Services*, *Personal Care Services*, and *Early Childhood Development and Services*. Many careers in human services are also included in other occupational categories. For example, careers in the early childhood development and services pathway are also in the education and training occupational category. Jobs in human services today are many and varied. This chapter will primarily focus on careers that require an understanding of how people develop and change throughout the lifespan, **17-1**.

# Counseling and Mental Health Services

Counseling and mental health services professionals such as counselors and psychologists work with people of all ages. They are aware of how people's needs, values, motivations, and subsequently their behaviors are different throughout the life stages. They also have an appreciation for human diversity. Overall, they are compassionate and have a sincere interest in helping people.

## Counselors

A **counselor** or therapist helps people manage and overcome problems and develop strategies needed to live a healthy and safe life. Counselors are good communicators who work with people individually and in groups. They possess high mental and physical energy to handle the daily stresses of working with people in difficult situations. Most counseling positions require a master's degree and some form of licensure or certification to practice.

| Human Services Careers | |
|---|---|
| **Career Pathway** | **Sample Careers** |
| **Counseling and mental health services** | Counselor, psychologist, sociologist, residential advisor |
| **Family and community services** | Adult day care worker, career counselor, community service director, dietitian, emergency and relief worker, human services worker, social worker |
| **Consumer services** | Consumer advocate, financial advisor, hospital patient account representative |
| **Personal care services** | Home care aide, personal fitness trainer |
| **Early childhood development and services** | Child care worker and director, nanny, elementary school counselor, parent educator, preschool teacher |

*Goodheart-Willcox Publisher*

**17-1**   These are just some of the many careers available in human services.

## Case Study ❓❓❓

### Confidentiality in Counseling

Dante is a mental health counselor who specializes in anxiety disorders. He has worked closely with one client, Felicia, for six months. When Felicia first started therapy sessions with Dante, she often felt overwhelmed and anxious. She also suffered occasional panic attacks. Throughout the therapy sessions, Felicia became less anxious and better able to manage stressors. The number of panic attacks she has now is significantly reduced.

Dante has a good friend, Michael, who recently began experiencing anxiety attacks. Over lunch, Michael explained some of his symptoms and stressors to Dante. While listening to Michael's condition, Dante is reminded of his patient, Felicia. Dante notices that Michael and Felicia share many similar qualities. They were raised in similar environments. As a mental health counselor, Dante wants to help Michael. Since Michael and Felicia have similar struggles, Dante is considering telling Michael about Felicia and her successes in dealing with her anxiety disorder.

- If Dante tells Michael about Felicia, how does this represent a breach in confidentiality?
- Why is confidentiality important in the counseling and mental health services career pathway?
- What other methods can Dante use to help Michael?

Counselors often specialize in a particular area, such as working with people to overcome grief, eating disorders, mental or emotional issues, substance abuse, or relationship conflicts. They may work with specific groups, such as children, adolescents, or older adults. A **marriage and family therapist** helps individuals, couples, and families resolve conflicts. Marriage and family therapists address such concerns as separation, divorce, and grief over the loss of a loved one by listening to clients and asking questions. They help clients deal with their problems in positive ways that can improve their lives. As they work with clients, marriage and family therapists enhance communication and understanding among family members.

A **mental health counselor** assesses, addresses, and treats mental and emotional issues such as anxiety, depression, trauma, stress, or grief. Mental health counselors often work closely with other mental health professionals such as psychologists, psychiatrists, and social workers. After diagnosis of a mental health issue, counselors provide a variety of therapeutic techniques to help their clients regain optimum mental health. Likewise, *substance abuse counselors* help people address problems with alcohol, drugs, or other substances. They also assist people with other behavioral disorders such as gambling or eating disorders.

A **rehabilitation counselor** helps people overcome effects of physical and emotional disabilities to achieve optimum independence. Rehabilitation counselors work in a variety of settings such as rehabilitation agencies, independent living facilities, prisons, schools, or private practice. They help individuals and their families deal with the personal, social, and physical ramifications of the disability. They also help individuals consider changes in employment if needed. They help clients come to terms with the disability and live as independently as possible.

## Psychologists

A **psychologist** studies human behavior and mental processes and develops theories to explain why people behave the way they do. Psychologists conduct studies and research to help understand and predict human emotions, feelings, and behavior. They look for patterns of behavior or cause-and-effect relationships between events.

Psychologists work with people of all ages, but may choose to work with a specific age group. They commonly have certain areas in which they specialize, **17-2**. Psychologists may work independently helping clients or conducting research. Some may work as part of a health care team to improve a person's overall health and well-being. Entrepreneurial opportunities exist for those who wish to be in private practice. To become a psychologist, a master's or doctoral degree is required. Practicing psychologists also require licensure.

## Checkpoint

1. Describe three occupational areas in which counselors specialize.
2. What are the typical educational requirements to become a counselor?
3. Differentiate between a counselor and psychologist.
4. List six occupational areas in which psychologists often specialize.
5. What are the typical educational requirements to become a psychologist?

| Common Occupational Specialties of Psychologists | |
|---|---|
| **Occupational Specialty** | **Description** |
| **Clinical psychologist** | Works with patients to assess, diagnose, and treat mental, emotional, and behavioral disorders. Conducts interviews with patients, performs diagnostic testing, develops treatment plans, and provides individual or group therapy sessions. |
| **Counseling psychologist** | Helps patients understand and deal with their problems through counseling. |
| **Developmental psychologist** | Studies psychological growth and development that occurs during various stages of the lifespan. |
| **Forensic psychologist** | Works in the legal and criminal justice system, often as an expert witness, to explain psychological findings involving a particular case. |
| **Industrial-organizational psychologist** | Studies workplace issues such as productivity, employee working styles, and morale to improve the quality of work life. |
| **School psychologist** | Provides counseling to students and families to help address students' behavioral and learning problems. |
| **Social psychologist** | Studies individual and group interactions to determine how behaviors are shaped by social interactions. |

Goodheart-Willcox Publisher

**17-2**    Psychologists often specialize in occupational areas such as these.

## Cultural Connections   Sociologists

Another job title in the counseling and mental health services pathway is a sociologist. A *sociologist* studies society and social behavior. Sociologists examine social interactions among groups, cultures, organizations, and nations to determine how social influences affect people. They observe activities in social, political, economic, religious, and business organizations. Sociologists test theories about social issues through data collection that involves observations, surveys, and interviews. They prepare detailed reports of their findings and may advise policymakers and other groups on sociological issues. Sociologists may specialize in such topics as families, health, education, gender, aging, poverty, crime, population, and racial and ethnic relations.

People with a sociology background are often teachers and professors. Others may find jobs outside the sociologist profession as statisticians, policy analysts, demographers, and survey researchers. To become a sociologist, a master's degree or Ph.D. is often required.

### Research Activity

Anthropologists and archaeologists are occupations that have similar job duties to those of sociologists. Research one of these careers to learn more about the job duties, education requirements, and job outlook. What similarities and differences do you notice between these careers?

## Family and Community Services

Careers in family and community services involve providing help to and care for people who are struggling to meet their basic needs. Daily activities of these professionals are many and varied. Depending on the organization, typical daily tasks include interviewing clients and family members to assess their needs and determine their eligibility for benefits and services. They also help clients fill out forms to receive benefits, such as food assistance and medical care.

Other activities of family and community services professionals include arranging transportation for clients, telephoning or visiting clients' homes, helping to provide emotional support, monitoring and maintaining case records, advising clients on budgeting and shopping for well-balanced meals, and organizing or leading support groups.

## Health Connections   Dietitians—Promoting Better Nutrition

A *dietitian* is an expert in food and nutrition. Dietitians advise people on ways to develop a more healthful lifestyle by making wise food choices. They assess clients' needs and then develop meal plans to best meet these needs. For example, a dietitian may plan meals that are low in fat and sugar for an overweight person who is trying to lose weight. Dietitians evaluate the effectiveness of their clients' meal plans and adjust them accordingly.

Dietitians give presentations to groups of people about promoting better nutrition through diet and good eating habits. They also teach people about

ways to prevent and manage specific diseases through good nutrition. Some dietitians work with specific groups such as pregnant women. Dietitians may work in hospitals, care facilities, cafeterias, food corporations, public health clinics, and government and non-profit agencies. To become a dietitian, a bachelor's degree and licensure is required.

### Listening Activity

Interview a dietitian to learn more about how good nutrition can help prevent and manage certain diseases such as high blood pressure or high cholesterol. Prepare a list of questions prior to the interview.

CREATISTA/Shutterstock.com

**17-3** Social workers determine the social and emotional needs of their clients by observing and interviewing them.

The daily tasks of family and community services professionals differ depending on the specific role and the people served. They also vary depending on the type of service organization. Job titles in family and community services include social worker, director, social and human services assistant, and emergency and relief worker.

## Social Workers

A **social worker** coordinates and plans programs and activities to meet client needs. Mostly, social workers are advocates for people who cannot or do not know how to help themselves. Typically, they work with clients to utilize community resources to meet individualized needs. Social workers often work with children, people with disabilities, people who are economically disadvantaged, and people with addictions. The job duties of social workers often include

- assessing clients' needs, situations, and support services to determine goals, **17-3**
- referring clients to community resources such as food or housing assistance programs
- helping clients adjust to challenges such as unemployment or illness
- responding to crises such as child abuse or natural disasters
- leading support and therapy groups
- preparing treatment plans for care and rehabilitation of clients and their families
- evaluating effectiveness of services and clients progress

The problems that social workers deal with are often complicated and many-layered. Sometimes social workers do not have the luxury of time to solve complex issues. Instead, they need to intervene on behalf of clients to resolve emergency problems or conflicts. For example, if an older adult enters a hospital with no known immediate family members or address, but displays evidence of abuse, the social worker must uncover the layers of the problem.

Social workers may work for the government, schools, private social services agencies, and health care organizations such as hospitals and treatment centers. Health care organizations represent one of the largest employment segments for social workers. School social workers bridge home, school, and community assets to provide resources to meet the needs of students. A social worker may work with family members, school personnel, and community resources such as a local Boys and Girls Club to help a child overcome social and personal problems. Social workers generally must possess a master's degree in social work. Licensure requirements vary from state to state, **17-4**.

Lisa F.Young/Shutterstock.com

**17-4** Advanced training allows social workers to handle more complex and responsible assignments or administrative positions.

## Agency Directors

A **community service director** oversees an organization's mission, goals, and programs. Community service directors develop and implement programs and evaluate whether programs meet the needs of clients and the objectives of the organization. Many community service directors spend a considerable amount of time working with state and federal agencies to secure grants and to maintain compliance with regulations. This is a supervisory position that usually requires a combination of educational expertise and experience.

A **development director** implements strategies for securing funding to meet program goals and objectives. These professionals write and help others to write grant proposals for funding. They cultivate relationships with potential donors and network with other support groups. The development director oversees special fundraising events such as charitable auctions, or other functions used to raise support. A development director in a larger organization generally has several grant writers and assistants. Development work can be very creative and often involves large event planning and detailed grant writing. Community service directors and development directors typically report directly to the executive director.

The **executive director** is responsible for the overall management and leadership of an organization. Executive directors oversee agency operations and act as liaison between the organization and the governing board. Successful executive directors are active in their community, serving as the face of the organization. They see the big picture and have a vision for the future while leading the agency to meet its mission.

## Social and Human Services Assistants

A **social and human services assistant** works under the direction of other workers, such as a social worker or community service director. Social and human services assistants work with clients and other professionals to help develop effective treatment plans. They also work directly with clients to provide help with daily activities and to make sure that programs run smoothly and efficiently. Each social and human services assistant plays a distinct role in the human services agency, 17-5. The minimum requirement to work as a social and human services assistant is a high school diploma, but many organizations require more education and/or experience.

Social and human services assistants may assume a more supervisory role by becoming case managers (sometimes called a *case coordinator* or *caseworker*). A **case manager** is responsible for developing appropriate case plans and making sure that direct care staff knows how to implement plans. Case managers work directly with clients from all representative populations. They are usually more involved in assessing client cases and supervising large caseloads.

---

### Roles of Social and Human Service Assistants

Social and human service assistants who work with

*children and families*
- ensure children are in a safe environment
- help families obtain resources such as food and housing assistance

*older adults*
- assist clients with daily living activities such as running errands and bathing
- coordinate meal deliveries

*people with disabilities*
- assist clients with daily living activities such as making meals and bathing
- work with employers to make positions accessible to people with disabilities
- help clients obtain rehabilitation services

*people with mental illnesses*
- assist clients in finding resources such as support and therapy groups
- help clients find group housing or personal care services as needed

*people with addictions*
- assist clients in finding rehabilitation centers to meet their needs
- help clients find support groups

*homeless people*
- help clients find temporary or permanent housing
- find places that provide meals, such as soup kitchens
- find other services to address problems such as joblessness

*former prison inmates*
- help clients re-enter society by finding job placement or training programs
- find housing assistance and other programs as needed

*Goodheart-Willcox Publisher*

**17-5**   The roles of social and human services assistants vary depending on the clients they serve.

Case managers are experienced in working with community resources to meet individual client needs. Social workers and community service directors depend on case managers to implement treatment plans. Case managers do not provide therapeutic care or counseling unless they have the required education, experience, and licensure. Case managers generally report directly to the community service director or executive director.

## Emergency and Relief Workers

An **emergency and relief worker** goes into communities to help people deal with the aftermath of a disaster. Emergency and relief workers start by performing search and rescue duties. They then provide or help people access health care and meet their basic needs of food, clothing, and shelter, **17-6**. They help with emotional and mental trauma and reconnect people with their loved ones. Eventually, they help people rebuild their lives. In their efforts, emergency and relief workers collaborate with many specialists who can provide needed resources. Emergency and relief workers may hold college degrees, but experience is most important.

## Checkpoint

1. List four job duties of a social worker.
2. Distinguish between a community service director, development director, and executive director.
3. Give examples of the roles of social and human services assistants for two different types of clients, such as people with addictions and people with disabilities.
4. Describe the responsibilities of a case manager.
5. What are the responsibilities of an emergency and relief worker?

*spirit of america/Shutterstock.com*

**17-6**   When natural disasters occur, such as hurricanes and tornadoes, emergency and relief workers help people meet their basic needs.

# Consumer Services

Careers within the consumer services pathway relate to providing services in the areas of finances, housing, and consumer products. Consumer services professionals provide assistance directly to or on behalf of the consumer. Professionals have specialized knowledge, such as financial management, and combine the specialization with the desire to help an individual, family, or group of people meet a need. Educational requirements for consumer services occupations vary, **17-7**.

Some professionals within the consumer services pathway are consumer advocates, financial advisors, and hospital patient account representatives. A **consumer advocate** helps protect the rights, safety, and health of consumers. Consumer advocates may work in government at the local, state, or national level or in consumer advocacy groups to represent consumer interests to various industries. For example, the Consumer Product Safety Commission evaluates the safety of products, such as electronics, toys, and appliances, to prevent injury or harm to consumers.

A **financial advisor** helps people set financial goals, establish and keep a budget, make investment decisions, and plan for future purchases and expenses. Knowledge in financial planning, insurance, investments, credit, and estate and

## Educational Requirements for Consumer Services Occupations

| Occupation | Education Requirements |
|---|---|
| Consumer advocate | Bachelor's or master's degree, state-issued license |
| Financial advisor | Bachelor's degree, state-issued license may be required |
| Hospital patient account representive | High school diploma or associate's degree, certification |

Goodheart-Willcox Publisher

**17-7** The amount of education, training, and licensing needed depends on the occupation.

## *Safety* Connections

### Consumer Product Safety Commission (CPSC)

The U.S. Consumer Product Safety Commission (CPSC) is an independent federal regulatory agency that Congress established in 1972 as part of the *Consumer Product Safety Act.* The CPSC issues and enforces safety standards that industries must meet when developing consumer products such as toys, cribs, sports equipment, tools, and appliances. These standards help protect the public against unreasonable injuries or deaths from consumer products. The CPSC informs the public when consumer products pose a fire, electrical, chemical, or mechanical hazard. They also provide safety guides for such topics as childproofing, bicycle safety, crib safety and SIDS reduction, pool safety, playground safety, and toy safety. Up-to-date product recall information is made available on www.cpsc.gov.

### Research Activity

Visit the CPSC's website to learn more about current product recalls. What are some of the products and why are they being recalled? What other information is available about the recalls? Share your findings with the class.

retirement planning is critical. Financial advisors may be self-employed, employed by an agency, or employed in a corporation.

Another specialized financial occupation is a **hospital patient account representative**. Also called *patient accounts representatives*, these professionals work in the medical field to help provide customer service and determine payment plans for patients. Account representatives understand insurance and explain to patients how their insurance applies to any medical expenses. Patient account representatives also help the patient establish a budget and payment plan for remaining medical bills. Most account representatives work in hospitals or private medical centers.

## Knowledge and Skills

For all occupations in the consumer services pathway, basic math, science, and language skills are needed to perform job functions, **17-8**. Communication skills are essential, since professionals work directly with clients, patients, and consumers. Professionals must listen to consumer concerns and provide feedback. Critical thinking and problem-solving skills are necessary to analyze a situation, apply their knowledge of the industry, and develop a plan for a solution.

*Blend Images/Shutterstock.com*

**17-8**  Consumer services professionals use a variety of knowledge and skills to perform job tasks.

Within each occupation, professionals will also have specialized knowledge. They must have thorough knowledge of the product or service and clearly communicate details to consumers. They must also be knowledgeable about the wider industry and related factors, such as any legal or safety regulations. They must be familiar with technology as it relates to their job occupation and develop additional skills as needed.

Human services workers must continue training to stay current in their professions as legal regulations, therapeutic measures, and demographics constantly change. Seminars, workshops, and government training are important parts of most human services workers' career development. Those who are licensed must take courses to keep their certification current. Employers who realize that an investment in educating employees pays big dividends often provide advanced on-the-job training.

## Checkpoint

1. Describe the duties of a consumer advocate.
2. How can a financial advisor help individuals or families reach financial goals?
3. Describe the duties of a hospital patient account representative.
4. List at least three skills needed to work in the consumer services career pathway.

# Pursuing a Career in Human Services

Human services professionals are as diverse as the agencies they work for and the people they serve. Human services professionals focus on helping others find safety, well-being, health, and success within their own lives. Many professionals in this field report that their work is personally gratifying, and they often cite this as their motivation for entering the field. For those who enjoy working closely with people, careers in this field are ideal. Daily tasks focus around the development of personal and professional relationships with others, **17-9**. Human services professionals work with infants, toddlers, children, teens, or adults.

Most personal care services focus on a person's appearance, but some are concerned with matters of health and well-being. For example, a **home care aide** helps clients who need assistance with daily living activities such as bathing and dressing. Home care aides often help older adults and people with disabilities so they can remain in their own home. Other job duties of home care aides may include doing light housekeeping, running errands, scheduling medical appointments, and providing companionship.

The field of human services is very hands-on. The perceived care that clients receive is important to their effective utilization of services offered. Good customer service is essential to building trust between the service provider and client. Human services professionals often deal with sensitive topics related to family life. Trust is needed to maintain honesty, open communication, and full disclosure. Knowledge of group behavior, cultural norms, societal trends, and influences are also important. Good communication skills, including speaking, writing, and listening skills are necessary.

| Typical Daily Tasks of Human Services Professionals | | | | |
|---|---|---|---|---|
| **Interpersonal** | **Legal** | **Family/People** | **Data/ Information** | **Business** |
| Utilize group dynamics | Compile evidence for court actions | Apply theories of lifespan development | Utilize research methodology | Utilize business principles |
| Provide counsel | Identify illegal/safety issues | Hold parent or family conferences | Compile social services data | Develop policies |
| Empathize with others | Apply local, state, federal laws | Identify abuse | Manage case details | Supervise staff |
| Encourage collaboration | Understand legal process | Refer clients to family resources | Obtain information from clients, coworkers | Prepare reports |

*Goodheart-Willcox Publisher*

**17-9**    Daily tasks of human services professionals are many and varied.

Specific knowledge can help human services professionals provide resources for families to meet their basic needs of food, clothing, and shelter. For example, some human services professionals teach people how to budget their money, prepare healthy food, and perform other daily living activities. They also teach communication and conflict resolution skills. They organize or lead discussion and support groups for pregnant teens or AIDS patients, and arrange support work in food banks and housing assistance programs.

Human services organizations often work with people who have different lifestyles and personal values, **17-10**. Education, economic, culture, or value differences become more apparent when working with intimate family issues. These differences can lead to challenges.

*lev radin/Shutterstock.com*

**17-10**   Human services professionals must be able to help others without being critical or judgmental.

## Rewards and Challenges

There are significant rewards that come from helping people improve their lives. First, people in human services careers have a vision of a better community and tend to be compassionate toward others. Second, human services careers promote collaborative working teams that share a common purpose. Working with like-minded colleagues in a collaborative effort is very gratifying. In this environment, there is often room for creative problem solving. Third, human services careers offer great diversity in interactions with people from various socioeconomic, ethnic, and cultural backgrounds.

Despite the rewards, there are challenges. Many human services workers find that the biggest challenge upon entering the field is finding the right balance between personal and professional roles. Establishing appropriate personal boundaries is paramount to long-term success in the field. Experienced professionals know this and supervisors often work with those who are new to the field to help them establish how much of a person's personal life is appropriate to share in the workplace.

 **Checkpoint**

1.  List five qualities of human services professionals.
2.  Give an example of how specific knowledge can help human services professionals provide resources for families to meet their basic needs of food, clothing, and shelter.
3.  List three rewards of having a career in human services.
4.  What is the biggest challenge many workers find upon entering the field of human services?

## Summary

Careers in human services focus on meeting the needs of people. Human services professionals work in five different career pathways: *Counseling and Mental Health Services, Family and Community Services, Consumer Services, Personal Care Services,* and *Early Childhood Development and Services.* Many careers in human services are also included in other occupational categories. Human services jobs vary greatly.

Human services professionals work with diverse clients including infants, children, teens, and adults. They work with older adults, the homeless, and people with mental illnesses, disabilities, and addictions. Because of this, daily tasks may also be very different. Common human services professional careers in the counseling and mental health services pathway include counselors and psychologists. Careers in the family and community services pathway include social workers and social and human services assistants. On the administrative level, program directors, development directors, and executive directors lead human services agencies. These professional careers typically require an advanced degree.

People are drawn to human services careers for different reasons. For those who enjoy working with people and value helping others, these careers are ideal. Whatever the motivation, there will continue to be a need for human services professionals as long as there are people and families.

## Vocabulary Activity

With a partner, choose two terms from the terms list to compare. Create a Venn diagram to compare your words and identify differences. Write one term under the left circle and the other term under the right. Where the circles overlap, write three characteristics the terms have in common. For each term, write a difference of the term for each characteristic in its respective outer circle.

## Critical Thinking

1. **Determine.** Should human services workers be held to a higher moral and ethical standard than others? Why or why not?

2. **Make inferences.** What information about clients do counselors need to keep confidential? When might counselors need to share client information with others?

3. **Predict.** What do you believe might be the biggest issue facing families in the next 10 years? What type of programs could best meet the needs of families?

4. **Identify.** Locate three family services in your community and identify the target audience served, resources made available, and methods of accessing the programs and services.

5. **Analyze.** Identify three consumer-spending trends for students today. How will these trends affect future interests, fads, and ultimately careers?

6. **Assess.** The effects of overspending can be financially devastating to individuals and families. What can government agencies, schools, community groups, and the public sector do to combat overspending and debt?

7. **Draw conclusions.** Make a list of the knowledge and skills human services workers need to have. How can workers obtain this knowledge and learn these skills?

8. **Evaluate.** Find information from five colleges or universities that offer degrees in a human services career that

interests you. List the advantages and disadvantages of each school based on information you gather and your personal wants and needs.

9. **Compare and contrast.** Use online or print sources to compare and contrast the job duties and educational requirements for three human services careers. Create a table of your findings to share with the class.

10. **Cause and effect.** The national and global economies are cyclical, hitting both highs and lows. How do economic lows affect the need for human services workers? How do economic highs affect the need?

## Core Skills

11. **Writing.** Volunteer a few hours at a food bank, crisis center, or homeless shelter in your community. Write a newspaper article about your experience.

12. **Speaking.** Share with your classmates about a government program, private organization, or community group that provides a service to improve quality of life.

13. **Listening.** Interview a human services professional to learn more about his or her job. What made this person decide to pursue a career in human services?

14. **Reading.** Read a book about disaster relief work in another country. Write a summary to share with the class.

15. **Math.** Calculate how much it would cost to feed 200 people a healthy meal at a homeless shelter in your community.

16. **CTE Career Readiness Practice.** Select two human services careers to research on O*NET. Read the summary reports for these careers, especially the knowledge, skills, abilities, and interests required

to do the work. Analyze whether your personal interests, skills, and abilities are a logical fit with one or both careers. Write a summary explaining why you think you are well suited for either career.

## Research

17. Research an environmental global concern that is affecting families today such as food scarcity, the lack of clean water, global warming, pesticide use, or homelessness following an act of nature or social conflict. Create a presentation of your findings to share with the class.

18. Professionals that work with families must understand the changing environment in order to meet their needs. Some examples include the aging population, increasing diversity, the global economy, technology, and work-life issues. Research what futurists are saying about future environmental trends and forecasts that may affect the family in the next 50 years.

## Event Prep

19. Careers in human services are all about helping people through life's many obstacles. One great way to learn about careers in human services is to spend time volunteering. Through volunteer or service learning opportunities, you can get hands-on experience helping others. Research existing volunteer opportunities in your community or identify a need that perhaps is not being addressed. Volunteer your time to help strengthen your community. You may wish to expand your project by developing an FCCLA *Leadership Service in Action* project. See your FCCLA adviser for further information.

# Glossary

## A

**abandonment.** When a person who has assumed responsibility for the care of another deserts, or leaves, that person. (14)

**abilities.** Acquired skills. (15)

**abstinence.** Choosing not to engage in sexual activity. (9)

**accredited.** Refers to child care centers that are licensed and meet additional standards set forth by a professional child care organization. (13)

**adolescence.** Stage in life when people go through the transforming process of changing from children to adults. (9)

**adult day care.** Centers that provide care for older adults during mornings and afternoons, and offer age-appropriate activities, physical activities, meals, hobbies, and social activities. (13)

**Adult Protective Services (APS).** The primary agency that investigates claims of elder abuse and neglect. (14)

**affectionate love.** Involves romantic ways of expressing love for each other, which are not necessarily sexual. (10)

**afterbirth stage.** The last stage of birth, after delivery, when the placenta and umbilical cord are expelled. (4)

**ageism.** Bias against, or unfair treatment of, persons based on their age. (12)

**AIDS.** A disease (acquired immune deficiency syndrome) caused by the human immunodeficiency virus, which destroys the body's immune system. (4)

**alcoholism.** Disease resulting from the addiction to alcohol. (10)

**allergy.** A reaction that develops because of the immune system's overreaction to a normally harmless substance in the environment. (7)

**Alzheimer's disease.** A progressive brain disorder that includes not only memory loss, but also progressively severe confusion. (12)

**amygdala.** Part of the brain responsible for emotional reactions such as anger. (9)

**andragogy.** Self-directed learning. (1)

**anorexia nervosa.** Eating disorder that involves the relentless pursuit of thinness through starvation. (9)

**anxious attachment style.** Results when people are often anxious, possessive, demanding, and tend to lack trust in relationship partners. (10)

**Apgar scale.** A measure used to determine the health of a newborn. It rates a baby's heart and respiratory rates, muscle tone and body color, and reflex irritability. (5)

**aptitudes.** Natural talents people possess. (15)

**assisted living housing.** An environment that provides older adults with gradually expanded oversight and help with their daily activities. (12)

**associative play.** When children interact while involved in parallel play. (7)

**asthma.** Disease that causes inflammation of the airways in the lungs. (7)

**asynchrony.** Body growth that occurs at different rates. (9)

**atherosclerosis.** Clogging of the arteries with plaque. (11)

**attachment.** Emotional connection between an infant and caregiver. (5)

**attention deficit hyperactivity disorder (ADHD).** A learning disability that includes hyperactivity, difficulty staying on task, and impulsiveness over time. (7)

**au pairs.** Child care providers that are often from a different culture and are hired to live in the home, providing occasional child care as well as performing light household duties. (13)

**authoritarian parenting style.** A parenting style that tends to be controlling and corrective. (7)

**autism spectrum disorder (ASD).** A broad term that describes a developmental disability that leads to problems with social behaviors and communication. (7)

**autonomy versus shame and doubt.** Erikson's stage in which young children begin to see themselves as separate from their caregivers, without feelings of embarrassment or uncertainty. (6)

**avoidant attachment style.** When adults tend to avoid "getting too close" to others or avoid commitment; often results in multiple, short-lived relationships. (10)

## B

**Baby Boomer Generation.** People born between the years of 1946 and 1964. (11)

**bacterial STIs.** Sexually transmitted infections caused by bacteria and can be cured with antibiotics if detected and treated early. (4)

**behaviorism.** Theory based on the belief that a person's developmental stage should be based on what can be observed or seen in his or her behavior rather than making assumptions about what cannot be directly observed. (2)

**beneficiaries.** People who are recipients of financial assets once a person dies. (12)

**benign.** Term used to describe growths or tumors that are noncancerous. (11)

**bereavement.** A term used to describe the state of losing a loved one through death. (12)

**binge drinking.** The heavy consumption of alcohol over a short period of time. (10)

**binge-eating disorder.** Eating disorder that involves eating large amounts of food without taking any actions to reduce the amount of food intake. (9)

**bingeing.** Consuming a large volume of food in a short amount of time. (9)

**biological generativity.** Giving back to future generations by having and raising children. (11)

**blastocyst.** When a fertilized egg begins dividing into cells. (4)

**body composition.** The proportion of body fat to lean mass (muscle, bone, and water) in a person's body. (8)

**body language.** Nonverbal signals such as facial expressions, gestures, posture, and eye contact. (15)

**bonding.** Emotional connection that a parent or caregiver develops with a baby. (5)

**Braxton-Hicks contractions.** The first mild contractions that begin labor, sometimes weeks before actual labor occurs. (4)

**Brazelton Neonatal Behavioral Assessment Scale.** A test given shortly after birth to measure a baby's reflexes and responses to light, sounds, and touch. Attention and ability to be soothed are also observed. (5)

**breech birth.** When the baby is in an upright rather than a head-down position through birth. (4)

**budget.** A written financial plan to manage income, expenses, and savings. (14)

**bulimia nervosa.** Eating disorder that uses a bingeing and purging pattern. (9)

**bullying.** The act of intimidating, threatening, or hurting someone else, often over a period of time. (8)

## C

**caesarean section.** Surgical procedure to remove the baby from the womb. (4)

**calcium.** A mineral important for strong bones and teeth. (4)

**capillaries.** Blood vessels. (2)

**cardiovascular disease.** Abnormal function of the heart or blood vessels. (11)

**career.** A progression of related jobs a person has over an extended period of time. (15)

**career and technical student organizations (CTSOs).** Groups that provide students with opportunities to demonstrate social skills such as loyalty, responsibility, and leadership. (9)

**career assessments.** Useful tools that help people to better understand their strengths by identifying their interests, aptitudes, and abilities. (15)

**career counselors.** Professionals who help people make career decisions by leading them through the process of choosing and preparing for a career. (16)

**career fairs.** Events where employers network with potential employees. Also called *career expos* or *job fairs*. (15)

**career plan.** A detailed plan outlining all the steps needed to reach a career objective. (15)

**case manager.** Professional who is responsible for developing appropriate case plans and making sure that direct care staff knows how to implement plans. (17)

**cataracts.** Eye condition in which the lens of the eye thickens and causes cloudy or distorted vision. (12)

**centenarian.** A person age 100 or older. (12)

**centering.** The tendency to focus on only one part of a situation. (8)

**centration.** The tendency of young children to focus on just one aspect of something seen. (7)

**cephalocaudal development.** Development that occurs from the top of the head down to the extremities. (5)

**certified nurse-midwives.** Nurses who specialize in pregnancy and birth. (4)

**chemotherapy.** The use of cancer-killing chemicals or drugs. (11)

**child abuse.** Threatening to or inflicting harm on a child. (14)

**child–caregiver ratio.** The appropriate number of caregivers available for each child in a child care setting. (13)

**child custody.** Determines who has the legal responsibility for a child. (3)

**child neglect.** Endangerment of or harm to a child caused by an adult's failure to provide for the child's basic needs. (14)

**children in self-care.** Unsupervised children who provide care for themselves when caregivers are away. Also called *latchkey children*. (13)

**children's librarians.** Professionals who specialize in children's literature and learning resources. (16)

**child support.** Financial responsibility and maintenance of children that is legally binding. (3)

**classical conditioning.** Behaviors associated with emotional responses. (2)

**climacteric.** When reproductive capacity declines or is lost for both men and women. (11)

**cognition.** All of the actions or processes involving thinking and knowing. (1)

**cognitive development.** The changes in how people perceive, sense, organize, memorize, recall, reason, problem solve, and imagine that occur as humans develop from birth through older adulthood. (1)

**cognitive theories.** Ideas about how people process information, think, and learn. (2)

**collaborative learning.** When students work in groups to discuss and solve problems together. (16)

**community service director.** Professional who oversees an organization's mission, goals, and programs. (17)

**compromise.** To reach an agreement by incorporating each partner's goals and ideas into one solution. (10)

**conception.** When the female egg is fertilized by sperm. (4)

**concrete operational stage.** Piaget's third stage of cognitive development in which children think logically based on past experiences. (8)

**conservation.** Understanding transformation of viewed objects. (7)

**constructive play.** Play that involves creating something. (7)

**consumer advocate.** Professional who helps protect the rights, safety, and health of consumers. (17)

**consumers.** People who purchase goods and services. (14)

**consummate love.** The combination of affectionate love and a desire to commit to the relationship through good times and challenges; often results in marriage. (10)

**continuity.** Refers to developmental changes that are relatively slow, but steady. (1)

**contractions.** Tightening of the uterus during the labor process of birth. (4)

**conventional morality.** Second level in Kohlberg's theory of moral development in which people's moral decisions are motivated by laws and how they might be perceived. (8)

**cooperative extension educators.** Community teachers that provide educational programs in family and consumer sciences, 4-H youth development, agriculture, and community and rural development. (16)

**cooperative play.** When children participate in constructive play together. (7)

**corporate trainers.** Workers who design, conduct, and supervise programs for company employees or members of organizations. (16)

**counselor.** Professional who helps people manage and overcome problems and develop strategies needed to live a healthy and safe life. (17)

**crawling.** Movement that is accomplished by laying on the stomach and pulling forward with shoulders and arms. (5)

**creeping.** When the stomach is raised off the floor and movement is achieved by moving the hands and knees to pull the body forward. (5)

**critical thinking.** Involves looking closely at a situation and weighing possible outcomes before determining a solution. (15)

**cross-sectional studies.** Method of data collection used to compare groups of various ages at the same time. (2)

**crystallized intelligence.** Aptitude that includes judgment, knowledge, and skills needed in life and work. (10)

**cultural generativity.** Giving back to future generations by passing on cultural values and traditions. (11)

**curriculum.** The material and content taught in a school or program. (16)

**curriculum developer.** A professional who helps develop course content in a program of study or specific course. Also called an *instructional coordinator*. (16)

**cyberbullying.** Harassment of others through a digital medium; includes cruel and hurtful messages. (9)

## D

**day care centers.** Center-based child care facilities that offer care to large groups of infants, toddlers, and children with several caregivers employed. (13)

**decision-making process.** Series of six steps that involves examining an issue, analyzing alternatives, and acting based on careful evaluation. (9)

**deductive reasoning.** Using general observation or theory to reach a detailed conclusion. (11)

**dementia.** A brain disorder that involves cognitive declines and memory loss. This also impairs a person's ability to perform everyday tasks, such as self-dressing, cleaning, eating, and remembering where items are placed. (12)

**democratic parenting style.** A parenting style that offers support with firm expectations. Also called *authoritative parenting style*. (7)

**dentures.** Manufactured, custom-made teeth that replace natural teeth. (12)

**descriptive studies.** Method of data collection used to obtain information that describes people and situations, such as their ages, attitudes, or behaviors. (2)

**developmental acceleration.** When a child's development exceeds the norms for other children the same age. (5)

**developmental delay.** When a child's development lags behind the norms for other children the same age. (5)

**developmentally appropriate practices (DAPs).** Age-appropriate activities and teaching methods that also consider each child's strengths, interests, and culture. (13)

**developmentally inappropriate practices (DIPs).** Activities that focus on infants, toddlers, or children as a group without considering developmentally appropriate activities or individual preferences. (13)

**developmental theories.** Comprehensive explanations about why people act and behave the way they do and how they change over time. (2)

**development director.** Professional who implements strategies for securing funding to meet program goals and objectives. (17)

**diabetic retinopathy.** Eye disease that involves damage to the blood vessels in the retina, which causes blurred vision. (12)

**dilation stage.** Labor stage that causes the cervix opening to widen. (4)

**disability.** Cognitive or physical impairment that impedes or limits common activities. (3)

**discontinuity.** The process of development, spurred by abrupt changes. (1)

**doula.** A kind of emotional coach used by some mothers during childbirth. (4)

**Down syndrome.** A disorder that causes a delay in physical, intellectual, and language development. (2)

**dyslexia.** Developmental reading disorder characterized by difficulty understanding and recognizing letters, symbols, and sentence meanings. (8)

## E

**eating disorder.** Serious condition that involves abnormal eating patterns that can cause severe or life-threatening physical problems. (9)

**ecological theory.** Assigning traits and behaviors based on a person's environment. (2)

**educational neglect.** Failure to conform to a state's legal requirements to provide for a child's education or special education needs. (14)

**egocentrism.** The inability to take another person's perspective. (7)

**elder abuse.** Any act that threatens or harms the health or well-being of an older adult. (14)

**embryo.** Term used to describe the developing baby during the embryonic period. (4)

**embryonic period.** Pregnancy stage that extends from conception to the ninth week of pregnancy. (4)

**emergency and relief worker.** Professional who goes into communities to help people deal with the aftermath of a disaster. (17)

**emotional abuse.** Involves constant criticism, threats, or rejection that harms a person's sense of self-worth and emotional development. Withholding love, support, or guidance is also a part of emotional abuse. (14)

**emotional neglect.** Failure to meet a person's emotional needs or to provide psychological care, or to allow a child to use alcohol or drugs. (14)

**empathetic.** To be understanding or sensitive to the feelings, thoughts, and experiences of others. (2)

**employability skills.** Basic skills needed to obtain and succeed on a job. (15)

**empty nest.** A void in a couple's life when the home is empty and they are no longer focusing their resources on rearing their children. (3, 11)

**energy balance.** Calories gained through foods consumed equal calories burned through everyday movements and physical activities. (9)

**entrepreneurship.** The process of creating and managing one's own business. (15)

**enuresis.** Difficulty in controlling bathroom habits overnight. (7)

**environment.** All of a person's surroundings and the people in them. (1)

**episiotomy.** A surgical cut that allows the baby to pass through more easily during delivery. (4)

**episodic memories.** Includes personal experiences or events such as remembering where the car keys were placed. (11)

**estrogen.** Hormone that is important in the development of female bodily characteristics. (11)

**ethnicity.** A person's identity with a particular racial, national, or cultural group and support of that group's customs, beliefs, and language. (3)

**ethnic or cultural diversity.** In the United States, people of different backgrounds, languages, races, ethnicities, religions, and socioeconomic classes live in one society. (3)

**ethological theory.** Assigning traits and behaviors based on a person's biology or genetic make-up. (2)

**executive director.** Professional who is responsible for the overall management and leadership of an organization. (17)

**executive strategies.** Skills used to solve problems, which involve assessing problems, making goals, and developing plans to meet goals. They also involve implementing and evaluating solutions. (8)

**expansion mode.** When the economy accelerates and increases. (3)

**expenses.** Goods and services that require payment. (14)

**expulsion stage.** The delivery stage of childbirth. (4)

**extracurricular activities.** Before or after school activities that promote group interactions and have a positive effect on social skills. (9)

## F

**family.** Two or more people living in the same household who are related by blood (birth), marriage, or adoption. (3)

**Family and Medical Leave Act (FMLA).** Federal law that allows full-time employed individuals to take job-protected leave without pay for the family transitions that involve close family members such as spouses, children, and parents. (3)

**family child care centers.** Programs operated in a caregiver's private home for a small number of children. (13)

**family life cycle.** Six basic stages that many families go through as a normal part of life. Includes the beginning, childbearing, parenting, launching, mid-years, and aging stages. (3)

**fetal alcohol syndrome (FAS).** Conditions such as cognitive disabilities caused by prenatal exposure to alcohol. (4)

**fetal monitoring.** Device used to track a baby's heart rate, the mother's contractions, and to alert the medical staff to any signs of distress. (4)

**fetal period.** Pregnancy stage that extends from the ninth week of pregnancy until birth at the end of the third trimester. (4)

**fetus.** Term used to describe the developing baby during the fetal period. (4)

**financial advisor.** Professional who helps people set financial goals, establish and keep a budget, make investment decisions, and plan for future purchases and expenses. (17)

**fine-motor skills.** Physical tasks involving small muscle movements such as cutting with scissors, typing on a keyboard, and writing with a pen or pencil. (1)

**first trimester.** Begins at conception and lasts until about the ninth week of pregnancy. (4)

**fixed expenses.** Costs that do not vary from time period to time period. (14)

**flexible expenses.** Costs that fluctuate or vary in price and frequency. (14)

**fluid intelligence.** The ability to reason abstractly, which includes calculating mathematical problems with speed or learning things quickly. (10)

**folic acid.** A vitamin that when taken prenatally, helps reduce brain and spinal cord birth defects. (4)

**food allergies.** When foods trigger a response by the body's immune system, which can cause severe reactions, including breathing problems or death. (7)

**food intolerances.** Reactions to foods that are unpleasant, such as digestive or behavioral problems. (5, 7)

**formal operations.** Piaget's fourth stage of cognitive development in which adolescents think in more abstract terms. (9)

**functional play.** Using repetitive motions in play such as moving a toy car in circles. (7)

## G

**gender identity.** A child's sense about being a boy or a girl. (7)

**gender roles.** Expectations about what is expected of boys or girls in how they should act, how they should feel, and what should be of interest to them. (7)

**generational cohorts.** People who are born in a similar time in history. (11)

**Generation X.** People born between the years of 1965 and 1979. (11)

**generativity versus stagnation.** Erikson's socio-emotional stage in middle adulthood when adults begin to either leave legacies of themselves to the next generation or live solely for themselves. (11)

**genes.** Part of a DNA molecule that determines individual traits. (2)

**genetics.** The study of genes. (2)

**germinal period.** The pregnancy stage that extends from conception until about two weeks later when implantation in the uterus occurs. (4)

**gestational diabetes.** A type of diabetes that occurs only during pregnancy. (4)

**giftedness.** Students who are ahead of their peers in at least one area of intelligence. (3)

**glaucoma.** Eye condition that involves damage to the optic nerve, and in which vision is distorted. (12)

**grief.** The mental anguish or sadness that accompanies bereavement. (12)

**gross-motor skills.** Physical tasks involving large muscle movements such as crawling, walking, and jumping. (1)

**growth spurts.** Rapid changes in both height and weight. (9)

## H

**hand and eye coordination.** Using visual input to guide a hand activity. (7)

**Head Start.** A government funded preschool program which focuses on preparing disadvantaged children for school. (7)

**heart attack.** Condition that occurs if the heart function is stopped. (11)

**heredity.** Traits that people are born with or have genetically acquired. (1)

**high school.** Includes grades 9 or 10 through 12. (16)

**HIV.** The human immunodeficiency virus which causes AIDS. (4)

**holophrases.** One word descriptors used for many different, but related objects. (6)

**home care aide.** Professional who helps clients who need assistance with daily living activities such as bathing and dressing. (17)

**hormones.** Chemicals that travel through the bloodstream and cause a change or development within the body. (9)

**hospice care.** A form of care given by trained medical professionals, which focuses on making a person comfortable in his or her last days and hours of life. (12)

**hospital patient account representative.** Professional who works in the medical field to help provide customer service and determine payment plans for patients. (17)

**hot flashes.** The feeling of suddenly being very warm and sweaty. (11)

**human behavioral environment.** All the societal systems that regulate behavior and relationships between people. (3)

**human constructed environment.** Products produced for consumers to use. (3)

**human development.** A gradual process through which humans change from birth to adulthood. (1)

**human papillomavirus (HPV).** A common STI virus linked to cervical cancer. (4)

**hyperopia.** An eye condition that results in difficulty seeing objects that are near. Also called *farsightedness.* (8)

**hypothesis.** Prediction about something that can be tested. (2)

## I

**identity versus identity confusion.** Erikson's stage when adolescents experiment with different roles and integrate opinions of others to formulate a sense of self. (9)

**idiom.** Figure of speech used as an expression that has cultural meaning, but does not necessarily make sense. (9)

**imaginary audience.** Adolescents' belief that everyone is watching them. (9)

**impulse buying.** Making unplanned purchases. (14)

**inclusion.** Placing students with special educational needs in a general education classroom setting all or most of the time so students will benefit from the whole class experience. (3, 8)

**income.** Money earned through work. (14)

**incontinence.** Involuntary urination or defecation. (12)

**independent living community.** Housing for older adults who can care for themselves, but desire the community support of those who are of similar age. (12)

**Individualized Education Plan (IEP).** Educational plan tailored to the specific educational goals of a child with special needs. (3)

**Individuals with Disabilities Education Act (IDEA).** Federal law that governs how states provide early intervention, special education, and other services to children with disabilities. (3)

**induced labor.** Labor that is hastened by medical intervention rather than occurring naturally. (4)

**inductive reasoning.** Making conclusions by moving from detailed facts to general theory. (11)

**industry versus inferiority.** Erikson's stage when children develop a sense of self-confidence by displaying skill, without feelings of inadequacy. (8)

**infancy.** The period from birth to the first birthday. (5)

**infatuation.** An obsession with someone based on appearance or ability. (10)

**initiative versus guilt.** Erikson's stage when young children begin to be productive for themselves, without feelings of blame or remorse. (7)

**inoculations.** Substances that when given in liquid or shot form, produce or boost immunity to a specific disease such as measles or mumps. (6)

**insomnia.** The inability to fall asleep or to sleep more than a few hours at a time. (10)

**integrity versus despair.** Erikson's final socio-emotional stage in which people either come to terms with their life or fall into despair over failings and unmet goals. (12)

**interests.** Things a person enjoys learning about or doing. (15)

**internships.** Work-based learning programs at the postsecondary level. (15)

**interview.** A formal meeting between an employer and a potential employee. (15)

**intestate.** To die without a will. (12)

**intimacy.** The self-disclosure and sharing of private thoughts and emotions. (10)

**intimacy versus isolation.** Erikson's socio-emotional stage for young adulthood in which he theorized that if people do not establish intimate relationships during young adulthood, they risk isolation from others. (10)

**intuition.** Perception or insight based on feelings. (7)

**invincible.** Incapable of being defeated, conquered, or having anything bad happen to oneself. (9)

**iron.** A mineral that when taken prenatally reduces the chance of babies being born at a low birthweight. (4)

## J

**jargon.** Content-specific language often used by experts and professionals in their field of study. (11)

**job application.** A document that contains information about the qualifications and skills of a person seeking employment with a company. (15)

**job shadowing.** Observing a worker in his or her job for a few hours or a day to get an idea about the job or career field. (15)

**joint custody.** Legal agreement in which both parents provide care and make decisions for the child. (3)

**junior high.** Includes grades 7 through 8 or 9. (16)

## L

**Lamaze method.** Natural childbirth method that focuses on relaxation techniques, using a focal point, and an emotional coach. (4)

**Last Will and Testament.** A legal document that gives explicit directions on how to divide a person's financial assets once he or she dies. (12)

**leadership.** A quality that involves organizing, guiding, and taking responsibility for a team. (15)

**learning diversity.** Differences in learning based on abilities or experiences. (8)

**learning styles.** Methods of taking in and processing information. (8)

**lease.** A legally binding rental agreement. (14)

**letter of application.** A written introduction to a résumé that provides additional details about why a person is qualified for a job. (15)

**letter of recommendation.** A formal written letter by a reference that outlines a person's qualifications to perform a job. (15)

**liver spots.** Harmless age spots that are flat gray, brown, or black, vary in size, and may appear on the face, hands, shoulders, and arms. (12)

**living will.** A legal document that informs family and medical workers of preferences for being kept alive by artificial means, or allows the decision to let them pass, when there is no chance of recovery. (12)

**longitudinal studies.** Method of data collection used to observe the same individuals over a period of time. (2)

**long-term goals.** Major goals that may take months or even years to achieve. (9)

**low birthweight.** Babies that weigh less than 5.8 pounds at birth. (4)

# M

**macular degeneration.** Eye disease that causes people to have difficulty seeing objects inside the center of the field of vision. (12)

**mainstreaming.** The placement of special needs students who show the ability to keep up with the curriculum into a regular classroom. (8)

**major.** Area of study that outlines classes needed to complete a program and achieve a particular degree. (15)

**malignant.** Term used to describe growths or tumors that are cancerous. (11)

**malnutrition.** A chronic problem caused by a significant lack of nutrients within a person's diet. (8)

**mammogram.** X-ray of the breasts that checks for unusual tissue growth, which can identify early signs of breast cancer. (11)

**manipulative experiments.** Method of data collection used to keep all the variables that affect behavior the same except for one. (2)

**marriage and family therapist.** Counselor who helps individuals, couples, and families resolve conflicts. (17)

**material exploitation.** The misuse of an older adult's financial resources, property, or possessions. (14)

**maternity leave.** Paid or unpaid time off from work to care for a new child. (3)

**matriarch.** The oldest and most influential female family member. (12)

**maturity.** The ability to adapt to the inevitable changes that happen in life. (11)

**medical neglect.** Failure to provide necessary treatment for injuries, illnesses, or other health conditions. (14)

**Medicare.** A government health insurance program that helps older adults pay for medical costs. (12)

**menopause.** When menstruation ceases for a year or more and women can no longer reproduce. (11)

**mental health counselor.** Therapist who assesses, addresses, and treats mental and emotional issues such as anxiety, depression, trauma, stress, or grief. (17)

**metacognition.** Thinking about thinking processes. (7)

**metamemory.** Thinking about memory. (7)

**metaphors.** Figure of speech used to connect two seemingly unlike objects or ideas that have something in common. (9)

**middle schools.** Includes grades 5 or 6 through 8. (16)

**Millennial Generation.** People born between the years of 1980 and 1995. (11)

**moral decisions.** Personal choices that evaluate what is right and what is wrong. (2)

**morphology.** Refers to word structures and formations. (7)

**mortality.** Eventual death. (12)

**mortgage.** A legally binding contract in which property is security for borrowed money. (14)

**mourning.** The period when people remember and grieve for the loss of a beloved one. (12)

**multiculturalism.** The idea that cultural identities should not be ignored, but instead should be maintained and valued. (3)

**myopia.** A condition that results in difficulty seeing objects that are far away. Also called *nearsightedness*. (8)

**MyPlate.** Food guidance system created by the USDA to help people ages 2 and older make healthful food choices. (7)

# N

**nannies.** Professionals hired to care for children in their own home. (13)

**natural childbirth.** Birth procedures that focus on relaxation techniques instead of medication to deal with pain. (4)

**natural environment.** All living and nonliving things on Earth not influenced by people. (3)

**naturalistic experiments.** Method of data collection used to only observe existing groups and record observations. (2)

**nature versus nurture debate.** The debate between genetic and environmental influences on development. (1)

**neonates.** Babies from birth to age 1 month. (5)

**networking.** The act of meeting and making contact with people who may be of help in finding a job. (15)

**nonsectarian.** Schools that are not based on any religious affiliation. (16)

**nutrient-dense.** Refers to foods that are rich in vitamins and minerals and contain relatively few calories. (8)

# O

**obesity.** An excessive amount of body fat. (8)

**object permanence.** The understanding that people, places, or objects still exist even when they are out of sight or can no longer be heard or touched. (5)

**observable behaviors.** Things people do and say or the way they act. (2)

**obstetricians.** Medical doctors who specialize in pregnancy and birth. (4)

**occupation.** The job a person does for a living. (15)

**operant conditioning.** Behaviors that continue when reinforced. (2)

**operations.** Formal or logical processes that are organized mental processes. (7)

**osteoarthritis.** The most common form of arthritis, which is caused by the chronic breakdown of cartilage in the joints. (12)

**osteoporosis.** Progressive bone loss when calcium is depleted, causing bones to become brittle and more porous. (11)

**overweight.** A high amount of body fat in relation to lean body mass. (8)

**oxygen deprivation.** When the baby's flow of oxygen is somehow interrupted during the birth process. (4)

## P

**Palmar grasp.** When a baby scrapes up an object using all of the fingers into the palm of the hand. (5)

**parallel play.** Play that occurs alongside another toddler with little reciprocal interaction. (6)

**parental generativity.** Giving back to future generations by participating in children's lives through passing on knowledge, skills, and cultural values. (11)

**parent educators.** Teachers or trainers who focus their content on parenting knowledge and skills. (16)

**paternity leave.** Paid or unpaid time off from work that fathers may take after the birth or adoption of a child. (3)

**patriarch.** The oldest and most influential male family member. (12)

**pedagogy.** Teacher- or parent-directed learning. (1)

**peer pressure.** Influence a group of people has on an individual in the same age group. (9)

**pelvic inflammatory disease (PID).** An infection of the uterus and fallopian tubes caused by some STIs that can lead to infertility. (4)

**perimenopause.** The time proceeding menopause when hormonal shifts begin and menstrual cycles become less regular. (11)

**periphery.** The outer edges of the center field of vision. (12)

**permissive parenting style.** A type of parenting that gives children control of situations with few limits. (7)

**personal fable.** Thinking pattern related to cognitive function that often occurs during adolescence when they distort and inflate the opinion of themselves and their own importance. (9)

**phonology.** Refers to the sounds that make up words. (7)

**physical abuse.** Inflicting injury through beating, hitting, shaking, biting, punching, kicking, or by other means. (14)

**physical dependency.** Develops when the body becomes reliant on the presence of a drug in the system to properly function. (9)

**physical development.** The changes in size, body composition, chemical make-up, and height that occur as humans develop from birth through older adulthood. (1)

**physical neglect.** Failure to provide such basic needs as food, clothing, shelter, or appropriate supervision. (14)

**pincer grasp.** Picking up items using a coordinated motion of thumb and forefinger. (5)

**pituitary gland.** Small organ at the base of the brain that releases hormones that regulate growth and reproduction. (9)

**placenta.** A mass attached to the uterus and the umbilical that provides nutrients from the mother to the baby. (4)

**plaque.** Fatty substance that clogs veins and arteries. (11)

**playgroups.** Parent-child groups that focus on socialization. (13)

**portfolio.** A dynamic, ever-growing, and changing collection of work that illustrates a person's abilities and achievements. (15)

**postconventional morality.** Kohlberg's final stage of moral development in which adults begin to care about the local community, environment, and society as a whole. (10)

**postformal stage.** Cognitive stage of development in which adults appear to be better at dealing with complex questions they may never fully answer. (10)

**postpartum depression.** A mother's intense sadness and oftentimes emotional withdrawal from others after giving birth. (5)

**postpartum period.** The time mothers need for both physical and psychological adjustment after giving birth. Usually lasts six weeks. (5)

**postural control.** Being able to achieve and maintain a state of balance while performing an activity, such as jumping. (7)

**pragmatics.** Refers to using language properly. (7)

**preconventional morality.** The first level in Kohlberg's theory of moral development in which people make decisions based on whether or not they will be punished or rewarded. (7)

**prefrontal cortex.** Part of the brain that regulates emotions and impulse control. (9)

**prejudice.** Unfounded negative bias often based on stereotyping. (3)

**prekindergarten programs.** Educational programs intended for children who will be attending kindergarten in the next year. Also called *Pre-K.* (16)

**prenatal vitamins.** Vitamins that contain extra folic acid, calcium, and iron. (4)

**preoperational stage.** Piaget's second stage of cognitive development in which young children are beginning to use more rational thought processes. (7)

**presbycusis.** Hearing loss associated with age, most often caused by damage to the inner ear. (12)

**presbyopia.** Eye condition common in middle age due to loss of elasticity of the lens of the eye, which results in a slow decrease in the ability to focus on nearby objects. (11)

**preschoolers.** Children between the ages of 3 through 5. (7)

**preschool programs.** Educational programs for 3- to 5-year-olds. (13)

**progesterone.** A hormone that prepares the female body for reproduction. (11)

**program director.** A professional who oversees the mission, goals, and programs of an organization, such as a child care center. (16)

**proximodistal development.** Pattern of development that occurs from the body core to the extremities. (5)

**psychoanalytic theories.** Ideas that analyze the symbolic meaning behind behaviors. (2)

**psychological dependency.** Develops when a person uses a drug for the feeling it causes. (9)

**psychologist.** Professional who studies human behavior and mental processes and develops theories to explain why people behave the way they do. (17)

**psychosocial development stages.** Erikson's theory consisting of eight stages in which people must successfully resolve a psychological and/or social conflict before moving to the next stage in life. (2)

**puberty.** Period of development marked by growth spurts and sexual maturation. (9)

**pullout programs.** School programs that allow gifted children to leave the regular classroom for certain periods of the day or week for advanced learning in a particular subject area along with social opportunities with peers. (3)

**purging.** Self-induced method of expelling food from the system by means such as vomiting or using laxatives. (9)

## Q

**quantifying.** Measuring the quantity of items. (8)

## R

**receptive language.** Understanding spoken language even without the ability to verbally respond. (5)

**recession mode.** When the economy slows or declines. (3)

**recovery mode.** When the economy begins to accelerate or look hopeful. (3)

**references.** People other than relatives who know a person and can attest to his or her work habits, skills, and abilities. (15)

**rehabilitation counselor.** Therapist who helps people overcome effects of physical and emotional disabilities to achieve optimum independence. (17)

**résumé.** An organized summary of a person's education, qualifications, and work experience. (15)

**retirement homes.** Living environment that provides more intense nursing care for older adults, usually with a medical staff that provides oversight as needed. (12)

**reversibility.** The ability to understand how actions can be reversed. (8)

**Rh Factor.** When the type of protein in red blood cells do not match between the mother and baby. (4)

**romantic love.** Develops from the combination of friendly love and affectionate love and creates the feelings of security in the relationship and care and appreciation for each other. (10)

**rooting reflex.** The natural inclination of newborns to turn their head toward the food source when the side of their mouth is stroked. (5)

## S

**sandwich generation.** A term used to describe the situation when adults are caring for needs of both their aging parents and their own children at the same time. (11)

**sarcopenia.** Term used to describe the loss of muscle mass and strength over time. (11)

**savings.** The remaining amount of money after income is received and expenses are paid. (14)

**scaffolding.** When caregivers and older peers or siblings help children learn at their level. (6)

**school-age child care programs.** Programs that provide care for children before and after school in safe, healthy, and stimulating environments. (13)

**school guidance counselors.** Trained professionals who help students learn social skills, solve issues, cope with personal crises, and make education and career decisions. (16)

**scientific method.** A means of increasing knowledge by observing, formulating a hypothesis, testing the hypothesis, and formulating a theory. (2)

**secure attachment style.** Occurs when people perceive relationships positively and often establish relationships smoothly and naturally. (10)

**self-contained classrooms.** Learning environment where the same teacher and group of students remain in one classroom most of the day, with most or all subjects taught by one teacher. (16)

**self-neglect.** Intentional or unintentional behaviors committed by an older adult that endanger his or her health, safety, and overall well-being. (14)

**semantic memories.** Includes knowledge such as how to change a flat tire on a car. (11)

**semantics.** Refers to the meaning of words. (7)

**sensorimotor stage.** Piaget's first stage of cognitive development that begins with reflexes and ends with the use of symbols. (5)

**separation anxiety.** Distress infants experience when their caregiver or parent leaves them in the care of a stranger. (5)

**sexual abuse.** Involves inappropriate behavior toward or with a child including touching, sexual acts, and exposure to pornography. (14)

**sexually transmitted infections (STIs).** Infectious illnesses spread primarily through sexual contact. Also known as *sexually transmitted diseases (STDs)*. (4)

**Shaken Baby Syndrome.** A brain injury that occurs as a result of shaking an infant. (5)

**short-term goals.** Goals that are achievable in the immediate to near future. (9)

**sleep apnea.** A condition in which the airway collapses or becomes blocked and causes a person to have pauses in breathing while sleeping. (12)

**social and human services assistant.** Professional who works under the direction of other workers, such as a social worker or community service director. (17)

**social clock.** Cultural expectations of when major life milestones should occur. (10)

**social cognitive theory.** Theory based on the assumption that people are affected by rewards and punishments, but that their reaction to rewards and punishments are filtered by their own perceptions, thoughts, and motivations. (2)

**Social Security.** A government retirement fund that provides supplemental income to Americans who are at least 62 years of age and who have met employment contribution eligibility standards. (12)

**social system.** The organization of individuals into groups based on characteristic patterned relationships. (3)

**social worker.** Professional who coordinates and plans programs and activities to meet client needs. (17)

**socio-emotional development.** The changes in the way a person's social relationships, feelings, social skills, self-esteem, gender identity, and ways of coping with situations develop from birth through older adulthood. (1)

**solitary play.** When infants play alone without interacting with others. (5)

**special education teachers.** Professionals who work with children and youth who have a variety of special needs. (16)

**special needs.** Includes physical disabilities, cognitive disabilities, emotional and behavioral problems, and learning disorders. Also includes speech, vision, and hearing disorders. (3)

**specific learning disability (SLD).** Disorder that involves basic psychological processes that impair using or understanding language including the ability to listen, speak, read, write, spell, or calculate. (3)

**speech-language specialists.** Professionals who are trained to diagnose and provide treatment for speech or language challenges. (16)

**standard of living.** A measure of the wealth, comforts, and material goods available to a family. (3)

**stereotypes.** Preconceived generalizations about certain groups of people. (3)

**stillbirth.** Delivery of a deceased baby. (4)

**stranger anxiety.** Fretfulness that occurs when around unfamiliar people, peaking in infants between 9 and 12 months. (5)

**stress.** The body's response when faced with pressures and demands. (8)

**stroke.** Clogging of the arteries in the brain. (11)

**substance abuse.** Misuse of drugs to a toxic, dangerous level. (9)

**sudden infant death syndrome (SIDS).** Unexpected death for unknown reasons during the first few months of a baby's life. (4)

**synonyms.** Different words with the same meanings. (11)

**syntax.** Refers to sentence structure. (7)

# T

**team member.** A person who works with other members of the group to help achieve a common goal. (15)

**telegraphic speech.** When two words are combined, usually a verb and a noun. (6)

**temperament.** A part of personality that reflects how a person interacts with the environment. (5)

**temper tantrums.** Emotional episode of upset behavior usually experienced by a toddler that may involve yelling and crying. (6)

**testosterone.** Hormone that is important in the development of the male reproductive system and characteristics. (11)

**tinnitus.** A ringing sound in the ears. (12)

**toddlers.** Children between the ages of 1 and 3 years. (6)

**trust versus mistrust.** Erikson's stage in which infants must learn to develop trust relationships with their caregivers. (5)

# U

**umbilical cord.** The tube of veins that connects the placenta with the baby (at the site later called the belly button). (4)

**unconditional love.** Love without limits or exceptions. (10)

**universal design.** Housing design that meets the physical needs of people of all ages and abilities. (11)

**unoccupied play.** When a baby observes and focuses on an object or activity. (5)

# V

**very low birthweight.** Babies that weigh less than 3.5 pounds at birth. (4)

**viral STIs.** Sexually transmitted infections caused by viruses and cannot be cured. (4)

**visual acuity.** The ability to visually perceive objects sharply at a given distance based on a fixed standard. (11)

**voice cracking.** Sporadic voice octave changes in males that occur when the vocal chords are lengthening and thickening during puberty and adolescence. (9)

# W

**weight management.** Achieving and maintaining a healthy weight over time. (9)

**widow.** A woman who has lost her husband to death. (12)

**widower.** A man who has lost his wife to death. (12)

**windows of opportunity.** Ideal time frames for optimizing the development of critical skills because the brain is most receptive to learning. (7)

**work ethic.** A personal belief in the value of work and its ability to strengthen character. (15)

**work generativity.** Giving back to future generations by passing on work knowledge, skills, and cultural values. (11)

# Z

**zone of proximal development (ZPD).** The level at which a child can learn with help, as theorized by Vygotsky. (6)

**zygote.** The cell that results from fertilization between a sperm and an egg. (4)

# Index